INNOVATIVE COMPARATIVE METHODS FOR POLICY ANALYSIS

INNOVATIVE COMPARATIVE METHODS FOR POLICY ANALYSIS

Beyond the Quantitative-Qualitative Divide

Edited by

Benoît Rihoux
Université catholique de Louvain, Belgium

Heike Grimm
University of Erfurt and Max Planck Institute of Economics, Jena, Germany

 Springer

Library of Congress Control Number: 2005933471
ISBN-10: 0-387-28828-7   e-ISBN 0-387-28829-5
ISBN-13: 978-0387-28828-4

Printed on acid-free paper.

© 2006 Springer Science+Business Media, Inc.
All rights reserved. This work may not be translated or copied in whole or in part without the written permission of the publisher (Springer Science+Business Media, Inc., 233 Spring Street, New York, NY 10013, USA), except for brief excerpts in connection with reviews or scholarly analysis. Use in connection with any form of information storage and retrieval, electronic adaptation, computer software, or by similar or dissimilar methodology now known or hereafter developed is forbidden.
The use in this publication of trade names, trademarks, service marks, and similar terms, even if they are not identified as such, is not to be taken as an expression of opinion as to whether or not they are subject to proprietary rights.

Printed in the United States of America.

9 8 7 6 5 4 3 2 1

springeronline.com

TABLE OF CONTENTS

		Page	
List of Figures			vii
List of Tables			ix
Acknowledgements			xiii

Chapter 1	Introduction. Beyond the 'Qualitative-Quantitative Divide: Innovative Comparative Methods for Policy Analysis *Benoît Rihoux and Heike Grimm*	1

Part One: Systematic Comparative Case Studies: Design, Methods and Measures

Chapter 2	The Limitations of Net-Effects Thinking *Charles Ragin*	13
Chapter 3	A Question of Size? A Heuristics for Stepwise Comparative Research Design *David Levi-Faur*	43
Chapter 4	MSDO/MDSO Revisited for Public Policy Analysis *Gisèle De Meur, Peter Bursens and Alain Gottcheiner*	67
Chapter 5	Beyond Methodological Tenets. The Worlds of QCA and SNA and their Benefits to Policy Analysis *Sakura Yamasaki and Astrid Spreitzer*	95

Part Two: Innovative Comparative Methods to Analyze Policy-Making Processes: Applications

Chapter 6	Entrepreneurship Policy and Regional Economic Growth. Exploring the Link and Theoretical Implications *Heike Grimm*	123
Chapter 7	Determining the Conditions of HIV/AIDS Prevalence in Sub-Saharan Africa. Employing New Tools of Macro-Qualitative Analysis *Lasse Cronqvist and Dirk Berg-Schlosser*	145

Chapter 8	Diversity, Ideal Types and Fuzzy Sets in Comparative Welfare State Research *Jon Kvist*	167
Chapter 9	Scenario-Building Methods as a Tool for Policy Analysis *António Brandão Moniz*	185

Part Three: Innovative Comparative Methods for Policy Implementation and Evaluation: Applications

Chapter 10	A New Method for Policy Evaluation? Longstanding Challenges and the Possibilities of Qualitative Comparative Analysis (QCA) *Frédéric Varone, Benoît Rihoux and Axel Marx*	213
Chapter 11	Social Sustainability of Community Structures: A Systematic Comparative Analysis within the Oulu Region in Northern Finland *Pentti Luoma*	237
Chapter 12	QCA as a Tool for Realistic Evaluations. The Case of the Swiss Environmental Impact Assessment *Barbara Befani and Fritz Sager*	263

Part Four: Conclusion

Chapter 13	Conclusion. Innovative Comparative Methods for Policy Analysis: Milestones to Bridge Different Worlds *Benoît Rihoux and Heike Grimm*	287

References	297
Contributors	319
Abstracts	323
Index	329

LIST OF FIGURES

3.1	Stepwise Heuristic of Comparative Analysis	61
4.1	Extreme Similarity with Different Outcomes (a/A) and Extreme Dissimilarity with Same Outcomes (a/b or A/B) when Outcome has (Only) Two Possible Values	68
4.2	Manhattan and Euclidean Distances Structure Space Differently	68
4.3	Distance Matrix for Category A	75
4.4	MDSO Pairs for Tight Cases	79
4.5	MDSO Pairs for Loose Cases	79
4.6	MSDO Pairs	80
4.7	MSDO Graph for Criteria h and h-1	81
4.8	Comparison Scheme for a Three-Valued Outcome	94
5.1	Step 1 of QCA Data Visualization Using Netdraw	114
5.2	Step 2 of QCA Data Visualization Using Netdraw	117
5.3	Step 3 of QCA Data Visualization Using Netdraw	118
7.1	Case Distribution of the 1997 HIV Prevalence Rate	156
7.2	Correlation between Change of HIV Rate 1997-2003 and the Mortality Rate	158
7.3	Case Distribution of the MORTALITY Variable	159
9.1	Representation of Distribution of Realization Time Responses in First and Second Round of a Delphi Questionnaire	195
10.1	Policies and Comparative Strategies	225
11.1	The Population Change in Oulunsalo since the Beginning of the 20th Century	241
12.1	Overview of the Evaluation Design	265

LIST OF TABLES

2.1	Hypothetical Truth Table with Four Causal Conditions and One Outcome	19
2.2	Logistic Regression of Poverty Avoidance on AFQT Scores and Parental SES (*Bell Curve* Model)	27
2.3	Logistic Regression of Poverty Avoidance on AFQT Scores, Parental Income, Years of Education, Marital Status, and Children	28
2.4	Distribution of Cases across Sectors of the Vector Space	31
2.5	Assessments of Set-Theoretic Consistency (17 Configurations)	33
3.1	Four Inferential Strategies	59
4.1	Formal Presentation of Binary Data	73
4.2	The Binary Data Set	73
4.3	Extremes and Thresholds for Each Category	76
4.4	Four Levels of (Dis)similarity for Each Category	77
4.5	Pairs Reaching the Different Levels of (Dis)similarity	78
4.6	Commonalities between Very Distant Cases Leading to a Same Outcome	82
4.7	Identified Variables from MDSO Analysis of Loose Networks	83
4.8	Identified Variables from MDSO Analysis of Tight Networks	84
4.9	Identified Variables from MSDO Analysis of Loose vs. Tight Networks	84
4.10	Dichotomizing a 3-Valued Variable	90
4.11	Another Attempt at Dichotomization	91
5.1	Advantages and Shortcomings of POE / POA	101
5.2	Implication of Network Measures for Each Type of Network	108

5.3	Network Measures	109
5.4	Truth Table	110
5.5	Truth Table of the Redding and Viterna Analysis	112
5.6	Co-Occurrence of Conditions (Redding and Viterna Data)	115
6.1	What Kind of Information Do You Offer? We Provide Information About...	132
6.2	What Kind of Counseling Do You Offer?	133
6.3	Are Federal Programs of High Importance to Entrepreneurs?	134
6.4	Are State Programs of High Importance to Entrepreneurs?	134
6.5	Are Regional Programs of High Importance to Entrepreneurs?	135
6.6	Are Municipal Programs of High Importance to Entrepreneurs?	135
6.7	Are Municipal Programs of High Importance to Entrepreneurs? (Output per Region)	136
7.1	Religion and HIV Prevalence Rates in 1997	151
7.2	Socio-Economic and Gender Related Indices and Prevalence Rates in 1997	152
7.3	Socio-Economic and Gender Related Indices and Prevalence Rates in 1997 Checked for Partial Correlations with Religious Factors (PCTPROT and PCTMUSL)	152
7.4	Multiple Regressions (HIV Prevalence Rate 1997)	154
7.5	Multiple Regressions (Change of HIV Prevalence Rate 1997-2003)	155
7.6	Truth Table Religion and the HIV Prevalence Rate in 1997	157
7.7	Change of HIV Prevalence Rate and Socio-Economic and Perception Indices	158
7.8	QCA Truth Table with MORTALITY Threshold at 4%	159

7.9	MVQCA Truth-Table with Trichotomized MORTALITY Variable	161
7.10	The Similar Cases Burkina Faso, Burundi, C.A.R., and Côte d'Ivoire	162
7.11	Experimental Truth Table without the Central African Republic (C.A.R.)	162
8.1	Assessing Change Across Two Policies	169
8.2	Specification of Empirical Indicators for Child Family Policies and the Translation of Raw Data into Fuzzy Membership Scores and Verbal Labels	178
8.3	The Analytical Property Space and Ideal Types: Child Family Policies and Welfare State Ideal Types	180
8.4	Fuzzy Membership Scores for Nordic Child Family Policies in Welfare State Ideal Types, 1990-99	182
9.1	Forecasting Methods	189
9.2	State of the Future Index--2002	205
11.1	The Distributions of the Variables Used as the Basis of the Truth Table in the Residential Areas	247
11.2	The Truth Table Based on the Former Table	248
11.3	Crisp Set Analysis: 9 Minimal Formulae	249
11.4	The Pearson's Correlation Coefficients	255
12.1	List of Test Cases	270
12.2	Basic Data for Output	272
12.3	Basic Data for Impact	273
12.4	New CMO Configurations and Related QCA Conditions Accounting for Implementation Quality with Regard to Political/Cultural Context	277
12.5	New CMO Configurations and Related QCA Conditions Accounting for Implementation Quality with Regard to Project Size	278
12.6	Overview of Combinations of Conditions for Output and Impact	279
12.7	New CMO Configurations and Related QCA Conditions Accounting for Final Project Approval	281

ACKNOWLEDGMENTS

This publication originated in the European Science Foundation (ESF) exploratory workshop on *"Innovative comparative methods for policy analysis. An interdisciplinary European endeavour for methodological advances and improved policy analysis/evaluation"* held in Erfurt from 25 to 28 September 2004 (ref. EW03-217). This volume brings together a selection of contributions to this workshop, which gathered specialists from many fields and countries.

The major scientific objective of this ESF exploratory workshop, which we jointly convened, was to further develop methods for systematic comparative cases analysis in a small-N research design, with a key emphasis laid on policy-oriented applications.

Without the support of the ESF, and in particular of the Standing Committee for the Social Sciences (SCSS), it would not have been possible to bring together such a wide range of academics and policy analysts from around the globe to further improve the development of methodologies for comparative case study analysis.

The completion of this volume was also made possible by the support of the Fonds de la Recherche Fondamentale Collective (FRFC), through the Fonds National de la Recherche Scientifique (FNRS, Belgium), with the research grant on "Analyse de l'émergence des nouvelles institutions à parties prenantes multiples (multi-stakeholder) pour la régulation politique et sociale des conditions de travail et de la protection de l'environnement dans des marchés globaux" (ref. 2.4.563.05 .F).

We would like to thank Sakura Yamasaki for the setting up and management of a restricted-access workshop web page, as well as Barbara Befani, Lasse Cronqvist, Axel Marx, Astrid Spreitzer and Sakura Yamasaki for helping us in the compilation of the workshop report. We thank those workshop participants, namely Robert Gamse, Bernhard Kittel, Algis Krupavicius, Carsten Schneider and Detlef Sprinz, who actively contributed to the workshop with useful and critical comments as well as oral and written contributions which greatly helped to push forward new ideas and discussions. We are very indebted to Nicolette Nowakowski for her organizational support to set up the workshop and for taking care of management duties like accounting, travel organization etc. which would have surpassed our forces - and maybe even our skills. And we would also like to thank Sean Lorre from Springer Science + Media, Inc. for co-operating with us professionally and reliably during the publication process.

Last but not least, this volume is dedicated to our respective spouses, Anne Thirion and Helmut Geist, for patiently making room for our workshop, book publication and intellectual development of our methodological ambitions, for listening to new ideas in the process of writing, and for their vital help in the management of our two families (both of which have grown in the course of this project and do not perfectly fit into the "small N" research design anymore...) while we were working on undue hours.

Benoît Rihoux and Heike Grimm

Chapter 1

INTRODUCTION
Beyond the `Qualitative-Quantitative´ Divide: Innovative Comparative Methods for Policy Analysis

Benoît Rihoux
Université catholique de Louvain

Heike Grimm
University of Erfurt and Max-Planck-Institute of Economics, Jena

> " *'Social phenomena are complex'. As social scientists we often make this claim. Sometimes we offer it as justification for the slow rate of social scientific progress. (...) Yet (...) we sense that there is a great deal of order to social phenomena. (...) What is frustrating is the gulf that exists between this sense that the complexities of social phenomena can be unraveled and the frequent failures of our attempts to do so.* " (Ragin 1987: 19)

1. CONTEXT AND MAIN ISSUES: THE HIGH AMBITION OF THIS VOLUME

The ambition of this volume is to provide a decisive push to the further development and application of innovative comparative methods for the improvement of policy analysis.[1] Assuredly this is a high ambition. To take on this challenge, we have brought together methodologists and specialists from a broad range of social scientific disciplines and policy fields including senior and junior researchers.

During the last few years, an increasing number of political and social scientists and policy analysts have been opting for multiple case-studies as a research strategy. This choice is based on the need to gather in-depth insight in the different cases and capture the complexity of the cases, while still attempting to produce some level of generalization (Ragin 1987). Our effort also coincides – and is in line – with a much renewed interest in case-oriented research (Mahoney and Rueschemeyer 2003; George and Bennett 2005; Gerring forthcoming), and also in new attempts to engage in a well-informed dialogue between the "quantitative" and "qualitative" empirical traditions (Brady and Collier 2004; Sprinz and Nahmias-Wolinsky 2004; Moses, Rihoux and Kittel 2005).

Indeed, in policy studies particularly, many relevant and interesting objects – from the viewpoint of both academics and policy practitioners – are 'naturally' limited in number: nation states or regions, different kinds of policies in different states, policy outputs and outcomes, policy styles, policy sectors, etc. These naturally limited or "small-N" (or "intermediate-N") populations are in many instances especially relevant from a policy perspective. This is particularly true in a cross-national or cross-regional context, e.g. within the enlarged European Union or the United States.

In many instances the (ex-post) comparison of the case study material is rather 'loose' or not formalized. The major objective of this volume is to further develop methods for systematic comparative cases analysis (SCCA) in a small-N research design, with a key emphasis laid on policy-oriented applications. Hence our effort is clearly both a social scientific *and* policy-driven one: on the one hand, we do engage in an effort to further improve social scientific methods, but on the other hand this effort also intends to provide useful, applied tools for policy analysts and the 'policy community' alike.

Though quite a variety of methods and techniques are touched upon in this volume, its focus is mainly laid on a recently developed research method/technique which enables researchers to systematically compare a limited number of cases: Qualitative Comparative Analysis (QCA) (De Meur and Rihoux 2002; Ragin 1987; Ragin and Rihoux 2004) and its extension Multi-Value QCA (MVQCA). In some chapters, another related method/technique is also examined: Fuzzy-Sets (FS) (Ragin 2000). An increasing number of social scientists and policy analysts around the globe are now beginning to use these methods. The range of policy fields covered is also increasing (De Meur and Rihoux 2002; Ragin and Rihoux 2004) (see also the exhaustive bibliographical database on the resource website at: http://www.compasss.org). So is the number of publications, papers, and also ongoing research projects.

In a nutshell, we ambition to confront four main methodological issues. These issues, as it were, correspond to very concrete – and often difficult to overcome – problems constantly encountered in real-life, applied policy research.

First, how can specific technical and methodological difficulties related to systematic case study research and SCCA be overcome? There are numerous such difficulties, such as case selection (how to select genuinely 'comparable' cases?), variable selection (model specification), the integration of the time dimension (e.g. path-dependency), etc.

Second, how can the 'quality' of case studies be assessed? Case studies are often refuted on the ground that they are ill-selected, data are biased, etc. In short, case studies are sometimes accused of being 'unscientific', as one can allegedly prove almost anything with case studies. We shall attempt to demonstrate, through real-life applications that, by using new methods such as QCA, all the important steps of case study research (selection of cases, case-study design, selection and operationalization of variables, use of data and sources, comparison of case studies, generalization of empirical findings, etc.) become more transparent and open to discussion. We believe that methodological transparency is especially relevant for policy-makers assessing case study material.

Third, what is the practical added value of new comparative methods for policy analysis, from the perspective of policy analysts (academics) *and* policy practitioners (decision-makers, administrators, lobbyists, etc)? Can the following arguments (De Meur, Rihoux and Varone 2004), among others, be substantiated?

- The newly developed methods allow one to systematically compare policy programs in a "small-N" or "intermediate-N" design, with cross-national, cross-regional and cross-sector (policy domains) comparisons, typically within or across broad political entities or groups of countries (e.g. the European Union, the ASEAN, the MERCOSUR, the OECD, NATO, etc), but also for within-country (e.g. across states in the USA, across *Länder* in Germany, etc.) or within-region (e.g. between economic basins, municipalities, etc.) comparisons;
- these methods also allow one to test, both *ex post* and *ex ante*, alternative causal (policy intervention) models leading to a favorable/unfavorable policy output and favorable/unfavorable policy outcomes (on the distinction between *outputs* and *outcomes*, see Varone, Rihoux and Marx, in this volume). This approach, in contrast with mainstream statistical and econometric tools, allows thus the identification of more than one unique path to a policy outcome: more than one combination of conditions may account for a result. This is extremely useful in real-life policy practice, as experience shows that policy effectiveness is often dependent upon national/regional settings as well a upon sector-specific features, and that different cultural, political and administrative traditions often call for differentiated implementation schemes (Audretsch, Grimm and Wessner 2005). For instance, this is clearly the case within the enlarged European Union, with an increased diversity of economic, cultural and institutional-political configurations;
- these methods also allow one to engage in a systematic quasi-experimental design: for instance, this design enables the policy analyst or

policy evaluator to examine under which conditions (or more precisely: under which combinations of conditions) a specific policy is effective or not;
- these methods are very transparent; the policy analyst can easily modify the operationalization of the variables for further tests, include other variables, aggregate some proximate variables, etc. Thus it is also useful for pluralist/participative analysis;
- these methods are useful for the synthesis of existing qualitative analyses (i.e. "thick" case analyses), as well as for meta-analyses.

Fourth and finally, from a broader perspective, to what extent can such comparative methods bridge the gap between quantitative and qualitative analysis? Indeed, one key ambition of SCCA methods – of QCA specifically – is to combine some key strengths of both the qualitative and quantitative tools, and hence to provide some sort of 'third way' (Ragin 1987; Rihoux 2003).

2. WHAT FOLLOWS

This volume is divided into three main sections, following a logical sequence, along both the research process and the policy cycle dimensions. The first section on *Research design, methods and measures of policy analysis* addresses some prior key methodological issues in SCCA research from a policy-oriented perspective, such as comparative research design, case selection, views on causality, measurement, etc. It also provides a first 'real-life' confrontation between set-theoretic methods such as QCA and FS with some other existing – mainly quantitative – methods, in an intermediate-N setting.

The second section on *Innovative methods to analyze policy-making processes (agenda-setting, decision-making): applications,* covers the 'first half' of the policy-making cycle. It pursues the confrontation between SCCA methods (including FS) and mainstream statistical methods. It also gathers some real-life QCA and MVQCA (Multi-Value QCA) policy-oriented applications and opens some perspectives towards another innovative method which, potentially could be linked with FS and QCA: scenario-building.

Finally, the third section on *Innovative methods for policy implementation and evaluation: applications*, concentrates on the 'second half' of the policy-making cycle. It contains some concrete applications in two specific policy domains, as well as some more methodological reflections so as to pave the way for improved applications, especially in the field of policy evaluation.

2.1 Part One: Research Design, Methods and Measures in Policy Analysis

Charles C. Ragin's opening contribution interrogates and challenges the way we look at social science (and policy-relevant) data. He concentrates on research which does not study the policy process *per se*, but which is relevant for the policy process as its empirical conclusions has a strong influence in terms of policy advocacy. He focuses on the *Bell Curve Debate* (discussion on social inequalities in the U.S.) which lies at the connection between social scientific and policy-relevant debates. He opposes the 'net-effect' thinking in the Bell Curve Debate, which underlies much social science thinking. In the discussion on social inequalities, it is known that these inequalities do intersect and reinforce each other. Thus, does it really make sense to separate these to analyze their effect on the studied outcome? Using FS to perform a re-analysis of the Bell Curve Data, Ragin demonstrates that there is much more to be found when one takes into account the fundamentally 'configurational' nature of social phenomena, which cannot be grasped with standard statistical procedures.

To follow on, David Levi-Faur discusses both more fundamental (epistemological) and more practical issues with regards to comparative research design in policy analysis. The main problem is: how to increase the number of cases without loosing in-depth case knowledge? On the one hand, he provides a critical overview of Lijphart's and King-Keohane-Verba's advocated designs, which meet respectively the contradictory needs of internal validity (by control and comparison) and external validity (by correlation and broadening of the scope). The problem is to meet both needs, while also avoiding the contradiction between in-depth knowledge and generalization. On the other hand, building on Mill and on Przeworksi and Teune, he attempts to develop a series of four case-based comparative strategies to be used in a stepwise and iterative model.

The contribution by Gisèle De Meur, Peter Bursens and Alain Gottcheiner also addresses, from a partly different but clearly complementary perspective, the question of comparative research design, and more precisely model specification. They discuss in detail a specific technique: MSDO/MDSO (Most Similar, Different Outcome / Most Different, Similar Outcome), to be used as a prior step before using a technique such as QCA, so as to take into account many potential explanatory variables which are grouped into categories, producing a reduction in complexity. MSDO/MDSO is then applied in the field of policy-making processes in the European Union institutions. Their main goal is to identify the variables that explain why certain types of actor configurations (policy networks) develop through the elaboration of EU legislative proposals. In particular, can institutional variables, as defined by historical institutionalist theory, explain the way policy actors interact with each other during the policy-making process? MSDO/MDSO ultimately enables them to identify two key variables, which in turn allows them to reach important conclusions on how 'institutions matter' in the formation of EU policy networks.

Finally, Astrid Spreitzer and Sakura Yamasaki discuss the possible combinations of QCA with social network analysis (SNA). First, they identify some key problems of policy analysis: representing and deciphering complexity, formalizing social phenomena, allowing generalization, and providing pragmatic results. It is argued that both QCA and SNA provide useful answers to these problems: they assume complexity as a pre-existing context, they assume multiple and combinatorial causality, they offer some formal data processing, as well as some visualization tools. They follow by envisaging two ways of combining QCA and SNA. On the one hand, a QCA can be followed by a SNA, e.g. for purposes of visualization and interpretation of the QCA minimal formulae. On the other hand, a QCA can complement a SNA, e.g. by entering some network data into a QCA matrix. This is applied on two concrete examples, one of them being road transportation policy. In conclusion, they argue that the combination of QCA and SNA could cover 'blind areas' in policy analysis, while also allowing more accurate comparative policy analyses and offering new visualization tools for the pragmatic necessity of policy makers.

2.2 Part Two: Innovative Methods to Analyze Policy-Making Processes (Agenda-Setting, Decision-Making): Applications

In her chapter focusing on entrepreneurship policy and regional economic growth in the USA and Germany, Heike Grimm develops several qualitative approaches focusing on `institutional policies´ a) to define the concept of `entrepreneurship policy´ (E-Policy) more precisely and b) to explore whether a link exists between E-Policy and spatial growth. She then implements these approaches with QCA to check if any of these approaches (or any combination thereof) can be identified as a causal condition contributing to regional growth. By using conditions derived from a previous cross-national and cross-regional qualitative survey (expert interviews) for respectively three regions in the USA and in Germany, no "one-size-fits-it-all" explanation could be found, confirming the high complexity of the subject that she had predicted. Summing up, QCA seems to be a valuable tool to, on the one hand, confirm (causal) links obtained by other methodological approaches, and, on the other hand, allow a more detailed analysis focusing on some particular contextual factors which are influencing some cases while others are unaffected. The exploratory QCA reveals that existing theory of the link between policies and economic growth is rarely well-formulated enough to provide explicit hypotheses to be tested; therefore, the primary theoretical objective in entrepreneurship policy research at a comparative level is not theory testing, but elaboration, refinement, concept formation, and thus contributing to theory development.

The next contribution, by Lasse Cronqvist and Dirk Berg-Schlosser, examines the conditions of occurrence of HIV prevalence in Sub-Saharan Africa, and provides a test of quantitative methods as well as Multi-Value QCA (MVQCA). Their goal is to explore the causes in the differences of HIV prevalence rate between Sub-Saharan African countries. While regression tests and factor analysis show that the religious context and colonial history have had a strong impact on the spread of HIV, the popular thesis, according to which high education prevents high HIV prevalence rates, is invalidated. In countries with a high HIV prevalence rate, MVQCA then allows them to find connections between the mortality rate and the increase of the prevalence rate, as well as between the economical structure and the increase of the prevalence rate, which might be of interest for further HIV prevention policies. Methodologically, the introduction of finer graded scales with MVQCA is proved useful, as it allows a more genuine categorization of the data.

Jon Kvist's contribution is more focused on FS. In the field of comparative welfare state research, he shows how FS can be used to perform a more precise operationalization of theoretical concepts. He further demonstrates how to configure concepts into analytical concepts. Using unemployment insurance and child family policies in four Scandinavian countries as test cases, he exemplifies these approaches by using fuzzy memberships indicating the orientation towards specific policy ideal types. Using longitudinal data, he is then able to identify changes in the policy orientation in the 1990s by identifying changes in the fuzzy membership sets. Thereby an approach is presented which allows to compare diversity across countries and over time, in ways which conventional statistical methods but also qualitative approaches have not been able to do before.

Finally, António Brandao Moniz presents a quite different method, scenario-building, as a useful tool for policy analysis. Scenarios describe possible sets of future conditions. By building a scenario, one has to consider a number of important questions, and uncertainties as well as key driving forces have to be identified and deliberated about. The goal is to understand (and maximize) the benefits of possible strategic decisions, while also taking uncertainties and external influences into consideration. He further discusses some of the forecasting methods used in concrete projects, and exemplifies them by presenting scenario-building programs in the field of technological research, performed in Germany, Japan and by the United Nations. Potential ways of cross-fertilizing scenario-building and SCCA methods (QCA, MVQCA and FS) are also discussed.

2.1 Part Three: Innovative Methods for Policy Implementation and Evaluation: Applications

To start with, Frédéric Varone, Benoît Rihoux and Axel Marx aim to explore in what ways QCA can contribute to facing up key challenges for policy evaluation. They identify four challenges: linking policy interventions to outcomes and identifying causal mechanisms which link interventions to outcomes; identifying a 'net effect' of policy intervention and purge out the confounding factors; answering the 'what if'-question (i.e. generate counterfactual evidence); and triangulating evidence. It is argued that QCA offers some specific answers to these challenges, as it allows for a three way comparison, namely a cross-case analysis, a within-case analysis, and a comparison between empirical reality and theoretical ideal types. However, they also point out that QCA should address the contradictions/uniqueness trade-off. If one includes too many variables, a problem of uniqueness might occur, i.e. each case is then simply described as a distinct configuration of variables, which results in full complexity and no parsimony (and is of limited relevance to policy-makers). On the other hand, if one uses too few variables the probability of contradictions increases. Some possibilities to deal with this trade-off are discussed.

To follow up, Pentti Luoma applies both QCA, regression analysis, and more qualitative assessments, in a study on the ecological, physical and social sustainability of some residential areas in three growing and three declining municipalities in the Oulu province (Finland). He presents preliminary results of a study of 13 residential areas in Oulunsalo, a municipality close to the city of Oulu with a rapidly growing population in connection with urban sprawl. He identifies several variables which might influence this sustainability, such as issues related to the attachment to a local place (local identities). The main substantive focus of this contribution is placed on social sustainability and integration, which are operationalized as dependent variables in terms of satisfaction with present living conditions in a certain neighborhood, inclination to migrate, and a measure of local social capital. QCA and regression are used to analyze the occurrence of social integration in a model which consists out of social, physical and local features. Though the QCA analysis yields some contradictions, it still provides useful results from a research and policy advocacy perspective.

Finally, Barbara Befani and Fritz Sager outline the benefits and challenges of the mixed realistic evaluation-QCA approach. A study from the evaluation of the Swiss Environmental Impact Assessment (EIA) is presented, in which

Introduction 9

three types of different outcomes are evaluated. Following the realist paradigm, initial assumptions are made on which Context-Mechanism-Outcome (CMO) configurations explain the different types of policy results. The propositions constituting this type of working material are then translated into a set of Boolean variables, thereby switching the epistemological basis of the study to multiple-conjunctural causality. A QCA model deriving from those initial assumptions is then constructed and empirical data are collected in order to fill in a data matrix on which QCA is performed. The QCA produces minimal configurations of conditions which are, in turn, used to refine the initial assumptions (on which mechanisms were activated in which contexts to achieve which outcomes). The theory refinement made possible by QCA covers both directions on the abstraction to specification scale: downward, it offers more elaborate configurations able to account for a certain outcome; upward, it aggregates relatively specific elements into more abstract ones ('realist synthesis'). The authors finally argue that QCA has the potential to expand the scope and possibilities of Realistic Evaluation, both as an instrument of theory refinement and as a tool to handle realist synthesis when the number of cases is relatively high.

3. ASSESSING THE PROGRESS MADE... AND THE CHALLENGES AHEAD

To what extent has this volume been successful in providing 'a decisive push to the further development and application of innovative comparative methods for the improvement of policy analysis'? This will be the main focus of the concluding chapter, in which we first argue that, in several respects, we have indeed made some significant progress in the task of addressing the above-mentioned four key methodological challenges.

On the other hand, building upon this collective effort, we also attempt to identify the remaining challenges. This enables us not only to pinpoint some key difficulties or "Gordian knots" still to be unraveled, but also the most promising avenues for research. Finally, we discuss ways in which the dialogue between policy analysts ('academics') and the policy community ('decision makers') could be enriched – around methods, not as an end in themselves, but as a means towards better policy analysis, and thus hopefully towards better policies.

NOTES

[1] We thank Axel Marx for his input in a preliminary version of this text.

PART ONE

SYSTEMATIC COMPARATIVE CASE STUDIES: DESIGN, METHODS AND MEASURES

Chapter 2

THE LIMITATIONS OF NET-EFFECTS THINKING

Charles C. Ragin
University of Arizona

1. INTRODUCTION

Conventional methods of data analysis such as multiple regression form the backbone of most policy-oriented research in the social sciences today. It should not be surprising that they do, for they are considered by many to be the most rigorous, the most disciplined, and the most scientific of the analytic methods available to social researchers. If the results of social research are to have an impact on policy, it stands to reason that such findings should be produced using the most rigorous analytic methods available.

While conventional quantitative methods are clearly rigorous, it is important to understand that these methods are organized around a specific kind of rigor. That is, they have their own rigor and their own discipline, not a universal rigor. While there are several features of conventional quantitative methods that make them rigorous and therefore valuable to policy research, in this contribution I focus on a single, key aspect--namely, the fact that they are centered on the task of estimating the "net effects" of "independent" variables on outcomes. I focus on this central aspect, which I characterize as "net-effects thinking", because this feature of conventional methods can undermine their value to policy.

This contribution presents its critique of net-effects thinking in a practical manner, by contrasting the conventional analysis of a large-N, policy-relevant data set with an alternate analysis, one that repudiates the assumption that the key to social scientific knowledge is the estimation of the net effects of independent variables. This alternate method, known as fuzzy-set/Qualitative Comparative Analysis or fsQCA, combines the use of fuzzy sets with the analysis of cases as configurations, a central feature of case-oriented social research (Ragin 1987). In this approach, each case is examined in terms of its degree of membership in different *combinations* of causally relevant conditions. Using fsQCA, researchers can consider cases' memberships in all of the logically possible combinations of a given set of causal conditions and then use set-theoretic methods to analyze--in a logically disciplined manner--the varied connections between causal combinations and the outcome.

I offer this alternate approach not as a replacement for net-effects analysis, but as a complementary technique. fsQCA is best seen as an exploratory technique, grounded in set theory. While probabilistic criteria can be incorporated into fsQCA, it is not an inferential technique, per se. It is best understood an alternate way of analyzing evidence, starting from very different assumptions about the kinds of "findings" social scientists seek. These alternate assumptions reflect the logic and spirit of qualitative research, where investigators study cases configurationally, with an eye toward how the different parts or aspects of cases fit together.

2. NET-EFFECTS THINKING

In what has become normal social science, researchers view their primary task as one of assessing the relative importance of causal variables drawn from competing theories. In the ideal situation, the relevant theories emphasize different variables and make clear, unambiguous statements about how these variables are connected to relevant empirical outcomes. In practice, however, most theories in the social sciences are vague when it comes to specifying both causal conditions and outcomes, and they tend to be silent when it comes to stating *how* the causal conditions are connected to outcomes (e.g., specifying the conditions that must be met for a given causal variable to have its impact). Typically, researchers are able to develop only general lists of potentially relevant causal conditions based on the broad portraits of social phenomena they find in theories. The key analytic task is typically viewed as one of assessing the relative importance of the listed variables. If the variables associated with a particular theory prove to be the best predictors of the outcome (i.e., the best "explainers" of its variation), then this theory wins the contest. This way of conducting quantitative analysis is the default procedure in the social sciences today – one that researchers fall back on time and time again, often for lack of a clear alternative.

In the net-effects approach, estimates of the effects of independent variables are based on the assumption that each variable, by itself, is capable of producing or influencing the level or probability of the outcome. While it is common to treat "causal" and "independent" as synonymous modifiers of the word "variable", the core meaning of "independent" is this notion of autonomous capacity. Specifically, each independent variable is assumed to be capable of influencing the level or probability of the outcome *regardless of the values or levels of other variables* (i.e., regardless of the varied contexts defined by these variables). Estimates of net effects thus assume *additivity*, that the net impact of a given independent variable on the outcome is the same across all the values of the other independent variables and their different combinations. To estimate the net effect of a given variable, the researcher offsets the impact of competing causal conditions by subtracting from the estimate of the effect of each variable any explained variation in the dependent variable it shares with other causal variables. This is the core meaning of "net effects" – the calculation of the non-overlapping contribution of each variable to explained variation in the outcome. Degree of overlap is a direct function of correlation: generally, the greater the correlation of an independent variable with its competitors, the less its net effect.

There is an important underlying compatibility between vague theory and net-effects thinking. When theories are weak, they offer only general characterizations of social phenomena and do not attend to causal complexity. Clear specifications of relevant contexts and scope conditions are rare, as is consideration of how causal conditions may modify each other's relevance or impact (i.e., how they may display non-additivity). Researchers are lucky to derive coherent lists of potentially relevant causal conditions from most theories in the social sciences, for the typical theory offers very little specific guidance. This guidance void is filled by linear, additive models with their emphasis on estimating generic net effects. Researchers often declare that they estimate linear-additive models because they are the "simplest possible" and make the "fewest assumptions" about the nature of causation. In this view, additivity (and thus simplicity) is the default state; any analysis of non-additivity requires explicit theoretical authorization, which is almost always lacking.

The common emphasis on the calculation of net effects also dovetails with the notion that the foremost goal of social research is to assess the relative explanatory power of variables attached to competing theories. Net-effects analyses provide explicit quantitative assessments of the non-overlapping explained variation that can be credited to each theory's variables. Often, however, theories do not contradict each other and thus do not really compete. After all, the typical social science theory is little more than a vague portrait. The use of the net effects approach thus may create the appearance of theory adjudication in research where such adjudication may not be necessary or even possible.

2.1 Problems with Net-Effects Thinking

There are several problems associated with the net effects approach, especially when it is used as the primary means of generating policy-relevant social scientific knowledge. These include both practical and conceptual problems.

A fundamental practical problem is the simple fact that the assessment of net effects is dependent on model specification. The estimate of an independent variable's net effect is powerfully swayed by its correlations with competing variables. Limit the number of correlated competitors and a chosen variable may have a substantial net effect on the outcome; pile them on, and its net effect may be reduced to nil. The specification dependence of the estimate of net effects is well known, which explains why quantitative researchers are thoroughly schooled in the importance of "correct" specification. However, correct specification is dependent upon strong theory and deep substantive knowledge, both of which are usually lacking in the typical application of net-effects methods.

The importance of model specification is apparent in the many analyses of the data set that is used in this contribution, the National Longitudinal Survey of Youth (NLSY), analyzed by Herrnstein and Murray in *The Bell Curve*. In this work Herrnstein and Murray report a very strong net effect of test scores (the Armed Forces Qualifying Test--AFQT, which they treat as a test of general intelligence) on outcomes such as poverty: the higher the AFQT score, the lower the odds of poverty. By contrast, Fischer *et al.* use the same data and the same estimation technique (logistic regression) but find a weak net effect of AFQT scores on poverty. The key difference between these two analyses is the fact that Herrnstein and Murray allow only a few variables to compete with AFQT, usually only one or two, while Fischer *et al.* allow many. Which estimate of the net effect of AFQT scores is "correct"? The answer depends upon which specification is considered "correct". Thus, debates about net effects often stalemate in disagreements about model specification. While social scientists tend to think that having more variables is better than having few, as in Fischer *et al.*'s analysis, having too many independent variables is also a serious specification error.

A related practical problem is the fact that many of the independent variables that interest social scientists are highly correlated with each other and thus can have only modest non-overlapping effects on a given outcome. Again, *The Bell Curve* controversy is a case in point. Test scores and socioeconomic status of family of origin are strongly correlated, as are these two variables with a variety of other potentially relevant causal conditions (years of schooling, neighborhood and school characteristics, and so on). Because social inequalities overlap, cases' scores on "independent" variables tend to bunch together: high AFQT scores tend to go with better family backgrounds, better schools, better neighborhoods, and so on. Of course, these correlations are far from perfect; thus, it is possible to squeeze estimates of the net effects of these "independent" variables out of the data. Still, the overwhelming empirical pattern is one of confounded causes – of clusters of favorable versus unfavorable conditions, not of analytically separable independent variables. One thing social scientists know about social inequalities is that because they overlap, they reinforce. It is their overlapping nature that gives them their strength and durability. Given this characteristic feature of social phenomena, it seems somewhat counterintuitive for quantitative social scientists to rely almost exclusively on techniques that champion the estimation of the separate, unique, net effect of each causal variable.

More generally, while it is useful to examine correlations between variables (e.g., the strength of the correlation between AFQT scores and family background), it is also useful to study cases holistically, as specific configurations of attributes. In this view, cases combine different causally relevant characteristics in different ways, and it is important to assess the consequences of these different combinations. Consider, for example, what it takes to avoid poverty. Does college education make a difference for married White males from families with good incomes? Probably not, or at least not much of a difference, but college education may make a huge difference for unmarried Black females from low-income families. By examining cases as configurations it is possible to conduct context-specific assessments, analyses that are circumstantially delimited. Assessments of this type involve questions about the conditions that enable or disable specific connections between causes and outcomes. Under what conditions do test scores matter, when it comes to avoiding poverty? Under what conditions does marriage matter? Are these connections different for White females and Black males? These kinds of questions are outside the scope of conventional net-effects analyses, for they are centered on the task of estimating context-independent net effects.

Configurational assessments of the type just described are directly relevant to policy. Policy discourse often focuses on categories and kinds of people (or cases), not on variables and their net effects across heterogeneous populations. Consider, for example, phrases like the "truly disadvantaged", the "working poor", and "welfare mothers". Generally, such categories embrace combinations of characteristics. Consider also the fact that policy is fundamentally concerned with social intervention. While it might be good to know that education, in general, decreases the odds of poverty (i.e., that it has a significant, negative net effect on poverty), from a policy perspective it is far more useful to know under what conditions education has a decisive impact, shielding an otherwise vulnerable subpopulation from poverty. Net effects are calculated across samples drawn from entire populations. They are not based on "structured, focused comparisons" (George 1979) using specific kinds and categories of cases. Finally, while the calculation of net-effects offers succinct assessments of the relative explanatory power of variables drawn from different theories, the adjudication between competing theories is not a central concern of policy research. Which theory prevails in the competition to explain variation is primarily an academic question. The issue that is central to policy is determining which causal conditions are decisive in which contexts, regardless of the (typically vague) theory the conditions are drawn from.

To summarize: the net-effects approach, while powerful and rigorous, is limited. It is restrained by its own rigor, for its strength is also its weakness. It is particularly disadvantaged when to comes to studying combinations of case characteristics, especially overlapping inequalities. Given these drawbacks, it is reasonable to explore an alternate approach, one with strengths that differ from those of net-effects methods. Specifically, the net effects approach, with its heavy emphasis on calculating the uncontaminated effect of each independent variables in order to isolate variables from one another, can be counterbalanced and complemented with an approach that explicitly considers combinations and configurations of case aspects.

2.2 Studying Cases as Configurations

Underlying the broad expanse of social scientific methodology is a continuum that extends from small-N, case-oriented, qualitative techniques to large-N, variable-oriented, quantitative techniques. Generally, social scientists deplore the wide gulf that separates the two ends of this continuum, but they typically stick to only one end when they conduct research. With fsQCA, however, it is possible to bring some of the spirit and logic of case-oriented investigation to large-N research. This technique offers researchers tools for studying cases as configurations and for exploring the connections between *combinations* of causally relevant conditions and outcomes. By studying combinations of conditions, it is possible to unravel the conditions or contexts that enable or disable specific connections (e.g., between education and the avoidance of poverty).

The starting point of fsQCA is the principle that cases should be viewed in terms of the combinations of causally relevant conditions they display. To represent combinations of conditions, researchers use an analytic device known as a truth table, which lists the logically possible combinations of causal conditions specified by the researcher and sorts cases according to the combinations they display. Also listed in the truth table is an outcome value (typically coded either true or false) for each combination of causal conditions. The goal of fsQCA is to derive a logical statement describing the different combinations of conditions linked to an outcome, as summarized in the truth table.

A simple, hypothetical truth table with four crisp-set (i.e., dichotomous) causal conditions, one outcome, and 200 cases is presented in table 2.1.

Table 2.1. Hypothetical Truth Table with Four Causal Conditions and One Outcome

	College Educated (C)	High Parental Income (I)	Parent College Educated (P)	High AFQT Score (S)	Poverty Avoidance (A)	Number of Cases
1	0	0	0	0	0	30
2	0	0	0	1	?	3
3	0	0	1	0	?	4
4	0	0	1	1	?	0
5	0	1	0	0	0	25
6	0	1	0	1	0	19
7	0	1	1	0	?	0
8	0	1	1	1	0	20
9	1	0	0	0	?	0
10	1	0	0	1	?	1
11	1	0	1	0	?	0
12	1	0	1	1	?	2
13	1	1	0	0	1	19
14	1	1	0	1	1	22
15	1	1	1	0	1	32
16	1	1	1	1	1	23

The four causal conditions are:

(1) Did the respondent earn a college degree?
(2) Was the respondent raised in a household with at least a middle class income?
(3) Did at least one of the respondent's parents earn a college degree?
(4) Did the respondent achieve a high score on the Armed Forces Qualifying Test (AFQT)?

With four causal conditions, there are 16 logically possible combinations of conditions, the same as the number of rows in the table. More generally, the number of combinations is 2^k, where k is the number of causal conditions. As the number of causal conditions increases, the number of combinations increases dramatically. The outcome variable in this hypothetical truth table is "poverty avoidance" – indicating whether or not the individuals in each row display a very low rate of poverty (1 = very low rate).

In fsQCA outcomes (e.g., "poverty avoidance" in table 2.1) are coded using set-theoretic criteria. The key question for each row is the degree to which the individuals in the row constitute a subset of the individuals who are not in poverty. That is, do the cases in a given row agree in not displaying poverty? Of course, perfect subset relations are rare with individual-level data. There are always surprising cases, for example, the person with every possible advantage, who nevertheless manages to fall into poverty. With fsQCA, researchers establish rules for determining the degree to which the cases in each row are consistent with the subset relation. The researcher first establishes a threshold proportion for set-theoretic consistency, which the observed proportions must exceed. For example, a researcher might argue that the observed proportion of cases in a row that are not in poverty must exceed a benchmark proportion of 0.95. Additionally, the researcher may also apply conventional probabilistic criteria to these assessments. For example, the researcher might state that the observed proportion of individuals not in poverty must be significantly greater than a benchmark proportion of 0.90, using a significance level (alpha) of 0.05 or 0.10. The specific benchmarks and alphas used by researchers depend on the state of existing substantive and theoretical knowledge. The assessment of each row's set-theoretic consistency is straightforward when truth tables are constructed from crisp sets. When fuzzy sets are used, the set-theoretic principles that are invoked are the same, but the calculations are more complex.

As constituted, table 2.1 is ready for set-theoretic analysis using fsQCA. The goal of this analysis would be to identify the different combinations of case characteristics explicitly linked to poverty avoidance. Examination of the last four rows, for example, indicates that the combination of college education and high parental income may be an explicit link – a combination that provides a good recipe for poverty avoidance. Specific details on truth table analysis and the derivation of the causal combinations linked to a given outcome are provided in Ragin (1987, 2000).

2.3 Key Contrasts between Net-Effects and Configurational Thinking

The hypothetical data presented in table 2.1 display a characteristic feature of nonexperimental data; namely, the 200 cases are unevenly distributed across the 16 rows, and some combinations of conditions (i.e., rows) lack cases altogether. (The number of individuals with each combination of causal conditions is reported in the last column). In the net-effects approach, this unevenness is understood as the result of correlated independent variables. Generally, the greater the correlations among the causal variables, the greater the unevenness of the distribution of cases across the different combinations of causal conditions. By contrast, in fsQCA this unevenness is understood as "limited diversity". In this view, the four causal conditions define 16 different kinds of cases, and the four dichotomies become, in effect, a single nominal-scale variable with 16 possible categories. Because there are empirical instances of only a subset of the 16 logically possible kinds of cases, the data set is understood as limited in its diversity.

The key difference between fsQCA and the net-effects approach is that the latter focuses on analytically separable independent variables and their degree of intercorrelation, while the former focuses on kinds of cases defined with respect to the combinations of causally relevant conditions they display. These contrasting views of the same evidence, net-effects versus configurational, have very different implications for how evidence is understood and analyzed. Notice, for example, that in table 2.1 there is a perfect correlation between having a college degree and avoiding poverty. That is, whenever there is a 1 (yes) in the outcome column ("poverty avoidance"), there is also a 1 (yes) in the "college educated" column, and whenever there is a 0 (no) in the "poverty avoidance" column, there is also a 0 (no) in the "college educated" column. From a net-effects perspective, this pattern constitutes very strong evidence that the key to avoiding poverty is college education. Once the effect of college education is taken into account (using the hypothetical data in table 2.1), there is no variation in poverty avoidance remaining for the other variables to explain. This conclusion does not come so easily using fsQCA, however, for there are several combinations of conditions in the truth table where college education is present and the outcome (poverty avoidance) is unknown, due to an insufficiency of cases. For example, the ninth row combines presence of college education with absence of the other three resources. However, there are no cases with this combination of conditions and consequently no way to assess empirically whether this combination of conditions is linked to poverty avoidance.

In order to derive the simple conclusion that college education by itself is the key to poverty avoidance using fsQCA, it is necessary to incorporate what are known as "simplifying assumptions" involving combinations of conditions that have few cases or that lack cases altogether. In fsQCA, these combinations are known as "remainders". They are the rows of table 2.1 with "?" in the outcome column, due to a scarcity of cases. Remainder combinations must be addressed explicitly in the process of constructing generalizations from evidence in situations of limited diversity (Ragin and

Sonnett 2004; Varone, Rihoux and Marx, in this volume). For example, in order to conclude that college education, by itself, is the key to avoiding poverty (i.e., the conclusion that would follow from a net-effects analysis of these data), with fsQCA it would be necessary to *assume* that if empirical instances of the ninth row could be found (presence of college education combined with an absence of the other three resources), these cases would support the conclusion that college education offers protection from poverty. This same pattern of results also should hold for the other rows where college education equals 1 (yes) and the outcome is unknown (i.e., rows 10-12).

Ragin and Sonnett (2004) outline general procedures for treating remainder rows as counterfactual cases and for evaluating their plausibility as simplifying assumptions. Two solutions are derived from the truth table. The first maximizes parsimony by allowing the use of any simplifying assumption that yields a logically simpler solution of the truth table. The second maximizes complexity by barring simplifying assumptions altogether. That is, the second solution assumes that none of the remainder rows is explicitly linked to the outcome in question. These two solutions establish the range of plausible solutions to a given truth table. Because of the set-theoretic nature of truth table analysis, the most complex solution is a subset of the most parsimonious solution. Researchers can use their substantive and theoretical knowledge to derive an optimal solution, which typically lies in between the most parsimonious and the most complex solutions. The optimal solution must be a superset of the most complex solution and a subset of the most parsimonious solution (it is important to note that a set is both a superset and a subset of itself; thus, the solutions at either of the two endpoints of the complexity/parsimony continuum may be considered optimal). This use of substantive and theoretical knowledge constitutes, in effect, an evaluation of the plausibility of counterfactual cases, as represented in the remainder combinations.

The most parsimonious solution to table 2.1 is the conclusion that the key to avoiding poverty is college education. This solution involves the incorporation of a number of simplifying assumptions, specifically, that if enough instances of rows 9-12 could be located, the evidence for each row would be consistent with the parsimonious solution (i.e., each of these rows would be explicitly linked to poverty avoidance). The logical equation for this solution is:

$C \longrightarrow A$

[In this and subsequent logical statements, upper-case letters indicate the presence of a condition, lower-case letters indicate its absence, C = college educated, I = at least middle class parental income, P = parent college educated, S = high AFQT score, A = avoidance of poverty, "⟶" indicates "is sufficient for", multiplication (·) indicates combined conditions (set intersection), and addition (+) indicates alternate combinations of conditions (set union).] Thus, the results of the first set-theoretic analysis of the truth table are the same as the results of a conventional net-effects analysis. By contrast, the results of the most complex solution, which bars the use of remainders as simplifying assumptions, are:

$C \cdot I \longrightarrow A$

This equation indicates that two conditions, college education and high parental income, must be combined for a respondent to avoid poverty.

As Ragin and Sonnett (2004) argue, in order to strike a balance between parsimony and complexity it is necessary to use theoretical and substantive knowledge to identify, if possible, the subset of remainder combinations that constitute plausible pathways to the outcome. The solution to table 2.1 favoring complex causation shows that two favorable conditions must be combined. In order to derive the parsimonious solution using fsQCA, it must be assumed that *if* cases combining college education and the *absence* of high parental income could be found (thus populating rows 9-12 of table 2.1), they would be consistent with the parsimonious conclusion. This logical reduction proceeds as follows:

observed: $C \cdot I \longrightarrow A$
by assumption: $C \cdot i \longrightarrow A$
logical simplification: $C \cdot I + C \cdot i = C \cdot (I + i) = C \cdot (1) = C \longrightarrow A$

According to the arguments in Ragin and Sonnett (2004) the logical simplification just sketched is *not* warranted in this instance because the *presence* of high parental income is known to be a factor that *contributes* to poverty avoidance. That is, because the assumption $C \cdot i \longrightarrow A$ involves a "difficult" counterfactual, it should not be made, at least not without extensive theoretical or substantive justification. More generally, they argue that theoretical and substantive knowledge should be used to evaluate all such simplifying assumptions in situations of limited diversity. These evaluations can be used to strike a balance between the most parsimonious and the most complex solutions of a truth table, yielding solutions that typically are more complex than the parsimonious solution, but more parsimonious than the complex solution. This use of substantive and theoretical knowledge to derive optimal solutions is the essence of counterfactual analysis.

In conventional net-effects analyses "remainder" combinations are routinely incorporated into solutions; however, their use is invisible to most users. In this approach, remainders are covertly incorporated into solutions via the assumption of additivity – the idea that the net effect of a variable is the same regardless of the values of the other independent variables. Thus, the issue of limited diversity and the need for counterfactual analysis are both veiled in the effort to analytically isolate the effect of independent variables on the outcome.

3. FUZZY SETS AND CONFIGURATIONAL ANALYSIS

Set-theoretic analysis is not limited to conventional, presence/absence sets, the kind used in table 2.1. With fuzzy sets it is possible to assess the degree of membership of cases in sets, using values that range from 0 (non-membership) to 1 (full membership). A fuzzy membership score of 0.90, for example, indicates that a case is mostly but not fully in a set. This score might be used to describe the membership of the U.S. in the set of democratic countries, as demonstrated in the presidential election of 2000. Fuzzy sets are useful because they address a problem that social scientists interested in sets of cases routinely confront – the challenge of working with case aspects that resist transformation to crisp categories. To delineate the set of individuals with high AFQT scores as a conventional crisp set, for example, it would be necessary to select a cut-off score, which might be considered somewhat arbitrary. The use of fuzzy sets remedies this problem, for degree of membership in a set can be calibrated so that it ranges from 0 to 1.

A detailed exposition of fuzzy sets and their uses in social research is presented in Ragin (2000; 2005). For present purposes, it suffices to note that the basic set-theoretic principles described in this contribution, including subset relations, limited diversity, parsimony, complexity, and counterfactual analysis have the same bearing and importance in research using fuzzy sets that they do in research using crisp sets. The only important difference is that with fuzzy sets each case, potentially, can have some degree of (nonzero) membership in every combination of causal conditions. Thus, the empirical basis for set-theoretic assessment using fuzzy sets is much wider than it is using crisp sets because more cases are involved in each assessment. Note, however, that it is mathematically possible for a case to be more "in" than "out" of only one of the logically possible combinations of causal conditions listed in a truth table. That is, each case can have, at most, only one configuration membership score that is greater than 0.50 across the 2^k configurations.

Because of the mathematical continuities underlying crisp and fuzzy sets, table 2.1 could have been constructed from fuzzy-set data (see Ragin 2005).

To do so, it would have been necessary to calibrate the degree of membership of each case in each of the sets defined by the causal conditions (e.g., degree of membership in the set of individuals with high AFQT scores) and then assess the degree of membership of each case in each of the 16 combinations of causal conditions defining the rows of table 2.1. For example, a case with a membership score of .4 in "high AFQT score" and membership scores of .7 in the other three causal conditions would have a membership score of .4 in the combined presence of these four conditions (see Ragin 2000 for a discussion of the use of the minimum when assessing membership in combinations of sets). After calibrating degree of membership in the outcome (i.e., in the set of individuals successfully avoiding poverty), it would be possible to evaluate the degree to which membership in each combination of causal conditions is a fuzzy subset of membership in this outcome. In effect, these analyses assess the degree to which individuals conforming to each row consistently avoid poverty. Such assessments are conducted using fuzzy membership scores, not dichotomized scores, and they utilize a stricter definition of the subset relation than is used in crisp-set analyses (Ragin 2005).

In fuzzy-set analyses, a crisp truth table is used to summarize the results of these fuzzy-set assessments. In this example there would be 16 fuzzy-set assessments because there are four fuzzy-set causal conditions and thus 16 configuration membership scores. More generally, the number of fuzzy-set assessments is 2^k, where k is the number of causal conditions. The rows of the resulting truth table list the different combinations of conditions assessed. For example, row 4 of the truth table (following the pattern in table 2.1) would summarize the results of the fuzzy-set analysis of degree of membership in the set of individuals who combine low membership in "college educated", low membership in "high parental income", high membership in "parents college educated", and high membership in "high AFQT score". The outcome column in the truth table shows the results of the 2^k fuzzy-set assessments – that is, whether or not degree of membership in the configuration of causal conditions specified in a row can be considered a fuzzy subset of degree of membership in the outcome. The examination of the resulting crisp truth table is, in effect, an analysis of *statements* summarizing the 2^k fuzzy-set analyses. The end product of the truth table analysis, in turn, is a logical equation derived from the comparison of these statements. This equation specifies the different combinations of causal conditions linked to the outcome via the fuzzy subset relationship.

Note that with fuzzy sets, the issue of limited diversity is transformed from one of "empty cells" in a k-way cross-tabulation of dichotomized causal conditions (i.e., remainder rows in a truth table), to one of empty sectors in a vector space with k dimensions. The 2^k sectors of this space vary in the degree to which they are populated with cases, with some sectors lacking cases altogether. In other words, with naturally occurring social data it is common for many sectors of the vector space defined by causal conditions to be void of cases, just as it is common for a k-way cross-tabulation of dichotomies to yield an abundance of empty cells. The same tools developed to address limited diversity in crisp-set analyses, described previously in this contribution and in Ragin and Sonnett (2004), can be used to address limited diversity in fuzzy-set analyses. Specifically, the investigator derives two solutions to the truth table, one maximizing complexity and the other maximizing parsimony, and then uses substantive and theoretical knowledge to craft an intermediate solution--a middle path between complexity and parsimony. The intermediate solution incorporates only those counterfactuals that can be justified using existing theoretical and substantive knowledge (i.e., "easy" counterfactuals).

The remainder of this contribution is devoted to a comparison of a net-effects analysis of the NLSY data, using logistic regression, with a configurational analysis of the same data, using the fuzzy-set methods just described. While the two approaches differ in several respects, the key difference is that the net-effects approach focuses on the independent effects of causal variables on the outcome, while the configurational approach attends to combinations of causal conditions and attempts to establish explicit links between specific combinations and the outcome.

3.1 A Net Effects Analysis of *The Bell Curve* Data

In *The Bell Curve*, Herrnstein and Murray (1994) compute rudimentary logistic regression analyses to gauge the importance of AFQT scores on a variety of dichotomous outcomes. They control for the effects of only two competing variables in most of their main analyses, respondent's age (at the time the AFQT was administered) and parental socio-economic status (SES). Their central finding is that AFQT score (which they interpret as a measure of general intelligence) is more important than parental SES when it comes to major life outcomes such as avoiding poverty. They interpret this and related findings as proof that in modern society "intelligence" (which they assert is inborn) has become the most important factor shaping life chances. Their explanation focuses on the fact that the nature of work has changed, and that there is now a much higher labor market premium attached to high cognitive ability.

Table 2.2. Logistic Regression of Poverty Avoidance on AFQT Scores and Parental SES (*Bell Curve* Model)

	B	S.E.	Sig.	Exp(B)
AFQT (z score)	.651	.139	.000	1.917
Parental SES (z score)	.376	.117	.001	1.457
Age	.040	.050	.630	1.040
Constant	1.123	.859	.191	3.074

Chi-Squared = 53.973, df = 3

Their main result with presence/absence of poverty as the outcome of interest is presented in table 2.2 (with absence of poverty = 1). The reported analysis uses standardized data (z scores) for both parental socio-economic status (SES) and AFQT score to facilitate comparison of effects. The analysis is limited to Black males with complete data on all the variables used in this and subsequent analyses, including the fuzzy-set analysis. The strong effect of AFQT scores, despite the control for the impact of parental SES, mirrors the *Bell Curve* results.

A major rebuttal of the *Bell Curve* "thesis", as it became known, was presented by a team of Berkeley sociologists, Claude Fischer, Michael Hout, Martin Sanchez Jankowsk, Samuel Lucas, Ann Swidler, and Kim Voss (1996). In their book, *Inequality By Design*, they present a much more elaborate logistic regression analysis of the NLSY data. Step by step, they include more and more causal conditions (e.g., neighborhood and school characteristics) that they argue should be seen as competitors with AFQT scores. In their view, AFQT score has a substantial effect in the *Bell Curve* analysis only because the logistic regression analyses that Herrnstein and Murray report are radically under-specified. To remedy this problem, Fischer *et al.* include more than 15 control variables in their analysis of the effects of AFQT scores on the odds of avoiding poverty. While this "everything-but-the-kitchen-sink" approach dramatically reduces the impact of AFQT scores on poverty, the authors leave themselves open to the charge that they have misspecified their analyses by being over-inclusive.

Table 2.3. Logistic Regression of Poverty Avoidance on AFQT Scores, Parental Income, Years of Education, Marital Status, and Children

	B	S.E.	Sig.	Exp(B)
AFQT (z score)	.391	.154	.011	1.479
Parental Income (z score)	.357	.154	.020	1.429
Education (z score)	.635	.139	.000	1.887
Married (yes = 1, 0 = no)	1.658	.346	.000	5.251
Children (yes = 1, 0 = no)	-.524	.282	.063	.592
Constant	1.970	.880	.025	7.173

Chi-Squared = 104.729, df = 5

Table 2.3 reports the results of a logistic regression analysis of poverty using only a moderate number of independent variables. Specifically, presence/absence of poverty (with absence = 1) is regressed on five independent variables: AFQT score, years of education, parental income, married versus not married, and one-or-more children versus no children. The three interval-scale variables are standardized (using z scores) to simplify comparison of effects. The table shows the results for Black males only. The rationale for this specification is that the model is more fully specified than the unrealistically spare model presented by Herrnstein and Murray and less elaborate and cumbersome than Fischer *et al.*'s model. In other words, the analysis strikes a balance between the two specification extremes and focuses on the most important causal conditions.

The results presented in table 2.3 are consistent with both Herrnstein and Murray and Fischer *et al.* That is, they show that AFQT score has an independent impact on poverty avoidance, but not nearly as strong as that reported by Herrnstein and Murray. Consistent with Fischer *et al.*, table 2.3 shows very strong effects of competing causal conditions, especially years of education and marital status. These conditions were not included in the *Bell Curve* analysis. More generally, table 2.3 confirms the specification-dependence of net-effects analysis. With an intermediate number of competing independent variables, the effect of AFQT is substantially reduced. It is not nearly as strong as it is in the *Bell Curve* analysis, but not quite as weak as it is in Fischer *et al.*'s analysis.

3.2 A Fuzzy-Set Re-Analysis

The success of any fuzzy-set analysis is dependent on the careful construction and calibration of fuzzy sets. The core of both crisp-set and fuzzy-set analysis is the evaluation of set-theoretic relationships, for example, the assessment of whether membership in a combination of causal conditions can be considered a subset of membership in the outcome. A fuzzy subset relationship exists when the scores in one set (e.g., the fuzzy set of individuals who combine high parental income, college education, high test scores, and so on) are consistently less than or equal to the scores in another set (e.g., the fuzzy set of individuals not in poverty). Thus, it matters a great deal how fuzzy sets are constructed and how membership scores are calibrated. Serious miscalibrations can distort or undermine the identification of set-theoretic relationships. By contrast, for the conventional variable to be useful in a net-effects analysis, it needs only to vary in a meaningful way. Often, the specific metric of a conventional variable is ignored by researchers because it is arbitrary or meaningless.

In order to calibrate fuzzy-set membership scores researchers must use their substantive knowledge. The resulting membership scores must have face validity in relationship to the set in question, especially how it is conceptualized and labeled. A fuzzy score of 0.25, for example, has a very specific meaning – that a case is half way between "full exclusion" from a set (e.g., a membership score of 0.00 in the set of individuals with "high parental income") and the cross-over point (0.50, the point of maximum ambiguity in whether a case is more in or more out of this set). As explained in *Fuzzy-Set Social Science* (Ragin 2000), the most important decisions in the calibration of a fuzzy set involve the definition of the three qualitative anchors that structure a fuzzy set: the point of full inclusion in the set (membership = 1.00), the cross-over point (membership = 0.50), and the point of full exclusion from the set (membership = 0.00). For example, to determine full inclusion in the set of individuals with high parental income, it is necessary to establish a threshold income level. All cases with parental incomes greater than or equal to the threshold value are coded as having full membership (1.00) in the fuzzy set. Likewise, a value must be selected for full exclusion from the set (0.00) and the remaining scores must be arrayed between 0.00 and 1.00, with the score of 0.50 representing the point of greatest ambiguity regarding whether a case is more in or more out of the set.

The main sets in the analysis reported in this study are degree of membership in the outcome, the set of individuals avoiding poverty, and membership in sets reflecting five background characteristics: parental income, AFQT scores, education, marital status, and children. The calibration of these fuzzy sets is explained in the appendix. At this point it is important to note that it is often fruitful to represent a single conventional, interval-scale variable with two fuzzy sets. For example, the variable parental income can be transformed separately into the set of individuals with high parental income and the set of individuals with low parental income. It is necessary to construct *two* fuzzy sets because of the *asymmetry* of these two concepts. Full *non*-membership in the set of individuals with high parental income (a membership score of 0.00 in high parental income) does *not* imply full *membership* in the set with low parental income (a score of 1.00), for it is possible to be fully out of the set of individuals with high parental income without being fully in the set of individuals with low parental income. The same is true for the other two interval-scale variables used as causal conditions in the logistic regression analysis (table 2.3), AFQT scores and years of education. Thus, the fuzzy-set analysis reported here uses eight causal conditions, two crisp sets: married versus not and one-or-more children versus no children, and six fuzzy sets: degree of membership in high parental income, degree of membership in low parental income, degree of membership in high AFQT scores, degree of membership in low AFQT scores, degree of membership in high education (college educated), and degree of membership in low education (less than high school).

After calibrating the fuzzy sets, the next task is to calculate the degree of membership of each case in each of the 2^k logically possible combinations of causal conditions, and then to assess the distribution of cases across these combinations. With eight causal conditions, there are 256 logically possible combinations of conditions. Table 2.4 lists the 55 of these 256 combinations that have at least one case with greater than 0.50 membership.

Recall that a case can have, at most, only one configuration membership score that is greater than 0.50. Thus, the 256 combinations of conditions can be evaluated with respect to case frequency by examining the number of empirical instances of each combination. If a configuration has no cases with greater than 0.50 membership, then there are no cases that are more in than out of the combination. As noted previously, this evaluation of the distribution of cases is the same as determining whether there are any cases in a specific sector of the vector space defined by the causal conditions.

Table 2.4 reveals that the data used in this analysis (and, by implication, in the logistic regression analysis reported in table 2.3) are remarkably limited in their diversity. Only 55 of the 256 sectors contained within the eight-dimensional vector space have empirical instances (i.e., cases with greater then 0.50 membership), and most of the frequencies reported in the table are quite small. The 11 most populated sectors (4.3% of the 256 sectors in the vector space) capture 70% of the listed cases. This number of well-populated sectors (11) is small even relative the number of sectors that exist in a five-dimensional vector space (32). (This is the number of sectors that would have been obtained if the three interval-level variables used in the logistic regression analysis--years of education, parental income, and AFQT scores--had been transformed into one fuzzy set each instead of two.)

Table 2.4: Distribution of Cases across Sectors of the Vector Space

Less than High School	College	Low parental income	High parental income	Low AFQT	High AFQT	Married	Children	Frequency	Less than High School	College	Low parental income	High parental income	Low AFQT	High AFQT	Married	Children	Frequency
0	0	1	0	1	0	0	1	118	0	1	0	0	1	0	0	1	4
0	0	0	0	1	0	0	1	51	0	1	0	0	1	0	1	1	4
0	0	1	0	1	0	1	1	51	1	0	1	0	1	0	0	0	3
0	0	1	0	0	0	0	1	35	0	0	0	1	1	0	1	0	3
0	0	1	0	0	0	1	1	34	0	0	1	0	0	0	1	1	3
0	0	1	0	1	0	0	0	34	0	1	0	1	0	0	0	1	3
0	0	0	0	0	0	0	1	32	0	0	0	0	0	1	0	0	3
0	1	0	0	1	0	1	1	30	0	1	0	0	0	0	0	1	3
0	0	0	0	0	0	0	0	29	0	1	0	1	0	0	1	0	3
0	0	0	0	1	0	1	1	24	0	1	1	0	0	1	1	0	2
0	1	1	0	0	0	0	1	20	0	1	0	0	0	0	1	0	2
0	0	0	0	0	0	0	1	17	0	1	1	0	1	0	0	0	2
0	1	0	0	0	0	1	0	15	0	0	0	1	0	0	0	0	2
0	0	1	0	0	0	1	1	14	0	1	0	1	1	0	1	1	1
0	1	0	0	0	0	0	0	12	1	0	1	0	0	0	0	0	1
0	1	1	0	0	0	1	1	12	1	0	0	0	1	0	1	0	1
0	1	0	0	0	0	1	1	10	1	0	0	0	1	0	0	1	1
0	1	0	0	1	0	0	0	9	0	0	0	1	0	0	1	1	1
0	1	1	0	0	0	0	1	9	0	1	1	0	0	1	0	1	1
0	0	1	0	0	0	0	0	8	0	0	0	1	1	0	0	0	1
0	1	1	0	1	0	1	0	7	0	1	0	1	0	0	1	1	1
0	0	0	1	0	0	0	0	6	0	1	1	0	0	1	1	1	1
0	0	0	0	1	0	0	0	5	0	0	1	0	0	1	1	0	1
0	0	0	1	0	0	0	1	4	0	0	0	1	0	1	1	1	1
0	1	1	0	0	1	0	0	4	0	1	1	0	0	1	0	0	1
0	1	1	0	1	0	0	1	4	0	0	1	0	0	1	1	0	1
0	1	0	0	1	0	1	1	4	1	0	1	0	0	1	0	1	1

continued...

In fuzzy-set analyses of this type, it is important to establish a strength-of-evidence threshold for combinations of conditions, using the information on the distribution of cases across sectors just discussed. Specifically, the causal combinations with too few cases should be filtered out and not subject to further empirical analysis. In addition to the fact that it would be unwise to base a conclusion about a combination of individual-level attributes on a small number of cases, the existence of cases in low-frequency sectors may be due to measurement or assignment error. In the fuzzy-set analysis that follows, I use a frequency threshold of 10 cases. Thus, 38 low-frequency rows of table 2.4 are filtered out of the analysis. Because these rows do not meet the strength-of-evidence threshold, they are treated as "remainder" combinations in the fuzzy-set analysis, along with the 201 combinations that lack cases altogether.

The next task is to assess the consistency of the evidence for each of the combinations of conditions (the 17 high-frequency rows of table 2.4) with the subset relation. Specifically, it is necessary to determine whether degree of membership in each combination of conditions is a subset of degree of membership in the outcome. As explained in Ragin (2000; 2005), the subset relation may be used to assess causal sufficiency. If the cases with a specific combination of conditions (e.g., the cases that combine college education, high parental income, high AFQT scores, being married, and having no children) constitute a subset of the cases with the outcome (e.g., cases avoiding poverty), then the evidence supports the argument that this combination of conditions is sufficient for the outcome. With fuzzy sets, the subset relation is demonstrated by showing that degree of membership in a combination of conditions is consistently less than or equal to degree of membership in the outcome.

One simple descriptive measure of the degree to which the evidence on a combination of conditions is consistent with the subset relation is:

$$\sum(\min(X_i, Y_i)) / \sum(X_i)$$

where "min" indicates selection of the lower of the two scores; X_i indicates degree of membership in a combination of conditions; and Y_i indicates degree of membership in the outcome. When all Xi values are consistent (i.e., the membership scores in a combination are uniformly less than or equal to their corresponding Y_i values), the calculation yields a score of 1.00. If many of the X_i values exceed their Y_i values by a substantial margin, however, the resulting score is substantially less than 1.00. Generally, scores on this measure that are lower than .75 indicate conspicuous departure from the set-theoretic relation in question ($X_i \leq Y_i$).

Table 2.5: Assessments of Set-Theoretic Consistency (17 Configurations)

Less than High School	College	Low parental income	High parental income	Low AFQT	High AFQT	Married	Children	Frequency	Consistency	Outcome
0	1	0	0	0	0	1	0	12	0.98	1
0	1	0	0	0	0	1	1	14	0.90	1
0	1	0	0	0	0	0	0	29	0.85	1
0	1	1	0	0	0	1	1	12	0.83	1
0	0	0	0	0	0	1	1	20	0.80	1
0	0	1	0	0	0	1	1	34	0.68	0
0	0	0	0	0	0	0	0	15	0.66	0
0	0	0	0	1	0	1	1	30	0.61	0
0	0	0	0	1	0	0	0	24	0.59	0
0	1	0	0	0	0	0	1	10	0.56	0
0	1	1	0	0	0	0	1	17	0.51	0
0	0	1	0	1	0	1	1	51	0.47	0
0	0	0	0	0	0	0	1	32	0.43	0
0	0	1	0	0	0	0	1	35	0.32	0
0	0	0	0	1	0	0	1	51	0.29	0
0	0	1	0	1	0	0	0	34	0.28	0
0	0	1	0	1	0	0	1	118	0.14	0

Table 2.5 reports the results of the set-theoretic consistency assessments for the 17 combinations in table 2.4 that meet the strength of evidence threshold (a frequency of at least 10 cases that are more in than out of each combination). The consistency scores for the combinations range from 0.14 to 0.98, indicating a substantial spread in the degree to which the subset relation is evident. In the truth table analysis that follows the five combinations with consistency scores of at least 0.80 are treated as subsets of the outcome; the remaining 12 fail to satisfy this criterion. Once this distinction is made, table 2.5 can be analyzed as a crisp truth table (Ragin 1987). The binary outcome, which is based on set-theoretic consistency scores, is listed in the last column of table 2.5.

Using fsQCA (Ragin, Drass, and Davey 2005) it is possible to derive two truth table solutions, one maximizing parsimony and the other maximizing complexity. The most parsimonious solution permits the incorporation of any counterfactual combination that contributes to the derivation of a logically simpler solution. This solution of the truth table yields three relatively simple combinations linked to poverty avoidance:

COLLEGE•children +
COLLEGE•MARRIED +
low_income•low_afqt•MARRIED

In this and subsequent fsQCA results the following notation is used: COLLEGE is the fuzzy set for college education; LESS_THAN_HS is the fuzzy set for less than high school; LOW_INCOME is the fuzzy set for low parental income; LOW_AFQT is the fuzzy set for low AFQT score; CHILDREN is the crisp set for at least one child; and MARRIED is the crisp set for married. A fuzzy set name in upper-case letters indicate original membership scores; lower-case letters indicate *negated* scores (e.g., "low_income" indicates membership in the set of cases with *not*-low parental income because the name is in lower case). Multiplication (•) signals combined conditions (set intersection); addition (+) signals alternate combinations of conditions (set union). The parsimonious solution reveals that there are three combinations of conditions linked to poverty avoidance: college education combined with either marriage or the absence of children, and not-low parental income combined with not-low AFQT scores and marriage.

While parsimonious, this solution involves the incorporation of many counterfactual combinations, and many of these, in turn, are "difficult" (Ragin and Sonnett 2004). For example, the combination of low income parents, low AFQT score, and having at least one child (along with having a college education and being married) is included in the second combination in the solution. There are too few empirical cases of this combination to allow its assessment (N = 4; see table 2.4), but the solution just reported assumes that individuals with this combination are able to avoid poverty. With 256 logically possible combinations of conditions, there are many combinations without cases or with very few cases, as table 2.4 indicates. The parsimonious solution just presented incorporates many such combinations, without regard for their empirical plausibility.

If, instead, the researcher evaluates the plausibility of the counterfactual combinations, a less parsimonious solution is derived. This intermediate solution is obtained by first deriving the most complex solution (not shown here) and then using only "easy" counterfactuals to produce an intermediate solution. The intermediate solution is a subset of the most parsimonious solution and a superset of the most complex solution. The intermediate solution indicates that there are three combinations of conditions linked to poverty avoidance:

COLLEGE·low_income·low_afqt·children +
COLLEGE·low_afqt·MARRIED +
less_than_hs·low_income·low_afqt·MARRIED

The three combinations linked to poverty avoidance are similar in that they all include education (COLLEGE or less_than_hs), *not* having low AFQT scores (low_afqt), and some aspect of household composition (MARRIED or children). Only the second combination lacks parental income as an ingredient, indicating that the second combination holds for cases with both low and high parental income. These results are important because they confirm that the causal conditions linked to poverty avoidance are combinatorial in nature and that it is possible to discern the relevant combinations when cases are viewed as configurations.

The results can be summarized with the aid of a branching diagram, starting with the common causal condition, not having a low AFQT score:

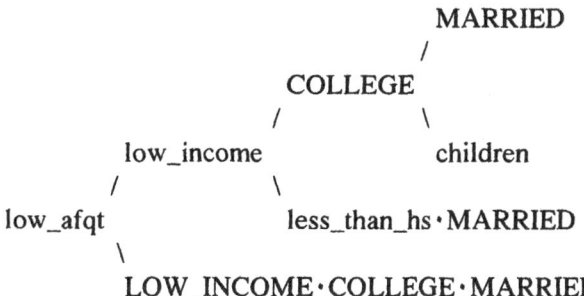

The first divide is low parental income versus not-low parental income. In the low income path, it takes both college education and marriage to stay out of poverty. In the not-low parental income path, it is possible to stay out of poverty with a high school education, if this characteristic is combined with marriage. If not-low parental income is combined with college education, however, it is necessary only to avoid being an unmarried parent in order to stay out of poverty.

In addition to revealing the combinatorial complexities of staying out of poverty for Black males, the results also challenge the interpretation of AFQT scores offered by Herrnstein and Murray. Recall that the core of their argument is that the nature of work has changed and that the labor market now places a premium on high cognitive ability. The image they conjure is one of a society that has many positions for the cognitively gifted but few slots for those who are more modest in their cognitive endowments. The results presented here are unequivocal: what really matters when it comes to avoiding poverty is to *not* have low test scores. In other words, the common ingredient across the three causal combinations in the solution is not vaunted cognitive ability, but having at least modest ability. Of course, this interpretation assumes that one accept the questionable claim that AFQT scores indicate cognitive ability. According to many of the critics of the *Bell Curve* thesis, AFQT scores indicate the acquisition of cultural capital. In this light, the findings reported here indicate that an important ingredient in the effort to avoid poverty is the possession of at least modest cultural capital.

The fuzzy-set results also show clearly that household formation and composition matter a great deal--they are part of every recipe for staying out of poverty. When it comes to important life outcomes such as avoiding poverty, these factors should not be ignored. These results reinforce the findings of Fischer *et al.*, and extend their argument by showing that household composition can best be understood as a key ingredient in recipes that include such things as education, test scores, and not having low-income parents. It is also worth noting that even the most advantaged of the pathways shown in the branching diagram (not-low test scores combined with not-low parental income and college education) include household composition as a factor (either marriage or no children--avoid being an unmarried parent).

4. DISCUSSION

The results presented here are preliminary findings drawn from a larger fuzzy-set analysis of the *Bell Curve* data. The primary goal of this illustrative research is to provide a contrast between a net-effects and a configurational analysis of the same data. The contrast between these two approaches is clear.

The findings of the net-effects analysis are expressed in terms of individual variables. They provide the final tally of the competition to explain variation in the outcome, avoiding poverty. Education and marital status win this competition, but AFQT is not eliminated, for it retains a modest net effect, despite the stiff competition (compare table 2.2 and table 2.3). The logistic regression results are silent on the issue of causal combinations. The analysis of causal combinations would require the examination of complex interaction models. The examination of a saturated interaction model, for example, would require the estimation of 32 coefficients in a single equation. Even if such a model could be estimated (extreme collinearity makes this task infeasible), the model would be virtually impossible to interpret, once estimated.

Note also that the assumptions of additivity and linearity in the logistic regression analysis allow the estimation of outcome probabilities for all 32 sectors of the vector space defined by the five independent variables, regardless of whether these sectors are populated with cases. Thus, the net-effects approach addresses the problem of limited diversity in an indirect and covert manner, by assuming that the effect of a given variable is the same regardless of the values of the other variables and that a linear relationship can be extrapolated beyond an observed range of values. To derive the estimated probability of avoiding poverty for any point in the vector space defined by the independent variables, it is necessary simply to insert the coordinates of that point into the equation and calculate the predicted value. The issue of limited diversity is thus sidestepped altogether.

By contrast, this issue must be confronted head-on in a configurational analysis. Naturally occurring data are profoundly limited in their diversity. This fact is apparent whenever researchers examine the distribution of cases across logically possible combinations of conditions, especially when the number of conditions is more than a handful. As the analysis reported here illustrates, the problem of limited diversity is not remedied by having a large number of cases.

When cases are viewed configurationally, it is possible to identify the different combinations of conditions linked to an outcome. The results of the configurational analyses reported in this contribution show that there are several recipes for staying out of poverty. The recipes all include not having low AFQT scores, a favorable household composition--especially marriage for those with liabilities in other spheres (e.g., lacking college education or having low parental income), and educational qualifications. Not having low parental income is also an important ingredient in two of the three recipes. Herrnstein and Murray dramatize the implications of their research by claiming that if one could choose at birth between having a high AFQT score and having a high parental SES (or high parental income), the better choice would be to select having a high AFQT score. The fuzzy-set results underscore the fact that the choice is really about combinations of conditions, about recipes, not about individual variables. In short, choosing to not have a low AFQT score, by itself, does not offer protection from poverty. It must be combined with other resources.

Appendix: Constructing Fuzzy Sets

As previously noted, the calibration of fuzzy sets is central to fuzzy-set analysis. Miscalibrations can seriously distort the results of set-theoretic assessments. The main principle guiding calibration is that the resulting fuzzy set scores must reflect both substantive knowledge and the existing research literature. While some might consider the influence of calibration decisions "undue" and portray this aspect of fuzzy-set analysis as a liability, it is, in fact, a strength. Because calibration is important, researchers must pay careful attention to the definition and construction of their fuzzy sets, and they are forced to concede that substantive knowledge is, in essence, a prerequisite for analysis. The main fuzzy sets in the analysis presented in this contribution are degree of membership in the outcome – the set of individuals avoiding poverty – and degree of membership in sets reflecting various background characteristics and conditions.

Avoiding Poverty. To construct the fuzzy set of individuals avoiding poverty, I use the official poverty threshold adjusted for household size as provided by the NLSY, the same measure used by both Herrnstein and Murray (1994) and Fischer *et al.* (1996). In their analyses, both Herrnstein and Murray and Fischer *et al.* use the poverty status variable as a binary dependent variable in logistic regression analyses. However, this places families whose income is just barely above the poverty level in the same category as those families that are far above the poverty threshold, such as comfortably upper-middle class families. The fuzzy set of cases in poverty avoids this problem. In accordance with the official poverty threshold, households with total family income at or below the poverty level are defined as having full membership in the set of households in poverty. Conversely, households with incomes that are four times the poverty level are defined as fully out of poverty. The fuzzy set of households in poverty is a symmetric set, that is, it is truncated at both ends and the crossover point is set exactly at the halfway mark. Accordingly, the fuzzy set of households *not* in poverty (poverty avoidance) is simply 1 minus membership in the original set.

High School and College Education. To measure educational attainment, the NLSY uses "Highest Grade Completed" (NLSY User's Guide: 138). This variable translates years of education directly into degrees (i.e., completing twelve years of education indicates a high school degree, while completing sixteen years completed indicates a college degree). Respondents with twelve or more years of school are fully excluded from the set with less than a high school education (a score of 0.0). On the other hand, those with only a primary school education (i.e., six years of school or less) are treated as fully in the set of respondents with less that high school (a score of 1.0). The fuzzy set thus embraces the six years of secondary school: 7 years = 0.15; 8 years = 0.30; 9 years = 0.45; 10 years = 0.60; and 11 years = 0.75. The fuzzy set of college-educated respondents was constructed similarly by defining respondents with sixteen or more years of education as having full membership in the set with a college education, while those with twelve years of education or less were coded as fully out of the set: 13 years = 0.20; 14 years = 0.40; and 15 years = 0.60.

Parental Income. The measure of parental income is based on the average of the reported 1978 and 1979 total net family income in 1990 dollars. It is the same measure used by Fischer *et al.* and was generously provided by Richard Arum. These data were used to create two fuzzy sets: respondents with low parental income and respondents with high parental income. The fuzzy set of respondents with low parental income is similar in construction to the fuzzy set of households in poverty. Using NLSY data on the official poverty threshold in 1979, adjusted by household size, respondents are defined as coming from a low parental income household if parental income was at or below the poverty threshold. Conversely, respondents are fully out of the set of those experiencing low parental income if family income was at least four times the poverty level in 1979. The cross-over point in the fuzzy set is pegged at two and a half times the poverty level. Truncation thus occurs for those below the official poverty level and for those with incomes exceeding the official poverty level by a factor of four or greater.

Multiples of the poverty ratio were also used to construct the fuzzy set of respondents with high parental income. At the bottom end, respondents are defined as fully out of the set of high parental income if their household had a poverty ratio of 2.5, thus indicating that their parental income was only two and a half times the official poverty level. This point corresponds to the cross-over point for membership in the set of respondents with low parental income, thus indicating that there is modest overlap between the two sets. (That is, some respondents have low membership in both sets--the set with low parental income and the set with high parental income.) To define full membership in the set of high parental income respondents, I used the median family income in 1990 dollars as a baseline. In 1979, the median family income in the U.S. was about 35,000 dollars. Respondents have full membership in the set of high parental income if their parental income was on average three times the national median income, or $105,000 a year. This translates to about fourteen times the poverty threshold. The crossover point was set at two times the median family income, which translates to about eight times the poverty threshold.

Test Scores. The AFQT scores used by Herrnstein and Murray are based on the *Armed Services Vocational Aptitude Battery* (ASVAB), which was introduced by the Department of Defense in 1976 to determine eligibility for enlistment. In *The Bell Curve*, Herrnstein and Murray pay special attention to those at the two ends of the AFQT score distribution. Specifically, they describe the top five percent as "the cognitive elite", and the bottom five percent as "very dull." While their arguments suggest that these groups are to some extent qualitatively different from the respondents in between, their measure of AFQT and their analysis of its effects largely ignore possible qualitative differences. While using the top and bottom 5 percent of the distribution has some intuitive appeal, it is still a largely arbitrary decision. To construct the fuzzy-set measures of those with high AFQT scores and low AFQT scores, I relied instead on categories used by the Department of Defense to place enlistees. Thus, the calibration of these fuzzy sets is grounded in practical decisions made by the military.

The military divides the AFQT scale into five categories based on percentiles. These five categories have substantive importance in that they determine eligibility as well as assignment into different qualification groups. Persons in categories I and II are considered to be above average in trainability; those in category III are about average; those in category IV below average; and those in category V are markedly below average. To determine eligibility for enlistment, the Department of Defense uses both aptitude and education as criteria. Regarding aptitude, the current legislated minimum standard is the 10th percentile, meaning that those who score in category V (1st to 9th percentile) are not eligible for military service. Furthermore, those scoring in category IV (10th to 30th percentile) are not eligible for enlistment unless they also have at least a high school education. Legislation further requires that no more than 20 percent of the enlistees be drawn from Category IV, which further indicates that respondents in this category are substantially different from those in categories I to III.

To construct the fuzzy set of respondents with low AFQT scores, I define those in category V (who are by law prohibited from enlistment because of their low aptitude) as having full membership in the set of cases with low AFQT scores. At the other end of the distribution, those scoring in category III or higher (and thus are of average or above average trainability) are defined as fully out of the set of low AFQT scores. Respondents in category IV (10th to 30th percentile), who need the additional criterion of a high school degree to be eligible for military service, have varying degrees of partial membership in the set of low AFQT scorers, with the crossover point in the middle of this category at the 20th percentile. Partial membership scores were directly tied to the percentile score, thus providing a continuous measure ranging from zero to one.

For the fuzzy set of respondents with high AFQT scores, I define those in category I (93rd to 99th percentile) as having full membership, while those in category II (65th to 92nd percentile) have partial membership in the set of high AFQT scores, with the crossover point at the 78th percentile. Respondents in categories III, IV, and V are thus fully out of the set of respondents with high AFQT scores. To calculate the fuzzy set scores, I use the percentile scores based on revised procedures established in 1989 and provided by the NLSY (NLSY79 User's Guide: 95).

Household Composition. Household composition has two main components: whether or not the respondent is married and whether or not there are children present in the household. All four combinations of married/not-married and children/no-children are present with substantial frequency in the NLSY data set. I code respondent's marital status as a crisp set, assigning a value of one to those who were married in 1990. In general, married individuals are much less likely to be in poverty. While Fischer *et al.* use the actual number of respondent's children in 1990, I code "having children" as a crisp set. The rationale for this is that being a parent imposes certain status and lifestyle constraints. As any parent will readily attest, the change from having no children to becoming a parent is much more momentous, from a life style and standard of living point of view, than having a second or third child. In general, households with children are more likely to be in poverty than households without children. The most favorable household composition, with respect to staying out of poverty, is the married/no-children combination. The least favorable is the not-married/children combination.

Chapter 3

A QUESTION OF SIZE?
A Heuristics for Stepwise Comparative Research Design

David Levi-Faur
University of Haifa and the Australian National University

1. INTRODUCTION

There are some areas where size doesn't not matter. Social Science is not one of them since size "Large *N*" is widely perceived as a necessary condition for the corroboration and falsification of generalizations. Valid generalizations, it is habitually asserted, are those that have been examined against a large number of cases. Despite a recognition of the importance of case-oriented research, the prevailing view is that when one faces the choice between small-*N* and large-*N*, the larger is the better.[1] This chapter offers some caveats regarding this conventional wisdom; it qualifies the fetishism attached to size through an ontological inquiry into the issues of inference, and proposes a practical solution for the problems of generalization in case-oriented analysis. This solution involves a stepwise comparative design, balancing internal and external validity, and a distinction among four different strategies of inference and case selection. The chapter discusses the challenges of comparative designs intended to increase the number of cases, and then offers a heuristic of comparative research design for comparative politics and policy analysis that allows a controlled, reasoned increase in the number of cases without compromising the strength of case-oriented analysis.

At the centre of the discussion are issues of generalization, control, and inference in case-oriented designs. These are basic issues as old as the social sciences, and are often framed in the social science textbooks through notions such as the quantitative-qualitative divide. Unsurprisingly, considering the importance of these issues, the literature on the "divide" is voluminous (certainly too large to cite in full here). Rather than advocating the advantages of the qualitative over the quantitative, or vice versa, this chapter aims to bridge the divide, a goal that is often considered as gracious and important. Gracious since it may help to create a more genial atmosphere in an environment that is often competitive in unconstructive ways. Important, since these divisions tend somewhat to impede mutually beneficial discourse across methodological barriers. So not surprisingly, considerable efforts are periodically made in this direction (Lijphart 1971; 1975; King, Keohane, and Verba 1994). Still, gracious and important as these efforts indeed are, they may lead us astray, if, say, bridging the divide compromises the meta-goal of all sciences, namely the production and dissemination of knowledge through adversarial or critical modes of inquiry.

To suggest that there is only one logic for all social science research is one example of unproductive ways of trying to bridge the divide. Not only does the advocacy of 'one logic' ignore the plurality of goals in social science research (seven according to Ragin 1994), it ignores the plurality of heuristics, which connects ideas and evidence in the social sciences. To argue for a monistic view of science is one problem, but even more problematic is to argue that the logic of social science research is best articulated in quantitative research, and this should serve as the model for qualitative research (Brady and Collier 2004). Quantitative research is grounded in several heuristics of analysis that are as revealing as they are constraining. If bridging the divide means less pluralism in scientific inference, and if this implies that one logic of research is to be enforced, we might best keep the barriers and the divide intact. This is not to suggest that we should maintain our methodological walls; the best option is certainly in the direction of bridging the divide.

In many respects I follow in the footsteps of Charles Ragin (1987, 1994, 2000; Ragin and Becker 1992) whose treatises on methodological problems of the social science have opened the way to the development of several heuristics of comparative analysis. Charles Ragin's own advocacy of Qualitative Comparative Analysis (QCA) and Fuzzy-Set inquiry stands independent of his contributions to our understanding of the limits and strength of case- and variable- oriented research. My discussion in this chapter, and the heuristic offered, are framed in Ragin's approach for social science inquiry, yet they are closer in spirit to the simpler and more easily applied small-N design, which does not involve Computer Mediated Methodology (CMM). The drive to formalize comparative techniques of inference follows Smelser's *Comparative Methods in the Social Science* (1976), where the explicit and implicit techniques of some great comparativists are discussed in detail.

The heuristic this chapter advances is grounded in four principals. First, a distinction between different cases according to their inferential roles in the research design. This justifies varied degrees of in-depth analysis of the cases under study, hence broadens the generalization without compromising the in-depth study of the primary cases. Second, a stepwise, research design with two major components. The first, based on a most-similar research design, aiming to enhance internal validity (via an in-depth study of primary cases). The second builds on a most-different research design, aiming to increase external validity (via the study of secondary and tertiary cases). Third, the application of four comparative inferential strategies in various stages of the research. Finally, a formalization of the analysis, in order to improve the consistency and transparency of case selection and of the inferential process. While I discuss and advocate here a particular heuristic I also suggest that that it may trigger the development of more heuristics that will bridge the divide between case- and variable-oriented analyses in creative ways.

This heuristic sets out to deal with six interrelated problems that I have encountered in my effort to enhance the validity of my own conclusions in the context of comparative political and policy-oriented research. These six problems are the subject of the first part of the chapter. The second part discusses the two major studies that advance various techniques of increasing the number of cases in the context of case-oriented designs (Lijphart 1971; King, Keohane, and Verba 1994). My discussion suggests that these techniques pay inadequate attention to the case-oriented logic of research. As an alternative, I outline the ontology of case-oriented research and discuss the criterion of consilience as it affects case selection and theory choice. The chapter then distinguishes four inferential techniques, which are framed by the interaction of Mill's methods of agreement and difference and Przeworski and Teune's distinction between a Most-Similar and a Most-Different System Design. The stepwise use of these different techniques to balance internal and external validity is then discussed. The chapter concludes with a formal presentation of a heuristic that allows an increase the number of cases in a comparative manner without compromising the strength of case-oriented analysis.

2. FROM POLICY ANALYSIS TO METHODOLOGICAL AGENDA

The particular heuristic advocated here derives from my interest in the dynamics of change in the contexts of globalization, liberalization, and Europeanization. In my own research on these issues, I found myself beset with doubt about the validity of my conclusions and insights beyond the nation and the sector that I and my colleagues had studied. The scholarly analysis seemed to be organized around particular issues and sectors with a limited comparative analysis. The problems I encountered are not new, but globalization, liberalization, and Europeanization seem to have complicated them still more. They have added an extra level of analysis in the sense that public policy in the national arena has become entangled in policies in the international arena. At the same time these changes have superposed new layers of institutions onto already crowded institutional structures, where 'institutional design' reflects the aspirations of analysts and academics rather than the realities of policy making. Instead of homogenization and convergence I found 'divergent convergent' and plurality of forms of governance, degrees of change, and complex causality. Generalizations, beyond the particular cases I studied, always seemed tricky. What I felt I should do was increase the number of cases in my research and to work in a more comparative manner.

Accomplishing this increase, I thought in the beginning, would be fairly painless. The difficulties I expected at the initial stages were basically about data collection and project funding. In practice, however, I also encountered methodological dilemmas that were far from easy to resolve. For one, the literature on techniques of increasing the number of case in the context of case-oriented research ranged from laconic to non-existent. Lijphart, who in his seminal paper *Comparative Politics and the Comparative Method* (1971) advocated an increase of number of cases – within the comparative case-oriented approach, changed his mind only four years later. In a special issue of *Comparative Political Studies* he suggested that a statistical approach was the best way to manage an increase in the number of cases (Lijphart 1975). While I found plenty of references to Lijphart's paper, I could not find much about how to increase the number of cases. The most notable exception, King, Keohane, and Verba's *Designing Social Inquiry* (1994) (hereafter, KKV) made some useful suggestions but these authors overlooked the costs of increasing the number of cases while still keeping an intimate knowledge of them; they advocated inferential procedures based on the ontology of the statistical method (or General Linear Reality: see Abbott 2001). Unfortunately, KKV were not particularly concerned with the distinct contribution of comparative procedures to an increase in the number of cases.

The challenges before me were multi-dimensional. My first case-study of telecoms liberalization in my own country, Israel, led me quickly in two comparative directions. The first one was the classic road in comparative politics, and I began comparing countries. In doing so I essentially moved towards an increase in the number of cases following Lijphart's (1971) and KKV's recommendations. The second direction followed the tradition of comparative public policy. Here I moved from my initial case-study, telecoms, to a comparative study of two sectors (telecoms vs. electricity) in one country. I increased the number of cases but did so using two different dimensions and following two different theoretical approaches. All these, I felt, carried certain important implications for the degree of control and the nature and scope of the generalization that could be produced. The gradual perception of these implications came about largely through my own efforts rather than the available literature on comparative methodology.

Consider the options of increasing the number of cases in the context of my interest in comparative analysis of political change. In the first approach, moving the comparison from one nation to another, while keeping the sector constant (a two-countries, one-sector design), I essentially moved along the national dimension of my cases. The decision to use this particular strategy of increasing the number of cases was not mechanical but theoretical. Changing the nation, while keeping the sector, reflects a research design taking what might best be labeled the National Patterns Approach (NPA). It suggests that political processes and outcomes are shaped by a country's unique national and historically determined characteristics embedded in specific state traditions, and that the nation-level community of policy-makers has effective control over domestic political processes.

The second strategy of increasing the number of cases, namely moving the comparison from one sector to another while keeping the nation constant (a two-sectors, one-country design) was also theoretically induced. Moving along the sectoral dimension of my cases, I worked on the assumption that sectoral variations are important, as suggested by the Policy Sector Approach (PSA).[2] The PSA emphasizes the autonomous political characteristics of distinct policy sectors, hence the multiplicity of political patterns in any one country. Sectors are expected to be embodied in policy communities and policy networks organized domestically in a regulatory regime. This approach anticipates finding distinct policy communities and policy networks around the production of energy through the generation, transmission, and distribution of electrical energy. These communities and networks are expected to be subject to a unique regime of controls that mainly reflect the characteristics of the technology as embedded in the specific national environment.

At a certain stage I felt that the sectoral and national variations were equally important; it might be useful to work by a research design using both, thus increasing the number of cases along both sectoral and national dimensions. I say 'felt', because at the time the decision was rather intuitive. I could find only a few research designs that followed the logic, and nothing at all on the methodological issues, involved in such a decision. An arbitrary decision regarding either of these dimensions seems to be acceptable and legitimate practice in the profession. Still, I was curious to find out, especially given some time and financial constraints, which dimension I should follow if I wanted to increase the number of my cases by one: should I add one more country or one more sector?

Things got more complicated when I realized that in different stages of my inferential process I was changing my implicit notion of a case. This was not an outcome of the increase in the number of cases, but thinking about 'casing' made me aware of it. Thus, in the study of telecoms liberalization in Israel, I held a notion of telecoms as a case for some purposes and Israel as a case for other purposes. In the study of European telecoms and electricity liberalization, I was reflecting on Europe, on the various member states, and on the two sectors. Each served as a case in my inquiry, but the emphasis was on different cases in different steps of the discussion and some cases certainly got more attention than the others. Each case represented some inferential constraints and limits, and these were different and needed some discussion. Each held some advantages, which required similar discussions. For example, in a certain research design whereby I was studying telecoms and electricity liberalization in the United States and Britain, I justified telecoms and electricity in terms of least likely cases (targeting validity beyond these concrete cases) and a most-similar research design (opting for the comparable case strategy). When considering my cases as the United States and Great Britain (rather than the sectors), case selection was indeed justifiable again on the grounds of a most-similar research design. However, being liberal countries, they were not in any reasonable way least-likely cases for liberalization. To top it all, the more I used the most-similar design, the more I traded generalization for control and the less I was able to generalize across different cases. I felt I needed to make use of Przeworski and Teune's most-different design, but then what about control in such a research design? In other words, how does one achieve control when the cases are not similar?

Let me summarize the methodological problems I had to tackle in increasing the number of cases. First, how was I to increase the number of cases without compromising in-depth knowledge of my cases? Second, how was I to win control without trading it for generalization? Third, how was I to justify and to clarify case selection when cases varied in their inferential role in the inquiry? Fourth, how was I to increase the number of cases in a framework of comparative analysis? Fifth, how was I to obtain validity not only from the number of cases but also from varied types of cases? Sixth, how could all these solutions to the problem of the inquiry be combined into one heuristic of research design?

3. FROM LIJPHART TO KING, KEOHANE AND VERBA: INCREASING THE NUMBER OF CASES

Generalizations and control, we are often reminded, are the two pillars of all major scientific methods - experimental, statistical and comparative. Here is the argument in Lijphart's authoritative words: *"All three methods (as well as certain forms of the case study method) aim at scientific explanation, which consist of two basic elements: (1) the establishment of general empirical relationships among two or more variables, while (2) all other variables are controlled that is, held constant. These two elements are inseparable: one cannot be sure that a relationship is a true one unless the influence of other variables is controlled*" (Lijphart 1971: 683).

Thus theory-construction and theory-testing are geared to generalizations (the broader the better, it would seem) on the one hand, and to validity (applied through three types of controls – experimental, statistical and comparative) on the other. Next Lijphart assesses these two goals against *two* major and interrelated problems of the comparative method: - the problem of many variables and the problem of a small number of cases (Lijphart 1971). Lijphart does not reflect on the sources of these two problems but takes them as given. Implicitly he seems to perceive the existence of many variables as a feature of the social world but to consider the problem of 'a small number of cases' a characteristic of the case-oriented research only. The possibility that the problems of 'many variables' and 'a small number of cases' are primarily ontological rather than methodological is not considered. Nor did Lijphart explore the possibility that method and ontology can be aligned better, in a way that will solve at least some of the problems of inference and validity that concern him.

For Lijphart the logic of the comparative method is "*the same as the logic of the experimental method*" (Lijphart 1971: 684). The comparative method is identical to the statistical method except for one crucial difference: "*The crucial difference is that the number of cases it deals with is too small to permit systematic control by means of partial correlations. (...) There is, consequently, no clear dividing line between the statistical and comparative methods; the difference depends entirely on the number of cases*" (Lijphart 1971: 684).

From Lijphart's perspective, since both control and generalizations depend on large N, the comparative method is thus second best and should be used in two circumstances: when the number of available cases does not allow statistical analysis, and whenever hypotheses have to be formulated rather than corroborated, that is, at the 'first stage of research'. For the final stage and for authoritative results one should turn to statistical analysis, where these hypotheses are tested against as large a sample as possible (Lijphart 1971: 685).

Lijphart's goals are not dissimilar to KKV's, whose major aim was to unify the logic of inference across the 'quantitative-qualitative' divide (KKV: 3). Differences between the two are described as a matter of style and specific technique but not of ontology or epistemology. As already pointed out by others, KKV tended at the time not only to unify the logic of inference, but also to apply the statistical world view to qualitative research (McKeown

1999; Tarrow 1995; Brady and Collier 2004). Missing from both Lijphart's and KKV's accounts is an appreciation of the relation between methodology and ontology in social science research. Ontologies are views or presumptions about the character and 'deep structures' of the world as it actually is. Methodologies are derivatives of these ontologies. An investigator's ontology may be implicit or explicit, depending on how reflexive he or she is, but the ontology is always there as all research is grounded in *"fundamental assumptions scholars make about the nature of the social and political world and especially about the nature of causal relationships within that world"* (Hall 2003: 374). Different methodologies are grounded in different ontologies and misalignment of methodology and ontology may result in confusion. The deep divide in social and political inquiry is ontological rather than technical or instrumental. The conceptions of causal relations underlying statistical methods and standard regression techniques are based on ontologies *"that assume casual variables with strong, consistent and independent effects across space and time"* (see also Ragin, in this volume); but the case-oriented approach advocates ontologies that acknowledge more extensive endogeneity, the ubiquity of complex interaction effects, reciprocal causation, distant events, sequencing, and multi-causality (Hall 2003: 387).

Beyond these assumptions as to the goals and logic of social science research, both Lijphart (1971) and KKV deal extensively with possible solutions to the problems of generalization and control. Lijphart suggests four remedies. The first two focus on the problem of 'many variables', the other two on the problem of 'a small number of cases'. Let me start with the problem of many variables. The first remedy is to focus the analysis on 'comparable' cases. One has to select cases which are similar in many important variables but dissimilar in the variables hypothesized to be related. If such cases can be found, they offer particularly good opportunities for the application of the comparative method because they allow the establishment of a relationship among few variables *"while many other variables are controlled"* (p. 687).[3] Lijphart's second remedy for the 'many variable' problem is to focus the analysis on 'key variables'. The idea is that the problems of 'many variables' can be controlled through the omission (after scanning) of all variables of 'only marginal importance' (p. 690). Comparative analysis must avoid the danger of being overwhelmed by large numbers of variables and Lijphart expresses reservations about 'configurative' and 'contextual' analysis which implies the exploration of more variables and the scanning of the entire context (ibid.).

What is common to these two remedies of Lijphart is the assumption that the problem of 'many variables' is one of control and that it can be overcome, if only partly, by either finding similar cases or by the creation of 'aggregative-variables'. In both cases his solutions to the problem of control are only partial. The existence and identification of 'key' variables and the existence of 'comparable cases' are contingent on the number of variables, in other words on the complexity of social phenomena. The more complex and diverse the social, political, and economic world, the harder it is to identify key variables and the more likely it is that "comparable cases" and "key variables" will not found. One can easily critique Lijphart's solutions, pointing to the practical problem of screening 'many variables' to find similar cases as well as to the puzzle of how to know what is a 'key variable' and what is not. Another problem with the comparable-case strategy is that it reduces the diversity of the social and political world and results in generalization on similar cases (e.g., Anglo-Saxon countries; developing countries with the British colonial heritage and parliamentary system, etc.). The more similar the cases, the more one may gain control, but the down side is a more narrow scope of the research argument and ability to generalize. The comparable-case strategy, in Lijphart's formulation, is therefore not only problematic with regards to the criterion of control, but also in its ability to provide generalization with broad scope.

Lijphart's remedies for the problem of a small number of cases are first to reduce the property-space of the analysis and second to increase in the number of cases as much as possible. First, reducing the 'property-space' requires the investigator to combine two or more variables (or categories) that express an essentially similar underlying characteristic into a single variable (or category). In this way the number of cells in the matrix representing the relationship between the different variables in the research is reduced, and the number of cases in each cell increases accordingly. This suggests that Lijphart intends to allow better control without *"increasing the sample itself"* (p. 687). A second remedy for the problem of a small number of cases is to increase the number of cases as much as possible by extending the analysis both geographically and historically, which *"improves the chances of instituting at least some control"* (p. 686). Lijphart is terse about how to increase the number of cases in his 1971 paper; in his follow-up paper he suggests that the increase in the number of cases is not part of the comparative method, and that a statistical rather than a comparative procedure should be employed when an increase in the number of cases is possible: *"I now think that it is more appropriate to reserve the term comparative method to the comparable cases strategy and to assign the first solution (i.e., maximizing the number of cases) to the category of the statistical method"* (Lijphart 1975: 163).

Unlike Lijphart in 1975, KKV seem to believe that there is a place for an increase in the number of cases in the framework of case-oriented analysis. Indeed, they make some important suggestions in this direction, but they fall short of supplying a heuristic of increase that recognizes the ontology of the case-oriented approach on the one hand and nurtures comparative designs on the others. What may appear, write KKV, *"to be a single-case study, or a study of only a few cases, may indeed contain many potential observations, at different levels of analysis, that are relevant to the theory being evaluated"* (p. 208). The way to go about increasing the number of cases involves *redefining the nature* of the case while still keeping the focus directly on evidence for or against the theory (p. 217). Three particular techniques are offered. First, one can study more units and thus keep the same explanatory and dependent variables intact. This is the most straightforward way to increase the number of cases. A scholar of regulatory governance, for example, devoting much time to the study of enforcement problems in the British water sector, may often choose to increase the number of cases he or she studies and to check the validity of his or her conclusions against enforcement problems either in the water sector in Germany (a one-sector, two-nation design) or in health and safety issues in Britain (a two-sector, one-nation design). Alternatively, he or she may manipulate the notion of a case and, without necessarily collecting extensive amount of additional data, compare the problems of regulatory enforcement in the British water sector before and after privatization (a one-nation, one-sector, two-era design). A second technique is to take new and different measures of the dependent variable. Regulatory enforcement in the water sector can be measured against several indicators, including the number of cases where regulations have been breached, the number of inspections, and the number of litigations (a design with one sector, one nation, and several measures of regulatory enforcement). A third technique is to increase both units and measures, that is, to observe more units while using new measures. This requires a new (or greatly revised) hypothesis that uses a new dependent variable and new explanatory variables (p. 218). In sum, to increase the number of cases it is possible to employ similar measures in additional units, use the same units but change the measures, or change both measures and units (p. 217).

Lijphart and KKV made important contributions to both the discussion of the role of comparative methods and the nature of scientific inference. Lijphart's input is mainly his identifying the two related problems of many variables and few cases and his mapping some major solutions. KKV take the increase in the number of cases farther and come up with useful techniques to overcome them. However, these contributions have something in common that stops them short of the desired end of increasing validity without compromising the strength of case-oriented analysis. First, Lijphart and KKV discuss the problems of and solutions to generalization and control without due appreciation of the ontology of case-oriented research. Second, they seem (certainly KKV) to build their discussion on the assumption of unity of inference across the social sciences. This unity is shaped in turn by a statistical worldview on the one hand and the philosophy of the natural sciences on the other. Third, neither pays attention to the comparative procedures of the increase in the number of cases. For example, if an increase in the number of cases follows the most-comparable-case strategy, validity of generalization may be obtained, but its scope may increase only slightly (as cases are very similar). Fourth, they do not suggest how the major benefit of case-oriented research, namely in-depth knowledge of one's cases, can be kept within the context of increasing the number of cases. Fifth, the inference process in their research design seems to be a one-shot inference rather than step-wise, iterative, and cumulative. It fits better the dominant statistical heuristic than the implicit heuristic of inference in case-oriented analysis. Finally, their cases seem to play the same inferential role and to serve the same purpose in different stages of the inferential process.

4. REFLECTING DIVERSITY, LEVERAGING COMPLEXITY

The goals and the logic of social science research can be grounded in different ontologies about the world and consequently in different appreciation of the divide. Probably the best discussion on the nature of the ontological divide is in the ground-breaking work of Charles Ragin (1987, 1994; 2000; Ragin and Becker 1992). For Ragin the major cleavage in the social sciences is not about the number of cases, the desired scope of generalization, or the aim of control but about different conceptions of the notion of "a case" and appreciations of the extent of diversity across cases. Ragin's perception of the nature of the divide led him to distinguish 'case-oriented approaches' from 'variable-oriented approaches' for social and political inquiry.

Case-oriented approaches are oriented towards comprehensive invariant examination patterns common to relatively small sets of historically defined cases and phenomena. The variable-oriented approach is concerned instead with assessing the correspondence between relationships discernible across many societies or countries, on the one hand, and broad theoretically based images of macro-social phenomena, on the other (Ragin 1987; 2000). This in turn is grounded in an ontological view of *"the nature of causal relationships within that world"* (Hall 2003: 374).

Instead, Ragin takes on board Verba's notion of a *'disciplined, configurative approach'* (Verba 1967: 114) and develops a notion of a case according to which a case is *"a particular configuration of attributes"* (Ragin 2000: 66). The attributes of interest are intimately connected to other attributes of the case which are captured as the relevant context and which may be highly relevant to our understanding of the theoretical value of the case: *"The logic of case study is fundamentally configurational. Different parts of the whole are understood in relation to one another and in terms of the total picture or package that they form. The central goal is usually to show how different 'parts' of a case interconnect ... What matters most is that the investigator makes sense of multiple aspects of the case in an encompassing manner, using his or her theory as a guide"* (Ragin 2000: 68).

To suggest that the investigator's aim to make sense of *"multiple aspects of the case in an encompassing manner"* is to say that the purpose of the inquiry is not necessarily generalization across cases. Indeed, what Ragin suggests is to balance the aims of generalization and intimate knowledge of a case by looking at limited number of cases. Instead of enforcing assumptions of homogenization on diverse units he suggests recognizing diversity (indeed seeing it as a major goal of social science research). He also implies that what may seem to be a population of homogeneous units is really a collection of diverse types of cases. Each of these different cases may be shaped by a particular pattern of causality. Ragin's ontology allows his methodological choices and explanations to reflect the diversity of multiple causality and the varied attributes that define these different types. It is this assumption of diversity that embodies his ontology and serves him to develop his defense of the case-oriented approaches and to advance some solutions to the problems of social science research.

The major goal of the social sciences, from this point of view, is to generalize in a way that reflects the diversity and complexity of the social world in general, and of cases in particular.[4] Instead of generalizations such as 'The greater the power of private business in a sector, the more likely it is to be liberalized', the comparative approach looks for generalizations such as 'The greater the power of private small business associations in a sector, the more likely its liberalization will also be accompanied by competition'. While the first generalization homogenizes both the notion of private business and the notion of liberalization, the second (i.e., the comparative) diversifies it to small and big business and allows a distinction between liberalization that leads to competition and liberalization that does not. The comparative and the quantitative method may both result in abstract conclusions, but a variable-oriented approach is more likely to result in abstract generalizations that do not reflect diversity.

Most would take diversity as a problem and see it as the fated burden of social scientists. But if we are to ground our research in an ontological view of the world that understands it as a complex and diverse entity, it may serve us to increase the legitimacy of case-oriented research. An assumption about diversity suggests that validity of theory is not necessarily the result of one's ability to control (as suggested by Lijphart) but rather of one's ability to show the robustness of the argument (or hypotheses) across diverse social and political spheres of action. Thus, instead of a burden diversity may be an advantage. The notion of consilience as a criterion of falsification and corroboration serves to clarify how validity can be increased through examination against diverse classes of facts and not only through the sheer number of facts of the same kind.

The term consilience originated in the work of the British philosopher of science William Whewell (1794-1866) (Tucker 2004). The evidence in favor of a theory, argued Whewell, is *"of much higher and more forcible character when it enables us to explain and determine cases of a kind different from those which were contemplated in the formation of our hypothesis"* (Whewell 1840: 230). Following Whewell, Thagard suggested that *"A consilient theory unifies and systematizes. To say that a theory is consilient is to say more than it 'fits the facts' or 'has broad scope'; it is to say first that the theory explains the facts, and second that the facts that it explains are taken from more than one domain. These two features differentiate consilience from a number of other notions, which have been called 'explanatory power', 'systematic power', 'systematicization', or 'unification'. (...) We are not concerned with the explanation of a horde of trivial facts from the same class. (...) In inferring the best explanation, what matters is not the sheer number of facts explained, but their variety and relative importance"* (Thagard 1988: 80, 81).

These criteria stand in contrast to the somewhat mechanical process of increase in the number of cases implied by Lijphart and KKV, as it suggests that validity is driven not necessarily by statistical control of possibly intervening variables, but rather by the robustness of the argument (or, in other words, by the relations between 'independent' and 'dependent' variables) across different kinds of cases. One of the most important implications of this argument is the distinction that it allows between cases and aspects of cases. Relations between aspects of cases (or variables) can be examined in varied contexts – similar and less similar, different and less different. The choice of cases and not only of the aspects of the case (within-case variation) is of great importance. This insight seems to be captured as well by Przeworski and Teune's (1970) distinction between most-similar and most-different systems design, and in turn allows me to distinguish between four different types of inferential techniques.

5. FOUR INFERENTIAL TECHNIQUES

Przeworski and Teune's *The Logic of Comparative Social Inquiry* (1970) is often considered, and rightly so, as an outstanding treatise on the comparative method. It was written with the problems of variable-oriented analysis in mind and therefore does not deal with the problem of increasing the number of cases. Yet, it does include some important insights for case-oriented comparative analysis. Their most important innovation, the notion of Most-Different System Design, was also conceptualized with reference to problems of variable-oriented comparative analysis but it may also serve the purpose of increasing the number of cases without compromising the strengths of the case-oriented approach. Presumably because they were oriented toward the variable-oriented problems, Przeworski and Teune (henceforward PT) apparently did not find it necessary to clarify the relation between their design and Mill's canons of comparative analysis. This is unfortunate since such a contribution could have made the impact of their treatise even stronger. Most importantly, it might have balanced the growing tendency in the discipline to compare most similar cases, possibly induced even more by Lijphart's forceful and clearer paper on the comparative method. In what follows, I first clarify the notions of most-similar and most-different designs, and then discuss their relation to Mill's canons. The section concludes with the isolation of four strategies of case selection that result from the interaction of Mill's and PT's designs.

The notion of "system" is critical to PT's logic of comparative inquiry in a way. Systems or cases may be sectors, nations, firms, or organizations. Systems and aspects of systems covary, and the goal of social inquiry is to clarify the source of variations by examining interactions on at least two levels of analysis: of the system and within the system. That much is evident when one compares the definition of the comparative method by Lijphart to that of PT:

"The comparative method can now be defined as the *method of testing hypothesized empirical relationships among variables on the basis of the same logic that guides the statistical method, but in which the cases are selected in such a way as to maximize the variance of the independent variables and to minimize the variance of the control variables."*
(Lijphart 1975: 164, italics in the original)

"Comparative research is inquiry in which more than one level of analysis is possible and the units of observation *are identifiable by name at each of these levels."*
(PT 1970: 36-7, italics in the original)

What PT recognizes, but Lijphart does not, is that any inquiry involves some unknown and uncontrollable variables (or aspects). These aspects are defined as systemic and can be assessed only against variations in the relations between within-system variables across systems. At the same time they recognize that selection in social science research consists at the same time in the selection of cases and in the selection of aspects of the cases. Ecological inferences[5] (hence ecological fallacies) are characteristic of all social science research, whatever the level of the analysis. Hence the comparative methods require us to compare once and at the same time both cases and aspects of the cases. This is a major argument of this chapter and its implications will be discussed shortly, after I have introduced PT's distinction between Most-Similar and Most-Different system designs.

The logic of comparison in Most-Similar System Designs (MSSD) is grounded in the assumption that the more similar the cases being compared, the simpler it should be to isolate the intervening factors: *"Inter-systemic similarities and inter-systemic differences are the focus of the 'most similar' systems designs. Systems constitute the original level of the analysis, and within-system variations are explained in terms of systemic factors (...). Common systemic characteristics are conceived of as 'controlled for', whereas inter-systemic differences are viewed as explanatory variables. The number of common characteristics sought is maximal and the number of not shared characteristics sought, minimal"* (p. 33).

For PT *"(t)he efficiency of the MSSD in providing knowledge that can be generalized is relatively limited"* (p. 34). Their critique rests on the limited number of cases that can be compared in the sense that they display a large number of common characteristics and a minimal number of not shared characteristics. They also seem to suggest that the comparative inquiry should focus not only on the variables (or aspects of the case) but also on the case, and in this sense it is a 'multi-level' inquiry. To this one can add the argument that selection of similar systems is yet another source of selection bias, and that the more similar the cases the less generalizable the findings (one is forced to trade control for generalization).

An alternative approach – which PT and others associated unnecessarily with statistical analysis – is to select the case on the principle of a Most Different System Design (MDSD). Here the logic is to compare cases as different as possible, demonstrating the robustness of a relationship between dependent and independent variables within the system. Such a design assumes that the argument of the research is better supported by demonstrating that the observed relationship holds despite the wide range of contrasting settings (pp. 31-46). This research design is important especially as it helps to release the comparative agenda from the "spell" of the 'comparable case strategy' that confined comparative analysts to similar cases ("Don't compare apples with pears," students are warned, as if both are not fruits!) and thus broadens the potential theoretical impact of the comparative method. The starting point of the researcher is the variation in aspects of the system (the lowest level of analysis): if these variations hold to the same extent in different systems, the analysis can and should continue at the intra-systemic level (or at the lowest level of analysis). If these relations vary across cases then one should turn to systemic variables or factors, and examine their impact across all cases. Unlike the most-similar system design, they write, *"(t)he question of at which level the relevant factors operate remains open throughout the process of inquiry"* (p. 36) and the aim is to eliminate irrelevant systemic factors.

To compare English and American systems of common law is to select cases that follow PT's Most-Similar-System Design. To compare the English (common law) and the French (civil law) legal systems is to select cases according to the Most-Different-System Design. Each of these selections is grounded in a different logic of scientific inquiry and represents different sets of inferential strengths and constraints. Similarly a comparative study that compares liberalization in Norway and Denmark (two corporatist systems) is based on the Most-Similar-System Design, while a study that compares Norway with France (the latter an étatist system) is based on the Most-Different-System Design. Most-similar and most-different cases are similar and different on sets of variables deemed highly relevant to the political process and its outcomes. That countries are of the same size or even at the same level of economic development does not necessarily make them similar in any theoretically relevant sense.

But what are the relations between case selection on system characteristics and Mill's canons? Let us deal with the two canons that are most relevant for case-oriented analysis: the method of difference and the method of agreement. The method of difference is based on comparison of similar aspects of different cases that differ in outcomes, for example, a case of privatization and a case of nationalization. Looking at the control and independent variables, the scholar is supposed to identify the critical variable that makes the difference. The method of agreement is based on comparison of similar aspects of different cases that are similar in their outcomes, for example, two cases of regulatory reforms in two different countries. Looking at the control and independent variables, the scholar is supposed to identify the common elements that are common to both cases, eliminate elements that differ in both, and come closer to the goal of identifying the causal and the spurious relations between the variables of interest.

The different logic of comparative analysis that characterizes Mill's methods on the one hand and PT's methods on the other was generally ignored by comparativists. Indeed, the only noted example appears to be Faure's (1994), who 'mirrored' Mill's canons in PT's two designs. Building partly on Faure, it is possible to suggest that these methods open the way to four strategies of case selection and inference in comparative studies (see table 3.1). These four combine, first, the most-similar system design and Mill's method of difference (MSSD+MMD). Here the comparative strategy involves selection of similar systems, for example, countries that belong to the Anglo-Saxon family of nations or economic sectors that have network characteristics (similar systems), but some cases opted for liberalization and others for nationalization (hence yielding different outcomes for their economic policies). The idea is to minimize variance of the control variables and maximize variance in the dependent variable (the choice of liberalization or nationalization) in the hope of identifying the few variables that may account for the difference in outcome.

Table 3.1. Four Inferential Strategies

	Mill's Method of Difference	Mill's Method of Agreement
Most-Similar System Research Design	MSSD+MMD (dealing with differences in Similar Cases) Minimize variance of the control variables, maximize variance in the dependent variable	MSSD+MMA (dealing with similarities in Similar Cases) Minimize variance of the control and dependent variables
Most-Different System Research Design	MDSD+MMD (dealing with differences in Different Cases) Maximize variance of the control and dependent variables	MDSD+MMA (dealing with similarities in Different Cases) Maximize variance of the control, minimize variance in the dependent variable

Key: MDSD= Most-Different System Design
MSSD= Most-Similar System Design
MMD = Mill's Method of Difference
MMA = Mill's Method of Agreement

The second of these strategies involves the most-similar system design and Mill's method of agreement (MSSD+MMA). Here the comparative strategy involves a selection of similar systems, for example, countries that belong to the Anglo-Saxon family of nations or economic sectors that have network characteristics (similar systems) and both opted for the same policy, say liberalization (hence with similar outcomes on their economic policies). The idea is to minimize variance of the control and on the dependent variables (the choice of liberalization or nationalization) in the hope of eliminating the variables that are less likely to exert a causal effect on the similar outcome since they appear in one of the cases but not in the other.

The third and fourth strategies involve the choices of cases according to the Most-Different System Design. The third combines it with Mill's method of difference (MDSD+MMD). The comparative strategy involves selection of dissimilar systems, for example, an Anglo-Saxon country with a 'lean' welfare state and continental European country with a comprehensive welfare state (dissimilar systems). These countries, to continue the example, but now in regard to the aspects of the case under investigation, have different educational policies (hence different outcomes by Mill's logic). The idea here is to maximize variance on both the dependent and control variables in order to eliminate the variables that are less likely to exercise a causal effect on the different outcomes since they appear in both cases. The fourth strategy combines the Most-Different System Design with Mill's method of agreement (MDSD+MMA). The comparative strategy involves a selection of dissimilar systems, for example, an Anglo-Saxon country with a 'lean' welfare state and continental European country with a comprehensive welfare state, but this time with similar policies on, say, monetary policy. The expectation of different policies, given the differences in welfare orientation, is met, oddly enough, with a similar policy. The comparative design maximizes variance on the control variables and minimizes variance on the dependent variable, and this allows the elimination of a set of variables that differ across the cases and thus are not likely to have a causal effect on the outcome of interest.

Here then are four strategies of elimination and corroboration. Each can take us forward only modestly, but together they may let us progress in a more significant way. The next part of the chapter demonstrates how.

6. A STEPWISE COMPARATIVE HEURISTIC

Figure 3.1 outlines the stepwise heuristic of comparative research that this chapter advances. It includes two major steps that can be further broken down internally to more steps. Inference is therefore a gradual and cumulative process of elimination, falsification, discovery, and corroboration. This is not a unique feature of the proposed heuristic as social science research rarely can avoid a stepwise, Sherlock Holmesian style of inference.

Figure 3.1. Stepwise Heuristic of Comparative Analysis

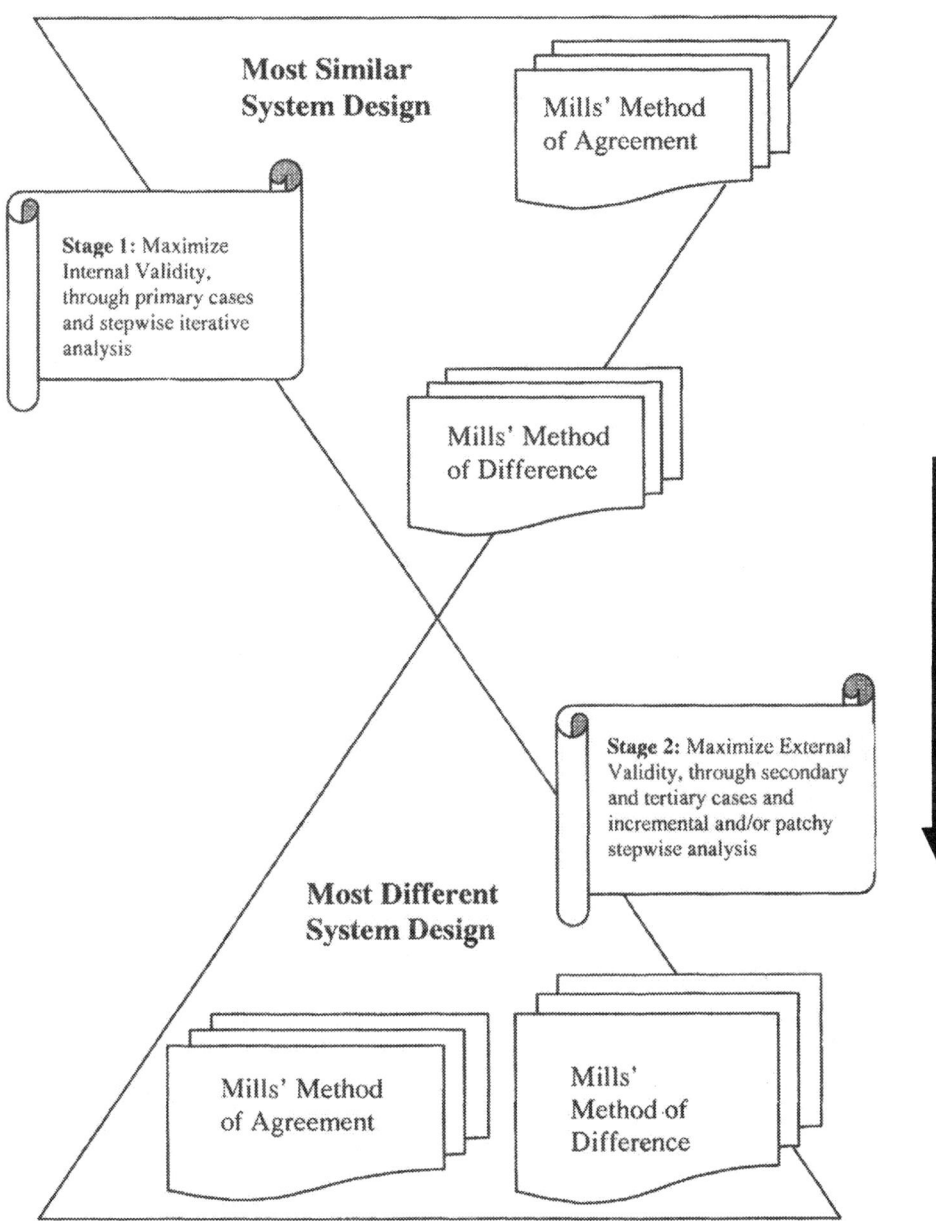

The heuristic only formalizes these repeated inferences and make the inferential process more transparent. Take, for example, the process of inference in PT's most-different system design, which as was mentioned before was formulated with the problem of cross-national/cross-level quantitative research problems in mind. The need to exert control on two different levels requires the application of two different steps of inference. The first is inference regarding co-variation of within-unit variables, while the second is a study of similarities and variations of correlations across the cases. For example in a cross-national study of education and electoral behavior, the first step is an analysis of co-variations of education and party-voting in Australia and Israel. The second step is then to compare the results from the two different cases. If the results are similar in Israel and Australia, one can eliminate country-level causes (or the "name" of the country) and stay with a variable-centered model. If these countries differ one needs to look at the variables in the level of the system (country in this case) and to identify the source(s) of the variations across the cases.

Let us return to the various stages of the proposed heuristic. The first step rests on comparative analysis where case selection is grounded in the Most-Similar System Design (MSSD) as well as either Mill's Method of Agreement (MSSD-MMA) or Mill's Method of Difference (MSSD-MMD). The research goal in this stage is to apply in-depth analysis of the primary cases and to enhance internal validity. Let me clarify the goals of the comparative method at this stage first by clarifying what primary cases are and then by distinguishing internal and external validities. To keep intact the strengths of case-oriented analysis, and primarily the in-depth knowledge of one's case, it may be useful to distinguish primary, secondary, and tertiary cases. In-depth analysis is a *sine qua non* for the primary cases on which theory was generated and where the primary purpose of the inquiry is to increase internal validity. Yet this in-depth knowledge is impossible, and even not desirable, for the secondary and tertiary cases against which the theory is examined in order to increase generalization. The element of explanatory surprise in one's research cannot be realized without imbalance in our knowledge, namely knowing more about one case than about another. Inference is a process of the examination of one case, which we know intimately, against another, about which we know much less. In this process we trade depth for breadth and dilute one type of knowledge for another. This also implies that cases vary in their 'inferential status' and that comparative analysis that rests on varying degrees of in-depth analysis is a legitimate scientific enterprise (Levi-Faur 2004; 2006).

The first step of the heuristic addresses the issue of internal rather than external validity. Validity, the authors of the most widely cited paper on this subject tell us, "*refers to the best available approximation to the truth or falsity of propositions, including propositions about cause*" (Cook and Campbell 1979: 37). The presence of the word 'best' in this definition means that all knowledge is approximate to the truth, and that there is always uncertainty about its validity. Internal validity refers to the approximate validity by which we infer that the relationship between two variables is causal. External refers to the approximate validity by which we can infer that the *"presumed causal relationship can be generalized to and across alternate measures of cause and effect and across different types of persons, setting, and times"* (ibid.).[6] These two types of validity are often in conflict, and it is suggested that they be worked out independently in the process of scientific inference. This independence is all the more important with reference to the requisite nature of internal validity. Problems of internal validity are chronologically and epistemologically antecedent to problems of external validity (Guala 2003). A theory, hypothesis, or argument that fails the test of internal validity is meaningless even if it holds across many cases. The tensions between these two kinds of validity are many; perhaps the most familiar is that of limited resources that require investment in one or other type of validity. To summarize, the first step in any case-oriented process of increase in the number of cases is to achieve internal validity through the study of primary cases. This is gained through a careful process of control and process-tracing analysis of the interrelated aspects under the examination, in the primary cases and in the first step of the proposed heuristic. One may want to use here the MSSD and apply one of Mill's methods, or alternatively apply both in a stepwise iterative manner.

In the second step of the analysis the focus of the research moves from issues of internal validity to issues of external validity or generalizability across diverse sets of cases. The study involves an analysis of secondary and tertiary cases, and instead of focusing on the issue of the validity of the relations between aspects or variables of the case in a small number of cases through in-depth study, the focus now is on the robustness of these relations across cases that differ in kind. The comparative analysis rests on of the Most-Different System Design (MDSD) through either Mill's Method of Agreement (MDSD-MMA) or Mill's Method of Difference (MDSD-MMD) or both. In both cases variance in the control variables across the cases is maximized. In the MDSD-MMA's strategy the variations in the dependent variable are minimized. The inquiry is then focused on the 'suspect' independent variables or aspects that can explain the similarity in the outcome. The relations that were found to be internally valid in stage 1 of the research are re-examined in order to gain some external validity. In the MDSD-MMD strategy the variations in the dependent variable are maximized and the investigator examines to what extent the relations that were found to be internally valid in stage 1 of the research are also valid against the new cases that were added to the analysis. Strategies of stepwise comparison here can be incremental or patchy, or both. Iterative strategy is not efficient here.

Let me give a brief example of the options for increasing the number of cases in a way that is sensitive to case-oriented analysis. It refers to a small-N comparative study which includes two sectors, say telecoms and electricity, in two countries, say Britain and the United States. Both sectors and nations are selected according to the MSSD principle of minimizing variations in the control variables across the cases. The number of sectoral cases is four and the number of national cases is two. One can compare the two countries; then one can compare the two sectors in the same country, move to the same two sectors in the other country, continue with a comparison of the same sector in the two countries, and finally compare the second sector in the two countries. One can move farther still, and add a temporal dimension to the analysis to compare sectors and nations before and after a critical event or a turning point. This can be done at the level of the sector or the nation as well as the international; for example, the creation of a new regime and the formalization of new international commitments. Indeed, the number of possible pairwise comparisons is given by the formula $n(n-1)/2$, where n is the number of cases in the study. Thus, for four sectoral cases the maximum number of pairwise comparisons is six $\{(4(4-1))/2\}$. If one distinguishes between old and new regimes in each of the sectors the number of cases doubles to eight, and the number of possible pairwise comparisons reaches 21. Only a small number of these possible comparative pairs might be used, but whatever the number the aim at this stage is to increase internal validity. The argument or the relations between variables or aspects of the cases that were established in the first stage are then examined against most different cases, so case selection in this case involves an increase in the type of sectors and the countries. Sectors such as finance or even natural resources might be added to telecoms and electricity, and countries such as France and Argentina might be added to the original set of countries of Britain and the United States. Following PT's recommendations, the analysis at this stage (though not statistical as they envisioned) examines the robustness of the relations that were defined in the first stage; the aim is to explain system-level variations, thereby to determine if the relations are determined by national or sectoral characteristics.

It is important to note that in both stages the increase in the number of cases is not random, but rather controlled and systematic. Case selection is a critical aspect of the inquiry as it has important implications of the validly of the research. Validity, as already argued by Eckstein (1975), is not driven necessarily by the number of cases under study. A large number of tests on the same cases may be an alternative trajectory for increasing the validity of one's conclusions. Yet, if one opts for the incremental stepwise strategy, one should not only increase the sheer number of cases but also add different types of cases, following the criteria of consilience and the strategy of most-different research design. Validity in this stage of the analysis is aimed at robustness, so the investigator should disregard the principles of the comparable case strategy (or the most-similar-system design) that were taken in the first stages of the research.

7. CONCLUSIONS

Why a heuristic of stepwise comparative research? A short summary might be useful and four reasons come to mind. First, it may help us balance the potentially conflicting demands of internal and external validity as well as those of different types of cases as they vary in terms of degree of in-depth analysis, and in terms of level of analysis. Second, the research design is formalized in a manner that increases the transparency of the inferential process. This is not a trifling issue. Since scientific advance rests on collegial criticism and on the examination of 'plausible rival hypotheses'; and since collegial criticism and rivalry are contingent on transparency of the inferential process, its formalization should be highly valued. Third, the comparative method is highly esteemed but very slightly practiced. One way to put it into more widespread use is to look for a new language, new terms, new procedures, and new instruments of inference; it is, in short, to innovate and to move on with a critical view of the dominance of both case studies and statistical approaches (see also Amenta and Poulsen 1994; Berg-Schlosser and De Meur 1997; Berg-Schlosser 2001).

Finally, the heuristic is an effort to bridge the divide between case- and variable-oriented research. However, unlike other such efforts, the heuristic rests on the particular ontology and epistemology of case-oriented analysis and does not force that of statistical analysis. The problem does not necessarily lie in the statistical worldview, or even in the general tendency to 'trust in numbers' (Porter 1995). For too long, methodological issues received only scant attention from the otherwise lively community of 'case-oriented' scholars. If there is a methodological divide across the discipline, and if distribution of prestige across the methodological divide is uneven, it is mainly a reflection of the *under*investment of case-oriented scholars in methodological innovations. Of course, some case-oriented scholars have made a heavy investment in methodological issues, but on balance the community of self-reflexive case-oriented scholars is small. It may well be that 'unconscious thinking' and the self-content of case-oriented researchers who are oblivious to methodological issues are the major impediments to progress. The challenge, in short, is for those on both sides of the divide.

NOTES

[1] Exceptions are mainly due to issues of sampling considerations that might limit the size in order to minimize measurement errors.

[2] The major suggestions of the PSA might be summarized in two major propositions: *"(First) that the style of policy making and the nature of political conflicts in a country will vary significantly from sector to sector... (And second) that policy making in a particular sector will exhibit strong similarities, whatever its national context"* (Freeman 1986: 486).

[3] One cannot reduce the total number of variables, yet it is possible to reduce considerably the number of operative variables and study their relationships under controlled conditions without the problem of running out of cases (Lijphart, 1971: 687).

[4] Cf. *"If the monographic literature provides us with few generalizations, the second kind of literature (i.e., variable-oriented literature) provides us with many generalizations that do not seem to fit many or any of the relevant cases"* (p. 113). *"A disciplined configurative approach is, thus, based on general rules, but on complicated combinations of them. Explanations may be tailored to the specific case, but they must be made of the same material and follow the same rules of tailoring. All this is easier said than done"* (Verba 1967: 115).

[5] Ecological inference is an inference from one level of analysis to another; for example, from individual behavior to aggregate behavior or from aggregate behavior to individual behavior.

[6] Guala defines the difference between external and internal validity succinctly: "Whereas internal validity is fundamentally a problem of identifying causal relations, external validity involves an inference to the *robustness* of a causal relation outside the narrow circumstances in which it was observed and established in the first instance" (2003: 4).

Chapter 4

MSDO/MDSO REVISITED FOR PUBLIC POLICY ANALYSIS

Gisèle De Meur
Université Libre de Bruxelles - MATsch

Peter Bursens
Universiteit Antwerpen

Alain Gottcheiner
Université Libre de Bruxelles - MATsch

1. MSDO/MDSO: THE FOUNDATIONS

The MSDO/MDSO procedure (Most Similar Different Outcome / Most Different Same Outcome) was elaborated by De Meur in order to reduce the huge complexity of a data set gathered by a large research team working during a dozen of years on the «Inter War Europe crisis». A selection of articles (e.g. De Meur and Berg-Schlosser 1994; De Meur 1996) describe the use of the procedure in that particular research field. Several indicators made the researchers understand there would be a similar methodological need in the field of public policy analysis, hence the present contribution.

Imagine a social (political, economical) phenomenon or some public policy matter observed through the values[1] attained on different empirical «cases» by some «<u>outcome variable</u>», e.g.:
- existence /absence of regulation concerning smoking in public area;
- strong/weak penalties for speeding (or drunk driving) on highways;
- existence/absence of «positive discrimination» policies to enforce gender equality.

You are trying to understand the observed differences in outcomes through the action of some «<u>condition variables</u>», e.g.:
- existence/absence of high taxes (thus State benefits) on tobacco sales;
- existence/absence of important (physicians, consumers, etc) lobbies against cancer/carcinogenic products;

- high/low costs of cancer treatments at charge of national social security system.

Our starting point is the following: An «ideal» comparison protocol would be, as summarized in the figure below, to look at three extreme configurations in each of which <u>one</u> single condition variable could emerge as «responsible» for the outcome:

Figure 4.1: Extreme Similarity with Different Outcomes (a/A) and Extreme Dissimilarity with Same Outcomes (a/b or A/B) when Outcome has (Only) Two Possible Values

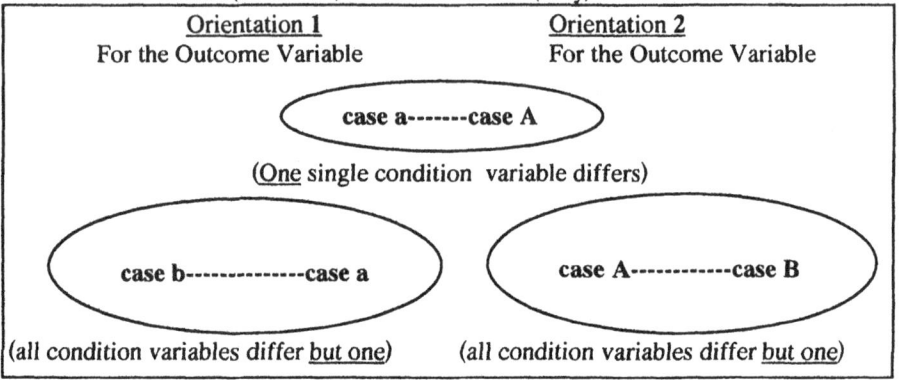

As a matter of fact, this ideal protocol is rarely applicable in the real world. This is the reason why we «softened» the rule: instead of the <u>absolute criterion</u> «different in only one condition» and «similar in all but one condition», we asked <u>for relative criteria</u> «most similar» and «most different».

Going from absolute to relative criteria will not only help keeping in touch with reality, and guarantee the existence of «solution(s)», but also require a new tool: intuitive notions of «most similar» - «most different» need to be conceptualized, well-defined and operationalized. This construction is neither obvious, nor unique or neutral. As would do any distance or measure, it will deeply structure the data space and influence the results.

See for example how two classical «distances» organize a plane

Figure 4.2: Manhattan and Euclidean Distances Structure Space Differently

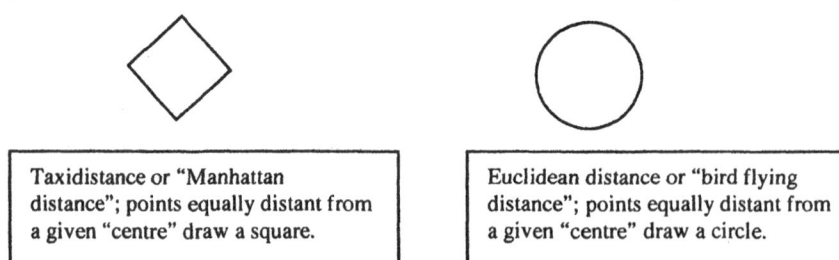

Thus the «distance» to choose will need to be in accordance with the characteristics of our data space: Euclidean distance is associated with spaces fully homogeneous in their directions, while Taxidistance will be more convenient for a space with two privileged directions (here, horizontal and vertical).

Which are the basic properties of our (future) data space?

a) unlike classical spaces (Euclidean spaces), which are linear, «naturally» metric and homogeneous in their elements as well as in their directions, our data set will produce a <u>non linear</u>, <u>non metric</u>, and essentially <u>non homogeneous</u> space. The variables' heterogeneity lies at different levels: quantitative or qualitative, some dealing with objective facts, others with experts' evaluations, measured with very different accuracy; moreover, nothing guarantees independence among variables.

b) our data space is structured by subsets, named «categories» (see further), and the number of variables by category is not constant; this also contributes to the heterogeneity of the space.

c) the degree of precision of the whole set depends on its weakest part; therefore, finely grained measures on some variables, while other are more roughly measured, bring more illusion than real precision.

First consequences (drawing of the «basic» model):
- we opted for a rough and robust measure, identical for each variable: each variable was dichotomized (strong/weak – yes/no – etc); hence the space will gain some homogeneity, and the Boolean distance[2] will be used as a basic tool;
- similarly, we opted for a similar weight to be assigned to each category, independently from their number of variables. Variables inside a category are considered as indicators of some specific «dimension». Within each category, each variable will be assigned the same weight.

Later (refinement to the model):
- we proposed a global measure of (dis)similarities taking into account both their intensity and their extension; this demand leads to simultaneous consideration of different levels of (dis)similarity: the lower levels pointing at pairs of cases very (dis)similar in a small number of categories
- higher levels revealing less sharp (dis)similarities more widely spread among categories.

In the following section, we elaborate on an example from the field of European public policy.

2. AN MSDO/MDSO APPLICATION IN (EUROPEAN) PUBLIC POLICY ANALYSIS

European integration studies - from a political science perspective - are conducted along many methodological lines and within a diverse set of theoretical schools. Most common are quantitative studies, often from a rational choice point of view, and interpretative single case studies, often from a sociological institutionalist perspective. Very scarce, on the contrary, are examples of qualitative comparative analyses (Bursens and Kerremans 1997; Schimmelfennig 2004). This contribution describes the use of both the MDSO/MSDO (and QCA) tools in the context of European public policy, based upon the design and results of work by Bursens (1999).

The general aim of this particular project was to identify the variables that explain why certain types of actor configurations develop through the elaboration of legislative proposals. More specifically, the research was intended to examine whether an institutionalist perspective could account for actor configurations that take shape on the European level. In other words, can institutional variables, as defined by historical institutionalist theory, explain the way policy actors interact with each other during the policy-making process?

The research design resulted in the identification of the outcome (independent) variable and the condition (dependent) variables and the selection of the empirical cases. First, the outcome variable was the type of configuration of actors that can be found during the policy-making processes. These configurations were conceptualized as policy networks and therefore defined through the structural and relational characteristics of a pair of actors instead of through the attitudinal variables of the individual actors. Based on the literature of policy networks on the one hand (cf. Rhodes and Marsh 1992; Smith 1992; Van Waarden 1992) and on the literature of the corporatism - pluralism spectrum on the other hand (cf. Schmitter 1979; Lehmbruch and Schmitter 1982), four main categories were constructed: relations among interest groups, involvement of decision-makers in interest groups, involvement of interest groups in the decision-making process and contacts between decision-makers and interest groups.

Second, the condition variables were chosen from an empirical point of view. In order to examine whether institutional variables matter, both rationalist actor-centered variables and institutional variables were selected. An exhaustive list of variables with potential explanatory power was established. Important to note is that, while the outcome variable was characterized by structural features, the condition variables are constructed by attitudinal features. Five main categories of condition variables could be defined: formal aspects of the decision-making process, characteristics of the interest groups, characteristics of the decision-making institutions, characteristics concerning the content of the legislative initiative and formal aspects of the policy concerned. These main categories could again be divided into several variables. In total, 44 condition variables were identified.

Thirdly, with regards to the selection of cases, from the perspective of a classic research design, a major problem occurred. The number of legislative initiatives that can be analyzed was limited while the number of potentially explanatory or condition variables was relatively large. The solution was found in the application of two qualitative comparative techniques: MDSO/MSDO and QCA. In total nine directives from EU environmental, agricultural and social policy were selected. Due to the use of small N techniques, all variables were first constructed as dichotomies and inserted in a matrix that could serve as the basis for the qualitative comparative analysis. The outcome variable was dichotomized into loose and tight actor configurations. The construction of this dichotomy was based upon the policy network and corporatism - pluralism literature. Both approaches use a spectrum that ranges from loose networks on the one hand to tight networks on the other. With respect to policy networks the far ends are respectively issue networks and policy communities; the other ideal-types are of course respectively pluralism and corporatism. Loose configurations were thus defined as 'pluralist issue networks' while tight configurations are defined as 'corporatist policy communities'. The condition variables, on the other hand, were dichotomized through various means. Sometimes this was obvious (e.g. a particular feature was present or absent), sometimes a threshold had to be depicted (e.g. long versus short procedures).

First, an MDSO/MSDO analysis was carried out to find out which variables could account for the occurrence of a tight or a loose configuration. The MDSO/MSDO technique is based on a particular two-step logic of comparison (cf. infra): firstly, the identification of the cases that must be compared with each other and secondly, the identification of the relevant (categories of) variables. For our research this logic sounded as follows:

- MDSO logic: to explain why within a set of legislative initiatives, all these initiatives result in the same decision-making pattern, one has to look for similarities in the characteristics of initiatives that differ the most from each other; firstly the identification of the most differing pair of cases and secondly the identification of similarities between those two cases.
- MSDO logic: to explain why within a set of legislative initiatives, some initiatives result in other decision-making patterns than other initiatives, one has to look for dissimilarities in the characteristics of initiatives that are similar to each other; firstly the identification of the most similar pair

of cases and secondly the identification of dissimilarities between those two cases.

Taking into account the data set of 9 cases, 4 with loose patterns and 5 with tight patterns, the two logics of comparison demand a total of three parallel analyses:

- An analysis of the 5 tight patterns following the MDSO logic to examine why they all resulted in tight patterns
- An analysis of the 4 loose patterns following the same MDSO logic to examine why they all resulted in loose patterns
- Analysis of the 5 tight patterns versus the 4 loose patterns to examine why some of them resulted in loose and other in tight patterns

The nine cases represent decision-making configurations that were developed around nine legislative dossiers (regulations and directives) in EU policy-making, more in particular in social policy (safety and security in workplaces and the European works councils), environmental policy (noise emissions, gas emissions and packaging waste) and agriculture policy (market organization of the rice and fodder sectors, price-setting in the sugar and fruit sectors). These cases describe the relations between all relevant actors during the decision-making process.

3. METHODOLOGICAL ELABORATION OF THE MDSO/MSDO ANALYSIS

Following the reasoning of the small N analysis, three different analyses had to be carried out: one among the tight networks, one among the loose configurations (both by means of the 'Most Different Same Outcome' logic) and one between the tight vs. the loose configurations (by means of the 'Most Similar Different Outcome' logic). The analysis among the loose networks identified the pairs Waste - Emissions and Waste - Health as being the most similar to each other.

To present the operation of our MSDO/MDSO algorithm on this « space » of cases, variables and categories, we make use of formal labeling of cases and variables:

- case 1 (**R**); case 2 (**Fo**); 3:**S**; 4:**Fr**; 5:**C**; 6:**N**; 7:**E**; 8:**W**; to case 9 (**H**)
- category 1 (or A),...to category 5 (or E)
- condition variables **A1** to **A11** (in category A); **B1** to **B7** ; **C1** to **C11**; **D1** to **D11**; and **E1** to **E4**.
- outcome variable: «Tight» (1) or «Loose» (0)

For practical reasons, we order the cases in such a way that all «Tight» cases come before all «Loose» cases. Our data would then appear under the form of a large binary table:

Table 4.1. Formal Presentation of Binary Data

Var/cat ↓	Cases →	Case1	Case2...	Case 9
$V_{A,1}$				
...				
$V_{E,4}$				

Table 4.2. The Binary Data Set

	R	Fo	S	Fr	C	N	E	W	H
Type of configuration (T = Tight and L= Loose)	T	T	T	T	T	L	L	L	L
Category A Formal aspects of the decision-making process									
A1 consultation procedure (0) –cooperation/co-decision procedure (1)	0	0	0	0	1	1	1	1	1
A2 protocol based (0) – treaty based(1)	1	1	1	1	0	1	1	1	1
A3 Commission's own initiative (0) – Council based initiative(1)	1	1	0	0	1	0	0	1	0
A4 short preparation (0) – long preparation(1)	1	1	0	0	1	0	0	1	0
A5 consultation of an advisory committee 0) – no consultation of an advisory committee (1)	0	0	0	0	1	0	0	0	0
A6 COREPER (0) – Special Committee Agriculture (1)	1	1	1	1	0	0	0	0	0
A7 implementation committee (0) – no implementation committee (1)	0	0	0	0	1	0	1	0	1
A8 Qualified Majority Voting (0) – unanimity (1)	1	1	0	0	1	0	1	0	1
A9 short procedure (0) – long procedure (1)	0	1	0	0	0	1	1	1	1
A10 package deal (0) – no package deal (1)	1	1	0	0	1	1	1	1	1
A11 time limit (0) – no time limit (1)	1	1	0	0	1	0	1	1	1
Category B Characteristics of the interest groups									
B1 large content-related interest (0) – small content-related interest (1)	0	0	0	0	0	1	1	0	0
B2 large institutional interest (0) – small institutional interest (1)	1	1	1	1	0	1	1	1	1
B3 representative groups (0) – also non-representative groups (1)	0	0	0	0	0	0	0	1	0
B4 European umbrella organizations (0) – also non-European umbrella organizations (1)	0	0	0	0	0	0	0	1	0
B5 social-economic groups (0) – also other groups(1)	0	0	0	0	0	0	0	1	0

B6 strong groups (0) – weak groups (1)	0	0	0	0	0	1	0	1	0
B7 organizations (0) – also individual actors (1)	0	0	0	0	0	1	0	1	0

Category C
Characteristics of the decision-making institutions

C1 closed Commission (0) – open Commission (1)	1	1	0	0	1	1	1	1	1
C2 much expertise inside Commission (0) – little expertise (1)	0	0	0	0	0	1	1	1	0
C3 large content-related interest Commission (0) – small content-related interest Commission (1)	0	0	0	0	1	1	1	0	1
C4 large institutional interest Commission (0) – small institutional interest Commission (1)	1	1	1	1	0	0	1	0	1
C5 much expertise inside European Parliament (0) – little expertise EP (1)	1	1	1	1	0	1	1	1	0
C6 much left – right opposition EP (0) – little left – right opposition EP (1)	1	1	0	0	0	1	1	0	0
C7 much materialism – non materialism opposition EP (0) – little materialism – non materialism opposition (1)	1	1	1	1	1	0	1	0	1
C8 much left – right opposition Council (0) – little left – right opposition Council (1)	1	1	1	1	1	1	1	0	1
C9 large institutional interest Council (0) – small institutional interest Council (1)	1	1	1	1	1	0	1	0	1
C10 much national interest opposition Council (0) – little national interest opposition Council (1)	0	1	0	0	0	0	1	0	0
C11 imminent presidency change Council (0) – no imminent presidency change Council (1)	0	1	0	0	1	0	0	0	0

Category D
Characteristics concerning the content of the legislative initiative

D1 polarization (0) – no polarization (1)	1	0	1	1	1	1	1	0	1
D2 radical changes (0) – marginal changes (1)	0	0	1	1	0	1	1	0	1
D3 broad scope (0) – small scope (1)	0	0	1	1	0	1	1	0	1
D4 technically difficult (0) – technically easy (1)	0	0	0	0	1	0	0	0	0
D5 spill-over (0) – no spill-over (1)	1	1	1	1	1	1	1	0	1
D6 exceptions for member states (0) – no exceptions for member states (1)	0	1	0	1	0	1	0	0	1
D7 social-economic basis (0) – other basis (1)	0	0	0	0	0	0	1	0	0
D8 heavy efforts required (0) – none or light efforts required (1)	0	0	1	1	0	0	0	0	0
D9 basic proposal (0) – complementary proposal (1)	0	0	1	1	0	1	1	0	1
D10 changing proposal (0) – new proposal (1)	0	0	0	0	1	0	0	1	0
D11 directive (0) – regulation (1)	1	1	1	1	0	0	0	0	0

Category E
Formal aspects of the policy concerned

E1 strong integration (0) – weak integration (1)	0	0	0	0	1	1	1	1	1
E2 young policy sector (0) – old policy sector(1)	1	1	1	1	0	0	0	0	0
E3 social-economic policy sector (0) – other sector(1)	0	0	0	0	0	1	1	1	0
E4 (re)distributive (0) – regulative (1)	0	0	0	0	1	1	1	1	1

Based on the general reflections above, the protocol of determination of most (dis)similar pairs follows these steps:
- construction and synthesis of distance matrices;
- construction and synthesis of (dis)similarity graphs;
- selection of configurations with the best concordance/discordance of key variables.

Distance Matrices:
For each of the (5) categories, one computes all distances among pairs of cases; this leads to (5) triangular matrices. Within each category, one looks for most similar pairs with different outcome (smallest distance: in the rectangular sub-matrix) and for most different pairs with similar outcome (largest distance: in the two triangular sub-matrices): see framed numbers in the figure below, showing the distance matrix for category A:

Figure 4.3. Distance Matrix for Category A

	case1	case2	case3	case4	case5	case6	case7	case8	case9
case1									
case2	1								
case3	5	6			Zone1				
case4	5	6	0						
case5	5	6	10	10					
case6	7	6	4	4	8				
case7	6	5	7	7	5	3		Zone2	
case8	4	3	7	7	5	3	4		
case9	6	5	7	7	5	3	0	4	
			Zone3						

Three zones are to be distinguished in the table:
- zone 1: pairs with same outcome „1" or „tight": triangular «Maximum distance, Same Outcome 1»
- zone 2: pairs with same outcome „0" or „loose": triangular «Maximum distance, Same Outcome 0»
- zone 3: pairs with different outcomes: rectangular «Minimum distance, Different Outcomes»

Each zone (1, 2, 3) of each matrix (1 to 5) produces such an extreme. When the Maximum value attained is smaller (respectively when the minimum value is bigger) than half the number of variables in the category, we decide not to take them into account. They do not reach the «threshold» separating large and small distances between cases.

We adopt the following presentation to summarize these extremes:

Table 4.3. Extremes and Thresholds for Each Category

	A (11 variables)	B (7 variables)	C (11 variables)	D (11 variables)	E (4 variables)
MAX for out 1: $D_0(1)$	10	(1)	(5)	8	3
MAX for out 0: $D_0(0)$)	(4)	6	7	7	(1)
Min for different out: $S_0(1/0)$	3	0	2	2	0
Thresholds	5,5	3,5	5,5	5,5	2

With only this information, one would point at pairs of cases with extreme distances (denoted by D_0 and S_0) for one category at a time, i.e. very (dis)similar inside one single category, without taking the other categories into account. Yet, it is interesting to consider pairs of cases possibly less close/distant, but in several categories at a time. Those considerations lead to define several levels of (dis)similarity spaced out by units between the Maximum (or minimum) and the threshold discriminating «similar» from dissimilar»: For example, for a category of 4 variables, the threshold is set at 2 (2 identical variables and 2 unequal variables): same number of similarities and dissimilarities; for a category of 11, the threshold is set at 5,5: 0 to 5 are considered «small» distances, and 6 to 11, «big» distances. Thus, if a Maximum distance (reached) D_0 equals 10 for a category of 11 the different values successively taken into account to build e.g. 4 levels of dissimilarity would be:

D_0	D_1	D_2	D_3
10	9	8	7

Conventions:
1) when the threshold is reached, the previous value is repeated (a star denotes the limit imposed by the threshold), without relaxing the constraint further;
2) when the first extremal distance computed is already beyond the threshold, the value is not retained, but replaced by a «--» mark.

By iteration on the 5 categories, one obtains the following values for four levels of (dis)similarity:

Table 4.4. Four Levels of (Dis)similarity for Each Category

	A (11 variables)	B (7 variables)	C (11 variables)	D (11 variables)	E (4 variables)
$D_0(1)$	10	--	--	8	3
$D_1(1)$	9	--	--	7	2*
$D_2(1)$	8	--	--	6*	2*
$D_3(1)$	7	--	--	6*	2*
$D_0(0)$	--	6	7	7	--
$D_1(0)$	--	5	6*	6*	--
$D_2(0)$	--	4*	6*	6*	--
$D_3(0)$	--	4*	6*	6*	--
$S_0(1/0)$	3	0	2	2	0
$S_1(1/0)$	4	1	3	3	1
$S_2(1/0)$	5*	2	4	4	2*
$S_3(1/0)$	5*	3*	5*	5*	2*

The different levels of (dis)similarities between pairs resulting from this procedure may then be presented in a synthetic matrix, showing most (dis)similar pairs of cases, for each category, at different levels of requirement. An empty cell means that the pair is not remarkably (dis)similar for the considered category.

As the requirement decreases when the level grows, (D_0 -> D_1 -> D_2 -> D_3 and S_0 -> S_1 -> S_2 -> S_3), we only indicate the strongest results (0 for the strongest level, then 1, 2 and 3 for the weaker levels).

To retain the coherence with the goal explained above («relaxing the constraint on maximally to extend to more categories»), one proceeds to the selection (for each zone, each level) of pairs reaching the value Di (or Si) in the largest number (denoted by **h**) of categories:

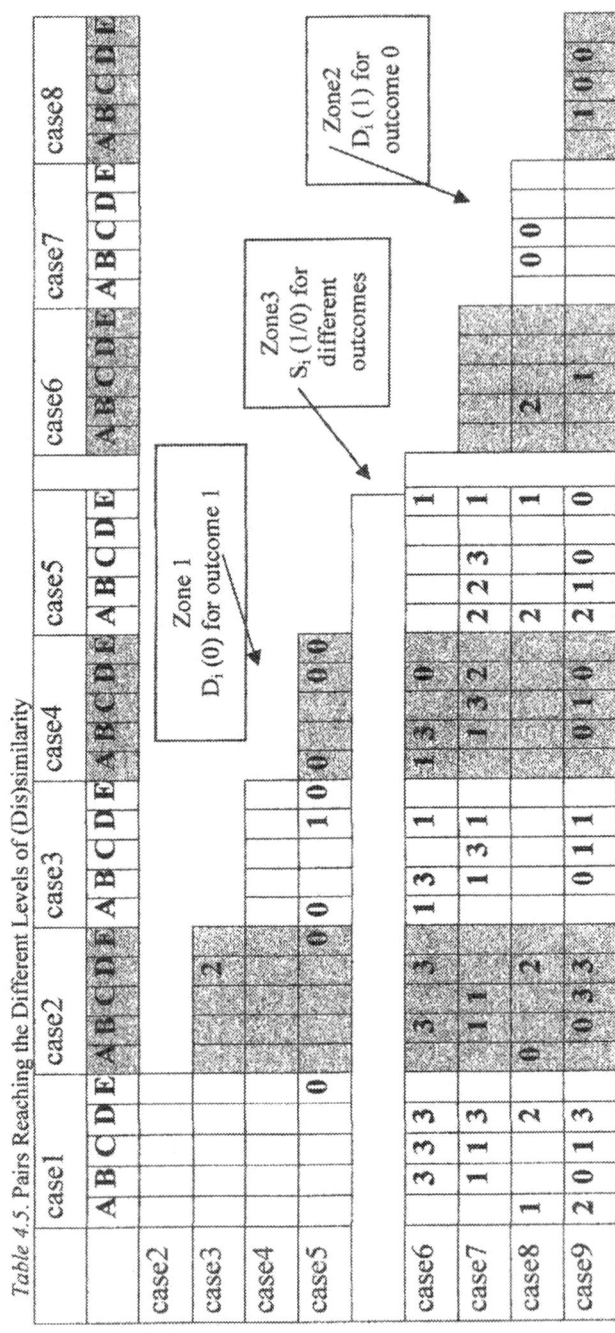

Zone1:
D_0: h=3, pair (Case4/case5); D_1: h=3, pairs (Case3/case5) and (Case4/case5); D_2 and D_3:same as D_1
Zone2:
D_0: h=2, pairs (Case7/case8) and (Case8/case9); D_1: h=3, pair (Case8/case9); D_2: and D_3:same as D_1
Zone3:
D_0: h=2, pairs (Case4/case9) and (Case5/case9); D_1: h=3, pairs (Case3/case9), (Case4/case9) and (Case5/case9); D_2: h=4, pair (Case5/case9) and D_3:h=4, pairs (Case1/case9), (Case5/case7) and (Case5/case9).

Pairs of cases selected by this process are then recorded in three (dis)similarity graphs, with a mark on the concerned level (D_i). Those graphs show the «result» produced by the «basic model» of a MSDO/MDSO algorithm:

Figure 4.4. MDSO Pairs for Tight Cases

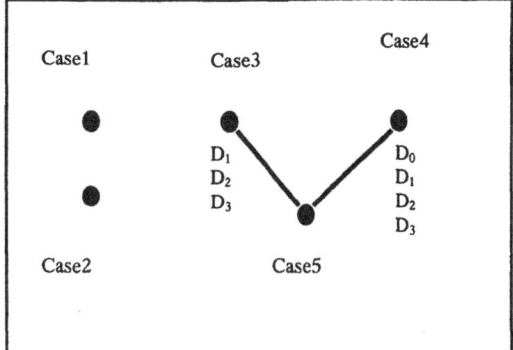

Figure 4.5. MDSO Pairs for Loose Cases

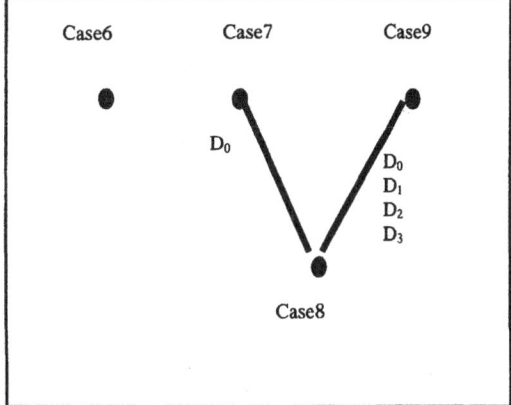

Figure 4.6. MSDO Pairs

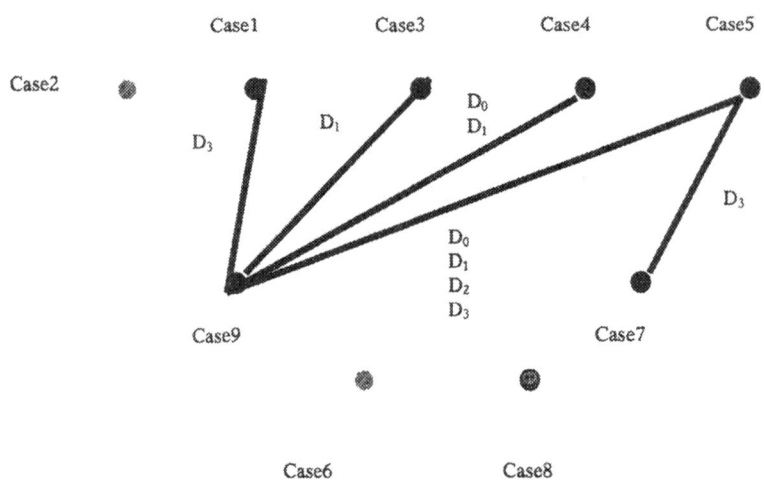

Zone3: most similar pairs with different outcomes, criterion **h**

One can now begin an analysis of the result: which categories, which variables are really involved in the graph relations.

One may also look for a richer graph (e.g. to ensure that no important variable is neglected: this will often be the case if the algorithm was used to «select» variables). Then, again, we make use of a less demanding second criterion: pairs reaching a (dis)similarity of level D_i for **h-1** categories are also taken into account, but with a weaker weight. A way to do this is to keep the «**h -1**» pairs only if they appear at least twice.

Zone1:
D_0: h=3, h-1=2: pairs (Case4/case5) and (Case3/case5); same pairs for D_1, D_2 and D_3.

Zone2:
D_0: h=2, h-1=1, pairs (Case7/case8), (Case8/case9), (Case6/case8), and (Case6/case9); D_1: h=3, h-1=2, pairs (Case8/case9) and pairs (Case7/case8); D_2: and D_3: same as D_1

Zone3:
D_o: h=2, h-1=1, pairs (Case1/case9), (Case2/case8), (Case2/case9), (Case3/case9), (Case4/case6), (Case4/case9) and (Case5/case9); D_1: h=3, h-1=2, pairs (Case1/case7), (Case1/case9), (Case2/case7), (Case3/case6), (Case3/case7), (Case3/case9), (Case4/case6), (Case4/case9) and (Case5/case9); D_2: h=4, h-1=3, pairs (Case1/case9) (Case3/case9), (Case4/case9) (Case5/case9) and D_3: h=4, h-1=3, pairs (Case1/case6), (Case1/case7), (Case1/case9), (Case2/case9), (Case3/case6), (Case3/case7), (Case3/case9), (Case4/case6), (Case4/case7), (Case4/case9), (Case5/case7) and (Case5/case9).

In this example, the graph for zone 3 would be enriched in the following way (full lines are retained, dotted lines are dropped)

Figure 4.7. MSDO Graph for Criteria **h** and **h-1**

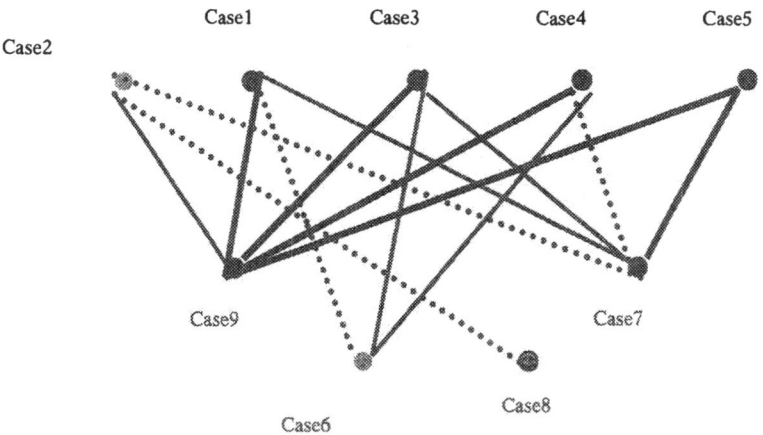

From this graph, at least two sub-configurations can emerge: the first, contrasting case 9 with cases 1, 2, 3, 4 and 5; the second, constituting of weaker lines, contrasting the pair 6, 7 with the triple 1, 3, 4. Each configuration may then be analyzed in depth, as suggested below, for the configuration «case 9 (loose) versus cases 1,2,3,4,5 (tight)».

At this stage, one has now to go back to cases, variables and categories, to interpret the table below, where commonalities are to be found, as potential key factors leading to a same outcome (in a configuration involving comparison between cases leading to different outcomes, one would search for differences): here the pair of cases 3 and 4 is contrasted with case 5, which is the most distant case for them, yet leading to the same «Tight» outcome.

Table 4.6: Commonalities between Very Distant Cases Leading to a Same Outcome

	S cases T	F cases T	C cases T
CatA			
A1	0	0	1
A2		1	0
A3	0		0
A4	0	0	
A5		0	1
A6	0		0
A7	0	0	
A8	0	0	
A9	0	0	0
A10	0	0	
A11	0		0
CatB			
B1	0	0	0
B2		1	0
B3	0	0	0
B4	0	0	0
B5	0	0	
B6	0	0	0
B7	0	0	0
CatC			
C1	0	0	0
C2	0	0	1
C3	0		
C4			
C5			
C6			
C7		1	
C8	1	1	
C9		1	
C10			
C11	0	0	
Cat D			
D1			1
D2	1		0
D3	1		0
D4		0	1
D5	1		
D6	0	1	0
D7	1		
D8	1	2	0
D9	1	1	0
D10	1	1	0
D11	1	1	0
Cat E			
E1	0	0	1
E2		1	0
E3	0	0	0
E4	0	0	1

Having reached that milestone, the researcher has to take the matter in hand and put forward his knowledge of the question under study. One can now look at the most contrasting configurations, and this table that shows which variables are most likely responsible of observed results (here, the same "tight" outcome despite many differences in starting conditions). The algorithm stops here; to go further, the researcher resumes one's analysis and interpretations.

4. INTERPRETING THE RESULTS OF THE MSDO/MDSO ANALYSIS

With respect to the analysis among the tight networks, the pairs Councils - Sugar and Councils - Fruit were identified as being the most similar. Finally, the analysis confronting the loose and the tight networks showed three pairs to be the least similar to each other: Emissions - Councils, Health - Councils and Fruit - Noise. The next step in the analysis was the identification of the variables that could be held responsible for the similarities (the two MDSO analyses) and differences (the MSDO analysis), respectively. This identification resulted in the following tables which show the pairs and the variables. The interpretation of these analytical results is given in the next paragraph.

Table 4.7. Identified Variables from MDSO Analysis of Loose Networks

Pair of Cases	Categories	Variables
Waste – Emissions	A	Treaty-based vs. Protocol based Coreper vs. Special Committee Agriculture qualified majority vs. unanimity (Treaty) long period vs. short period
	B	representative actors vs. not representative financially strong actors vs. weak actors geographically spread interest vs. not spread
	C	no secrecy within Commission vs. secrecy no expertise in EP vs. expertise in EP presidency change near vs. not near
Waste – Health	A	use of consultative committee vs. not use Treaty-based vs. Protocol based Coreper vs. Special Committee Agriculture qualified majority vs. unanimity (Treaty) long period vs. short period
	C	no secrecy within Commission vs. secrecy national tension within Council vs. no tension presidency change near vs. not near

Both pairs generate the dimensions formal aspects of the decision-making process and characteristics of the decision making institutions as potentially explanatory. Looking only at this analysis, the dimension characteristics of the interest groups seems to be important as well.

Table 4.8. Identified Variables from MDSO Analysis of Tight Networks

Pair of Cases	Categories	Variables
Councils – Sugar	A	Qualified majority vs. unanimity (Treaty) short period vs. long period
	B	representative actors vs. not representative social-economic actors vs. not social-economic financially strong actors vs. weak actors geographically spread interest vs. not spread
	E	time limit vs. no time limit part of a package deal vs. no part intervening policy vs. regulating policy
Councils – Fruit	A	qualified majority vs. unanimity (Treaty) short period vs. short period
	B	representative actors vs. not representative social-economic actors vs. not social-economic financially strong actors vs. weak actors geographically spread interest vs. not spread
	E	time limit vs. no time limit part of a package deal vs. no part intervening policy vs. regulating policy young vs. old policy domain

This analysis points again to the first dimension and to the same variables within this dimension. It furthermore adds the dimension of formal aspects of the policy to the list. The dimension discussing the characteristics of the interest groups is indeed identified but, after a detailed examination, cannot be treated as having explanatory power (cf. infra).

Table 4.9. Identified Variables from MSDO Analysis of Loose vs. Tight Networks

Pair of cases	Categories	Variables
Emissions – Councils	A	Consultation vs. co-operation Treaty-based vs. protocol based short preparation vs. long preparation long period vs. short period
	E	complementary proposal vs. basic proposal no package deal vs. of package deal
Health – Councils	A	Treaty-based vs. protocol based Commission initiative vs. council question short preparation vs. long preparation

		no use of consultative committee vs. no use long period vs. short period
	C	no institutional interest vs. interest Com. no presidency change near vs. change near
	E	complementary proposal vs. basic proposal replacing proposal vs. new proposal no package deal vs. of package deal
Fruit – Noise	A	consultation vs. co-decision Special Committee Agriculture vs. Coreper short period vs. long period
	B	little interest vs. a lot of interest financially strong actors vs. weak actors
	C	institutional interest vs. no interest Com. left right tension Council vs. no tension no materialism tension vs. tension Council
	D	no grave efforts vs. grave efforts
	E	distributive vs. regulative regulation vs. directive package deal vs. no package deal strong integration vs. weak integration

The MSDO analysis shows the formal aspects of the decision making procedure and of the policy as important variables. As will be discussed in the next section, the same variables again pop up: the length of the procedure and the use of package deals.

5. DISCUSSION

5.1 Overall Analysis: Length of Procedures and Package Deals

Two variables pop up in all three analyses: the length of the procedure in the category that discusses the formal aspects of the decision making procedure, and the use of package deals in the category that deals with the formal aspects of the policy concerned.

The length of the procedure seems to be a determinant factor for the type of network. A long procedure, defined as a period lasting more than one year, coincides almost in all cases with a loose network, while a short procedure corresponds always with a tight network. This can be explained by the fact that a short procedure forces interest groups to build intensive contacts and networks. Moreover, decision making institutions who are confronted with a short procedure, are not always able to maintain contacts with a large number of private actors, but, on the contrary are obliged to restrict their consultative contacts to a limited number of actors. Representative peak organizations then become the obvious interlocutors because they are able to provide decision makers with expert information.

The second important explanatory variable is the use of package deals within Council decision making. If the legislative proposal is part of such a deal, a tight network is almost always the case. If on the other hand the Council decides separately on each proposal, a loose network is found. The following argumentation can be developed. The most crucial feature of a package deal is the simultaneous treatment of several, mostly similar, policy proposals within the Council of Ministers. At such occasions, negotiations resemble very much a play of give and take: one member-state gives way with respect to one issue and in turn expects to win with respect to other issues. This negotiation mechanism has far-reaching consequences for the involved interest groups because they cannot be sure that the governments they have persuaded of their interests will persist in defending their viewpoint until the end of Council deliberations. Confronted with package deals, member-states make calculations, which not necessarily result in policy outcomes in favor of the interest group concerned. This puts off some interest groups and only stimulates the participation of those groups which can be relatively sure that governments will not abandon their viewpoints. The result is a tight policy network with a small number of actors who co-operate very intensively.

No other variables from all three analyses can be considered as explanatory, even though two variables from the category that discusses the formal aspects of the decision making procedure, pop up twice. The first one is required qualified majority voting within the Council of Ministers. Looking at the data set we can only conclude that this is not of any explanatory use because all cases had to be decided by means of qualified majority anyway. The second one is the distinction between the involvement of the Committee of Permanent Representatives (all loose networks) vs. the involvement of the Special Agricultural Committee (4 out of 5 tight networks). Since the latter four coincide with the four cases from the agricultural policy domain, it is obvious that we are confronted rather with a distinction between agricultural policy and the other policy domains than with a distinction between tight and loose networks.

It is furthermore striking that variables from the category that discusses the characteristics of the interest groups do not have any explanatory power. Neither the representativeness nor the financial strength of interest groups nor the geographical spreads of interests give a univocal result. In some cases they coincide with loose networks, in other cases with tight networks.

5.2 Analysis of the Loose Networks: Decision Makers Matter

With respect to the loose networks, attention was focused on the characteristics of decision making institutions. The absence of a culture of secrecy within the Commission during the policy formulation stage is an important feature of the cases that result in a loose network. If the administration is open during the drafting of policy proposals, interest groups are aware of the Commission's ideas in an early phase, which allows them to act very soon. This transparency also gives interest groups the opportunity to communicate their opinions and demands in an informal way. Indeed, a loose network is marked by multiple and informal contacts between private actors and public decision makers. If, on the contrary, the Commission does not want to give any information concerning its proposals until the publication in the Official Journal, less interest groups will be aware of the contents and therefore able to carry out useful lobby activities. Preliminary information is after all an essential prerequisite to succeed in influencing decision makers. The Commission, on the other hand, is not capable of collecting all essential data in order to elaborate realistic proposals and therefore has to rely on some expert information from the sector concerned. This is especially true with respect to price setting in agricultural policy. The Commission receives these data from a small number of privileged interest groups, i.e. the members of a tight policy network.

The absence or presence of expertise within the European Parliament is another variable that can be decisive in the construction of a policy network. Indeed, if the Members of the European Parliament don't have enough expertise themselves in order to treat proposals in an adequate way, they have to look for it elsewhere. Considering that one of the most fruitful ways to lobby consists of providing expert information, contacts with interest groups become an obvious strategy. If the Parliament has enough information at its disposal, for instance with respect to a technically less complex proposal, it has to rely less on the input of private actors and becomes less open to contacts, which impedes interest groups' access. One of the features of a tight network is indeed a low frequency of contacts between the players in the field.

An imminent presidency change can also be considered as an important variable but is less outspoken because of a less clear differentiation between loose and tight networks. We can only think of a minor stimulus, i.e. the expectation of interest groups that an issue will be concluded in due course which forces interest groups to enhance their lobby activities and turn more to unofficial, informal contacts, hence establishing a loose network. A polarization between two or more member-states within the Council of

Ministers doesn't lend itself to a univocal interpretation either. The only correlation we see is the use of informal channels to set member-states against each other when they are already in dispute.

5.3 Analysis of the Tight Networks: the Policy Domain Matters

The category that discusses the formal aspects of the policy becomes relevant when discussing analysis of the tight networks. Firstly, a time limit on the conclusion of a proposal, as can be the case with respect to price setting in agricultural policy, can restrict the opportunities for interest groups to establish contacts with decision makers. This equally limits the number of interlocutors for the decision making institutions. Both features lead to a rather tight network. Secondly, the age of a policy field can play a role. Young policy domains are normally characterized by less established concertation and consultation bodies and more by informal channels. Agricultural policy, for instance has got a long tradition during which consultative committees have been set up and semi-institutionalized relations have been established. Younger policy domains, such as environmental and social policy, simply have not yet been able to construct these.

5.4 Analysis of the Loose vs. the Tight Networks: the Legislative Proposal Matters

Again the categories covering the characteristics of the decision making institutions and formal aspects of the policy pop up as having explanatory power, although much less striking. Variables such as the institutional interest of the Commission and basic proposal vs. complementary proposal differentiate rather vaguely. Weak vs. strong integration of the policy is slightly more important since a strong integration can correspond with institutionalized mechanisms - hence tight networks - and weak integration with rather informal mechanisms - hence loose networks.

Finally, the category discussing characteristics concerning the content of the legislative initiative seems to have some explanatory power as well, More specifically, it concerns the variable on the degree of efforts that can be caused by a legislation. Serious efforts coincide with a loose network, while less serious efforts correlate with tight networks. This seems obvious: if a legislative proposal results in a situation in which interest groups have to make serious efforts to comply with the prescribed norms, more interest groups will try to influence the decision in their own favor, using very intensively a large number of channels and strategies. These are all features of a loose network. The cases from environmental policy in general and the

Packaging and Packaging Waste directive in particular can serve as excellent examples.

5.5 Conclusion: Do Institutions Matter?

The identification of the variables with explanatory power is not only interesting from an empirical point of view, but is also revealing with respect to political theory. The most remarkable result is that the characteristics of the interest groups themselves are no determinants for the type of policy network. On the contrary, characteristics of decision makers and formal aspects of the decision making procedure and of the policy domain seem to be much more decisive. Based on our empirical data, it would be going too far to say that the preferences of private actors don't matter at all, but the analysis does show that private actors' actions and strategies, and thus the policy networks they build, are highly restricted by the institutional setting they are operating in.

These findings suggest that an new-institutionalist approach of European governance is promising to explain what is really going on. The notion that 'institutions make politics' is not new within political science but it has taken a few years for scholars of European policy-making to follow the new-institutionalist research agenda. Only in the last few years, the European governance setting is being analyzed in the tradition that has been initiated by March and Olsen (1984 and 1989), Steinmo, Thelen and Longstreth (1993) and others. Both the European integration process (Pierson 1996) and the EU governance system (Bulmer 1994; Kerremans 1996; Pollack 1996; Schneider and Aspinwall 2001) are now being examined from a new-institutionalist perspective. These authors all stress different aspects but share a core belief in the determinant role of institutions, defined as legal arrangements, procedures, norms, conventions, organizational forms and routines, in the understanding of European governance.

The results of our analysis seem to confirm the importance of these institutions in two ways. Firstly, the developed policy network which is the result of the strategies of the participating actors, is largely determined by institutional constraints such as various aspects of the decision making procedure and the policy domain. Variables such as the length of the procedure and the use of package deals are the main examples. These aspects are in their turn products of the 'hard' and 'soft' institutional setting of the European Union, i.e. they are caused by the provisions of the treaties and legislation on the one hand and by the administrative culture and routines of institutional actors on the other hand. Secondly, private actors' strategies are influenced by the institutional actors themselves. The culture of secrecy and the presence of expertise within the institutions shape the choices interest groups make with respect to their participation in the policy making process.

The characteristics of those decision making institutions are again products of other new-institutionalist factors. The Commission lacks sufficient expertise because of its small size, which is in its turn caused by its internal organization and budget constraints. The culture of secrecy is a good example of a 'soft' implicit institutionalist variable. To sum up, the conclusions suggest that further research from a new-institutionalist point of view is likely to be promising with respect to the study of European governance.

6. METHODOLOGICAL OBSTACLES

This last section deals with some methodological observations with respect to the analysis used in the example from European public policy. It serves as a list of suggestions that can take the technique further in future applications.

6.1 Qualitative Variables with More Than Two Values

Sections 2-5 consider mainly Boolean variables, that is, variables that have but two possible values, or whose values could be grouped in two categories (*dichotomized*). But some variables have three or more possible values, which we often can't group in a natural way:

- answers to a poll may be "yes", "no", "don't know";
- a government may be left wing, right wing, or an ideologically non-connected coalition (i.e. a coalition in which the left-right dimension is not relevant);
- a student may answer a multiple-choice question right, or wrong, or not answer at all;
- a (pre-1990) European country could be member of NATO, the Warsaw pact or neither.

It would be very artificial, and subject to debate, to group the "don't know" answers with either the ayes or noes. The best answer, in such a case, is to create two variables. In the case of a government's orientation, for example, one could get a "left" (L) variable and a "right" (R) variable, and their values would be as follows:

Table 4.10. Dichotomizing a 3-Valued Variable

Government's orientation	variable L	variable R
left-wing	1	0
right-wing	0	1
neither	0	0

When computing distances between cases, the distance between a left-wing government and a right-wing one will be counted as 2, because both variables display different values in the table above. In contrast, the distance between a union government and a homogeneous one will be counted as 1. To cut a long story short, the three possible values are in a way graded: one of them lies in some sense "between" the other two. This makes sense in that particular case, as in the other cases mentioned above, but we might also be faced with variables with three distinct values and no possible gradation whatsoever. For example, if islands are classified as lying in the Atlantic, Pacific or Indian Oceans (and their respective adjacent seas), none of those groups can be deemed to lie "between" the other two. And it would look very artificial, if the results of the analysis were to depend from which two of those three oceans are taken as variable labels.

In such a case, we need to resort to another description, which statisticians call the *disjunctive form* : one separate Boolean (two-valued) variable for each value

Table 4.11. Another Attempt at Dichotomization

Situation	variable A	variable P	variable I
Atlantic Ocean	1	0	0
Pacific Ocean	0	1	0
Indian Ocean	0	0	1

Thus two units of distance will be computed whenever the situation of the islands differs.

Another problem now arises: when a variable has several different values, it will "count more" than a variable with only two values. Any difference will be counted multiple times. One may wonder, however, whether dichotomization is necessary in this case; in MSDO/MDSO, as first devised, all variables had to be Boolean; but this is not compulsory. The whole study may be conducted on variables with more than two values. When the outcome variable has several values, as is pointed below (see note 1, Figure 4.7), we will need to conduct a number of separate studies; but when "plain" (condition) variables do, no supplementary intricacies will be generated. However, if there are too many different values for one variable, nearly all pairs will be counted as being at distance 1 for this variable. This will make the method less efficient. The need for grouping will then be felt. For example, if one variable is the country (among EU countries), it has of course 25 possible values. However the use of a 25-valued variable will be impractical. It could even happen that each single case has a different value for this variable. We will then need to group countries in batches, as homogeneous as possible, or to use several variables, whose choice will be guided by the knowledge of the problem at study. For example, we might use two variables, with three values each:

"founding member / old member / 2004 member"
and
"small / medium / large country"
each of which may be treated as in table 4.10., as the values are in some way graded.

Using multi-valued variable makes no difference in the technicalities of the method; one only needs to be wary of variables with too many values.

6.2 Grouping Quantitative Values

Let us now turn to quantitative variables. When using such variables, if dichotomization appears less "natural", it is possible to split the field of possible values in more (but still few) parts. Consider a "GNP" variable. If the observed values for 10 countries were, say, $7000, 8000, 8500, 9000, 9500, 14000, 15000, 19000, 19500, 20000, it would be natural to consider a three-valued variable :

"high"   =   more than 15000
"medium"   =   10000 to 15000
"low"   =   less than 10000

From there on, we may use either the table 4.10. method, which will put "high GNP" and "low GNP" countries at distance 2, or just consider GNP as a three-valued variable.

6.3 Choosing Categories

For the method to make any sense, one needs to distribute variables among categories. To avoid the objection of arbitrariness, these should look as "natural" as possible, i.e. all variables in one category should pertain to some specific field. Ideally, any researcher with sufficient knowledge of the subject under study should create more or less the same categories. For example, if cases were cities, all variables related to the geographical environment of a city (climate, position relative to sea, central/peripheral position in its country...) may be put into one category, while variables of socioeconomic nature (richness, main activities, tourist center, openness to the outside...) will make up another one and so on. One should be especially wary of any "other" category that would encompass all variables that were not classified in any "obvious" category.

6.4 Conducting Successive Studies

Some variables could be felt as possibly pertaining to more than one category. For example, is "proportion of citizens participating to the vote" a sociological or political variable? Putting a variable into one category rather than another could change the results. We like to consider this as the method's strong point. The aim of the whole MSDO/MDSO endeavor is to select variables that may play some important role in the outcome. Let us consider two separate studies. In the first one, the variable "proportion of citizens participating to the vote" is put into the "sociological variables" category. In the second one, it is put into the "political" category. In those two separate studies, the results (in terms of which variables are selected as potentially important) may differ. However any variable that is nominated as important by both studies is a very strong candidate to the title of "decisive variable". Other variables, which would disappear from the selection after a small change in organization of variables, could be deemed to have appeared incidentally.

In a similar way, when no obvious grouping of quantitative values, as described above (section 6.2), appears (that is, values are more or less regularly spread), it could be useful to test several plausible groupings, in the hope that the same variable(s) will be nominated by all (or most) iterations of the study.

NOTES

[1] Values considered here are binary values; yet this limitation could - if necessary - be softened by the use of «multi value» variable, with a few number of values. Use with care! See section 6.1 and Figure 4.8. (here below) for the case when the outcome has several possible values.

Figure 4.8. Comparison Scheme for a Three-Valued Outcome

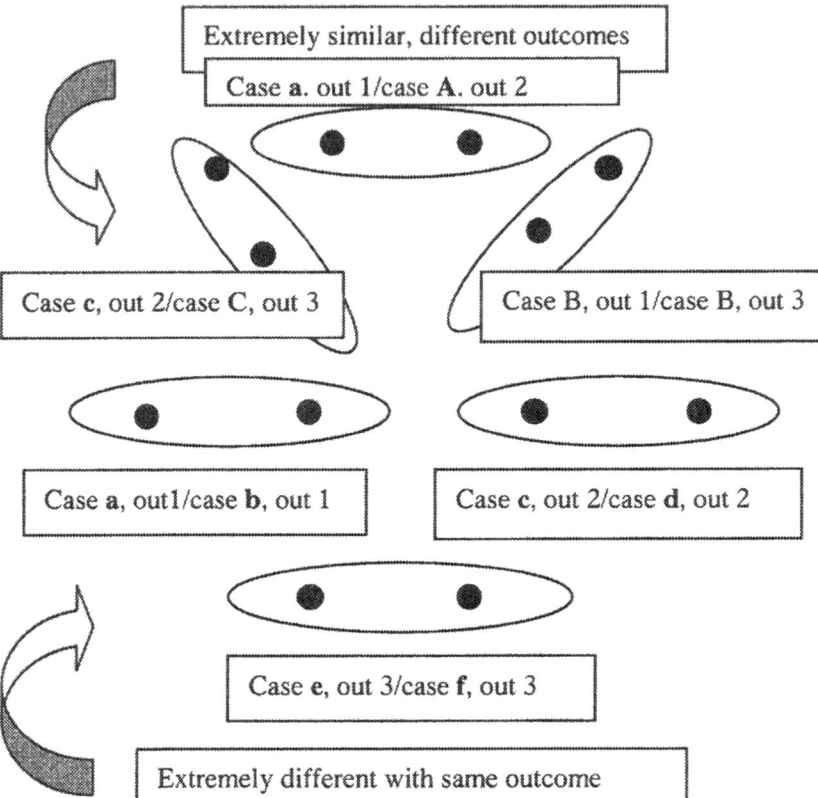

One notes that the number of comparisons to be performed will rapidly increase with the number of values of the outcome variable.

[2] The Boolean distance between two elements computes the total number of (binary) variables on which they differ.

Chapter 5

BEYOND METHODOLOGICAL TENETS
The Worlds of QCA and SNA and their Benefits to Policy Analysis[1]

Sakura Yamasaki
National Fund for Scientific Research and Université catholique de Louvain

Astrid Spreitzer
University of Vienna

1. INTRODUCTION

The aim of this study is to present combinations of Social Network Analysis (SNA) and Qualitative Comparative Analysis (QCA) and their benefit to Policy Analysis. We think that QCA and SNA are particularly suited to explain complex meso- or macro-social phenomena, just like policies. SNA gives access to a set of actors (individuals, groups, organizations, etc.) and allows to quantitatively measure and to visualize the relationships between these actors. The main goal is to model these relationships in order to study action and structure in their mutual dependence (Wasserman and Faust 1997). QCA on the other hand helps to uncover regularities across cases while maintaining within-case complexity; its strength lies on its ability to reduce complexity without loosing the analytical insights, a feature complemented by formalized "multiple conjunctural explanations" (Ragin 1987, 2003a). We first expose our understanding of Policy Analysis followed by the main challenges that research on the topic faces. We then explain why we think that SNA and QCA can answer these issues. As such, we shed some light on the main principles of the methods, and the main points for which they appear as supplementing to each other. Finally, we illustrate our arguments through two combinations of SNA and QCA applied to the field of Policy Analysis. We conclude on the main benefits as well as limitations of a combinatorial approach of the two methods vis-à-vis Policy Analysis.

2. POLICY ANALYSIS: CORE ELEMENTS, APPROACHES AND ITS CHALLENGES

2.1 Principles of Policy Analysis – in Brief

If we try to cover the principal dimensions of Policy Analysis (PA), we have to describe a multi-faceted area of research, ranging from pragmatic evaluation to theoretical contributions. In this respect, Héritier mentions that the ideas on science of scholars in this research area range between Post-Positivism (describing the values of groups) and the scientific neutrality of a utility-cost-analysis (scientific instrumentalism) (Héritier 1993a: 21f). As a very general statement, we can say that PA aims to classify policies alongside their effects, their use of political steering instruments and their character (Windhoff-Héritier 1987: 21ff; Schumann 1996: 74ff). This may be considered as a holistic approach in so far as it looks at politics, polity and the content of political decisions – the policies. Therefore it has to deal with the beliefs, interests and ideas of actors involved in political bargaining, the institutional framework they are embedded in and the process of interest aggregation with its formal and informal rules. PA was initially developed for the analysis in a national setting. In a modified style, it experienced a revival in the analysis of the European integration process. Here, our intention lies less in giving a detailed account of what Policy Analysis is, but rather in providing an overview of the two main branches of PA and in identifying the methodological shortcomings which evolved with the recent expansion of this research area.

When browsing the literature related to PA, two broad categories emerge. Considering the concept of a policy cycle as the general framework, a rough division of the field goes alongside the principles of policy formation and policy implementation. The former deals with the process of decision-making, concluding temporarily with the moment a legislative measure is created. Therefore, we can talk about policy formation analysis as the exploration of the analysis of a policy output. The second strand focuses instead on the outcome, by evaluating policy net effects in order to give recommendations to political practitioners (see also Varone, Rihoux and Marx, in this volume). As such, PA can be applied both in a descriptive, explanatory and counseling way (Héritier 1993a: 9).

2.1.1 Policy Implementation and Policy Outcome Evaluation

Within the policy evaluation category, an evaluation can be conducted before the policy is implemented (ex-ante analysis) or after implementation (ex-post analysis). Generally speaking, the evaluation of outcomes is a quantitative exercise where all measures of costs and benefits are expressed in monetary values. Several ways of conducting policy evaluation exist (Cost-Benefit Analysis, Cost-Efficiency Analysis, impact analysis, etc.) and the choice of the method as well as the measuring of some uncertainty parameters (such as depreciation level) is left to the discretion of the evaluator. The principal goal of Policy Outcome Evaluation (POE) is to *"evaluate public expenditure decisions"* (Stockey and Zeckhauser 1978: 134) and is guided by a Kaldor-Hicks criterion which is fulfilled if there is a *"guarantee that the benefits of any project undertaken will be large enough so that those who gain by the project* could *compensate those who lose, with everyone thus made better off"* (ibid: 137, emphasis in original). As such, POE implies *"a transparent and replicable methodological step. The major difficulty consists here in distinguishing, analytically and in reality, effects which are directly generated by the policy under evaluation from those which stem from contextual factors, thus not manageable by the actors of the policy"* (Varone 2001: 30, our translation; see also Varone, Rihoux and Marx in this volume).

Thus, POE is an analysis performed in view of formulating recommendations or reports to policymakers. It has a strong pragmatic orientation, as opposed to academic knowledge accumulation. However, as a consequence of its pragmatism, one of the main shortcomings of POE is the lack of theoretical insight throughout the analysis, which in turn leads to the fragmentation of PA results. We will come back to this issue later.

2.1.2 The Genesis of a Policy: Policy Output Analysis

As opposed to POE, the goal of Policy Output Analysis (POA) is to understand the complex mechanisms, which create, transform and sometimes "kill" a policy. Judging or assessing is not the keyword here. Rather, understanding and describing a policy as a research object is the purpose of such studies. For example, how policy changes occur (external events, macro political contexts, etc.) (Birkland 2004, Hall 1993), the nature of these changes (incremental, sudden) (Lindblom 1959, Baumgartner and Jones 1991), the role of ideas in the policy process (Sabatier and Jenkins-Smith 1999), the existence and role of policy networks (Sager 2001, Kriesi and Jegen 2001) are some of the phenomena policy process analysts try to explain. The analytical starting point of POA concerns – as its name already implies – the contents of politics. However, it also considers the institutional framework and the political processes, or the "environment" of the policy content in order to describe and explain policies.

In this regard, the evaluation and counseling function of PA, the analysis of the output (POA) is concerned with the policy itself in a more holistic sense than POE. As such, POA looks at components that go beyond the mere measurable impacts; equity, transparency, coordination, negotiation procedures and good governance are some of these other components. For example, on the basis of an identification of the actors involved, policies can be called distributive or re-distributive (Windhoff-Héritier 1987: 21ff; Schumann 1996: 74ff). Catching the complexity of the possible factors in their interactions and cumulative effects, which might influence a policy output, is the main difficulty here.

2.2 Challenges of Policy Analysis

As mentioned earlier, Policy Analysis was originally a concept of national politics. Challenged by the new area of research on European Integration, the shortcomings of PA became more obvious (Marks, Hooghe et al. 1995, 1996). Although there are certainly many more challenges for PA, we focus on two of them which are, in our opinion, the most important.

2.2.1 The Challenge of Causal and Subject Complexity

The variety of approaches and perspectives in the field of PA reveals that PA has to deal with a multifaceted subject that is embedded in a complex social context. All the different perspectives in PA[2] share only a minimum of common explanatory factors and, as Togerson commented almost some 20 years ago, this field *"often appears as a jungle of diverse and conflicting modes of inquiry, full of inconsistent terminologies, divergent intellectual styles – perhaps, indeed, incommensurable paradigms"* (1986: 33, cited in Hendrick and Nachmias 1992: 311). This assessment maintained its legitimacy until today: PA is challenged by the complex causalities of social reality.

It is not a single one, but rather a plurality of factors which might lead to a certain policy. the kinds of factors are multiple: Greenberg et al. (1977) suggest that *"the phenomena public policy theories seek to explain are radically different from other phenomena that social scientists study"* and that *"the difference is due to the objects of analysis being more complex in the policy science than phenomena such as voting, elite ideologies or revolutions"* (paraphrased in Hendrick and Nachmias 1992: 311). Policy Analysis is indeed often characterized as a complex subject, because of the multiple actors involved (policy makers, administration, beneficiaries, target groups, etc.) in a multi-level context (local level, national level, sub- and supra-national levels) and with conflicting goals or interest (e.g. redistribution issues) (a.o. Hendrick and Nachmias 1992; Owen 1995; Schön 1973, 1979; van Buuren 2004)[3].

In a nutshell, the difficulty in PA lies in adopting a viable strategy of analysis, where causal and subject complexity can be systematically analyzed (as opposed to non-formalized case studies, for example) and can be understood by practitioners (e.g. as opposed to stochastic modeling of PA). For example, a viable strategy would be a combinatorial one, between Social Network Analysis and Qualitative Comparative Analysis. As Lempert and Popper (2002) would suggest, within a complex world where uncertainty rules, we need to be adaptive in order to be robust. However, the strategies in PA rarely appear formalized and, therefore, seem to lack a level of pragmatism necessary for policy practitioners. As such, we suggest investigating PA by combinations of potentially influencing factors (Ragin 1987: 24). In order to clearly identify causal explanations, it is not an additive but a conjunctural logic which should be applied in the analysis (see also Varone, Rihoux and Marx, in this volume), by neutralizing the complexity of the object under study with a relational view on actors to preserve their interdependency and heterogeneity features.

2.2.2 The Pragmatism Challenge

Along with causal and subject complexity of explaining policies, the challenge to solve the difficulties in research design is still in the air: do we seek in depth knowledge of cases or results which we can generalize? These are the extreme points of a continuum, determined by a trade-off between the two ideal scientific notions. As Ragin reminds us, *"[n]either view is incorrect. Ultimately, the degree to which a set of observations or cases is one population or many depends on the interests of the investigator and on those of the intended audience"* (1987: 22). The issue of generalization is, of course, closely linked to the one of pragmatism, or, in other words, to the (re-)usability of the results.

On the one hand, in-depth knowledge of cases is attained when the intertwining of actors, institutions, the external environment, etc. are taken into account. However, formalization is an absent feature most of the time, or when present as in stochastic modeling, its practical interpretation becomes nearly impossible. Falsification and comparability become thus possible only at the cost of heroic re-interpretation of analytical factors and other choices.

On the other hand, the potentials for generalization and formalization are defining characteristics of POEs, where OLS regressions, for example, propose measurable net effects of a policy. The downside of it, as most quantitative analysts would admit, is the measurement errors inherent to any empirical quantitative studies. However, the appeal of generalization potentials and thus pragmatism is so strong that researchers (as well as policy-makers) usually close their eyes to these possible pitfalls, after, of course, having done their best to attenuate the size of the errors. Policy-makers seek for precise and simple results that are easily interpretable into decision-making. The point is then to draw simple, robust and elegant conclusions from the analysis of a complex phenomenon.

2.2.3 The Re-distribution of Challenges...

Policy Output Analysis (POA) deals much more with normative and subjective aspects of the policy than Policy Outcome Evaluation (POE), hence the analysis is generally conducted using qualitative methods. The objective herein is less to judge the effects of a policy and more to ponder the normative criteria a policy should fulfill, from its emergence to its adoption through all the iterative negotiations among the involved actors. Another reason for using qualitative tools in POA is the necessarily holistic approach of such an analysis. To assess the genesis of a policy requires looking at the complex societal or politico-administrative environment as well, and not just the policy "hardware". The main caveat of POA, though, is its lack of a systematic analytical approach, and hence the quasi-impossibility of producing comparable data for different policy areas in different national settings (Medda and Nijkamp 1999). With the development of sub-national policy analyses within the European integration frame, this problem looms over this PA category. Indeed, case studies (one policy in a specific context, sometimes over time)[4] represent the large majority of studies conducted in this PA field.

Conversely, Policy Outcome Evaluation (POE) induces quantitative analysis, focusing on "hard" measures such as: What is for the benefit of whom? The main caveats of POE are its underlying assumptions about what a "good" policy is, and the validity of statistical tools as appropriate for evaluating policy outcomes. POE supposes that a policy is good based on the Kaldor-Hicks criterion and, therefore, dismisses the power dilemma of re-distribution. Statistical tools such as OLS regression (multi-variate regression) for measuring the (potential) impact of a policy assumes that it can correctly measure most of the factors in term of monetary values, as well as identify the net effects of a policy by controlling other factors (see also Varone, Rihoux and Marx, in this volume). Such an epistemological assumption is generally acknowledged as being too strong, but accepted as a second-best choice. The problem is that analysts often fail to remind themselves or the client when producing their final assessment. Table 5.1 summarizes the strengths and shortcomings of each type of PA.

Since we seek for both, in-depth knowledge (complexity) and generalizations (applicability), the next section of the paper focuses on how to cope with complexity and formalization. We suggest that two methods, Qualitative Comparative Analysis and Social Network Analysis, may prove particularly helpful in providing some answers to these issues.

Table 5.1. Advantages and Shortcomings of POE / POA

TYPE OF PA	MAIN PITFALLS:	RESULTING IN:	STRONG POINTS:
Policy Output Analysis (POA)	• Lack of generalizability • Too theoretical and no applicability	Exaggeration in display of complexity	Complexity
Policy Outcome Evaluation (POE)	• Lack of theory • Too pragmatic, flawed measurements	Exaggeration in reduction of complexity	Pragmatism

3. HOW QCA AND SNA ANSWER TO SOME METHODOLOGICAL PROBLEMS OF POLICY ANALYSIS

As discussed above, we have to take into account complexity and in-depth knowledge as well as the ability to generalize in Policy Analysis. What we suggest here is the application of a combination of Social Network Analysis (SNA) and Qualitative Comparative Analysis (QCA) in order to achieve these aims to a certain extent. Before exposing the operational description of how to combine QCA and SNA to answer these problems, we found it necessary to address two questions, which might naturally come to the mind of the reader. First, why SNA and QCA? How do they answer the challenges of PA? Second, are QCA and SNA really compatible? At the same time, it will present our understanding of the two methods and their subjects.

Qualitative Comparative Analysis (QCA) and Social Network Analysis (SNA) have never been combined as a technique, and neither have they ever been compared and contrasted as an approach (for an exception, see Mohr 1998). Their realm of application differs in many respects and this has kept respective users insensitive to each other. For example, while QCA principally deals with macro-social phenomena and hence has macro-level units of analysis, SNA copes more with micro or meso-level issues such as individual performances or organizational structures. While QCA is a comparative method by definition and hence analyses more than three cases, SNA can be understood as a case study where the network constitutes the case. Also, while QCA is considered leaning more towards the qualitative camp of social science methodology, SNA is generally identified as a quantitative data analysis technique. These differences are the consequences of perceived incompatibility between QCA and SNA (for a recent state-of-the-art discussion on QCA, see Rihoux 2003). We shall demonstrate that on the contrary these two methods share deep-rooted assumptions that shape their approach to social science, and help answer some problems arising in the PA field.

3.1 The Complexity Issue

3.1.1 The View on Cases

Both QCA and SNA require analyzing cases as a whole and thus accepting and assuming complexity as a pre-existing context. That is, for both methods, there is no possibility to talk about causality (or regularities) if the cases have not been looked at as one entity. The opposite stance would be to look at cases as if they were composed of 'independent' variables, and hence in a fragmented and simplified manner, as in classical statistical approaches. Instead, QCA uses combinatorial logic to represent its cases: each case is a combination of conditions, therefore allowing within-case complexity that is comparable across cases (Ragin 2003a, and in this volume).

With SNA, there is no meaning in measuring anything without looking at the whole network, be it complete network or ego network. Just looking at one or several nodes or cliques is senseless, since any interpretation is relative to the whole network (all nodes and all cliques). This emphasis on the inter-related character of the world makes SNA furthermore suited for the analysis of complex phenomena. As Kenis and Schneider put it for SNA in policy analysis, *"[the network concept] helps us to understand not only formal institutional arrangements but also highly complex informal relationships in the policy process"*, since *"contemporary policy processes emerge from complex actor constellations and resource interdependencies, and decisions are often made in a highly decentralized and informal manner"* (1991: 27).

3.1.2 The Causal Interpretation

Furthermore, both QCA and SNA display a structural logic in their causal interpretations. QCA assumes multiple and combinatorial causality. This rejects the "one factor-one consequence" view on causality. This suggests two important points: first, that a set of conditions (or a term) is the *"full cause"* (Mackie 1974: 62) of an outcome, as opposed to one condition leading to an outcome. This 'full cause' view adequates with 'chemical' causation: the presence of A alone or B alone does not lead to an outcome, but the presence of both simultaneously (A and B) does lead to the outcome[5]. The second important point QCA makes is that there exists multiple "paths" to an outcome[6]. These two concepts (chemical causation and the plurality of causes) is the essence of what Ragin has labeled "multiple conjunctural causation" (1987: 121-122). Thus, the conditions (or independent variables) in QCA react in a "chemical" manner, as opposed to a linear and additive manner[7].

As for SNA, it presents one way to cope with a dilemma of Social Theory: the causal relationship between social action and social structure. Its focus lies on the complexity of the subject as it deals with the in-between of social entities, a societal space of interactions between individual and collective actors. In this sense, the understanding and conceptual framework of SNA assumes the interdependence of actors with their environment. Actors are able both to adopt successful strategies in reaction to environmental influences and to affect a given social structure (Hasse and Krücken 2002). As Wilks and Wright (1987: 298) note, *"The properties of the network are not reducible to those of individual actors. The network is the outcome of their combined actions"*[8]. Social Networks are *"lasting patterns of relations among actors"* (Wasserman and Faust 1997: 7) and in that sense they are the social structure which constrains individual behavior, but are also the product of actors' behavior. The "embeddedness" of social action in social structure is a basic assumption of SNA. This relational view is the main difference to more common approaches in social sciences.

As such, QCA and SNA appear to be appropriate tools for the study of complex phenomena, since both methods' ontological basis assumes complexity as a starting point.

3.2 Pragmatic Matters: Formalization and Visualization

Pragmatic matters such as formalization and thus the potential to generalize, and visualization are synonymous with systematic analyses. Their importance should not be dismissed lightly with a proud academic backhand, especially in PA, where studies can and most of the time should be used as advice to policy makers.

Two main techniques are behind QCA and SNA's formalization features: Boolean algebra for QCA and Multidimensional Scaling (MDS) for SNA. The former allows a systematic reduction in complexity by virtues of Boolean rules[9], such that redundant information will be dropped off until the most minimal formula accounting for all cases is obtained[10]. Generalization is made possible through the use of 'logical' (i.e. non-observed) cases, as well as hypotheses-testing through still other Boolean calculations. All these operations are made through available freeware such as fs/QCA and TOSMANA[11].

The latter technique is much more focused on the visualization effect. Indeed, the principle of MDS is to spatially represent a network of actors so that the distance among themselves represent their similarity and dissimilarity vis-à-vis their connection to each other. One of the fundamental features which make SNA so attractive in many fields of social sciences is the possibility to visualize networks. Unequal distribution of power, the overall distribution of information or the patterns of relational evolution can all be grasped in an intuitive understanding via the graphical visualizations of network structures[12].

So, the next question to ask would be "Why combine?". If QCA and SNA both deal with complexity and pragmatism in a well-suited manner, why not use them separately?

3.3 The Complementarities of QCA and SNA

In fact, both methods have potentials to mutually enrich one another. Although networks do preserve the complexity of Policy Analysis, comparisons of networks do not take into account the contextual factors, at least not in an explicit manner. As such, structural or institutional factors are "guessed" through the network analysis and not separately identified. Therefore, a well coordinated policy, for example, would be explained by a network attribute and maybe by other institutional factors which would not have been tested in a formalized way. In the next section; we will demonstrate how the combination of QCA and SNA allows for a distinction of the network attribute as a potentially relevant condition. This strategy is mainly possible thanks to the common ontological assumption underlying both methods: phenomena are conjunctural and stochastic rather than linear and additive; hence multi-colinearity is not seen as a problem (up to a certain degree).

QCA has an accurate but less intuitive visualization procedure through Venn diagrams. The "world" is divided into the presence or absence of variable spaces which can overlap. This allows an analytical (variable based) display of cases as opposed to the disappearance of cases behind variables. This usually does not immediately tell the viewer about the weight of a variable or combinations of variables. Instead, it provides a highly accurate account of variables and combinations of conditions leading to an outcome. This remark is not to say that accuracy is wrong (!), but when the analysis has a pragmatic purpose, like in some Policy Analyses, results or recommendations should also be made available in a convincing fashion (Simple, Straightforward and Sexy). Pragmatism ought not to be an accessory concern when dealing with PA. As the natural sequel to complexity, pragmatism here is understood as the technique to extract the most useful and complete data from the complex multi-dimensional web of information. Therefore, if QCA data could be displayed in an intuitive network mode, and so that the results are concordant, it might enlarge its audience from researchers to include practitioners as well.

Hence, although counter-intuitive, QCA and SNA share some deep-rooted ontological assumptions in terms of causality and epistemology. This shared basis provides a solid ground on which to build answers to some needs arising in PA. We have seen that they might enable each other to gain strength where a weakness was spotted.

Now that a tangible common basis has been laid across both methods, we would like to demonstrate how they could both contribute to the scientific advancement of PA.

4. ILLUSTRATION THROUGH TWO CASES: THE SWISS HEAVY TRUCK TRANSPORTATION POLICY NETWORK AND THE EMERGENCE OF LEFT-LIBERTARIAN PARTIES

At our exploratory stage we have identified two conjunctions of QCA and SNA, with a variation of different dependent and independent variables, all of them including attribute and relational data. The following models consider only meso-level phenomena, which should be useful for PA.

4.1 Network Data for QCA Analysis[13]

A first fusion of QCA and SNA allows network features to be compared through QCA. One aspect which could be seen as problematic with network analysis is that there is no "ideal" network. Therefore, it is difficult to assess which network features are relevant for the topic under investigation. This problem can partially be resolved by entering network data and other purely structural data into a QCA matrix. Therewith, we follow the central ideas of Network Analysis in assuming that "...*patterned relationships between multiple actors jointly affect network members' behavior*" (Wellman 1988: 20). As such, the network structure constraints the activities of involved actors.

One can think of analyzing network data with QCA in order to explain a particular policy outcome, where entire network attributes are the independent variables (conditions in QCA). The relational data (such as centrality measures) has to be transformed into attributes (usually gender, ethnic group, belonging to a particular group, etc.) to fit in QCA. The research question could on the one hand deal with a temporally static topic of how different types of networks (across nations or policy sectors) produce different kinds of policies during a given period of time and why. For example, health policy networks in different countries would be the cases, the outcome would be an efficient implementation of the policy, explained by several network attributes. Centrality is such a network feature, measured for example with the Bonacich's power based centrality measure (see below), and indicating how much a network is centralized around "powerful" actors. On the other hand, it is also possible to enter processes and dynamics in the analysis, for example by comparing one policy network at several points in time.

Our demonstration of entering network data into QCA-software deals with the latter, tracing the dynamic transformation of a policy network. We are grateful to Fritz Sager, for ceding us the data on the Swiss network on the policy of 28-tons truck transportations limits (hereafter the 28-tons policy). Therein, Sager *et.al.* (2001) show that it is the institutional givens (the national and supranational polity) rather than the policy sector (thematic division) that influence the boundary delineation of a policy network. In other words, it is the formal structural dimension first, and then the sector membership that matter for the formation of a policy network. Sager et al. measure 4 different network ties[14]:

- the quantity of the contacts among actors of the 28-tons policy network (0 value if none, 3 value if very frequent);
- the quality of the contacts among the actors (0 value if no contact, 3 value if crucial contact for decision-making);
- the sharing of interests (0 if no common interests, 3 value if complete matching of interests);
- the opposing interests (0 if no opposite interests, 3 value if competing interests).

About 30 actors of different backgrounds are involved in the 28-tons policy networks, namely governmental and private actors in Switzerland, its neighboring countries and the European Union (EU). The investigation started in the mid-1980s and was finalized in 1996. This period falls into three categories of dominating issues: a first period from 1984 to 1988 where transport and environmental policy were the most important issues within the 28-tons policy, a second period runs from 1989 to 1992 and represents a transition period to a prevailing integration policy, and the third period runs from 1992 to 1996 and is dominated by integration policy.

In our meta-application, the data enables us to compare 12 "different" networks: the Swiss 28-ton policy re-defined through a 4 by 3 matrix: 4 networks describing four types of relations (the quality of the relationship among actors, the quantity of the relationship, the sharing of common goals, and the sharing of opposing or competing goals, as explained above) along 3 periods in time (1984-8; 1989-92; 1992-96). These 12 networks are defined as our cases in QCA and the network features of clustering coefficient, centrality and transitivity depict the conditions (or independent variables). These three network features represent different measures of power inequality within a network (more below). Analyzing the data in QCA could bring us insights into the evolution of the network by explicitly determining how network attributes are combined at several points in time. As such, we call upon one of the underutilized functions of QCA: *typology building*. Our goal is not to explain a phenomenon, but rather to identify common factors across these networks (and a rigorous typology always contributes to an explanatory analysis). Summing up, the research questions to be answered by our application are:

- Do these networks expressing different ties at several points in time show regularities along clustering coefficient, centrality, and transitivity measures?
- If yes, can these regularities be regrouped along a time factor (periods of the network), or a type of tie factor (quality/quantity of contacts, shared/opposing interests)?

To obtain the different network measures, Sager *et.al.*'s network data has to be explored in UCINET first, a software tool for research on Social Networks. First, clustering coefficient measures "how "cliquish" the graph is, as in how closely the neighbors of a particular node interact with each other" (Indiana University 2004). As opposed to measure of network density, which tells us how "active" the overall network is, the clustering coefficient thus measures the level of activity in small groups. Hence, a high clustering coefficient tells us that the network is not homogeneous in terms of power[15]. Second, power centrality (or the Bonacich's centrality measure) indicates the degree to which the network concentrates on powerful (i.e. well-connected) actors. It is also often referred to as a measure of inequality (Hanneman 1999). Third and finally, transitivity focuses on the density of transitive triples in a network and indicates how well information or opinions circulate but at a local level. In this sense, transitivity measure is quite close to the clustering coefficient measure. Table 5.2 summarizes the implications of each of these measures for each type of network.

Table 5.2. Implication of Network Measures for Each Type of Network

MEASURE	TYPE OF NETWORK	IMPLICATIONS
CLUSTER	Quality of contacts	A high network clustering coefficient indicates a clique structure of crucial decision making contacts
	Quantity of contacts	A network in which actors communicate a lot (regardless of the quality of the communication) in cliques
	Sharing of interests	A network in which actors are cliqued in terms of shared interests (within the frame of the 28 tons policy)
	Opposing of interests	A network in which actors with competing interests form clique structures.
CENTRALITY	Quality of contacts	A high network centrality indicates that the crucial contacts are highly centralized around powerful (well connected) actors
	Quantity of contacts	The most frequent contacts usually go through powerful actors
	Sharing of interests	The strongest agreements in terms of interests are concentrated around powerful actors
	Opposing interests	The strongest disagreements in terms of interests are concentrated around powerful actors
TRANSITIVITY	Quality of contacts	A high network transitivity indicates that the most important contacts with regards to decision making are fluid at local levels
	Quantity of contacts	The most active exchanges are fluid at local levels
	Sharing of interests	The strongest agreements are fluid at local levels
	Opposing interests	The strongest disagreements circulate at local levels

Next, the results of the analysis in UCINET are summarized in table 5.3, showing all of the network measures for the 12 policy networks (cases). As a reminder, the cases contain two different informations: the type of the relations (contact frequency, contact quality, common and opposing interests) and the different points in time (1984-8; 1989-92; 1992-96)

Table 5.3. Network Measures

CASES	CLUSTERING COEFFICIENT (%)[16]	CENTRALITY (%)	TRANSITIVITY (%)
Quality of contacts, period A (1984-8)	59	3	60
Quantity of contacts, period A	67	4	58
Sharing of interests, period A	71	16	68
Conflicting interests, period A	38	10	32
Quality of contacts, period B (1989-92)	49	6	55
Quantity of contacts, period B	50	8	55
Sharing of interests, period B	71	17	69
Conflicting interests, period B	41	11	34
Quality of contacts, period C (1992-6)	64	4	57
Quantity of contacts, period C	69	14	63
Sharing of interests, period C	81	21	82
Conflicting interests, period C	33	9	28

In the next step, the data is fit into TOSMANA, a tool to analyze cross-case regularities in Small-N-Analysis. By means of Boolean algebra, dichotomized or multi-valued variables can be processed in MVQCA, a particular procedure, which results in a formula explaining the outcome by a combination of conditions (see Cronqvist 2005). In our analysis, however, and as mentioned above, the aim is to build a typology. Therefore, we create a false outcome condition, coded with the same value for all cases, so that the minimized equation results in a categorization of all cases.

The main added value of QCA consists in a comparison of network attributes between different relations (quality and frequency of contact, common and different interests) over time. The outcome of QCA is expected to show, how the network structure of the policy characterizes these cases. By letting the TOSMANA software establish a dichotomization threshold through the clustering technique, we obtain a truth table (table 5.4).

Table 5.4. Truth Table

CASES	CLUSTERING COEFFICIENT	CENTRALITY	TRANSITIVITY	[Outcome] (for typology)
Quality of contacts, period A (1984-8)	1	0	1	1
Quantity of contacts, period A	1	0	1	1
Sharing of interests, period A	1	1	1	1
Conflicting interests, period A	0	0	0	1
Quality of contacts, period B (1989-92)	0	0	1	1
Quantity of contacts, period B	0	0	1	1
Sharing of interests, period B	1	1	1	1
Conflicting interests, period B	0	0	0	1
Quality of contacts, period C (1992-6)	1	0	1	1
Quantity of contacts, period C	1	1	1	1
Sharing of interests, period C	1	1	1	1
Conflicting interests, period C	0	0	0	1

The minimization procedure (without the logical cases) allows us to view how these 12 networks can be categorized. Note that this categorization is valid only with the selected conditions; here, we selected conditions (network measures) which focus on information/opinion flow, and thereby on power structure of the networks. Hence, the typology is built along network features of power. The TOSMANA results reads[17]:

Minimized value: 1

cluster * centrality　　　　　+　　　　**CLUSTER * TRANSITIVITY**
(OpposeA,OpposeB,OpposeC　　　　(ShareA,ShareB,ShareC,QuantiC+
QualiB,QuantiB)　　　　　　　　　　QualiA,QualiC,QuantiA)

The TOSMANA result brings interesting additional information about the Swiss 28-tons policy. First, we obtain two groups of networks: one characterized by a combination of low levels of clustering coefficient and centrality measure (cluster * centrality), and a second group characterized by a combination of high levels of clustering coefficient and transitivity measure (CLUSTER * TRANSITIVITY). Based on this first observation, we can advance a preliminary conclusion: there are two groups of networks differentiated by levels of network power structures. Indeed, the first group of networks displays a low level of network measures (a combination of lower case conditions) indicating a low level of power inequality, while the second group of networks share a high level of power inequality measures (a combination of upper case conditions).

Second, by looking at the corresponding cases, we observe a certain pattern in the groups. If we look at the first term [cluster * centrality], we see that it brings together all the networks of opposing interests (OppoA, OppoB, and OppoC) as well as the contact quality and quantity networks of period B (QualiB and QuantiB). As such, this category regroups network along a type of tie (opposing interests) and along a particular time period (period B, which is a transition period in the 28-tons policy).

The second term of the formula [CLUSTER * TRANSITIVITY] regroups the networks of shared interests (ShareA, ShareB, and ShareC) and the networks of contact quality and quantity at periods A and B (QualiA, QualiC, QuantiA, and QuantiC). Again, we observe a clustering of networks along the tie type (shared interests) and also along a time period (A and B, which are the periods where the dominating issue within the 28-tons policy was quite clear). We will not go any further in the analysis of the reasons of this categorization: it is not the subject of this study, even if policy network scholars might want to take this issue on board for their future research agendas.

Thus, by using the QCA method and the TOSMANA software, we created a typology of network based on an existing policy network analysis. We extracted two distinct groups of power networks, differentiated not only by their types of tie (opposing interests, for example) but also by the time period they represent (transition or stable dominant issues within the network).

The added value of QCA can be described as a clarifying function: where the relations between various network features were implicit, they are now formalized. For further steps, we could for instance test a hypothesis out of this typology, such as: *Networks of opposing interests and networks of transition periods differ from others vis-à-vis network power inequality measures.* In conclusion, this example shows how crossing the boundaries between SNA and QCA can give us insights on former blind regions in our map of data analysis.

4.2 QCA Data for Network Analysis

We propose another combinatorial model which in turn treats QCA data as relational data. In other words, QCA data would be transformed into a symmetrical matrix and thus into SNA data to be analyzed with network software. This would allow network measures to represent/describe QCA models. The main innovation here is the visualization of QCA data in a network fashion. Although visualization techniques for QCA already exists (Venn diagrams), we think that network visualization might be more intuitive in terms of interpretation for practitioners who are not very familiar with the language of logic. Also, apart from being more intuitive than Venn diagrams, the use of network software allows to visualize data with more than four conditions, whereas it becomes difficult, even for the trained eye, to interpret a Venn diagram with more than four conditions. In addition, we will advance the merits of a visualization using Multi-Dimensional Scaling (MDS), a method to visualize spatial representations of (dis-)similarity and closeness measures. Therefore, one can think of plotting cases to a policy, conditions to a policy or matching all of them into one graph, by the use of SNA software[18].

This combination (or even fusion) might be best understood through an application using an existing QCA analysis. The purpose of this exercise is to show the applicability of SNA technique on QCA data but also to identify some added-value of this combination of methods. Since there are not yet so many fine-grained applications of QCA on policy analysis, we chose Redding and Viterna's analysis on the success of left-libertarian parties in 18 OECD countries during the 1980s and 1990s[19] (Redding and Viterna 1999).

Table 5.5. Truth Table of the Redding and Viterna Analysis

SUCCESS	PNB	SOCS	CORP	LEFT	PROP	CASES
0	0	0	0	0	0	JP, NZ, AUS
0	1	0	0	0	0	CAN, USA
0	0	0	0	1	0	UK
0	0	0	0	0	1	IT
0	1	1	0	0	0	FR
0	0	1	0	0	1	IR
1	0	0	1	1	1	FI
1	1	0	1	1	1	CH
1	0	1	1	1	1	AT
1	1	1	0	1	1	BE
1	1	1	1	1	1	DK, West DE, SW
1	1	1	1	0	1	NL

The outcome (SUCCESS) is present when there was a successful left-libertarian party formation[20]. Redding and Viterna propose a model with five explanatory factors (or conditions). The presence of the conditions PNB and SOS express respectively high GDP per capita and high social security expenditures. They represent the demand-side hypothesis by assuming that: the more economically developed a society is, the more it creates post-materialist values, which, in turn, support the emergence of left-libertarian parties. The presence of the conditions CORP, LEFT and PROP express respectively a high level of corporatism, the presence of left parties in government and the presence of a proportional representation system. They together represent the supply-side hypothesis or the speculation that these institutional factors are conducive to successful left-libertarian party formations. Table 5.5 (above) exposes Redding and Viterna's truth table, once their raw data has been dichotomized.

The authors obtain the following results after the minimization procedure (without including the logical cases) of the "1" outcome (success of the left-libertarian party):

SUCCESS   =   CORP LEFT PROP +
                (AT, DK, FI, DE, NO, SE, CH)
                GDP SOS LEFT PROP +
                (BE)
                GDP SOS CORP PROP
                (NL)
           =   PROP (CORP LEFT + GDP SOS LEFT + GDP SOS CORP)

The minimized formula obtained by Redding and Viterna identifies PROP (presence of a proportional representation system) as a necessary condition for the success of a Left Libertarian Party (the condition PROP is observed whenever the outcome SUCCESS is observed, too) and the strong corroboration of the second institutional hypothesis.

Next, we transform QCA data into a 2 × 2 network matrix of n conditions × 2 rows. Each cell represents the number of times a presence/absence of the row condition is observed with the presence/absence of the column condition. For example, we count the number of times the presence of GDP is observed in co-occurrence with the presence of SOS, with the absence of SOS ("sos"), etc. This is repeated for all conditions, present and absent. At the end, we obtain a network data matrix (Table 5.6).

Finally, we process the QCA data for visualization using a SNA software (here, UCInet) and a network visualization tool (here Netdraw in UCInet), with the ties expressing co-occurrence of conditions for the explanation of the 1 outcome. We set the parameters of visualization such that the stronger the ties, the thicker the ties appear. The presence of conditions is indicated by white nodes and the absence by black nodes. In the same way, demand factors (SOS and GDP) display square nodes whereas supply factors (CORP, LEFT and PROP) display circle nodes. Once the parameters are thus set to intuitively grasp the essential information, we can also "play" with the level of complexity we wish to see. As such, we present here three levels of complexity. The first visualization displays all strength of ties. The second is an intermediary step where only the nodes that are connected more than three times are displayed as a network. Finally, the third level allows us to look at the most strongly co-occurring nodes (or conditions).

The first level of visualization (all ties are drawn) already gives some interesting insight into the relationship between conditions (figure 5.1).

Figure 5.1. Step 1 of QCA Data Visualization Using Netdraw

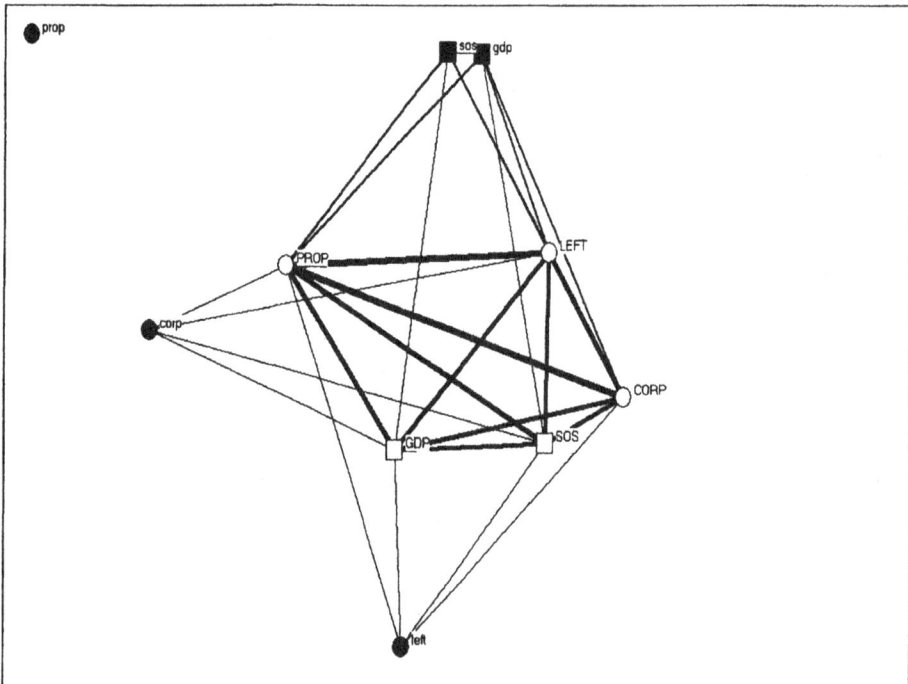

Table 5.6. Co-Occurrence of Conditions (Redding and Viterna Data)

	GDP	gdp	SOS	sos	CORP	corp	LEFT	left	PROP	prop
GDP	0[21]	0	5	1	5	1	5	1	6	0
Gdp	0	0	1	1	2	0	2	0	2	0
SOS	5	1	0	0	5	1	5	1	6	0
Sos	1	1	0	0	2	0	2	0	2	0
CORP	5	2	5	2	0	0	6	1	7	0
corp	1	0	0	0	0	0	1	0	1	0
LEFT	5	2	5	2	6	1	0	0	7	0
left	1	0	1	0	1	0	0	0	1	0
PROP	6	2	6	2	7	1	7	1	0	0
prop	0	0	0	0	0	0	0	0	0	0

We can see that there is one "isolate", i.e. a node that has no tie to any other: the absence of proportional representation ("prop"). And indeed, in the QCA truth table, we note that "prop" is never observed in connection with successful left-libertarian party formation. On the contrary, PROP or the presence of proportional representation has a central position within the network. Here again, the conclusion drawn from network visualization provides an information consistent with PROP's necessary character in the QCA minimal formula. Moreover, the strong ties (thicker lines) link the present conditions (white nodes) together quite obviously, whereas the absent conditions (black nodes) are represented at the periphery of the network. This intuitively shows that the hypotheses are generally corroborated since the presence of conditions correctly leads to the outcome. The display of the network is done using the MDS (Multi-Dimensional Scaling) function of Netdraw, which allows to spatially bind nodes that are "similar", i.e. conditions that share similar co-occurrence with other conditions, while conditions that are "dissimilar" or share minimal co-occurrence with other conditions are represented far away from each other. At this first level of visualization, this MDS added value is not fully appreciated, but we will see how it can contribute to Policy Analysis at subsequent levels.

The second level of visualization (figure 5.2), with the threshold set to "more than 3 times of co-occurrence" greatly reduces the "noise" surrounding the relationship between the most relevant conditions. Indeed, this network represents the most often observed co-occurring sets of conditions leading to the success of a left-libertarian party formation. As such, all the conditions with a "0" value are now isolates in the upper left corner of the graph, and only conditions with a "1" value are still part of the network. This is a stronger corroboration of the authors' hypotheses than what was observed in the first level visualization of the data.

In networks, a tie is the relationship between two nodes only, but the diffusion of these relationships to unite all nodes and thus compose a "network" is assured by the transitivity assumption (if A and B are strongly connected and B and C are also strongly connected, then there is a big probability that A and C are also strongly connected). In the present case, since PROP and LEFT are strongly co-occurring (7 co-occurrences) and PROP and CORP, too (7 co-occurrences), LEFT and CORP also display a strong relationship (6 co-occurrences)[22].

Figure 5.2. Step 2 of QCA Data Visualization Using Netdraw

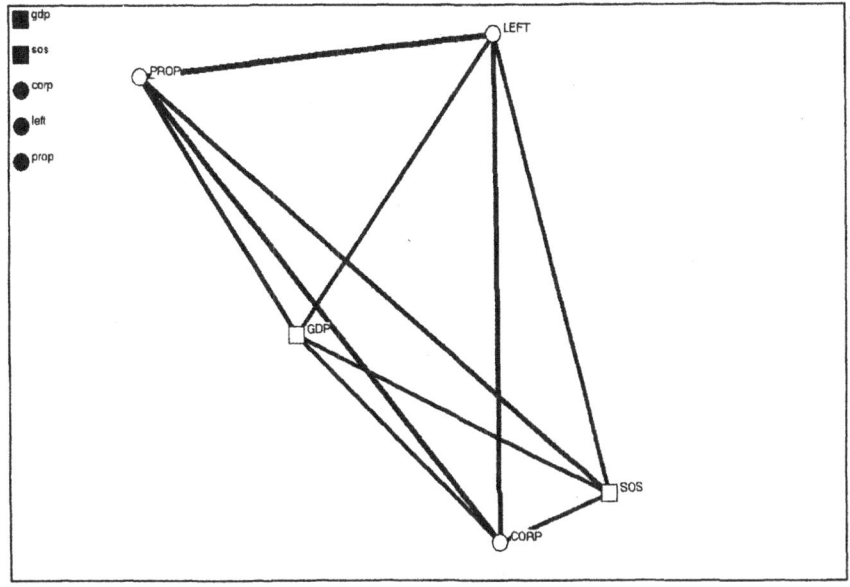

Of course, we do not forget the combinatorial logic that is fundamental to QCA, but by transforming QCA data into network data, we add a probabilistic character to the interpretation of the policy analysis results. We are not implying that all QCA analyses should incorporate this probabilistic element, but that seen the pragmatic concerns of an exercise such as Policy Analysis, the analyses should respond to these specific needs. However, this second level of visualization of the data may still throw a too broad "net" on the relevant conditions for policy analysts.

Finally, the last level of visualization leaves the analyst with three conditions, LEFT, PROP and CORP (figure 5.3). The threshold is set to "7 or more ties": LEFT and PROP co-occur 7 times and CORP and PROP also. If we were to visualize the same data with "6 or more ties", there would be a line between LEFT and CORP. The analyst can now conclude that a successful left-libertarian party formation is observed when there is a strong positive relationship between proportional representation and the presence of a leftist party in government or between proportional representation and a high level of corporatism. In any case, PROP is central since it is linked to both other conditions, whereas the latter ones are not (as strongly) linked.

Since PROP and LEFT are closer to each other on the MDS scale (they are spatially closer to each other than to CORP), the analyst would consider the combination of the two conditions as more relevant (because more probable in the real world) than the other two possible combinations of conditions (PROP and LEFT or LEFT and CORP). We would again like to stress that there is a concordance of results between QCA formulae and SNA visualization. In other words, Netdraw does not go counter to

QCA results (isolates, centrality of PROP, coherence of direction of conditions).

Figure 5.3. Step 3 of QCA Data Visualization Using Netdraw

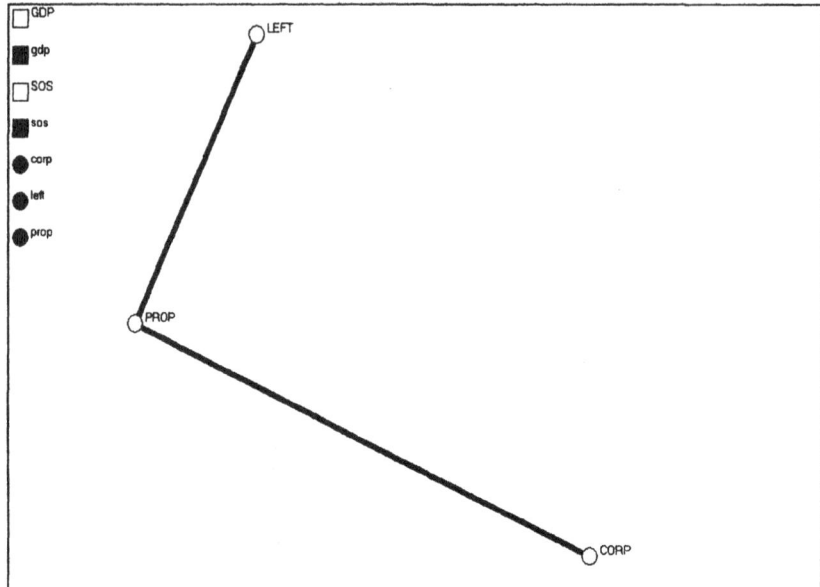

Another added value of analyzing QCA-data in SNA software is - besides the more intuitive visualization - that the visualization technique plugs in a probabilistic parameter to the interpretation. Indeed, the most traveled paths are directly identified, along with the distance (expressing the proximity) between conditions. Some probabilistic flavor is particularly welcome for PA since it is economically and ethically problematic for policy makers to implement several policies for one societal issue (Ragin 2003b). One might argue that this path probability is taken into account when a term is matched with the observed cases, with software such as TOSMANA. However, we argue that visualizations with network analysis software provide another interpretation of the relationship between conditions: the rigidity or the determinism of 100% case matching is dropped for a more flexible causal interpretation through conditions[23].

One last added value of transforming QCA data into a network matrix is the possibility of testing the significance of the results. Since the non-independence of variables and the non-random selection of cases are common assumptions to both methods, classical statistical significance tests remain invalid. To counter this, network analysis relies on permutation technique such as the QAP procedure to test hypotheses under such assumptions. It will be interesting to use this technique with QCA data in future research.

5. CONCLUSION: THE BENEFIT FOR POLICY ANALYSIS

The aim of this article was twofold. First, we clarified the boundaries of Policy Analysis, and identified the main streams composing this area of research as well as its main caveats. In our opinion, PA asks for a holistic approach given that policies are macro-social phenomena of extreme complexity. If one seeks to explain policy outputs and outcomes properly, one has to include polity as well as politics in the research design. However, this leads to one of the main shortcomings in this field: most research on Policy Analysis does not go beyond case studies. Therefore, comparisons and generalizations are hardly possible as we deal with case studies of small N. Comparative policy analysis represents a rapidly growing need in the field of Policy Analysis, because of the recent extension of its application from a primarily national setting towards a more comparative European setting. Moreover, Policy Analysis has to deal with the inherent complexity of its research subject, making general causal explanations rare. Indeed, classical statistical methods and solely qualitative studies are only partly able to bring research further in this field.

The second aim of this paper was to propose a combinatorial strategy of Qualitative Comparative Analysis and Social Network Analysis capable of covering these above mentioned "blind areas" in PA. We showed how these two apparently different methods prove to share some fundamental views on science and explanation. Indeed, the combination of these methods allows preserving complexity and still bringing about formalization in order to allow more accurate comparative policy analyses, or offer new visualization tools for the pragmatic necessity of policy makers. One of the main messages that we wished to be retained is the necessary concordance of assumptions among theory, methods and data. In other words, we should seek to clarify the epistemological and ontological bases of one's own research and select theories, methods and data in accordance to the declared assumptions.

NOTES

[1] We are grateful for the many comments we received from the ESF workshop participants, and especially to Bernhard Kittel and Fritz Sager.

[2] At least three different strands resting upon POA can be found: Policy Intertwining (Scharpf 1997, 1995, 2003), Constructivist elements in PA (Sabatier 1993, Majone 1993, 2001, Peters 1999) and Policy Network Analysis (Héritier 1993b, 1993c, Schumann 1996). These strands do not, of course, have clear cut boundaries between them and their approach often overlap in many respects (Thatcher 1998: 406).

[3] The latter explains that complexity theory has recently been flourishing within PA for several reasons: ontological changes concerning the growing interconnectedness of the real world, epistemological changes concerning the acknowledgment of uncertainty as a way of understanding the world, and changes in the nature of

decision-making where participatory style is becoming more common and additional dimensions such as new social actors, human rights or the environment are added (van Buuren 2004: 7; see also Gallopin et al. 2001: 222-3).

4 On case-studies, see Gerring (2004; forthcoming).
5 Mill even argues that one cannot talk about a 'cause' if one individualizes its components: *"We have, philosophically speaking, no right to give the name of cause to one of them, exclusively of the others"* (1872: III, v, 3).
6 This was also suggested by Mill, and he called this a "plurality of causes": *"It is not true that one effect must be connected with only one cause, or assemblage of conditions; that each phenomenon can be produced only in some way. There are often several independent modes in which the same phenomenon could have originated"* (1889, cited in Mackie 1974: 61).
7 Similarly to system theory where *"the whole is more than the sum of the parts, not in an ultimate, metaphysical sense but in the important pragmatic sense that, given the properties of the parts and the laws of their interaction, it is not a trivial matter to infer the properties of the whole"* (Simon 1981: 86).
8 Note here again the similarity with the system theory approach on causality.
9 For Boolean algebra, refer to Boole (1854), Carvallo (1970).
10 For the application of Boolean algebra in QCA, see Ragin (1987: 85ff), De Meur and Rihoux (2002). A bibliography of QCA applications as well as discussions around QCA is available at http://www.compasss.org .
11 All downloadable at http://www.compasss.org .
12 Visualization is possible in two dimensions through NetDraw, a package part of UCINet, or in three dimensions through the Pajek software.
13 The idea of having networks as independent or dependent variables is also presented in Kenis and Schneider 1991: 44ff.
14 A fifth variable obtained is the reputation of the actors, used in order to classify them. For our purpose it is sufficient to focus on the four main relations, and leave the analytical tool of reputation aside.
15 In network analysis, power is often associated with the level of activity of the network (information and opinion flow, contacts frequency, etc.).
16 To obtain the clustering coefficient, the network centralization measure and the transitivity measure, we first dichotomize the network data, such that $y(i,j) = 1$ if $x(i,j) >= 2$, and 0 otherwise.
17 The conditions in lower case indicate a low level of the network measure, while conditions in upper case show a high level of the network measure. Corresponding cases are shown in parentheses below each term (or combinations of conditions). "OpposeA" stands for the network of opposing interests in period A. "ShareB" stands for the network of shared interests in period B. "QualiC" stands for the network of contact quality in period C. "QuantiA" stands for the network of contact quantity in period A. Etc.
18 For a comprehensive overview of the available software and free downloads, the International Network for Social Network Analysis gives the details on its homepage. <http://www.insna.org/INSNA/soft_inf.html>, 30.08.04.
19 We analyze only one part of their study, the 1980s. We are grateful to the authors for letting us use their data.
20 For thresholds and their justifications, please refer to the original article.
21 Of course the co-occurrence of a condition with itself is not counted.
22 On transitivity, see Wassermann and Faust 1997: 150ff, 241ff.
23 This explanation-oriented example (POPA) might not prove as illustrative of the visualization strength as a recommendation-oriented example (POCE) with real policy evaluation data, but we hope that the essence of the advantages offered by such a technique has been made clear.

PART TWO

INNOVATIVE COMPARATIVE METHODS TO ANALYZE POLICY-MAKING PROCESSES: APPLICATIONS

Chapter 6

ENTREPRENEURSHIP POLICY AND REGIONAL ECONOMIC GROWTH
Exploring the Link and Theoretical Implications[1]

Heike Grimm
University of Erfurt and Max-Planck-Institute of Economics, Jena

1. INTRODUCTION

The key to promoting a place is a comprehensive knowledge and understanding of policies and strategies which successfully contribute to economic development. Whereas the story of economic development has often been the story of a nation-state, the unit of analysis has shifted to the sub-national level - the region - during the last years. Successful national "models" of development have been studied extensively, and national policy prescriptions and recommendations have been drawn up for less successful nations (i.e., Reynolds et al 2003). Nonetheless, it is mostly a matter of specific regions lagging behind the rest of a nation and a matter of specific regions within a nation developing successfully. In this context, it is also a matter of specific policy mix which is appropriate to promoting a region's economic development.

This leads to one of the core question of spatial economic development: Why do some regions take the lead while others lag behind? This question has not been answered yet due to a lack of regional case studies and due to a missing understanding and analyses which policies and strategies contribute to economic development at the local level. Rather, there is an increased risk that existent strategies favorable to the nation-states are interchangeably used at the national and local levels, and that the meaning and differences that lie behind them are not understood thoroughly. In addition, there is a rising tendency to transfer policies across nations and sub-national economies that seem to contribute to economic development at one place but may not have any impact on another place due to historical, cultural and institutional peculiarities which might differ greatly from one another. Clearly, there is no one-size-fits-all-solution. Each place - a nation, region or city - has to develop a perfect policy mix based on individual historical, cultural, social, economic and political experiences. In this contribution, I will focus specifically on one policy dimension, 'entrepreneurship policies', and their potential impact on regional economic development.

2. THEORETICAL FRAMEWORK

My research picks up Ann Markusen's critique that many analyses about the drivers of the competitiveness of regions have been accompanied by an increasing detachment from political and policy advocacy. Greater efforts to entering the policy debate and to making results accessible and informative to policymakers would contribute to the impact and usefulness of policy research (Markusen 1999, 1996a, 1996b). The relative neglect of successful policies which shape regional development, for example, widens the gap between research and policymakers. No doubt, in a global world, policies matter for the promotion of the entrepreneurial environment of places. Policies matter to induce regional economic growth as long as institutions and policymakers interfere with policies to shape the market economy. But what are successful 'entrepreneurship policies' designed for an 'entrepreneurial economy' (Audretsch and Thurik 2001) which is dependent on the input of knowledge and ideas?

In a global world, new policies need to be developed and old policy approaches need to be re-defined for the "strategic management of places" (Audretsch 2003:20). Nonetheless, there seems to be a vacuum of innovative policies which successfully promote an entrepreneurial society in the early 21st century. Above all, there is no comprehensive approach yet on how to define and measure policies which contribute to the attractiveness of places. The objectives of entrepreneurship policies implemented by policymakers are multifaceted and mostly not specified and, therefore, can not be evaluated (Reynolds and Storey 1994, Storey 2003). This deficit matters since locations do not just become attractive *per se*, but public policies contribute greatly to turn them into attractive ones. The question is which ones are really applicable to face the challenges of an entrepreneurial society.

Despite of much tribute given to the role of human capital for economic growth, not enough attention been paid to entrepreneurship policies implemented by individuals and institutions in order to attract entrepreneurial human capital. Some regional economies are innovative and grow because people turn them into innovative and prosperous locations. My hypothesis is that policymakers can actively contribute to the attractiveness of a region if they are provided a comprehensive knowledge, and a precise understanding of successful hands-on entrepreneurship policies which have been evaluated – and not just moderated – comparatively at a global level.

2.1 Content and Major Research Questions

In section 3, I review a variety of already existing concepts of entrepreneurship policy (E-Policy)[2] in order to deduce which causes and promoters of regional economic growth exist (Harkness et al. 2003). I will specifically focus on one indicator, 'institution policies', and explore whether this indicator is, indeed, causing regional economic growth or not. When using the term 'institutional policies', I refer to organizations or structural mechanisms which are created by people (intentionally or unintentionally, often both) and persist over time. In this article, the term 'institutional policies' refers primarily to 'formal' institutions and policies created and applied by 'formal' organizations, such as the U.S. Congress, the Ministry of Economics and Labor in Germany or Chambers of Commerce. Besides this formal dimension, institutions also stand for 'informal' organizations reflecting human psychology, habits and customs (North 1990, 1995). Applying Douglass North's concept to entrepreneurship, institutions are both 'formal' and 'informal' constraints contributing to a fruitful entrepreneurial environment. As Friederike Welter (2005: 95) points out, a clear-cut distinction between formal and informal institutions is difficult to achieve. In any case, we observe the development of a set of rules which are actually used by a set of individuals to organize repetitive activities that produce outcomes affecting those individuals and potentially affecting others.[3]

In my research, I am focusing on policies designed by formal organizations, and on rules of action which are related to the creation of an entrepreneurial environment (for more details see section 5). The institution policies' indicator as used in my exploratory research will be further clarified by introducing the research design and a summary of findings of an already finalized qualitative cross-national and cross-regional comparative study, below. With this qualitative survey I assessed design, focus and location of institution policies to find out whether they contribute to an entrepreneurial-friendly environment and, if so, to which extent. Understanding developmental outcomes requires a focus on institutional endowments and policy traditions of different regions. In this respect, my research follows in the tradition of a growing number of studies that have reoriented their attention to the local level of a political economy focusing on the fit between the local institutional framework and policies and the regional development (Segal and Thun 2001; Sternberg and Tamásy 1999).

By assessing some selected findings of an already finalized qualitative study and by synthesizing it with the latent construct (see sections 3 and 5), I aim to explore whether Qualitative Comparative Analysis (QCA) is an 'alternative' methodology for evaluating this link, after using SPSS as a tool for generating first descriptive insights and statistical explorations (see section 4 and Norusis 2002).

By applying such a three-fold approach (literature review, qualitative cross-national survey and QCA) I aim to test various qualitative methods to find out whether

- the performance of QCA and the use of Boolean variables is, in particular, suitable for exploring the correlation between E-policy and regional economic growth in comparison with a statistics-driven approach;
- we are able to assess whether E-policy matters for generating an entrepreneurial-friendly environment (according to initial QCA and statistical findings) and, if so, to which extent;
- there is a pattern or configuration of institutional policies across regions and nations which is inherent to the successful promotion of entrepreneurs.

2.2 Methodology

There is no comprehensive study to date that looks specifically at the correlation of entrepreneurship policy and regional or national economic growth. This lack of analysis is rooted in the difficulty to define what is exactly meant with the 'E-Policy' term, and consequently in the difficulty to measure whether E-Policy is important for the promotion of economic growth. David Hart (2003) emphasizes the need for a comprehensive definition of the concept of entrepreneurship policy. He provides an historical review of the "emergence of entrepreneurship policy" with the goal to comprehensively define the terms 'entrepreneurship' and 'entrepreneurship policy'. In order to illustrate the uniqueness of entrepreneurship policy, Hart underlines that entrepreneurial endeavors are not necessarily a synonym for small businesses. Entrepreneurship policy, therefore, has to be defined and measured in a considerably different manner from small business policy. Although Hart discusses the importance of making this crucial difference, and although he underlines the importance of specifying the term E-Policy, a comprehensive definition fails to appear. Hart's critical assessment is that the impact of policies on entrepreneurship processes has not been measured until today, and that no (empirical) method seems appropriate to do so. In particular, little is known about the impact of policies on the level of entrepreneurship in a certain spatial context.

This issue is also discussed by Heike Grimm (2004a, 2004b, 2003) with special reference to 'institution policies', such as the impact of government programs, counseling and access to information on the entrepreneurial environment. Not much is known about any correlation between a configuration of the above-mentioned institution-linked policies and entrepreneurship. Therefore, Grimm builds upon a qualitative cross-national survey, using SPSS to evaluate and analyze institution indices. According to her results, one may establish the existence of a positive correlation between the locality of policy and the level of entrepreneurship within a region: the stronger the local focus of entrepreneurship policy, the more prosperous a region seems to be (see section 4).

Whereas scientific studies attempt to compare public policies of different nation-states, some information and definitions are still missing, such as:

(a) What specifically is meant by public policies designed for promoting start-ups?
(b) To what extent do these policies differ across nations and regions?
(c) Can they be compared across nation-states and regions, at all?

These deficits matter, as public policies contribute greatly to turn places and regions into attractive ones (Audretsch 2003; Sternberg and Bergmann 2002; Reynolds et al. 2000, 2001, 2002), and as we are not yet able to evaluate to a fully satisfying extent the correlation between E-Policy and regional economic growth at a global or even cross-national level.

In the following, I will apply two qualitative-comparative approaches for a better understanding of the above discussed questions. I will also discuss whether a qualitative-comparative policy analysis is useful at all for clarifying if entrepreneurship policy matters for regional economic growth. We have been inspired to move along this methodological path by Berg-Schlosser, de Meur and Ragin who state that *"(...) the realm of qualitative methods in macropolitical inquiry (...) lies between conventional case-study research (countless variables, but only one case) and conventional quantitative research (many cases, relatively few variables)"* (Berg-Schlosser, de Meur and Ragin 1996: 749/750; Ragin 1994). The authors refer to Qualitative Comparative Analysis (QCA) which is an approach based on Boolean algebra devised by Charles C. Ragin (1987; see also Ragin, in this volume). In a nutshell, QCA is a data analytic strategy which selectively unites certain features of variable-oriented (quantitative) and case-oriented (qualitative) methods. In common with the variable-oriented strategy, it allows the examination of a large number of cases. In common with the case-oriented strategy, it allows the assessment of complex patterns of multiple and conjunctural causation. This merger of certain features of the two strategies offers the possibility of a middle road between emphasizing relationships among variables and structural explanations, on the one hand, and emphasizing the chronological particularities of cases and human agency, on the other. In other words the QCA is an intermediate path between generality and complexity (Ragin 2000; Rihoux 2003).

There are three distinct phases in the application of QCA to cross-case evidence:

(1) selecting cases and constructing the property space that defines kinds of cases (initial configurations);
(2) testing the necessity and the sufficiency of causal conditions;
(3) and evaluating the results, especially with respect to simplifying assumptions.

The summary equation ('minimal formula') that results from the application of QCA should be viewed as part of the larger dialogue between ideas and evidence.

The application of QCA is, according to my hypothesis, a promising step towards a more comprehensive understanding of the E-Policy term, mainly because a lot of reconsideration and rethinking of its basic elements is inherent to the application of QCA. However, the complexity of the research topic and the complexity of the practical application of the method made us aware that the final results might be used rather to further improve methodologies and devices for developing a better understanding of E-policies, on the one hand, and the link between E-policies and economic growth, on the other hand.

3. WHAT IS ENTREPRENEURSHIP POLICY?

In the following, I will review existent definitions and concepts of E-Policy in order to conceptualize the indicators of E-Policy which aim at promoting regional economic growth, and thus to develop an hypothesized latent construct of E-Policy (Harkness et al 2003).

(1) The Swedish researchers Lois Stevenson and Anders Lundström (2001, 2002) associated with the Swedish Foundation for Small Business Research made first efforts to comprehensively define the term. They emphasize three elements ("Motivation, Skills, and Opportunity") which form the E-Policy framework. In a nutshell, they define E-Policy as *"(...) policy measures taken to stimulate entrepreneurship, aimed at the pre-start, start-up and early post start-up phases of the entrepreneurial process, designed and delivered to address the areas of Motivation, Opportunity and Skills, with the primary objective of encouraging more people to consider entrepreneurship, to move into the nascent stage and proceed into start-up and early phases of a business"* (Stevenson and Lundström 2002: 4).

(2) This definition has much in common with Richard Florida's (2002: 49) idea and concept of the "3Ts" (Technology, Talent and Tolerance) as driving forces of economic development: each of the 3Ts is a necessary condition for the promotion of regional economic development. According to Florida, growing and prospering regions are characterized by the concentration of all "3Ts" at one place.

(3) The AICGS New Economy Study Group (2003) points out that public policy has responded in two fundamental ways to globalization and its impact on the comparative advantage of nations and regions, primarily affecting the target and the locality of public policies. The first has been to shift the policy focus away from traditional policy instruments essentially constraining the freedom of firms to contract (like regulation, competition policy or antitrust policy in the United States, and public ownership of business). The second has been a fundamental shift of the locality of policies, which are increasingly to be found at the regional and local level.

(4) As Sander Wennekers and Roy Thurik (1999) point out: *"(...) somewhat understated (...) is the primal of the economic agents who link the institutions at the micro level to the economic outcome at the macro level. It remains veiled how exactly institutions and cultural factors frame the decisions of the millions of entrepreneurs in small firms and of entrepreneurial managers"*. Both researchers take into consideration that cultural and institutional causes of entrepreneurship are not as obvious to policy-makers as economic causes and have not been fully taken into account by policymakers and researchers alike, also due to a lack of measurability. Nonetheless, they underline that the cultural and institutional environment are crucial features of a successful E-Policy: *"Both, culture and the institutional framework, are important conditions codetermining the amount of entrepreneurship in an economy and the way in which entrepreneurs operate in practice. But also technological, demographic and economic forces are at play"* (Uhlaner and Thurik 2004: 5-7).

(5) A very comprehensive framework on E-Policy is provided by the Global Entrepreneurship Monitor (GEM) Consortium. GEM draws a difference between general national framework conditions (including financial markets, labor markets; technology and R&D etc.) and entrepreneurial framework conditions (including government policies and programs, R&D transfer, cultural and social norms etc.). Rolf Sternberg (2003), who serves as managing director of the German GEM team, explains that *"the regional entrepreneurial framework conditions, along with the entrepreneurial attitudes and the entrepreneurial skills of the population, have a significant impact on actual entrepreneurial activities"*. It is a widespread view that the regions with the best framework conditions and the most favorable attitudes among the population also stand out with above-

average levels of entrepreneurial activities or a particularly high proportion of self-employed people. In other words, E-Policies are not only government programs but also policies promoting an entrepreneurial education and research.

After reviewing a variety of existent 'definitions' of E-Policy it can be assumed that economic indicators do play an important role, albeit not the exclusively important role, for the promotion of entrepreneurship at a national and regional level. In an entrepreneurial economy, cultural as well as institution-related indicators both contribute to the entrepreneurial environment.

4. DOES ENTREPRENEURSHIP POLICY MATTER?

In the following, initial results of an exploratory qualitative cross-national survey conducted in the U.S.A. and Germany will be presented to discuss characteristics and importance, as well as similarities and differences of E-Policy across nations and regions, with a specific focus on institution-linked policies.

4.1 Research Objectives and Research Design

Which public policies specifically exist in a nation-state or region for the successful promotion of entrepreneurs? What is their specific design, their content, their goal? Who is implementing these public policies: the federal government, the (federated) state government, and/or a municipal institution?

These questions are best answered by comparing existing policies cross-nationally and cross-regionally. The goal of this research is to discover significant local public policy patterns and to generate further hypotheses for public policy research at a cross-national level.

At this exploratory stage, a quota sample was chosen for the survey by dividing the population into geographic regions using the regional classifications of the metropolitan areas in the U.S.A. and the German Chamber of Commerce and Industry (CCI). The survey took place between December 2002 and June 2003. A questionnaire was designed containing 30 questions, some of them in the form of open questions, some answered following a yes/no filter, and most of them following a Likert scale (ranging from 1 (yes), 2 (mostly), 3 (partly), 4 (rather not), 5 (no)).

A sample of ten public experts per region, responsible for counseling entrepreneurs and providing information on public assistance programs, were interviewed in a structured face-to-face interview. We decided to approach ten experts in each region with a quota sample because it turned out that there are currently no more than ten to fifteen public institutions per region which are consulting start-ups. Among these institutions and organizations are district and municipal economic development centers, Chambers of Industry and Commerce, Chambers of Handicrafts, City Chambers of Commerce, Small Business Administration offices, economic technology transfer institutions, associated entrepreneurship institutes at universities and research institutes, capital venture companies, business angels, initiatives for the promotion of entrepreneurship networks and women in business, and credit institutes.

In June 2003, we finalized the personal interviews with 10 experts from each region selected for this case study.[4]

4.2 Cross-National and Cross-Regional Approach

The study focused on three metropolitan regions in the U.S.A. and three greater urban areas in Germany:
- Munich and Upper Bavaria (CCI District in Bavaria) and Atlanta (metropolitan area in Georgia),
- the Leipzig region (CCI District in Saxony) and the Research Triangle (greater metropolitan areas of Durham, Raleigh, Chapel Hill in North Carolina),
- the so-called *Bergische Städtedreieck* comprising the cities of Solingen, Wuppertal, and Remscheid in North Rhine-Westphalia (CCI District) and the Baltimore metropolitan region (Maryland).[5]

These six cases comprise two highly developed regions (Munich and Atlanta), two regions which successfully coped with socio-economic problems (Leipzig and the Research Triangle), and two regions which are still trying to cope with socio-economic problems (*Bergische Städtedreieck* and Baltimore metropolitan area).[5]

4.3 Selection of Findings

In order to generate first-hand, detailed information about public policies in both countries across the selected regions, we began the interviews by addressing questions relating to the design and availability of rather general information on how to successfully start up a business, and on the design and availability of public subsidies for start-ups. In other words, the first questions were intended to generate information from the supply-side with regard to the kinds of information provided by local public institutions, and to the kinds of subsidies which are offered within a region for the financial support of start-ups. We addressed the following question to respondents: "*What kind of information does the public institution you work for provide?*"

We have only tabled the answers "yes", "mostly", and "partly", aggregated into one category (frequencies in total numbers per country), with the respective percentages per country shown for each answer item (kind of information).

It is worth noting that the provision of most public information is given similar emphasis in both countries. Interestingly, all consultants interviewed confirmed that they see it as a major task for them to provide general and/or specific information on public financial assistance programs to entrepreneurs.

Nonetheless, some interesting cross-national differences exist, for example regarding information about (f) the opportunities for joint ventures, (k) personnel, and personnel management, and (l) the regional conditions such as regulations, taxes etc. U.S. consultants more frequently provide information on these three topics.

Table 6.1. What Kind of Information Do You Offer? We Provide Information About...

	U.S.A. (N=30)		Germany (N=30)	
	Total No./ Country[a]	% within Country	Total No./ Country	% within Country
(a) ... region, the state...	25	83,3	23	76.7
(b) ... legal form of an enterprise...	25	83.3	21	70.0
(c) ... business concept...	28	93.3	27	90.0
(d) ... market potentials of an idea...	27	90.0	26	86.7
(e) ... partners for regional co-operation...	26	89.7	28	93.3
(f) ... opportunities for a joint venture...	25	83.3	19	63.3
(g) ... public advisory bureaus...	25	83.3	26	86.7
(h) ... regional networks...	24	80.0	29	96.7
(i) ... public programs of financial assistance..	29	96.7	29	96.7
(j) ... venture capitalists. business angels...	24	80.0	20	66.7
(k) ... personnel and personnel management...	24	80.0	16	53.3
(l) ... regional conditions such as regulations..	26	86.7	20	66.7
(m) ... visa and residents permits...	6	20.0	8	26.7

(a) Responses on a Likert scale: (1) yes/ (2) mostly/ (3) partly

After familiarizing the interviewees with the questionnaire by beginning with questions related to the supply-side (*"which information do you offer?"*), we pursued with questions on the demand-side (*"what kind of counseling do you offer?"*).

Table 6.2. What Kind of Counseling Do You Offer?

	U.S.A. (N=30)		Germany (N=30)	
	Total No./ Country[a]	% within Country	Total No./ Country	% within Country
...website (entrepreneurs receive all information online)...	27	90,0%	22	73,3%
...release of information...	30	100,0%	29	96,7%
...individual counseling with appointment...	25	83,3%	30	100,0%
...specific consultation days open to the public without appointment (open days)...	15	50,0%	13	43,3%
...seminars for entrepreneurs...	29	96,7%	26	86,7%
...lectures on specific topics...	27	90,0%	25	83,3%
...road shows...	27	90,0%	27	90,0%
...participation in fairs...	26	86,7%	23	76,7%
...others...	2	--	4	--

(a) Responses on a Likert scale: (1) yes/ (2) mostly/ (3) partly

In Germany, high emphasis is placed on individual counseling. In contrast, in the U.S.A., a strong emphasis is placed on the release of information; websites, in particular, are a very prominent source of information for entrepreneurs. There seems to be some backlog of demand in Germany with regard to the availability of such online and virtual information. Nonetheless, it is worth noting that most public information is provided with similar emphasis in both countries (see table 6.2), and that the forms of counseling and of access to information are also quite similar.

To collect further information on which kind of public programs are important and whether federal programs are rated as more or less important as (federated) state, regional, and/or municipal programs, we addressed the following question: "*Are the following public assistance programs of high importance to entrepreneurs?*" The interviewees were asked to rate the importance of federal, (federated) state, regional, and municipal subsidies for the promotion of start-ups within their region, again using a Likert scale ranging from 1 (yes), 2 (mostly), 3 (partly), 4 (rather not), to 5 (no).

In both the U.S. and German regions under scrutiny, <u>federal</u> assistance programs play a very important role for the promotion of start-ups.

Table 6.3. Are Federal Programs of High Importance to Entrepreneurs?

		Federal Programs		
		Yes/ mostly/ partly	Rather not/ no	Total
Germany	Total No. / Country	28	2	30
	% within Country	93.3	6.7	100.0
U.S.A.	Total No. / Country	28	2	30
	% within Country	93.3	6.7	100.0
Total	Total No. / Country	56	4	60
	% within Country	93.3	6.7	100.0

Furthermore, (federated) state programs play a crucial role in promoting start-ups in both countries; in Germany such state programs are even of higher importance than in the U.S.A. (see table 6.4).

Table 6.4. Are State Programs of High Importance to Entrepreneurs?

		State Programs		
		Yes/ mostly/ partly	Rather not/ no	Total
Germany	Total No. / Country	29	1	30
	% within Country	96.7	3.3	100.0
U.S.A.	Total No. / Country	26	3	29[a]
	% within Country	93.3	6.7	100.0
Total	Total No. / Country	55	4	59[a]
	% within Country	93.3	6.7	100.0

a) One missing value

As demonstrated below, the role of regional subsidies was rated with different emphasis (see table 6.6). There is a strong demand for regional financial assistance programs – specifically in the U.S. regions. Indeed, a high proportion of U.S. respondents (25 out of 29) stated that regional financial assistance programs are of "very", "rather" or "partly high" importance for the promotion of start-ups, much more so than their German counterparts (only 16 out of 30).

Table 6.5. Are Regional Programs of High Importance to Entrepreneurs?

		Regional Programs		
		Yes/ mostly/ partly	Rather not/ no	Total
Germany	Total No. / Country	16	14	30
	% within Country	53.3	46.7	100.0
U.S.A.	Total No. / Country	25	4	29[a]
	% within Country	86.2	13.8	100.0
Total	Total No. / Country	41	18	59[a]
	% within Country	69.5	30.5	100.0

a) One missing value

To summarize these findings: in the U.S.A., regional financial assistance programs are of high importance for the promotion of start-ups and for regional economic development, whereas in Germany, it is federal and state (*Land*) programs that play the major role.

Further, local public policies for the promotion of entrepreneurs and entrepreneurial companies are rated with far more importance in the U.S.A. than in Germany. Although competition among regions is continuously increasing due to the challenges of a global economy, the strong focus, in the German case, on federal and state subsidies and the apparent absence of emphasis on regional and municipal programs come as a surprise.

Table 6.6. Are Municipal Programs of High Importance to Entrepreneurs?

		Municipal Programs		
		Yes/ mostly/ partly	Rather not/ no	Total
Germany	Total No. / Country	8	22	30
	% within Country	26.7	73.3	100.0
U.S.A.	Total No. / Country	23	6	29[a]
	% within Country	79.3	20.7	100.0
Total	Total No. / Country	31	28	59[a]
	% within Country	52.5	47.5	100.0

(a) One missing value

Moreover, the majority of German interviewees confirmed that there is a lack of <u>municipal</u> financial assistance programs. The latter are still non-existent in their region. Indeed, 22 out of 30 German respondents (76.9%)

stated that municipal programs play no or relatively little role for entrepreneurs in their region. On the contrary, 23 out of 29 U.S. experts stressed the high, rather or partly high importance of municipal financial assistance programs. Only 8 out of 30 German public consultants came to the same conclusion.

Above all (and particularly in the region which I focused on in this study that clearly has to cope with socio-economic challenges – the *Bergisches Städtedreieck* in North-Rhine Westphalia), municipal programs do not play any significant role in the promotion of start-ups (see table 6.7). Conversely, an American region which is facing similar challenges (the Baltimore metropolitan region) sees municipal financial assistance programs as a major prerequisite of a prosperous entrepreneurial environment and for contributing to a rising number of start-ups

Table 6.7. Are Municipal Programs of High Importance to Entrepreneurs? (Output per Region)

		Municipal Programs		
		Yes/ mostly/ partly	Rather not/ no	Total
Atlanta	Total No. / Country	8	1	9[a]
	% within Country	88.9	11.1	100.0
Triangle Region	Total No. / Country	6	4	10
	% within Country	60.0	40.0	100.0
Baltimore	Total No. / Country	9	1	10
	% within Country	90.0	10.0	100.0
Munich	Total No. / Country	3	7	10
	% within Country	30.0	70.0	100.0
Leipzig	Total No. / Country	5	5	10
	% within Country	50.0	50.0	100.0
Berg. Städtedreieck	Total No. / Country	0	10	10
	% within Country	.0	100.0	100.0
Total (all regions)	Total No. / Country	31	28	59[a]
	% within Country	52.5	47.5	100.0

(a) One missing value

4.5 Preliminary Summary

With a qualitative-exploratory survey it was possible to show that institution-linked policies differ across nations and regions with regard to the locus of their implementation. Although the design and content of E-Policy does not differ greatly across the U.S. and German regions, the locus of E-policy seems to be very different. This difference matters since public policy has responded in two fundamental ways to globalization and its impact on the comparative advantage of nations and regions, strongly affecting the locus of public policies. In the U.S.A., we observe a fundamental shift of public policies towards the regional or local level. This shift is missing in Germany. Further study needs to reveal whether this is also a missing link for the promotion of economic development at the local scale.

5. SYNTHESIS AND QCA

Based on the initial findings of the literature review and the qualitative cross-national and cross-regional study, we then attempted to synthesize findings with QCA.

We first developed a hypothesized concept of institution policies (see Grimm and Gamse 2004; Grimm 2004 for information on methodological issues). We re-fined the term institution-related policies, as well as the conditions which are either displayed as "present" (= "1") or "absent" (= "0") by using the questionnaire and interviews introduced here above. The idea is to reconstruct data for developing a truth table. Box 1 clarifies which questions/answers have been used to pinpoint the term institution policies, as represented in the hypothesized concept above. In total, we selected six causal conditions after re-assessing the literature review and the qualitative survey (see tables 6.1 to 6.7).

Box 1: Hypothesized concept of conditions of 'institution-related policies'

Access to public financial assistance programs ("A")
Offer of public financial assistance programs ("P")
Access to public information ("I")
Offer of information ("R")
Counseling ("C")
Degree of Centralization ("D")

We drew a difference between the mere existence (offer) of public financial assistance programs within a region and the potentials to get access to them, and similarly between the mere existence (offer) of public information on "How-to-start-up-a-business"-issues and the quality of access to this kind of information. We focused on the quantity and quality of counseling provided by public institutions to (potential) entrepreneurs and the degree of centralization of services offered by public institutions.

The focus on the offer of (*versus* access to) public financial assistance programs and information, on counseling services for entrepreneurs and on the degree of centralization of these services is ascribed to the following very interesting findings from the Regional and Global Entrepreneurship Monitor: in 2000, the Regional Entrepreneurship Monitor (REM) Executive Report for Germany analyzed a set of entrepreneurial framework conditions including financial start-up assistance and government programs for start-ups. The researchers came to the conclusion that content and design of the public programs and financial subsidies were positively evaluated by the survey respondents. However, when it came to public policies (distinct from public programs geared to entrepreneurship), the respondents criticized the policy framework conditions for entrepreneurs in Germany, referring to the implementation of policy regulations such as building regulations, police law, taxes etc. and also to the lack of a deeper understanding of entrepreneurship by public officials (Sternberg and Bergmann 2002; Sternberg et al. 2000).[6]

We performed an exploratory QCA analysis (Grimm and Gamse 2004), comparing the German regions of Munich, Leipzig and the *Bergische Städtedreieck*. With this procedure we tried to guarantee the comparability of regions and cases. QCA seemed an appropriate approach, since we have few cases and many variables, and since we are interested in a potential configuration of conditions – or possibly different configurations of conditions, depending on the local or regional context (see Varone, Rihoux and Marx, in this volume) of institution-related policies which have to be existent at a regional level for the promotion of economic growth.

Before performing we re-constructed the data by differentiating cases displaying economic growth ("prosperous regions" = "1") from cases with no or weak economic growth ("non-prosperous regions" = "0"). The outcome (significant regional economic development = "1" versus non-significant regional economic development = "0") was defined according to the statements and assessments of the public policy experts we had previously interviewed. In other words, we operationalized the outcome by defining economic growth not only as aggregated rise in employment within a region (this procedure is most common in economic analyses by applying quantitative methods, as discussed for example by Kirchhoff and Greene (1998)), but also by re-coding the qualitative statements of policy experts by applying qualitative breakpoints (qualitative measurement).

In the first place, we performed QCA by specifically looking at prosperous German regions and by minimizing the value "1" configurations (17 cases). The Boolean minimization procedure yielded a minimal formula which was not useful for interpretation due to the high number of contradictory configurations (covering 13 out of the 17 cases). The high number of contradictions is, among others, due to qualitative statements of policy experts who responded to our questionnaire, and to a high extent to the insufficient heterogeneity of the cases we have chosen.

In a next step, we thus reviewed the questionnaires and omitted all contradictory configurations. The QCA performance, then, led to a 'minimal formula' which we could have interpreted; but after omitting 13 out of 17 cases, the formula would not have been so useful in empirical terms, as it only covered the 4 remaining cases.

In an attempt to lift these contradictions and to improve the model as well, we then tried to re-configurate the data (for example, by re-coding the Likert scale and by the re-configuration of causally relevant conditions) and performed QCA after re-developing simplified truth tables to study a selection of locational factors promoting economic development, such as municipal taxes, prices for offices and buildings, public transportation, access to highways, leisure/ recreation activities etc. In spite of these modifications, we were not able to obtain minimal formulae (neither for the "1", nor for the "0" outcome) which were useful for interpretation, again due to too many contradictory configurations. This led us to the conclusion that it would have been suitable to choose fewer cases which differ more substantially from one another (more cross-case heterogeneity). The answers provided by the policy experts in our survey differed in too few cases so that the heterogeneity of test cases needed for QCA was not guaranteed – in other words, there was not enough variation on some of the causally relevant conditions we were focusing on. Nonetheless, the answers of policy experts in our survey differed in a few cases very strongly (as displayed with the SPSS tables above), so that we were able to pinpoint a few results and differences existent across two nations (U.S.A. and Germany) and six regions.

On the one hand, the simplification of indicators turned out to be a very useful methodology to pinpoint which policy field is under survey (in this example, we specified the conditions which fall in the 'institution-related policies' category). On the other hand, though, re-considering the approach to simplify regional patterns on differing economic development paths and status quos across one country, such as Germany, holds advantages as well disadvantages. The re-configuration in so-called "prospering" and "not prospering regions" did not provide us with a region's "full story" (such as: what are the region's distinctive strengths or local assets? Which challenges will it face in the near future?). Indeed, all German regions have to cope with different challenges in a global environment. Regions do compete globally but the challenges as well as the developmental status quos of places are so different across cases that rather a more in-depth analysis is necessary to exploring the core challenges of a place than a simplification of indicators.

In spite of these difficulties, the strength and usefulness – both in conceptual and in empirical terms – of the application of QCA in the context of the research question we raised was, among others, the re-consideration of conditions falling in one specific public policy category. Keeping in mind the many definitions of entrepreneurship policy which currently circulate and which are related to a variety of policy fields, we identified a need to get back to the roots and ask ourselves: what is meant by the term E-Policy in a general and comprehensive sense? Which policy fields fall in the category E-Policy, and what conditions are to be observed and analyzed in a case study analysis while keeping in mind the historical, cultural, socio-political and economic peculiarities of places?

With the exploratory QCA tests (summarized here above), we were not able to produce 'exploitable' empirical results for the cross-national and cross-regional qualitative survey introduced in section 4. However, these tests led us to re-examine our concepts, models and theories which have been developed on the basis of already existent definitions and concepts of E-Policy, as summarized in section 3. Above all, the tests made us aware that existent concepts are only fragmentary. Hence, the QCA tests turned out as a useful heuristic tool for a rich *"dialogue between ideas and evidence"*, more from a conceptual and theoretical perspective (Ragin 1987).

After having synthesized both quantitative and qualitative results (or approaches), I believe that the focus of current practices (i.e., to use either a quantitative or qualitative survey in *separation*) is misleading. For a thorough answer to the above raised questions, I suggest to follow Charles Ragin in proposing a middle way to be taken between (qualitative, narrative, descriptive) case study and (quantitative) variable-oriented research. The vision of such a middle path is to combine the strengths of within-case analysis and cross-case analysis (such as the identification of causes and pathways of economic growth). According to Ragin (2003), the approach is called 'configurational comparative research', and has the following characteristics:

- Role of theory: existing theory of the correlation between policies and economic growth is rarely well-formulated enough to provide explicit hypotheses to be tested; therefore, the primary theoretical objective in entrepreneurship policy research at a comparative level is not theory testing, but elaboration, refinement, concept formation, and thus contributing to theory development.
- Number of cases: to make strategic comparisons, comparative researchers use diverse cases; at the same time, they establish case homogeneity because the cases should all be instances of, or candidates for the same outcome (i.e., a certain degree of prosperity which is existent across all German regions).

- Conception of outcomes: comparative research starts by intentionally selecting cases that do not differ greatly from each other with respect to the outcome that is being investigated, i.e., 'positive cases' only; the constitution and analysis of these positive cases is usually a prerequisite for the specification of relevant negative cases. In our analysis, we also performed QCA by looking at prosperous German regions ('positive cases'), in the first place, and by minimizing the value "1" configurations. Instead of looking specifically at the 'positive cases' while raising the question: "why do some regions take the lead?" it would have been worthwhile to rather concentrate the question on: "why do some regions lag behind?" to analyze which policies are missing, not suitable or have just been copied because they have been labeled "best practice policies" in other, well developed regions. Again, this means that one of the core questions and research paths yet taken in economic development and entrepreneurship policy research has to be refined and the approach has to be re-developed.
- Understanding of causation: comparative research looks at causation in terms of multiple pathways, with positive cases often easily classified according to the general path which each followed to reach the outcome; each path, in turn, involved a different combination of relevant causal conditions and other factors such as system properties (e.g., feedbacks from policies) and pre-disposing initial conditions (e.g., economic history, cultural setting). According to our exploratory QCA tests, the classification of 'positive cases' (in terms of different pathways leading to a favorable outcome) of regional development has to be further refined not only in the present study, but also in most comparative analyses which aim at linking policies with economic development.
- Within versus cross-case analysis: comparative research focuses on configurations of causally relevant characteristics of cases, with the goal of determining how relevant aspects fit together; cross-case analysis is used to strengthen and deepen within-case analysis, and vice-versa; to the extent possible, comparative research tries to balance both analyses. Whereas we were able to focus on configurations of causally relevant characteristics of cases, the heterogeneity of test cases has not been sufficient. In other words, we were able to deepen the within but hardly the cross case analysis when performing QCA (this became evident after using QCA and would not have been evident by solely relying on the SPSS findings).

6. SUMMARY AND THEORETICAL IMPLICATIONS

With the initial results presented in this contribution we aimed to clarify whether E-Policy matters for and contributes to regional economic growth. To this end, we performed a qualitative exploratory survey. We selected regions characterized of different socio-economic profiles in order to assess the causal conditions which lead to a rise of economic growth. We then aimed at finding out whether these conditions are missing in less prosperous regions.

While the findings of the qualitative exploratory survey show that qualitative studies are useful to pinpoint the causal conditions of economic growth and that further studies have to be focused on this interdependence, it is not possible to link the causal conditions with economic growth.

Therefore, we aimed at applying QCA, in an exploratory way, in order to assess the role of institution policies for regional growth (usually defined as aggregated rise of job employment). We conceptualized and operationalized six conditions by applying the initial results and the questionnaire of the previous finalized qualitative cross-national and cross-regional qualitative survey.

In a nutshell, we can conclude that there is no one-size-fits-all-solution which can be transferred across regions. QCA made us aware of the complexity of the original "area of investigation" (Ragin, Berg-Schlosser and de Meur 1996: 760). As a result, the rising tendency to transfer policy concepts which contribute to economic development across regions and nations is misleading, without reflecting that regional and national differences exist. Interestingly, the approach to look at prosperous regions (instead of non-prosperous ones) in order to assess causal conditions of economic growth should be seriously re-considered.

Nonetheless, we see strong advantages of QCA for assessing the complex correlation between E-Policy and regional economic growth, such as the additive combination of presence/absence variables. In a Boolean-based qualitative comparison causes can be viewed within the context of presence and absence of causally relevant conditions.

Also, we agree with the introductory critic of Ann Markusen (Markusen 1999, 1996a, 1996b) that the sharpening of the concepts but also theory of entrepreneurship policies has to be pursued. Performing QCA 'forced' us to re-consider existent concepts, as well as conditions and outcome. This can potentially mean a valuable step forward to further exploring the link between E-Policy and regional economic growth. With the exploratory QCA as performed in this paper it became evident that existing theory of the link between policies and economic growth is rarely well-formulated enough to provide explicit hypotheses to be tested; therefore, the primary theoretical objective in entrepreneurship policy research at a comparative level is not theory testing, but elaboration, refinement, concept formation, and thus contributing to theory development.[7]

Further analysis is needed to conceptualize and evaluate the diverse conditions and features of E-Policy and to link them with regional economic growth. QCA has shown us that it is useful to move away from a "simple" correlational view of causality to a more "complex" view such as "multiple conjunctural causation" (Ragin and Rihoux 2004). Also, initial findings from the above introduced studies indicate a new field of researching causal clusters which has been labeled 'multiple-conjunctural causation' (Ragin 2003).

With my research still in progress, I believe that future in-depth case studies of the developmental status quo of places are necessary in regions across the world in order to develop strategies and policies to successfully cope with local challenges. Through the SPSS analysis, we achieved initial results which led to the insight that differences across places exist, though the differences are small and complex. However, these insights provided by quantitative variable-oriented research across cases clearly need to be complemented (and probably re-assessed) through insights geared from the qualitative perspective of within-case analysis and in-depth studies on a case-to-case basis.

These methods – e.g., system approach, multivariate statistical analysis, qualitative comparative analysis (QCA), simulation modeling and narratives/counterfactuals – need to be viewed as a toolbox of complementary approaches to uncover causal relationships in complex systems.

NOTES

[1] I am grateful to Robert Gamse for helpful comments and co-authoring the draft discussion paper "Entrepreneurship Policy and Regional Economic Growth. Exploring the Correlation", presented at the ESF exploratory workshop.
[2] The term 'E-Policy' was created and defined by Lundström and Stevenson (2001).
[3] For more information on the link between institutional theory and entrepreneurship see Welter (2005: 94-98).
[4] For a comprehensive list of the experts' names and affiliations interviewed in the survey see Grimm (2004: 12-14; 2005: 159-161). I would like to thank Iris Beckmann, research fellow of the Entrepreneurship, Growth and Public Policy Group at the Max-Planck-Institute for Economics in Jena, Germany, for her contribution to this research funded by the German Federal Ministry of Economics and Labor.
[5] The selection of the German cases is also ascribed to three studies which were completed between 1996 and 2002 and which provide findings and data specifically relating to new entrepreneurship policies and the entrepreneurial environment for start-ups within the selected German regions: the *"Münchner Gründerstudie"* (Brüderl, Preisendörfer and Ziegler 1996 and 1992), the *"Leipziger Gründerstudie"* (Hinz 1998), and a survey

conducted in the Ruhr area with special focus on Dortmund and Essen (Jansen and Weber 2003) in North-Rhine Westphalia.

[6] According to the so-called "Policy Regulation Index" set up by the researchers in 2000, Germany held the poor position of 17 in an index of 20 countries, and in 2002 it held the low rank of 20 out of 34 countries (Reynolds et al 2001). Particular criticism was directed towards a bureaucratic administration which lacks flexibility, transparency, and has a "civil servant mentality". Other points of criticism were bureaucratic rivalry, a lack of centralized information services (one-stop shops) within the German regions and lack of economics and business skills in public institutions.

[7] The necessity to refine the theoretical framework to improve policy analyses has also been emphasized by Befani and Sager as well as Varone, Rihoux and Marx in this volume (see chapters 11 and 13).

Chapter 7

DETERMINING THE CONDITIONS OF HIV/AIDS PREVALENCE IN SUB-SAHARAN AFRICA
Employing New Tools of Macro-Qualitative Analysis

Lasse Cronqvist
University of Marburg

Dirk Berg-Schlosser
University of Marburg

1. INTRODUCTION

Comparative methods in political science are often applied at the 'macro'-level of political systems, that is, at the nation-state level and different aspects of the overall system. At this level, the number of cases to be examined is by necessity limited, even if one takes the present number of approximately 200 independent states worldwide. Furthermore, the number of cases exhibiting a level of commonality on certain issues and the availability of specific data (for example the OECD states, certain regions of the Third World, etc.) are often even more limited. At the same time, these systems and their interaction exhibit a high level of complexity. Thus, the classic 'many variables - small N dilemma of this sub-discipline of political science comes into being (see Lijphart 1971, 1975; Collier 1993; Aarebrot and Bakka 2003).

There are various ways to deal with this dilemma, among which two dominant camps or schools, a 'macro-quantitative' and a 'macro-qualitative', can be observed. In line with Kuhn's proposition (1976), that scientific paradigms demonstrate not only a theoretical nucleus, but also a social environment which has been formed in a specific manner, the two sides have not spared mutual accusations of applying unscientific procedures, unproven premises, unwarranted conclusions and similar polemics (see Lieberson 1991, 1994; Savolainen 1994). So, the debate is characterized by an astounding amount of selective perceptions, misunderstandings and unjustifiable insinuations. Misunderstood or misleading formulations and deceptive claims by the protagonists of both sides have contributed to this situation. Attempts at conciliation (for example King/Keohane/Verba 1994; and, with certain limitations, Goldthorpe 1994; Ragin, Berg-Schlosser and De Meur 1996, and now, more explicitly, Brady and Collier 2004) are rare.

This chapter first outlines the central tenets and concrete procedures of both positions. It then exemplifies these methods by testing some possible explanations of differences of the HIV prevalence and effects of respective policies in Sub-Saharan Africa.

2. BASIC CHARACTERISTICS AND ASSUMPTIONS OF THE OPPOSING PARADIGMS

2.1. Macro-Quantitative Methods

Macro-quantitative methods and comparative aggregate data analyses have enjoyed increasing popularity since the 'behavioral revolution' in political science (see Falter 1982). Although this was concentrated mostly on the 'micro' level of politics using individual survey data, the preference for statistical analysis (as a result of a large number of cases) and a certain 'scientistic' position also colored corresponding macro analyses. Inspired by such untiring innovators as Karl Deutsch and Stein Rokkan, comprehensive data handbooks have been compiled since the 1960's (see for example Russett et.al. 1964; Taylor and Jodice 1982; Flora et.al. 1983, 1987), which together with official and unofficial (primarily economic) statistics formed the starting point for numerous macro-quantitative analyses (Niedermayer and Widmaier 2003).

The largest possible number of cases (usually states) with comparable data formed the foundation of such studies. However, due to the relatively limited level of basic similarities and in the face of frequently occurring data problems and lack of information, especially in the more 'sensitive' political areas, random sampling, which forms the basis for representative interpretations of the survey results on the 'micro' level, and 'normal distributions' cannot be applied. Thus, the 'inferential' statistics which are based on such prerequisites, as even simple Chi-Square-tests used for calculating levels of significance, are, strictly speaking, out of the question. This consequence is often ignored at peril.

Quantitative methods can provide useful descriptive averages of certain frequency distributions or serve as a basis for presumably 'universal' explanations based on the actual number of cases, as in linear (also an often unjustified assumption) regressions. Specific characteristics of individual cases are usually not taken into account. If such characteristics differ too crassly in the observed distributions, they are often dismissed and neglected as 'outliers'.

The fact that the limited number of cases increases the possibility that including one or a few deviating cases can drastically change the end results, is often not respected.

The causal relationships observed are 'probabilistic', that is they are usually based on correlations between a dependent and one or more independent variables. Such correlations can, of course, be 'spurious' (that is they may have occurred due to a third factor which has not been taken into account). The direction of a causal relationship is also not always clear (What came first? What depends on what?). The assumed causality is, as already stated, 'universal' in nature that is relating to the average of the observed totality. But, in view of the unrepresentative nature of the selection of cases, 'inferential' generalizations are clearly inadmissible. 'Conjunctural' causalities (which are based on differing combinations of variables) such as described by J. S. Mill (1974, 1975 [1843]) must also be discarded.

All of these criticisms and others are, of course, obvious and have been known for a long time. They are taken partly into account by more 'robust' statistics (see Hampel et.al. 1986). However, there still remains a considerable amount of dissatisfaction with regard to the one-sidedness, superficiality and limited theoretical implications of many macro-quantitative investigations. If an impression of the present authors' favoring comparative-qualitative methods arises here, this is explained by the dominance to date of quantitative-statistical methods in political science curricula, existing deficits in the comparative field and more recent developments we were involved in and which are not yet known amongst a wider public. However, we are interested in dealing fairly and constructively with the above mentioned problems and in bridging certain gaps between the two camps.

2.2. Macro-Qualitative Methods

Over the last decade, „macro-qualitative" and „diversity-oriented" methods have been more intensively employed and improved using new technological developments such as "Qualitative Comparative Analysis" (QCA) (see Ragin 1987, Drass and Ragin 1992, Ragin, Berg-Schlosser and De Meur 1996, Ragin 2000). Others have applied systematic 'most different' and 'most similar' research designs (see Przeworski and Teune 1970, De Meur and Berg-Schlosser 1994, 1996; see also Levi-Faur, in this volume), or more historically oriented comparative analyses as those by Theda Skocpol (1979, 1984) or Dietrich Rueschemeyer, Evelyne Huber Stephens and John Stephens (1992). The specific characteristics of such methods, which at least provide certain compensatory aspects to the quantitative procedure, will be briefly dealt with in this section.

The term 'macro-qualitative' is employed here to signify the presence or absence of characteristics at the level of entire political systems. This term should not be confused with qualitative methods at the micro-level (such as participant observations in ethnology) or with qualitative interpretative methods (for example in hermeneutics). Some of the techniques presented here rely on a dichotomization of the observed variables (yes/no, high/low, 0/1 etc.). In the case of originally more varied characteristics, certain 'thresholds' must be established for this purpose or a number of 'dummy' variables be formed (as for the conversion of nominal characteristics to variables for certain statistical procedures which require dichotomous or interval variables).

In a number of instances, this entails a loss of information. Such losses of information are also present in numerous statistical methods, for example in 'cluster' or 'correspondence' analysis, where multidimensional 'clouds' of cases are projected on a two-dimensional surface, without all the users being fully aware of such limitations. The necessary dichotomization allows the implementation of new more complex methods on the basis of Boolean algebra, of set theory and elaborated 'similarity' and 'dissimilarity' levels, which represent a certain 'compensation' for the occurring information loss (De Meur and Rihoux 2002).

In contrast to overall statistical methods, macro-qualitative analyses are more strongly *case*-oriented, i.e. each case which is taken into account has in principle the same value for the analysis. The selection of cases must, therefore, be as hypothesis- and theory-guided as the selection of variables. A minimum amount of homogeneity amongst the cases to be chosen, e.g. historical-regional similarities, must be ensured in order to analyze them meaningfully. Among the more limited number of cases selected in this way, a high level of heterogeneity not only with regard to the dependent variable but also for the possible independent variables is desirable. In this manner, the smaller and less studied countries or strongly 'deviating' cases can often supply interesting information relating to the validity and range of certain hypotheses.

Such a 'case orientation' should not be confused with a 'case-based' in contrast to a 'variable-based' statistical method. Naturally, the cases selected *and* a wide spectrum of possible variables form the basis of the analysis. The range of complexity of the examined cases is, of course, subject to theoretical and practical limitations. However, a high level of familiarity with a large number of cases is a prerequisite for every 'macro-qualitatively' inclined political scientist in order to obtain the necessary sensibility for the often complex and historically determined facts.

In contrast to more 'universal-statistical' attempts at explanation on the one hand and exclusively historical-ideographical (individualizing) case studies on the other, macro-qualitative analyses can also expose 'conjunctural' causal relationships, that is different patterns of factor combinations ('variation finding' in the sense of Charles Tilly 1984). The range of these patterns can be ascertained and in certain cases modified by a step by step expansion of the field of examination. A technique such as 'Qualitative Comparative Analysis' (QCA, see below) offers the further possibility of including hypothetically possible case constellations ('logical remainder cases') in the analysis and of developing at least a hypothetical generalization over and above the cases taken into account (see also Spreitzer and Yamasaki, in this volume).

3. APPLICATIONS TESTING THE CONTEXT OF THE AFRICAN HIV PROFILE

In 2003, an estimated number of 2.9 million people died of the consequences of the Acquired Immune Deficiency Syndrome (AIDS), of whom 2.3 million in Sub-Saharan Africa, with an estimated 23.8 million more adults and children infected with the Human Immunodeficiency Virus (HIV) (UNAIDS 2004: 193). Despite these facts, few social scientists have been studying the AIDS epidemic in a comparative perspective attempting to explain the differences in the development of the current HIV infection profile in Sub-Saharan Africa.

In this part of our contribution, we will present some preliminary steps for an in-depth analysis of HIV policies. It is our goal to describe first some characteristics of more general patterns of the spreading of HIV in Sub-Saharan Africa. Furthermore, we want to develop some causal explanations of the current tendencies in the HIV prevalence rate, showing why the HIV prevalence rate is falling in some countries while it increases strongly in others.[1]

3.1. The Current Situation

Although HIV is a major disease in almost all Sub-Saharan states, a closer look at the available data shows major differences in the growth or decline of the HIV prevalence rates across these countries. While the HIV rate seems to explode in a number of the southernmost states (Botswana, Namibia, South Africa, Zimbabwe) reaching an unimaginable estimated value of 38.8% in Swaziland (2003), the efforts to prevent future spreading of the virus seem to be successful to some extent in a number of other countries, where the rate has declined or at least has not risen any further in the last five years. It, therefore, seems of interest to study which factors have led to these divergent trends in the infection rate.

There are a number of theories to explain the HIV infection profile in Africa among which explanations based on cultural factors and those relying on socio-economic and historical factors can be regarded as the major competing ones (see Hunt 1996; Mufune 2003). We will now review these approaches and explore their use for our purposes.

3.2. Cultural Explanations

In Sub-Saharan Africa, unlike in Europe and Northern America, HIV is primarily transmitted by heterosexual intercourse and not by homosexual intercourse or blood transmissions (e.g. as a result of drug injections). Based on certain stereotypes derived from the writings of explorers and missionaries in the 19th century, whose intent was to shock their readers or to show the lack of moral attitudes of Africans, some emphasis has been laid to explain the AIDS epidemic by the extensive promiscuity supposedly found in Africa, although highly variable patterns of social regulation and norms which affect sexual behavior can be found (Mufune 2003: 44). Unfortunately, there are no detailed data available on an ethnic basis which reflects this variety.[2] Nevertheless, it is important to include some cultural factors such as religious influences in our set of possible explanatory variables, as the differences among countries can explain some differences in the HIV prevalence rate.

As HIV is primarily transmitted by sexual intercourse, factors influencing sexual behavior are of major concern: The risk of being infected with HIV increases with each sexual contact with different partners without protection. Therefore, attitudes toward sexual behavior must be considered: Is premarital and extra-marital sex socially disapproved, or is there a tradition towards a more risky sexual conduct among young people? Is HIV treated as a taboo or are HIV risks and the consequences of AIDS discussed freely?

Finding quantifiable data on these questions is difficult, especially if all countries of Sub-Saharan Africa have to be covered. As the goal of our contribution is to perform a first analysis on this topic and a broad data set on questions of sexual behavior covering all cases is not available, we will use the overall religious composition of countries to see whether this factor has any influence on the HIV prevalence rate. In Islamic countries, for example, the rights and movements of women are often restricted, affecting their contacts with the outside world. Among Catholics, pre-marital sexual contacts, but also the use of condoms, are strongly disapproved.

If we check for correlations between the religious affiliation (percentage of citizens adhering to traditional religions, Catholicism, protestant denominations and to Islam) and the HIV prevalence rate of 1997, we obtain correlations measures as shown in table 7.1.

Table 7.1. Religion and HIV Prevalence Rates in 1997

	PCTTRAD	PCTCATH	PCTPROT	PCTMUSL
r	0,273	-0,031	0,621**	- 0,478**

**: Significant at the 0.01 level (1-sided)
Notes: PCTTRAD: Percentage of population adhering to traditional religions, circa 1985, PCTCATH: Percentage of population adhering to Catholicism, circa 1985, PCTPROT: Percentage of population adhering to Protestant denominations, circa 1985, PCTMUSL: Percentage of population adhering to Islam, circa 1985, Source: Bratton and van de Walle 1997.

For the correlation between adherents of protestant denominations and a high HIV prevalence rate, it must be noted that the PCTPROT variable also can be considered as a proxy for the colonial impact: In historically grounded explanations, the AIDS epidemic resulted from the effects of European and especially British colonialism by which Protestant and Anglican churches were established. In a similar way, the economic system created in these countries based on migrant labor, where males had to live away from their homes for longer periods to earn money to ensure the survival of their families in the rural areas, has been one factor affecting the spread of the AIDS epidemic (Hunt 1996: 1284).

3.3. Socio-Economic Theories

The second major theory for the HIV prevalence profile is derived from dependency theory (Mufune 2003). Its advocates argue that the spread of HIV can only be understood by taking the global and national inequalities into account. There are several paths leading to this argument:

First of all, a lack of formal education as a result of extreme poverty leads to a lack of knowledge about HIV. As people do not know the risks, they do nothing to protect themselves, which results in a high HIV prevalence rate. If we test for a correlation between HIV and literacy, we would therefore expect a negative correlation: the higher the literacy, the lower the prevalence rate. However if we perform such a test on the HIV prevalence rate and the degree of literacy in 1997, the correlation is moderately positive ($r = 0.493$, $p < 0.01$). This is mainly due to a number of cases with a high degree of literacy as well as a high HIV prevalence rate (e.g. South Africa, Zimbabwe, and Namibia). But this correlation is spurious: If we perform a partial correlation checking for the influence of the two religious factors mentioned above, the correlation disappears ($p > 0.1$).

This is due to the high literacy rate found in former British colonies (with a high number of HIV positive citizens) and the low literacy found in Muslim dominated countries. So, seen at least at the level of national aggregation, a low level of literacy does not explain the rise of HIV. In the same way the prevalence of HIV cannot be attributed to poverty alone (see table 7.2). Similarly, within countries, it is not necessarily the poorest strata which are most affected by HIV (e.g. the high number of deaths among teachers in Uganda – UNAIDS 2004: 167)

A further connection between dependency theory and the spread of HIV has focused on gender issues. In current reports (e.g. UNAIDS 2004) it is argued that the poverty of African women affects their right of sexual autonomy and, to put it simply, that women cannot afford to say no to higher-risk sex, even if they do know about the risks, as their situation forces them to agree to such sexual relationships, as they depend on their husbands. A number of indices do attempt to quantify the development of women rights. The Gender Equity Index created by Robert Prescott-Allen (2001) combines the difference of income and school enrolment between males and females with the number of seats held by women in parliament.[3] The Gender Development Index (GDI) provided in the Human Development Reports focuses on such socio-economic factors as women's life expectancy, adult literacy, school enrolment and contribution to real GDP, similar to the factors employed in the overall Human Development Index (HDI). Finally, the Gender Empowerment Measure (GEM), also found in the Human Development Reports, combines political participation of women (seats in parliaments) with the share of women in better qualified jobs. While the latter index is too incomplete for our cases to allow any reliable analysis, the GDI and the Gender Equity Index are available for almost all Sub-Saharan countries. As the literacy rate, these variables seem to correlate positively with the prevalence rate (see table 7.2), but when checked for the religious factor, the correlations disappear (see table 7.3). Thus, there seems to be no independent connection between gender issues and the HIV prevalence rate.

Table 7.2. Socio-Economic and Gender Related Indices and Prevalence Rates in 1997

	LIT97	GENDEREQ	GDI97	HDI97	PPP97
r	0,473**	0,309*	0,311*	0,265	0,231

**: Significant at the 0.01 level (1-sided)
*: Significant at the 0.05 level (1-sided)

Notes and sources: LIT97: Literacy 1997, in % of population of 15 years and above (UNDP 1999), GENDEREQ: Gender Equity Index (Prescott-Allen 2001), GDI97: Gender Development Index 1997 (UNDP 1999), HDI95: Human Development Index 1995 (UNDP 1999), PPP97: Real GDP per capita (PPP$) (UNDP 1999).

Table 7.3. Socio-Economic and Gender Related Indices and Prevalence Rates in 1997 Checked for Partial Correlations with Religious Factors (PCTPROT and PCTMUSL)

	LIT97	GENDEREQ	GDI97	HDI97
r	-0,208	0,163	-0,165	-0,103

All p>0.1
Notes and sources: see table 7.1 and table 7.2.

Another possible cause for the spread of HIV may be labor migration. Hunt (1989) has shown for Uganda that rural poverty forced males to seek jobs in other regions, where HIV was already prevalent. Separated from their wives for a long time, these workers caused an increase of prostitution and sexually transmitted diseases (STDs). In a similar way, the "Truck Thesis" (see Hunt 1996:1291) considers the African transportation system as one of the main factors of the spread of HIV, as the truck drivers, separated from their wives, are spreading HIV from one area to another by frequent contacts with prostitutes. Overall, regional migration seems to be of importance, as in the situation described for Uganda. But there are no data available for intra-national migration in the Sub-Saharan countries, so we cannot include this in our analysis here.

Instead, we will use the share of agricultural products of GDP as a possible explanatory factor. Functioning agricultural economies to some degree prevents dependency on migrant labor and so the factors leading to spreading of HIV as indicated above are avoided. In fact, the share of agriculture correlates negatively (albeit weakly) with the HIV prevalence rate at a significant level ($p<0.05$), but this does not hold when controlled by religion. (In our QCA analysis below this variable nonetheless becomes important when studying the differences in the development of the HIV prevalence rate.)

3.4. Awareness of the HIV / AIDS Threat

One problem of educating people about HIV / AIDS is the long time between the infection with HIV, the outbreak of AIDS and the final death of a person. This may lead to a misperception of the cause of a person's death, relating it to other circumstances than the initial HIV infection. The actual impact of HIV is, consequently, underestimated or rejected. This misperception is strengthened by the fact that people often die of an illness (e.g. tuberculosis), from which they suffered because their immune system was weakened by AIDS, and not by the virus itself.

For the explanation of current trends of the African HIV infection profile, we have included some indicators on the awareness of HIV / AIDS. These are based, on the one hand, on UNAIDS (2004) figures on the knowledge about HIV and on subsequent changes in sexual behavior, although the data are not available for all countries. On the other hand, the estimated cumulative percentage of AIDS-related deaths until 1997 is included for each country, examining if a high number of victims has influenced the trend of the HIV prevalence rate. Our tests show that the cumulated number of people dying of AIDS until 1997 correlates moderately with the change of the HIV prevalence rate ($r=-0.414$, $p<0.05$).

It has to be discussed, of course, if this is merely an autocorrelation as a high number of deaths lowers the number of HIV infected people, or if there is a genuine change in HIV perception among citizens when they see many people dying of this disease. We have no separate survey data confirming such changed perceptions, but individual country reports confirm that a high level of mortality changes the awareness of people about HIV and subsequently changes their sexual behavior taking fewer risks.

3.5. Multiple Regressions

If we combine some of the more significant factors in a multiple regression analysis, we obtain the following results for the HIV prevalence rate in 1997 and the changes (in a positive or negative direction) of this rate between 1997 and 2003. In a first run, we included dominance of protestant denominations, literacy, share of agriculture and the gender equity index. The results are reported in table 7.4.

Table 7.4. Multiple Regressions (HIV Prevalence Rate 1997)

Model	Non-standardized coefficient B	Standard error	Standardized co-efficient Beta	T	Significance
(Constant)	-1.746	5.359		-0.326	0.746
PCTPROT	0.166	0.051	0.506	3.209	0.002
LIT97	5.437E-02	0.055	0.163	0.987	0.330
AGRAR	1.647E-03	0.058	0.004	0.028	0.978
GENDEREQ	8.108E-02	0.106	0.108	0.765	0.449

Dependent variable: ADULT97

Notes and sources: AdultHIV97: Estimated number of Adults (15-49) living with HIV/AIDS rate % end 1997 (UNAIDS 1998), PCTPROT: Percentage of population adhering to Protestant denominations, circa 1985 (Bratton and van de Walle 1997), LIT97: Literacy 1997, in % of population of 15 years and above (UNDP 1999), AgrarGDP: Agriculture, value added (% of GDP) (World Bank 2002), GENDEREQ: Gender Equity Index (Prescott-Allen 2001)

As can be seen, religion again is by far the strongest single factor, the others not being significant. The overall variance explained ($R^2 = 0.441$) remains, however, relatively low. Similarly, when we included the dominance of Islam with the socio-economic factors, religion was again the strongest single factor, the others not being significant ($R^2 = 0.327$).

In a second run, we only included cases with a high HIV prevalence rate in 1997 (above 6%, i.e. 19 cases out of the original 42) and their changes until 2003 in order to see whether in these high prevalence cases some policy changes may have occurred. Since no comparative data on the kind and strengths of respective policy measures (e.g. AIDS education, distribution of condoms, etc.) are available, in this context, we restricted ourselves to some of the overall conditioning factors. The regression results are reported in table 7.5.

Table 7.5. Multiple Regressions (Change of HIV Prevalence Rate 1997-2003)

Model	Non-standardized coefficient B	Standard error	Standardized coefficient Beta	T	Significance
(Constant)	4.483	11.515		0.389	0.703
LIT97	5.042E-02	0.127	0.122	0.397	0.697
AGRAR	-7.39E-02	0.137	-0.153	-0.539	0.598
GENDEREQ	-9.36E-02	0.179	-0.119	-0.524	0.609
PCTPROT	0.147	0.083	0.444	1.773	0.098
MORTALITY	-1.579	0.859	-0.392	-1.838	0.087

Dependent variable: HIVChange

Notes and Sources: LIT97: Literacy 1997, in % of population of 15 years and above (UNDP 1999), AgrarGDP: Agriculture, value added (% of GDP) (World Bank 2002), GENDEREQ: Gender Equity Index (Prescott-Allen 2001), PCTPROT: Percentage of population adhering to Protestant denominations, circa 1985 (Bratton and van de Walle 1997), Mortality: Cumulated AIDS related deaths until 1997 / population (UNAIDS 1998

As displayed in the previous regression, protestant denomination is the strongest single factor (in a negative sense). The cumulative AIDS death rate until 1997, as a factor indicating a possibly increased awareness, is the strongest positive factor affecting a decline in HIV rates. The overall variance explained is moderately high ($R^2 = 0.493$). None of the cases with a predominant Muslim population was still included among our high HIV incidence cases here.

4. QUALITATIVE COMPARATIVE ANALYSIS

Our statistical analysis resulted in some evidence for the HIV prevalence profile in Sub-Saharan Africa, but none of the correlations was very strong and the overall picture remains vague. We will now use QCA and MVQCA to see if we can find clearer constellations of factors explaining the HIV profile and current tendencies in Sub-Saharan Africa.

In order to perform a QCA, we have to dichotomize our data. For all variables we seek to obtain meaningful subsets. We either apply theoretically based thresholds or, if no such thresholds exist, we may use the median value or a cluster analysis to establish such thresholds. A purely mechanical use of the median, however, may result in misleading configurations as artificial cuts between close data points may be made. By using the threshold-setter, a feature of the TOSMANA software (Cronqvist 2004), such misleading thresholds can be avoided, as the data distribution is shown when the threshold is selected.

For the HIV prevalence rate in 1997, a simple single linkage cluster analysis results into a division in three subsets with the thresholds at 6% and 16% providing the best fit. We will use these thresholds, but merge the two upper clusters, so that the dichotomized value for the prevalence rate is 0 for cases with a HIV prevalence rate below 6% and 1 for cases with a HIV prevalence rate above 6% (see figure 7.1).

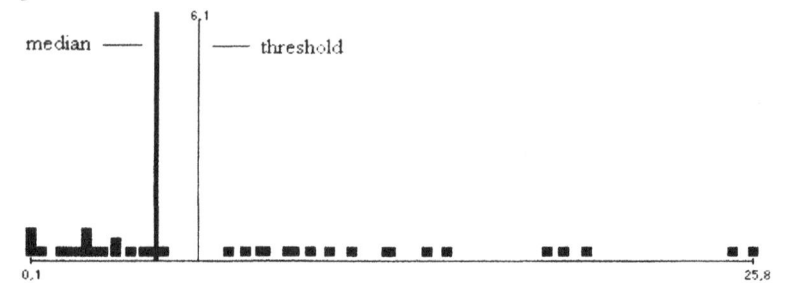

Figure 7.1. Case Distribution of the 1997 HIV Prevalence Rate

4.1. Contextual Factors

As shown above, there is a negative correlation between the predominance of Islam and the HIV prevalence rate, as well as a positive correlation with the predominance of protestant churches. If we dichotomize the variables indicating religious adherence by defining a religion as dominant if more than fifty percent belong to it, we see that this factor is strongly confirmed (see table 7.6).

Although this finding should not be overestimated, some connection between the major religion of a country and the HIV prevalence rate can be established (see rows 3 and 4 of table 7.6, covering a total of 14 countries; for the other rows, the "C" outcome value stands for "contradiction" – see below). This may be some evidence for the fact that Islam influences the sexual behavior of people to avoid high-risk activities, while there seems to be no such restraining driving force among members of the protestant churches.

The other factors discussed above do not produce any clear solutions with QCA (truth tables not displayed here). The relation between literacy and HIV prevalence is also confirmed to be spurious, as literacy is included in some QCA solutions for high as well as low HIV prevalence rates. There remains, however, a relatively great number of contradictory cases, which means that other more discriminating variables such as inter- and intra-state migration should be introduced which, unfortunately, are not available on a large-scale comparative basis.

Table 7.6. Truth Table Religion and the HIV Prevalence Rate in 1997

Country	PCT-TRAD	PCT-CATH	PCT-PROT	PCT-MUSL	Adult-HIV97
Zimbabwe, Zambia, Uganda, Tanzania, Mozambique, Mauritius, Lesotho, Guinea-Bissau, Ghana, Ethiopia, Cote d'Ivoire, Congo-Brazzaville, Cameroon, C.A.R., Benin	0	0	0	0	C
Togo, Sierra Leone, Rwanda, Madagascar, Liberia, Kenya, Burkina Faso, Botswana, Angola	1	0	0	0	C
Swaziland, South Africa, Namibia, Malawi	0	0	1	0	1
Senegal, Nigeria, Niger, Mauritania, Mali, Guinea, Gambia, Eritrea, Comoros, Chad	0	0	0	1	0
Gabon, Equatorial-Guinea, Congo. D.R., Burundi	0	1	0	0	C

Notes and sources: AdultHIV97: Estimated number of Adults (15-49) living with HIV/AIDS rate % end 1997 (UNAIDS 1998), Other variables: see table 7.1.

4.2. Explaining Changing Trends in HIV Prevalence Profile with QCA

The main question of this contribution is concerned with the contextual factors for the success of HIV prevention policies. Therefore, in the remaining part, we will examine these 18 cases with a high prevalence rate in 1997 (above 6%)[4], to see which factors affected significant changes in this rate until 2003. Again, we included some of the socio-economic and perception-based variables as mentioned above. For the impact of migration we de not have any data available, so we decided to use again the share of agrarian production of the GDP. For the other socio-economic factors discussed above, the 2000 literacy rate has been included, and to indicate the situation of women the Gender Equity Index was used. This index was preferred, as it is based on measures of differences between males and females, whereas the GDI is indicating the general development of the female part of a population of a country, and it is not an index on gender equivalence. Finally, to test the awareness of the HIV threat, the mortality rate (cumulated AIDS related death until 1997/ population) was employed.

If we check for correlations between these variables and the HIV change rate for the cases with a high HIV prevalence in 1997, we obtain correlations as shown in table 7.7.

Table 7.7. Change of HIV Prevalence Rate and Socio-Economic and Perception Indices

	LIT00	AgrarGDP	GenderEQ	Mortality
r	0.404*	-0.519*	0.246	-0.414*

**: Significant at the 0.01 level (1-sided), *: Significant at the 0.05 level (1-sided)

Notes and sources: LIT00: Literacy 2000, in % of population of 15 years and above (UNDP 2002), GENDEREQ: Gender Equity Index (Prescott-Allen 2001), AgrarGDP: Agriculture, value added (% of GDP) (World Bank 2002), Mortality: Cumulated AIDS related deaths until 1997 / population (UNAIDS 1998)

Our hypothesis of the impact of a high AIDS-related mortality on the awareness of the danger of HIV / AIDS and a subsequent change in sexual behavior is confirmed in table 7.7, as a moderate correlation was found. Also, the share of agricultural production of GDP again correlates negatively with the change rate, and the literacy rate shows still a moderate positive correlation. But these latter correlations do not hold when controlled for protestant religion.

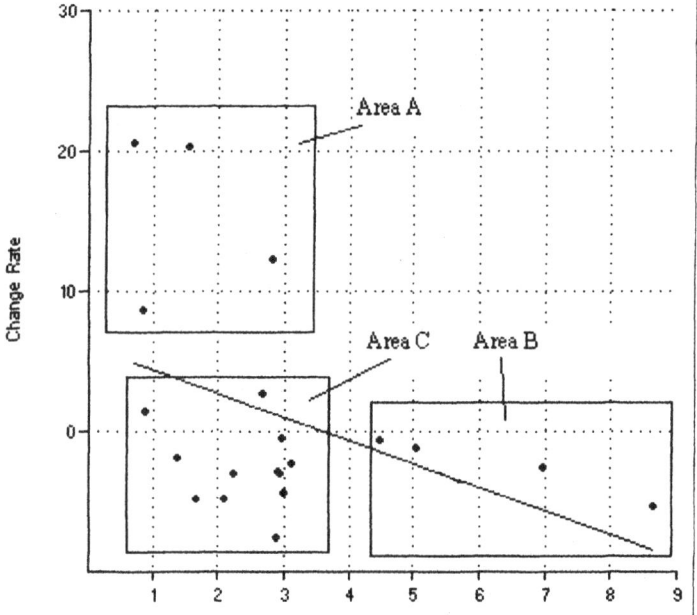

Figure 7.2. Correlation between Change of HIV Rate 1997-2003 and the Mortality Rate

As this statistical analysis only gives some first hints, we will now perform again a QCA analysis. As outcome, we use a dichotomized version of the changes of the HIV prevalence rate between 1997 and 2003. 0 indicates a falling HIV rate, while 1 indicates a rising rate. The thresholds of the agrarian share of GDP (above 25%), the literacy rate in 2000 (above 50%), and the

Conditions of HIV/AIDS Prevalence in Sub-Saharan Africa

gender equity index (above 40 index points) can be established quite easily with cluster analysis. The threshold for the cumulated AIDS mortality is, however, difficult to define, as the values are distributed continuously (see figure 7.3).

Figure 7.3. Case Distribution of the MORTALITY Variable

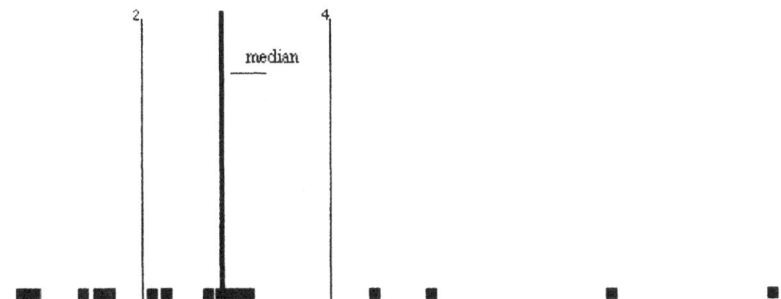

To show the differences between dichotomized QCA and Multi-Value QCA (MVQCA), we will, therefore, use different thresholds for the mortality variable. In a first step, we set the threshold at 4%, which creates a truth table as found in table 7.8.

Table 7.8. QCA Truth Table with MORTALITY Threshold at 4%

Country	LIT00' (L)	GENDER-EQ (G)	MORTA-LITY (M)	AGRAR-GDP (A)	HIV-Change
Ethiopia, Burkina Faso, C.A.R., Cote d'Ivoire, Burundi	0	0	0	1	C
Lesotho, Kenya, Congo-Brazzaville	1	0	0	0	C
Malawi, Uganda	1	1	1	1	0
Mozambique	0	1	0	0	0
Tanzania	1	1	0	1	0
Togo	1	0	0	1	0
Zambia	1	0	1	0	0
Zimbabwe	1	1	1	0	0
South Africa, Namibia, Swaziland, Botswana	1	1	0	0	1

Notes and sources: LIT00: Literacy 2000, in % of population of 15 years and above (UNDP 2002), GENDEREQ: Gender Equity Index (Prescott-Allen 2001), AgrarGDP: Agriculture, value added (% of GDP) (World Bank 2002), Mortality: Cumulated AIDS related deaths until 1997 / population (UNAIDS 1998), HIVChange: Change in the HIV/AIDS rate 1997 – 2003 (see Appendix A)

Though it still contains some contradictory configurations (see rows 1 and 2), this truth table can be minimized, leading to the following QCA minimal formulae[5]:

HIVCHANGE (0 , R) = M{1} *(Uganda, Malawi, Zambia, Zimbabwe)*

$\quad\quad$ + L{1}*A{1} *(Uganda, Malawi, Togo, Zambia, Tanzania)*

$\quad\quad$ + $L\{0\} * \begin{Bmatrix} G\{1\} \\ A\{0\} \end{Bmatrix}$ *(Mozambique)*

HIVCHANGE (1 , R) = M{0} * A {0} * G{1} * L{1}
$\quad\quad$ *(South Africa, Swaziland, Botswana, Namibia)*

In spite of the remaining contradictions, a first trend is visible. The prevalence rate has increased where the experienced death toll of AIDS has not been higher than 4% and modernization is high. For the opposite outcome, a high level of mortality or high literacy and high agricultural production explain most cases.

These solutions follow the trend using 2% as a threshold, but the importance of high mortality is much clearer here: A high degree (above 4%) of mortality is sufficient to explain a decrease in the prevalence rate of a country.

Altogether, however, the number of cases not explained – as they are expressed by the contradicting configurations – is too high to be satisfying.

4.3. Improved Analysis with MVQCA

One of the main problems with QCA is the compulsory transformation of data into dichotomous values, which entails a loss of information and may result in a relatively large number of contradicting configurations, as seen in this example. For this reason, we have developed a procedure for the use of non-dichotomized data. Multi-Value Qualitative Comparative Analysis – MVQCA (Cronqvist 2003) keeps the idea of minimizing Boolean expressions, while also allowing non-dichotomized literals to be included in the analysis. A truth function is assigned for each literal, so that the literals can be combined like Boolean literals in QCA. This allows the use of multiple values, for the minimization of complex data sets into parsimonious expressions. MVQCA thus allows the use of multi-value variables as they are also employed in fuzzy-set applications (see Ragin 2000), but instead of using probabilistic criteria to identify sufficient and necessary conditions, the veristic synthesis of data sets in QCA is still used in MVQCA.

Therefore, in a final step, we make use of this possibility. We divide the mortality variable employing thresholds of 2% and 4% (see also the distribution shown by the TOSMANA "thresholdsetter" in figure 7.3), while the thresholds for the other variables remain unchanged. The resulting truth table is given in table 7.9.

As this table shows, all but one contradicting configuration are eliminated. The solutions are somewhat similar to the solution found before, although one more prime implicant is included for each outcome.

HIVCHANGE (0 , R) = M{2} (Uganda, Malawi, Zambia, Zimbabwe)

$$+ A\{1\} \begin{Bmatrix} L\{1\} \\ G\{1\} \end{Bmatrix} \text{ (Uganda, Malawi, Tanzania, (Zambia, Togo)}^6)$$

$$+ G\{0\}M\{1\} * \begin{Bmatrix} L\{1\} \\ A\{0\} \end{Bmatrix} \quad \text{(Kenya, Togo (Congo-Brazzaville)}^7)$$

+ M{0}*L{0} *(Ethiopia, Mozambique)*

HIVCHANGE (1 , R) =   M{0}* L{1}   + M{1}* A {0} * G{1}
     (South Africa, Swaziland, Namibia, Lesotho) + (Botswana)

Table 7.9. MVQCA Truth-Table with Trichotomized MORTALITY Variable

Country	LIT00 (L)	GENDER-EQ(G)	MORTA-LITY(M)	AGRAR-GDP(A)	HIV-Change
Burkina Faso, C.A.R., Cote d'Ivoire, Burundi	0	0	1	1	C
Ethiopia	0	0	0	1	0
Kenya, Congo-Brazzaville	1	0	1	0	0
Malawi, Uganda	1	1	2	1	0
Mozambique	0	1	0	0	0
Tanzania	1	1	1	1	0
Togo	1	0	1	1	0
Zimbabwe	1	1	2	0	0
Botswana	1	1	1	0	1
Lesotho	1	0	0	0	1
South Africa, Namibia, Swaziland	1	1	0	0	1

Notes and sources: See table 7.8.

Still four cases (Burkina Faso, Burundi, C.A.R., and Côte d'Ivoire) are found in a contradicting configuration, but for the variables included in our analysis, it must be said that the values are too similar to allow a separation of these cases (see table 7.10).

Table 7.10. The Similar Cases Burkina Faso, Burundi, C.A.R., and Côte d'Ivoire

	LIT00	GEN-DEREQ	MOR-TALITY	AGRAR-GDP	HIVChange
Burkina Faso	23,9	38	2,3	35	-3,0
Burundi	48	40	3,1	55	-2,3
C.A.R.	46,7	34	2,7	40,8	+2,7
Côte d'Ivoire	46,8	26	2,9	29	-3,1

Notes and sources: See table 7.8.

Table 7.10 shows that three (Burkina Faso, Burundi, and Côte d'Ivoire) of the four cases do not have a rising HIV prevalence rate while one case (Central African Republic) does. There, apparently, some other factors are at work (for example certain ethnic traditions), which we cannot capture with the available data. If we exclude the C.A.R., we receive a contradiction free truth table as found in table 7.11.

Table 7.11. Experimental Truth Table without the Central African Republic (C.A.R.)

Country	LIT00 (L)	GENDER-EQ (G)	MORTA-LITY(M)	AGRAR-GDP(A)	HIV-Change
Burkina Faso, Cote d'Ivoire, Burundi	0	0	1	1	0
Ethiopia	0	0	0	1	0
Kenya, Congo-Brazzaville	1	0	1	0	0
Malawi, Uganda	1	1	2	1	0
Mozambique	0	1	0	0	0
Tanzania	1	1	1	1	0
Togo	1	0	1	1	0
Zambia	1	0	2	0	0
Zimbabwe	1	1	2	0	0
Botswana	1	1	1	0	1
Lesotho	1	0	0	0	1
South Africa, Namibia, Swaziland	1	1	0	0	1

Notes and sources: See table 7.8.

If we minimize this truth table, we get two even more parsimonious solutions:

HIVCHANGE (0,R) = M{2} (Malawi, Uganda, Zimbabwe, Zambia)
+ L{0} (Mozambique Ethiopia, Burkina Faso, Cote d'Ivoire, Burundi)
+ A{1} (Ethiopia, Burkina Faso, Cote d'Ivoire, Burundi, Tanzania, Togo, Malawi, Uganda)
+ M{1}*G{0} (Kenya, Congo-Brazzaville, Burkina Faso, Cote d'Ivoire, Burundi, Togo)

HIVCHANGE (1,R) = M{0}*L{1} (Lesotho, South Africa, Namibia, Swaziland)
+ M{1}*G{1}*A{0} (Botswana)

Here, the trends found above can be demonstrated again: a high AIDS-related mortality rate or a high share of agriculture imply most of the cases with a falling HIV rate, but also a low level of literacy can explain this outcome. By contrast, a low mortality rate combined with high literacy implies four out of the five cases with a strongly rising HIV rate.

5. CONCLUSION

Although the overall picture still produces many questions for further consideration, some conclusions for a policy analysis framework can be drawn.

First, the religious context and the colonial history had a strong impact on the spread of HIV in the 1980s and 1990s. In Islamic societies, a low prevalence rate is found, whereas a high rate exists in societies with dominant protestant (or Anglican) churches originally introduced by British colonialism.

Second, a high GDP share of agricultural production was found in many countries in which the HIV prevalence rate has fallen during the last years. This may indicate that the currently applied policies work better in areas without many migrating workers and that different policies are needed to combat the disease, in particular convincing migrant workers to adopt a more responsible sexual behavior.

Third, there seems to be a connection between the number of AIDS casualties and the development of the HIV prevalence rate. One explanation is that the death toll of AIDS must be high enough to show people the threat of HIV. If the death toll is low, people tend to ignore the danger, but if the death toll is high, people realize the consequences of high-risk sexual behavior. Combined with the apparently failing effect of a high level of education alone, this may lead to the recommendation that people do not only have to be educated about the dangers of HIV, but that a major effort should be made to clarify the connection between AIDS-related casualties of friends and relatives and the sexual behavior of the individual. Therefore, as the macro-qualitative analysis has highlighted, differentiated policies are required according to level of development. In the future, when more detailed policy-specific data become available, not only the conditions of occurrence but also the relevant policies as such may be tested and evaluated in this way.

As far as the strengths and weaknesses of our methodological tools are concerned, these also could be exemplified quite clearly. The "averaging out" of most statistical procedures certainly is a major weakness when we deal, as almost by necessity in comparative politics at the macro level, with a limited and small number of cases. Correlations and regressions then may be misleading when influenced by some strong outliers (an example is also discussed in Berg-Schlosser and Quenter 1996) or when further controls are not considered. Conversely, QCA and similar tools are helpful for a more diversified case-oriented "variation-finding". The use of multi-value variables proved useful in our example, as a more fine-graded subdivision of the cases could be employed to display the differences between low, medium and high mortality rates. At the extreme, however, the extensive use of fine-graded multi-value variables may lead to "individualizing" results describing the historical uniqueness of each case (see also Varone, Rihoux and Marx, in this volume). Between the extremes of over-generalizing and "universalizing" macro-quantitative approaches, on the one hand, and purely individualizing case-oriented approaches, on the other, as our analysis has demonstrated, a meaningful "medium-range" social science can be built which, at the same time, has a higher explanatory power and a greater social, political and policy relevance.

NOTES

[1] The data used can be found in Appendix A. All Sub-Saharan countries with available data were included in the analysis, only for the Cape Verde Islands, Sao Tome, the Seychelles and Somalia no statistics on the HIV prevalence were available. In addition, Djibouti and Sudan were excluded as the data seemed to be too incongruent for comparative purposes.

[2] Some attempts have been made to measure sexual behavior and knowledge of the risk involved, e.g. in the 2004 UNAIDS report on the HIV / AIDS epidemic.

[3] It must be mentioned, that this index must be used with care, as not all countries in Sub-Saharan Africa have a parliament. In these cases, Robert Prescott-Allen (2001: 179) simply bases his index on the two remaining factors: Gender and Wealth (ratio of male income to female income) and Gender and Knowledge (differences in school enrolment rates).

[4] Rwanda is excluded due to missing data on some of the variables, but the main conclusions drawn are compatible with this case.

[5] As multi-value variables can have more than two states, the QCA notation with lowercase and uppercase letters can no longer be used, and set notation has to be used to represent the cases and implicants as formal expressions. Each expression consists of one or more literals $X_i^{S_n}$ where X_i is a variable of the data set and S_n is a set of values of the variable. $I=A\{0,1\}$ indicates that the implicant I represents all cases having a value of A which is either 0 or 1. For the HIVCHANGE (1,R), for example, the logical expression

M{0}*L{1} indicates that a low mortality rate (M) combined with a high literacy rate (L) is the logically minimal Boolean expression when including "logical remainders" (R) in the analysis. As with QCA, '+' stands for a Boolean OR and '*' for an AND. Expressions in the long brackets show alternative combinations of variables for the same cases.

[6] Togo and Zambia are included with the prime implicant A{1}L{1} but not with A{1}G{1}.

[7] Congo-Brazzaville is included with the prime implicant G{0}M{1}L{1} but not with G{0}M{1}A{1}.

APPENDIX

Appendix A. HIV Prevalence Rate in Sub-Saharan Africa

NAME	Adult HIV prevalence rate 2003	Adult HIV prevalence rate 1997	Change 1997-2003
Angola	3.9	2.1	1.8
Benin	1.9	2.1	-0.2
Botswana	37.3	25.1	12.2
Burkina Faso	4.2	7.2	-3
Burundi	6	8.3	-2.3
C.A.R.	13.5	10.8	2.7
Cameroon	6.9	4.9	2
Chad	4.8	2.7	2.1
Comoros	0.1	0.1	0
Congo, D.R.	4.2	4.35	-0.15
Congo-Brazzaville	4.9	7.8	-2.9
Cote d'Ivoire	7	10.1	-3.1
Djibouti	2.9	10.3	-7.4
Equatorial-Guinea	0.5	1.2	-0.7
Eritrea	2.7	3.2	-0.5
Ethiopia	4.4	9.3	-4.9
Gabon	8.1	4.3	3.8
Gambia	1.2	2.2	-1
Ghana	3.1	2.4	0.7
Guinea	3.2	2.1	1.1
Guinea-Bissau	2.5	2.3	0.2
Kenya	6.7	11.6	-4.9
Lesotho	28.9	8.4	20.5
Liberia	5.9	3.7	2.2
Madagascar	1.7	0.1	1.6
Malawi	14.2	14.9	-0.7
Mali	1.9	1.7	0.2
Mauritania	0.6	0.5	0.1
Mauritius	0.1	0.1	0
Mozambique	12.2	14.2	-2
Namibia	21.3	19.9	1.4
Niger	1.2	1.5	-0.3
Nigeria	5.4	4.2	1.2
Rwanda	5.1	12.8	-7.7
Senegal	0.8	1.8	-1
Sierra Leone	3	3.2	-0.2
South Africa	21.5	12.9	8.6
Swaziland	38.8	18.5	20.3
Tanzania	8.8	9.4	-0.6
Togo	4.1	8.5	-4.4
Uganda	4.1	9.5	-5.4
Zambia	16.5	19.1	-2.6
Zimbabwe	24.6	25.8	-1.2

Notes and sources: AdultHIV97: Estimated number of Adults (15-49) living with HIV/AIDS rate % end 1997 (UNAIDS 1998), AdultHIV03: Estimated number of Adults (15-49) living with HIV/AIDS rate % end 2003 (UNAIDS 2004), HIVChange: Change in the HIV/AIDS rate 1997 – 2003.

Chapter 8

DIVERSITY, IDEAL TYPES AND FUZZY SETS IN COMPARATIVE WELFARE STATE RESEARCH

Jon Kvist
The Danish National Institute of Social Research

1. INTRODUCTION

Assessing diversity remains a big challenge in social science. Diversity implies qualitative and quantitative differentiation, that is of similarities and differences in kind and degree. One hundred years ago Max Weber suggested to study the conformity of cases to analytical constructs by way of constructing ideal types as yardsticks (Weber 1904).

In the last 15 years diversity and ideal types have taken centre stage in comparative welfare state research, a growing field of the social sciences characterized by a fruitful dialogue between qualitative and quantitative oriented researchers (Amenta 2003). With the influential *Three Worlds of Welfare Capitalism*, Gøsta Esping-Andersen (1990) placed diversity firmly on the research agenda. The Liberal, Conservative, and Social Democratic welfare state regimes depict ideal types for different groups of real welfare states that have undergone distinct political-institutional trajectories, or paths, in their historical development. At the same time, the ideal types also encapsulate distinct political economies with regard to the role of the state vis-à-vis the market and the family (further elaborated in Esping-Andersen 1999). These ideal types have become starting points for most subsequent studies of the causes and consequences of welfare state diversity.

Political scientists, for example, interested in current welfare reforms take issue with the idea that reforms follow distinct paths mainly given by their welfare state's (ideal typical) institutional setup, as argued perhaps most notably by Paul Pierson (1994, 1996, and 2001). Issues of key interest concern the extent to which welfare states are similar and different across time and place. Main questions addressed concern whether welfare state reforms amount to qualitative change, that is differences in kind, or quantitative change, that is difference in degree, and whether reforms amount to convergence or divergence across welfare states. Despite the rich dialogue between researchers there is no consensus on the nature of welfare state reform (e.g. Gilbert 2002). In part disagreement derives from different conceptualizations of the welfare state (Clayton and Pontusson 1998). Indeed different operationalizations and data may account for large part of the controversy surrounding the assessment of contemporary welfare reform.

Fortunately a new method for the social sciences, Fuzzy Sets (FS), may help researchers to rigorously study diversity and thus shed new light on such issues. This method has most recently been promoted in Charles Ragin's *Fuzzy Set Social Science* (2000). Ragin eloquently set out the rationale and logical operations for using FS in social science. But not everybody likes the new kid on the block. Most notably, Ragin has been criticized for not paying more attention to the construction of sets and the assignment of fuzzy set membership scores (see, for example, Verkuilen 2001). As also made clear by Ragin the very potential of fuzzy set social science stands and falls with the quality of this part of the work in the analysis. This chapter will therefore focus on the construction of sets and the use of FS in analyzing concepts and ideal types using an example from comparative welfare state research.

The chapter proceeds as follows. First, we briefly set out the scene of welfare state diversity. Second, we present and discuss the first main element of fuzzy-set analysis, namely the idea that concepts, aspects, or variables can be conceived and operationalized as FS. Then we present and discuss the second main element of fuzzy-set analysis, i.e. that cases can be seen as configurations of aspects, which we demonstrate by setting up two analytical constructs, or ideal types, for, respectively, social citizenship of unemployment and child family policy models. Third, we look at the categorization of cases in two illustrative analysis of the conformity of Nordic countries in the 1990s to a number of ideal types. We conclude by discussing the usefulness of the method advanced.

2. WELFARE STATE DIVERSITY

Comparative welfare state research took off after the Second World War. T.H. Marshall argued that the welfare state constituted the triumph of modern societies with social rights epitomizing the realization of full citizenship (Marshall 1950). Today it is largely uncontested that social rights constitute the cornerstone of the welfare state (Esping-Andersen 1990, Barbalet 1988). Whereas scholars differed in their theoretical starting points (see Huber *et.al.* 1993, Myles and Quadagno 2002) they shared to differing extent a neglect of interest in the welfare state itself as was evident in Marshall's work. Not seldom the empirical indicator for the welfare state was boiled down to share of GDP used on public social expenditures, as this, it was argued, reflected the 'welfare effort' of individual states. As made clear repeatedly by Esping-Andersen, Pierson, and Adema just to mention a few, an expenditure measure has little to do with levels or distribution of welfare, nor does it reflect on actors' motives (Esping-Andersen 1990, Pierson 1994, Adema 1999).

At the heart of the dispute on the nature and extent of recent welfare reform is the study of the dependant variable, the welfare state (Palier 2002). Whereas most scholars share a general, theoretical understanding of the welfare state they differ in how they translate theoretical concepts into empirical indicators, their view of cases and in their categorization of cases. Different methodological approaches, operationalizations of the dependant variable and empirical data go a long way to explain the divergent interpretations of welfare reforms.

The welfare state resembles Pandora's box since it consists of an interwoven bundle of different policies on taxation, housing, health, education, social affairs and labor markets, just to mention a few, that in turn is made up by a variety of policy programs. Against this complex reality generalizing statements like proclaiming 'resilience' or 'convergence' appear rather bold. They heroically assume homogeneity of the direction and scope of changes across different types of welfare states, across policy areas within given national welfare states, and, even, within different policy areas.

For illustrative purposes table 8.1 looks at two welfare state policies, and show that 'resilience' makes up only one out of nine possible combinations of less, the same or more of these policies. The other eight quadrants demonstrate situations of 'retrenchment' depicted by the crisis literature and defined by less of one or both policies (quadrants 1, 2 and 4), 'restructuring' with more of one policy and less of the other (3 and 7) or 'expansion' of one or both policies (6, 8 and 9).

Table 8.1. Assessing Change across Two Policies

		Policy 1		
		Less	Same	More
Policy 2	Less	(1) Retrenchment	(2) Retrenchment	(3) Restructuring
	Same	(4) Retrenchment	(5) Resilience	(6) Expansion
	More	(7) Restructuring	(8) Expansion	(9) Expansion

Operating with more than two welfare state policies evidently increase the complexities at hand. In any case, whether one or the other type of change characterizes a given policy, national welfare state, welfare state type, or, ultimately, all welfare states is a question to be addressed in empirical investigations.

Nevertheless, the picture becomes further complicated as table 8.1 in fact mimics the crude one-dimensional view of change which, as Pierson rightly argues, is dominant in the literature, i.e. that change is measured along a single continuum stretching from the intact or even expanding welfare state on one end to the seriously eroded or dismantled on the other (Pierson 2001: 421). When an aspect of a policy, say, the coverage of child family policies increases, this is by most sociologists and political scientists taken to be a case of expansion, preserving status quo is perceived as resilience and benefit decreases as retrenchment.

Such approaches to the study of welfare state diversity reflect the view of cases when approached by quantitative methods. They excel in making generalizations, but do not provide an informed understanding of specific cases. This is partly because these methods primarily conceive aspects or variables as separable identities, whereas these variables interact meaningfully according to the ideal typical logic (Becker 1998; Mahoney 2003; see also Cronqvist and Berg-Schlosser, in this volume).

This is a simplistic notion of change as mainly involving differences in degree. It runs the risk of ignoring, at least, two important types of changes in kind. The first takes place within given types of welfare states. Welfare states are not static but change over time. For example the Liberal welfare state of today is different from the one prevalent thirty years ago. We may thus want to argue that even incremental changes in degree at some point in time have accumulated to become a change in kind. The second change in kind takes place between welfare states types, i.e. developments mean that the very nature of a given welfare state has changed so that it belongs to another welfare state ideal type than at the onset of the period in question. Both changes in kind follow from Esping-Andersen's (1990) work on the complexities of the political economy of welfare states: welfare state diversity and change cannot be boiled down to a crude dichotomy of more or less on one or more separate dimensions. Welfare state ideal types are sites for configurations of aspects or variables, the latter cannot be examined in isolation.

Therefore the concept of 'path dependency' that is frequently used to note that welfare states develop within given ideal type trajectories by having the same or more of something (e.g. Pierson 1996) must be supplemented not only by concepts like 'path reversal' (less of the same) but, more importantly, also 'path change' (something else instead of the same), if, in theory, such classificatory concepts are to encompass all possible types of welfare state change. On the backdrop of the historical-institutional trajectories of Esping-Andersen's welfare state ideal types and Pierson's work on feedback mechanisms, it is of little surprise that the concept of path dependency has gained so much currency in contemporary welfare state research. But just as the welfare state ideal types have been accused of providing a static view on welfare states, the path dependency concept may be accused of providing a one-dimensional view on change.

In qualitative studies of the welfare state, configurations of variables or aspects take centre stage. A holistic view of the social world, *in casu* the welfare state, dominates studies using qualitative methods. This allows qualitatively oriented researchers to appreciate how differences in the level or configurations of cases constitute differences in type or kind rather than in degree or level (Yin 1994). However, appreciating the complexity of the social world comes at a price. For qualitative researchers, the price is a more limited number of cases than in most quantitative studies, and a general weakness in formalizing the extent of differences between cases of the same kind. In sum, quantitatively variable-oriented research focuses on generality and variation among cases within categories, whereas qualitatively case-oriented research focuses on complexity and categorization of cases (Ragin 2000).

To make sense of current welfare state reforms we thus need an approach that allows us to simultaneously access quantitative and qualitative differentiation, i.e. the diversity among welfare states and the kind of change they undergo. Fortunately, the outline of a diversity-oriented approach is emerging, namely the application of fuzzy-set theory to social science research (see Ragin 2000).

Here we will demonstrate how this new method can be used to study ideal types by first sketching out the main elements and basic operations in fuzzy-set theory, and, second, by applying it in a simple illustrative example of comparative social policy analysis. It will show that fuzzy-set theory allows for the simultaneous study of differences in kind and in degree, i.e. diversity. Because of these inherent features it is particularly well-suited to study conformity to ideal types as it can assess both to which ideal type a particular part of the real world belongs as well as the degree to which it belongs to this ideal type. Fuzzy-set theory was originally conceived by Lotfi Zadeh in 1965, and its application to the social sciences is advanced by Charles Ragin (2000). Here we will not deal with fuzzy-set causal analysis, but merely concentrate on what could be called 'fuzzy-set ideal type analysis'. At the core of fuzzy-set social science is a perception of cases as configurations of aspects so that a difference in one aspect may constitute a difference in kind and not just in degree. At the same time, the fuzzy-set approach allows partial membership of a case in a given configuration. Consequently, using the fuzzy-set approach allows us to study differences in both kind and degree at the same time. Among other things, this makes it possible to evaluate cases relative to their membership of specified ideal types.

The evidence concerns the Scandinavian welfare states in the area of child family policy in the 1990s. This is close to perfect data for this ideal type analysis. Theoretically, the existence of a 'Nordic welfare model' was solidified by Esping-Andersen's 'Social Democratic regime', and the Nordic countries is the most distinctive of all country groups (Castles 1993). Of relevance for the two policy areas, the model is characterized by a universal and generous income transfer system, local and publicly funded social services to cater for all needs and the whole population (Erikson *et.al.* 1987, Kangas 1994, Korpi and Palme 1998, Kvist 1999, Sipilä 1997). Moreover, these various attributes are thought to interact and reinforce each other, only together do they constitute the whole that we may describe as the Social Democratic model (Esping-Andersen and Korpi 1987, Kvist 1999).

These characteristics commonly result in the Social Democratic regime being portrayed as 'big and fat' compared to the more 'lean and mean' models in Anglo Saxon and Continental European countries. Nordic countries should thus be the most likely candidates for retrenching their welfare state with speed and determination if called for by economic or political pressures. And indeed, the period and policy areas in question provide near laboratory like settings for an examination of diversity and change due to the very different economic and political experiences of these countries in the period. For example, Denmark and Norway experienced a favorable economic development, especially in the second half of the decade, whereas Sweden and Finland faced a recession in the first half. Finland and Sweden became members of the EU while Norway opted to cooperate within the EEA-agreement. Denmark was the sole member of the EU at the start of the 1990s and the first of these countries to experience a shift from Conservative to Social Democratic led coalition government.

3. CONCEPTUALISATION – BRIDGING THE GAP BETWEEN THE WORLD OF LANGUAGE AND THE WORLD OF EMPIRICAL ANALYSIS

Perhaps the most salient aspect of fuzzy-set theory is that it allows researchers to bridge the gap between the world of language and the world of empirical analysis. As we saw above, quantitative researchers tend to study variables whereas qualitative researchers look at aspects of cases and their possible combinations. In contrast, the fuzzy-set approach takes its starting point in concepts. Concepts belong to the world of natural language. In social science theoretical, qualifying, and other abstract and verbal concepts are abundant. Within comparative welfare state research take, for example, a key theoretical concept like 'social citizenship' constituted by 'social rights' and 'social obligations' (Marshall 1950), qualifying concepts like 'universal' and 'generous', and an ideal type like the 'Social Democratic welfare state regime' (Esping-Andersen 1990, 1999) constituted by universal, generous social rights (Korpi and Palme 1998, Kvist 2002). All these theoretical concepts and analytical constructs have precise meaning to the researchers using them.

However, cases have differing degrees of membership in the set of cases with 'social citizenship', 'universality', 'generosity', and 'Social Democratic welfare states', and there are no crisp boundaries between, for example, being a case with generous benefits and a case without. Fuzzy-set theory provides a framework that gives the opportunity to measure verbal concepts in a precise way. Thus, fuzzy-set theory does not mean imprecise or fuzzy measurement, nor that concepts are vague or fuzzy in the conventional meaning, but rather that the concepts or phenomena under study can be operationalized as fuzzy sets allowing cases to have graded membership in such sets. Fuzzy-set theory provides a method for dealing with social science concepts. In fact, fuzzy-set theory offers a precise way of analyzing theoretical concepts. This first main element of fuzzy-set theory builds on crisp set theory.

3.1 The Crisp Set Approach

Crisp set theory underlies much of social science research as, for example, when qualitatively oriented researchers make typologies and quantitatively oriented researchers dichotomize variables. At its heart crisp set theory works as an exclusion mechanism. Either something is in or out of a set. Sets have crisp boundaries defining which cases or elements are in or out of sets. For example in set A, elements which are not members of set A are members of the complement set not-A. This is also called the negation principle, and is denoted by the set theoretical symbol '~'. The intersection operation represents logical AND, for example, whether case x is in set A AND in set B. In set theory it is denoted by the symbol '*'. The union operation represents logical OR, that is, whether case x is in set A OR B. In set theory it is denoted by the symbol '+'.

Crisp set theory can be seen as a framework for Aristotelian logic. Over 2,000 years ago, Aristotle formulated the law of the excluded middle and the law of non-contradiction. In crisp set theory these laws are formalized:

- The law of the excluded middle. A OR not-A. This law deals with the union of sets, where one takes all binary unit lists and takes the highest value for the corresponding slots. For example, the two sets (1 0) OR (0 1) equals (1 1).
- The law of non-contradiction. A ≠ not-A. This law deals with the intersection of sets, where one takes all binary unit lists and takes the

smallest value for the corresponding slots. For example, the two sets (1 0) AND (0 1) equals the empty set (0 0).

But how does the crisp set approach deal with theoretical concepts? We can illustrate this with an example. Imagine the situation of the unemployed. How do we determine whether their social rights are strong or weak, good or bad? It boils down to the classic problem in social science of where to draw the line.

A common research strategy to help set the line is to make use of averages or medians, and let cases be categorized accordingly. Benefit with payment levels above the median or average are then typically portrayed as strong social rights and those with payment levels below as weak social rights. However, this translation of mathematical language into formal language is problematic in a number of ways. First, it portrays the world as black and white when in reality the world is mostly shades of grey. Benefits, for example, are rarely fully generous or fully not-generous, but somewhere in between. Second, the practical procedure of rounding off raises a series of problems in itself. Averages are sample specific, theoretical concepts and ideal types are not.

Evaluating change and identifying qualitative breakpoints is another problem. If, for example, a benefit equals 100% of previous earnings, most would agree that this is a truly generous benefit. If we deduct 1% income compensation, most would still regard this as an incremental change and the benefit would still be judged to be generous. However, how many times can we deduct 1%, before the benefit can no longer be seen as generous? Clearly, when the income compensation moves towards zero, it becomes absurd to call it a generous benefit. For this reason, it seems fruitful to operate with shades of grey, in this case with differing degrees of benefit generosity.

A particularly troubling case of the conventional rounding off to A or not-A, to generous or not-generous, arises in situations of meaningful ambiguity. A well-known example is that of judging whether the glass is half-full or half-empty. In this situation one stage or category involves the other; a benefit that is half generous suggests that it is at the same time half not-generous. Or, in the language of set theory, sometimes A = not-A.

3.2 The Fuzzy Set Approach

In practice, fuzzy set theory works by drawing a curve between opposites, between A and not-A, between generous and not-generous. Information, substantive knowledge and theories help us to draw this curve. FS can take all possible shapes (linear, S-function, Bell-curve, etc), where the specific shape should resemble the given concept as closely as possible. So the creation of a fuzzy set is a process of operationalizing a concept – vague or not – into the 0 to 1 metric, from being fully out to fully in the set.

By having to draw a curve reflecting the particular concept under consideration, the focus of the researcher becomes centered on the concept rather than the variables themselves. In fact, this moves the analysis closer to the theoretical body that deals with concepts in the first place (Ragin 2000). It is more informative to talk of 'generous countries' than 'countries with a net replacement rate above X percentage'. This does not mean, however, that variables should be left behind, but rather that they should be transformed to FS. For example, replacement rates can be transformed to a fuzzy set on generosity. This involves setting a number of qualitative breakpoints to help the translation of raw data, or replacement rates, to FS. The first qualitative breakpoint is when the benefit is fully not-generous, below which variation is meaningless as it does not make sense to distinguish between the degree that benefits exceed fully not-generous benefits. The second qualitative breakpoint is when the benefit is fully generous, above which variation is meaningless as it does not make sense to distinguish between the degree that benefits exceed fully generous benefits. The third qualitative breakpoint is the cross-over point, where the benefit goes from being more not-generous than generous to become more generous than not-generous. As a benefit increases, it enters a world where it has properties of both generosity and not-generosity at the same time. A benefit that is not fully generous is also somewhat not-generous. This violates the Aristotelian Law of non-contradiction.

3.3 Empirical Indicators and Fuzzy Sets

Fuzzy set theory demands a high degree of correspondence between concepts and fuzzy membership scores in sets established to reflect such concepts. Therefore it is essential that great attention is paid to the analytical construction of the concepts, the criteria for establishing qualitative breaking points, and the empirical evidence. These crucial decisions should be made on the basis of theories, substantive knowledge, and the availability and nature of data. In any case, the decisions made should be explicit to allow for scientific dialogue and replication of the analysis.

Let us illustrate this. In the analysis of child family policies we use three sets for concepts related to the generosity of child allowances, and the universality and quality of childcare. These have been chosen as the literature has identified the generosity of child family allowances as a hallmark within child family policy since it reflects the public-private division of the economic costs of raising children. Universality of childcare reflects on the similar division of care responsibilities and hence also the autonomy of traditional care givers, most notably women in families (e.g. Orloff 1993). Finally, the quality of childcare is identified to inform about the priority given to children and their later life chances (e.g. Esping-Andersen 2002).

Having identified valid empirical indicators for the relevant theoretical concepts we must now calibrate the sets. Again this must be done informed by theoretical and substantive knowledge as it impacts on the measurement of fuzzy membership scores. Here fuzzy-set theory is helpful in that it allows for neighboring concepts to be linked via subsets. Whereas fully generous and fully not-generous each equal an extreme, there are many intermediary concepts which link these two categories. Depending on substance of the concept and raw material, various fuzzy category intervals may be used (see Ragin 2000). Here we use a nine value fuzzy set where continuous fuzzy scores between 0 (fully out) and 1 (fully in) indicate partial membership in the following way:

- Scores between 0.83 and 0.99 indicate that the case is almost fully in the set of, for example, 'generous' countries;
- 0.67 to 0.82 indicate fairly in;
- 0.51 to 0.66 is more or less in;
- 0.5 is the cross-over point where the case is neither more in nor more out;
- 0.33 to 0.49 is more or less out;
- 0.17 to 0.32 is fairly out; and
- 0.01 to 0.16 is almost fully out.

This nine value fuzzy set is used throughout the chapter to help us to translate interval fuzzy membership scores into verbal concepts or *verbal qualifiers*. For example, if a benefit gets a fuzzy score of 0.75 this is translated into the verbal concept 'fairly generous' and a fuzzy score of 0.60 translates to 'more or less generous'. This illustrates the 'second translation' in fuzzy-set theory. As described above, the first translation concerns translating a theoretical concept to a line connecting two opposites. After measurement and computation, the result is then translated back into natural language for presentational purposes - the second translation.

3.4 Child Family Policies

Returning to the example of child family policies, we shall now explain the reasoning behind the identification of the empirical indicators, criteria for qualitative breaking points, and procedures for translation of raw data into fuzzy membership values.

Generosity of child family allowances is assessed according to their impact on the net disposable income on families. From three stylized family types (with different number and age of children) we find the average increase in disposable income per child caused by child family allowances.

Based on substantive knowledge from national studies of household budgets we have established qualitative breaking points for when benefits can be judged to cover or more the costs associated with raising children (e.g. CASA 1993, and Hansen 1998). If child family allowances make the disposable income to increase with more than six percent, this country is seen as being fully in the set of countries with generous child family allowances. Since increases of less than 1.4 percent are judged to be trivial in relation to the costs of having children, such countries are therefore fully out the set.

Universality of childcare is measured by the share of children in childcare. Since the policy aim is not to place all children at all times in childcare we cannot use an interval scale from 0 to 100 %. Instead we introduce a qualitative breaking point at 80% coverage above which countries are seen as having fully universal child care. The relative high cut-of point takes account of the relative high employment rate of Nordic women and grandmothers that have traditionally cared of children (Leira 1992). The qualitative breaking point at the other end is set at 20% coverage. Data concerns coverage in publicly supported childcare facilities like kindergartens and day care, independently of whether there are in the public or private sector. Informal childcare, which is of considerable scope in some countries, is not included as the ideal type concerns the welfare *state*. A number of other schemes may bias our measure on universality of child care. Leave schemes for maternity, father and parents granted for children below three years of age invalidate any measure of coverage. Children above five years of age mostly go to schools or in preschool schemes. For these reasons we focus on the situation of children between three and six years of age (alternatively pre-school age if this is lower than six years of age)

Quality of child care is measured by child/staff ratios which has been identified in American clinical studies as of importance for children's welfare, cognitive development and later life chances, including social mobility (Howes 1997, Peisner-Feinberg and Burchinal 1997). Other relevant empirical indicators like the education of careers were not possible to establish due to limited comparative reliable information. With regard to the calibration of child/staff ratios to fuzzy membership scores, this must take into account the age of the children and other characteristics. Based on Brazelton' studies, average child/staff ratios for three to six year olds should be less than three children per staff to be a sign of high quality, the upper qualitative breaking point, less than six children is sign of good quality (cross-over point), and more than nine children is a sign of fully bad quality (the lower qualitative breaking point) (Brazelton 1992).

Table 8.2. Specification of Empirical Indicators for Child Family Policies and the Translation of Raw Data into Fuzzy Membership Scores and Verbal Labels

Empirical Indicators			Translation of raw data into:	
Child family policies				
Generosity	*Universality*	*Quality*	Fuzzy membership scores	Verbal labels
≥6.00	>80	<3.00	1	Fully in the set
5.20-5.99	71-80	3.00-3.99	0.84-0.99	Almost fully in the set
4.40-5.19	61-70	4.00-4.99	0.68-0.83	Fairly in the set
3.60-4.39	51-60	5.00-5.99	0.51-0.67	More or less in the set
3.50-3.59	50	6.00	0.50	Cross-over point
2.80-3.49	40-49	6.01-7.00	0.34-0.49	More or less out of the set
2.10-2.79	30-39	7.01-8.00	0.18-0.33	Fairly out of the set
1.40-2.09	20-29	8.01-8.99	0.01-0.17	Almost fully out of the set
<1.40	<20	≥9.00	0	Fully out of the set

Notes: *Generosity* of child family policies measured by the average increase in disposable net income caused by Child family allowances (%). *Universality* measured by the share of children between 3 and six years of age in child care (%). *Quality* measured by the child/staff ratio in child care.

Table 8.2 shows how fuzzy membership scores are translated into nine verbal labels, ranging from, for example 'fully accessible' to 'fully not accessible'. These labels are used in the analysis of cases' conformity to concepts and ideal types below. For example, if a child care benefit scores 4.5 in the set on quality this is translated into and presented as a benefit of a 'fairly good quality'.

After having established empirical indicators and procedures for translating raw data into fuzzy scores and verbal labels, we may now proceed to the operations on FS. That is, we can now set out how FS on concepts can be configured in various ways to construct ideal types.

3.5 Operations on Fuzzy Sets

In short, fuzzy-set theory can be said to provide a calculus of compatibility that can be applied in ideal type analysis (but for causal analysis, see Ragin 2000). Figure 1 shows the operations on FS that are particularly useful in studying ideal types, i.e. complement, union and intersection.

Operations on FS are generalizations of operations on crisp sets (see Zadeh 1965; Ragin 2000). Suppose case x has membership value v^a in fuzzy set A, membership value v^b in fuzzy set B, and membership value v^c in fuzzy set C:

- Complement. The value of x in ~A is $1-v^a$. This operation finds the complement to A, and is called *principle of negation* in fuzzy set theory.
- Intersection. The value of x in A*B*C is the minimum value of v^a, v^b, and

v^c. This operation represents logical AND, and is called the *minimum principle* in fuzzy set theory.
- Union. The value of x in A+B+C is the maximum value of of v^a, v^b, and v^c. This operation represents logical OR, and is called the *maximum principle*.

The complement operation is particularly helpful when looking only at one aspect of a case, e.g. the generosity and non-generosity of a case, whereas the intersection and union operations are useful when analyzing analytical constructs such as ideal types that consist of specific configurations of aspects. And this is exactly what we will turn to now.

3.6 Configuration - Ideal Types and Cases as Configurations of Aspects

The second main element of fuzzy-set theory that we will touch upon here concerns its configurational or holistic view (Ragin 2000). In short it implies that cases are seen as configurations of aspects (or sets) so that a difference in one aspect may constitute a difference in kind and not just in degree. The configurational view of cases is salient within qualitative case-oriented research where different aspects of a case are understood in relation to each other and to the whole they form. In contrast, conventional quantitative variable-oriented research is alien to understanding a case's variables in relation to each other. Instead variable-oriented research tends to look for variation among variables across cases (for an example on benefit generosity, see Scarpetta 1996). Variables are thus seen as independent of each other, and when they are not, researchers often find themselves busy trying to control for interaction effects among variables. However, in fuzzy-set ideal type analysis it is the very combination of variables, or aspects, which forms the analytical construct, the ideal type.

3.7 The Analytical Property Space

We found three aspects of relevance for child family policy models. Their possible eight combinations are set out in the analytical property space in table 8.3. The first two aspects, generosity and universality, are perhaps the least contested as they echo the work on social rights quoted above. The third aspect, quality of childcare, is not new in a theoretical sense, but is rarely included in empirical analysis. At the same time, the distinction between high and low quality which are associated with, respectively, new and old versions of the various models, e.g., New versus Old Social Democratic Model, aims to catch the increased attention paid by some politicians and academics to the importance of early, high quality interventions to secure children's welfare and later life chances.

In table 8.3 the New Social Democratic Child family policy model can be expressed in fuzzy-set terms as the ideal typical location: GENEROUS*UNIVERSAL*QUALITY, or as the combination of generous child family allowances with universal child care of good quality.

Table 8.3. The Analytical Property Space and Ideal Types: Child Family Policies and Welfare State Ideal Types

Child family policies			Welfare state
Generosity (G)	Universality (U)	Quality (Q)	ideal type
G (high)	U (encompassing)	Q (high)	New Social Democratic
G (high)	U (encompassing)	~Q (low)	Old Social Democratic
G (high)	~U (limited)	Q (high)	New Labour
G (high)	~U (limited)	~Q (low)	Old Labour
~G (low)	U (encompassing)	Q (high)	New Conservative
~G (low)	U (encompassing)	~Q (low)	Old Conservative
~G (low)	~U (limited)	Q (high)	New Liberal
~G (low)	~U (limited)	~Q (low)	Old Liberal

In general, this view of cases as configurations of aspects implements the idea that a single difference in an aspect between two cases may constitute a difference in kind - a qualitative distinction. Moreover, the analytical property spaces or truth tables show that aspects should not be seen as independent, separable variables, but rather as elements of configurations (Ragin 2000). Even though the aspects are not taken out of the blue, it may be that not all eight possible combinations have empirical instances or are of theoretical relevance. When some of the ideal types may lack empirical cases or be irrelevant, their listing still help the researcher to get an overview of the subject matter (see Ragin 1987, Becker 1998, and Ragin 2000 for set theoretical ways to reduce the property space).

3.8 Categorization – Studying Cases' Proximity to Ideal Types

Graphically, the eight possible models can be said to constitute corners in a cube: each corner represents an ideal typical location in the analytical space. The configurational view of cases within fuzzy-set theory has in this way allowed us to make a typology of possible ideal types. They are the analytical constructs formed by the possible combinations of the identified relevant aspects of cases; the corners of the cube. In reality, however, not all corners or ideal types will find empirical instances as the social world is characterized by limited diversity (Ragin 1987). Also, very rarely will a given concrete phenomenon be placed in a corner – a perfect match to the ideal type. Instead cases will be situated somewhere inside the cube.

By combining FS with the configurational view of cases, fuzzy-set theory gives us the opportunity to interrogate the inside of the cube, to find out which corner, or ideal type, a case belongs to as well as its degree of membership of the various possible combinations. Quantitative change is when a case's membership of an ideal type changes over time – the degree of membership changes.

In contrast, qualitative change is when a case shifts from having membership of one ideal type to another. This happens when the membership score shifts over the cross-over point for one or more of the constitutive aspects. This is why the cross-over points are considered one of the qualitative breakpoint anchors. At the same time is has to be kept in mind that a qualitative change only occurs to the extent that the cross-over points have true substantive meaning. In our example, if a case goes from 0.51 to 0.49 on generosity of benefits, this is a trivial change insofar as it has moved from being the weakest possible member of one type to become the weakest possible member of another, a mere shift within the region of great ambiguity. In other examples, where the cross-over point has greater substantive significance than in the example of generosity, however, such a shift could amount to real qualitative change.

After having identified our analytical constructs and their constitutive aspects, the next step is to transform these aspects into FS, and then apply the operations of fuzzy-set theory to determine the locations of cases outside the corners, but inside the cube. In the previous section we constructed the FS, so we can move on the analysis of our cases' conformity to ideal types.

4. IDEAL TYPE ANALYSIS

Table 8.4 above sets out countries' fuzzy membership scores on the eight possible welfare state ideal types for child family policy. Using these qualitative distinctions we can analyze not only which ideal type a country belongs to and its degree of membership, but also which ideal types the country is closest to and furthest away from. This enables us to make nuanced judgments on the (shifting) character of the national welfare states. As table 8.4 shows, all four countries belonged to the New Social Democratic model throughout the 1990s. There were, in other words, no qualitative changes brought about by recent welfare reforms. However, they did result in noticeable changes in degree. Denmark and Norway moved from 'more or less' to 'fairly' New Social Democratic child family policies. Finland moved

Table 8.4. Fuzzy Membership Scores for Nordic Child Family Policies in Welfare State Ideal Types, 1990-99

Country	Year	New Social Democratic	Old Social Democratic	New Labour	Old Labour	New Conservative	Old Conservative	New Liberal	Old Liberal
Denmark	1990	.53	.47	.44	.44	.13	.13	.13	.13
	1995	.65	.29	.35	.29	.01	.01	.01	.01
	1999	.68	.29	.32	.29	.00	.00	.00	.00
Finland	1990	.51	.49	.00	.00	.37	.37	.00	.00
	1995	.58	.37	.00	.00	.42	.37	.00	.00
	1999	.63	.37	.21	.21	.19	.19	.19	.19
Norway	1990	.62	.25	.32	.25	.38	.25	.32	.25
	1995	.68	.25	.32	.25	.32	.25	.32	.25
	1999	.75	.25	.32	.25	.09	.25	.09	.09
Sweden	1990	.71	.29	.11	.11	.27	.27	.11	.11
	1995	.63	.37	.24	.24	.13	.13	.13	.13
	1999	.63	.37	.33	.33	.03	.03	.03	.03

Sources: Hansen (various years); NOSOSKO (various years); Kvist (2000, 2001)

in the same direction but because of a lower initial membership it still belongs more or less to the New Social Democratic model. In contrast Sweden moved in the exact opposite direction going from 'fairly' to 'more or less' in. In 1999 Sweden thus belonged less to the New Social Democratic welfare state ideal type than Denmark and Norway with regard to child family policies.

4. IDEAL TYPE ANALYSIS

Table 8.4 above sets out countries' fuzzy membership scores on the eight possible welfare state ideal types for child family policy. Using these qualitative distinctions we can analyze not only which ideal type a country belongs to and its degree of membership, but also which ideal types the country is closest to and furthest away from. This enables us to make nuanced judgments on the (shifting) character of the national welfare states. As table 8.4 shows, all four countries belonged to the New Social Democratic model throughout the 1990s. There were, in other words, no qualitative changes brought about by recent welfare reforms. However, they did result in noticeable changes in degree. Denmark and Norway moved from 'more or less' to 'fairly' New Social Democratic child family policies. Finland moved in the same direction but because of a lower initial membership it still belongs more or less to the New Social Democratic model. In contrast Sweden moved in the exact opposite direction going from 'fairly' to 'more or less' in. In 1999 Sweden thus belonged less to the New Social Democratic welfare state ideal type than Denmark and Norway with regard to child family policies.

5. CONCLUDING REMARKS

We have now illustrated how fuzzy-set theory can be used to study the conformity of specific phenomena to concepts and, in turn, ideal types. It entails four basic steps:

1. Informed by theoretical and substantive knowledge, identify the ideal types' aspects (equal to sets) and their configuration. This leads to the construction of a useful analytical property space.
2. Specify the cases' membership scores in the sets comprising this property space, i.e. scores reflecting the degrees to which cases are in or out of sets where 0 is fully out, 1 is fully in, and 0.5 is the crossover point, being neither more in nor more out.
3. Compute the membership of each case in the ideal typical model, i.e. the given location in the property space, using the principles of fuzzy-set theory.

4. Evaluate the homogeneity of cases by using the information from the previous step to measure the conformity of each case to the ideal typical instance.

The examples of analysis on policy change demonstrated a series of advantages of the fuzzy set approach with regard to conventional qualitative case-oriented methods and quantitative variable-oriented methods. Fuzzy-set theory demands on an explicit definition of the subject under investigation stimulated the exchange of ideas and knowledge accumulation. This helps contributions to theory development as exemplified by the impact of adding a new dimension, quality of child care, in ideal types on child family policy. Fuzzy-set theory also showed potential in bridging the world of natural language and empirical analysis in new ways (for a similar demonstration with 'crisp' dichotomous sets, see Sager and Befani, in this volume). The configurational view of cases gave a holistic view of cases that is not present in conventional statistical methods. Allowing for partial membership of the various aspects provided a better way to convey the diversity of the real world than dichotomies of yes/no assignments common in case-oriented approaches. In turn this made it possible to investigate the conformity of cases to ideal-typical locations and to evaluate the homogeneity of cases. In other words, fuzzy-set theory gives the opportunity to compare diversity - differences in kind and degree - across countries and over time in ways that have not been possible before. Thereby fuzzy-set theory gives us a new approach to study Weberian ideal types and to investigate how empirical phenomena are similar and how they deviate from some predefined measure.

Also we have argued that no fancy set theoretic operations can save an analysis with lousy sets. The old saying that researchers should spend about 75% of their time on the dependant variable indeed applies to fuzzy set analysis. The chapter demonstrates how researchers can construct good sets, analytical constructs and use the operations in fuzzy set theory to analyze concepts and ideal types and thereby categorize cases by engaging into a laborious dialogue with evidence and theory. The example illustrates how the fuzzy set approach enables fine-grained, theoretically informed analysis of diversity.

Chapter 9

SCENARIO-BUILDING METHODS AS A TOOL FOR POLICY ANALYSIS

António Brandão Moniz[1]
Universidade Nova de Lisboa

1. INTRODUCTION

In terms of innovative methods for policy analysis, the foresight and scenario building methods can be an interesting reference for social sciences. A scenario – as a central concept for the prospective analysis – can be considered as a rich and detailed portrait of a plausible future world. It is a useful tool for policy-makers to grasp problems clearly and comprehensively and to better pin-point challenges as well as opportunities in an overall framework. The purpose of scenario-building is policy decision making. A scenario is not the prediction of a specific future. Rather it can better be considered as a plausible description of what *might* occur. In this sense, scenarios describe events and trends as they could evolve. They are not simulations.

The term "scenario" comes from the dramatic arts. In theatre, a scenario refers to an outline of the plot; in movies, a scenario is a summary or set of directions for the sequence of action. Often in creating a scenario, the questions that are considered are of the following types: What is uncertain? What is inevitable? What are the driving forces of...? In general, this term has been used in two different ways: first, to describe a snapshot in time or the conditions of important variables at some particular time in the future; second, to describe the evolution from present conditions to one of several futures. The latter approach is generally preferred because it can lay out the causal chain of decisions and circumstances that lead from the present. Some authors try to introduce exclusive quantitative techniques to the method. The results are normally not very consistent and in this case it proves the need for a balanced use of qualitative as well quantitative techniques for data analysis.

In a book entitled *Toward The Year 2000*, Kahn and Weiner examined the future possibilities of world order, describing potential power alignments and international challenges to American security.[2] One of their scenarios depicted an arms control agreement between the United States and the former Soviet Union; another assumed the former Soviet Union would lose control of the Communist movement; a third projected construction of new alliances among countries. These authors also described the technology "hardware" of the future, which included centralized computer banks with extensive information on individuals as well as parents able to select the gender and personal characteristics of their children through genetic engineering (cf. UN-Millenium project, below).

Some corporations also developed scenarios as their planning became more sophisticated. For example, Shell International Petroleum Company used scenarios before the 1973 oil shock. The method proved useful in allowing Shell to anticipate the rise and subsequent fall of oil prices. In the mid-80s, this same corporation created scenarios that focused on the future of the Soviet Union because that country was a major competitor in the European natural gas market. This kind of applications of the method are well disseminated in the economic structures, although mainly with large-sized and internationally operating firms, or with state institutions and public administration (Ministry of Economy or Finances, Ministry of Health, central planning departments, statistical bureaus).

Thus, a scenario is a *policy analysis tool* that describes a possible set of future conditions. The most useful scenarios (for corporations, for policy decision makers) are those that display the conditions of important variables over time. In this approach, the quantitative underpinning enriches the narrative evolution of conditions or evolution of the variables; narratives describe the important events and developments that shape the variables. In this respect one may say that there is, to a certain extent, some compatibility with Charles Ragin's (1987, 2000) approach underpinning both QCA and Fuzzy Sets. However the specificity of scenario-building is that it is specifically aimed at *future* sets of conditions. Techniques such as QCA and its extensions have (thus far) not been used specifically for scenario-building.

Some examples of these exercises will be presented in this paper, either related to vision in science and technology developments, social and technological futures, or related to aggregated indicators on human development. Two cases (Japan and Germany) are held on behalf of the ministries of science and education (respectively, Ministry of Education, Culture, Sports, Science and Technology (MEXT) and the *Bundesministerium für Bildung und Forschung* (BMBF)), and another with the support of United Nations.

2. APPROACHING SOME FORECASTING METHODS

One of the main references to the topic of foresight and policy analysis is Peter Schwartz, a member of the Royal Dutch/Shell scenario team, and he describes several steps in the scenario development process. In his main work, *The Art of the Long View,* he presents these process steps that include the following (Schwartz 1991):

a) identification of the focal issue or decision;
b) identification of the key forces and trends in the environment;
c) ranking the driving forces and trends by importance and uncertainty; selecting the scenario logics;
d) filling out the scenarios;
e) assessing the implications;
f) selecting the leading indicators and signposts for monitoring purposes.

Another reference author is Michel Godet, from the Laboratory for Investigation in Prospective Studies in Paris (Godet 1993). He begins the scenario development process by constructing a base image of the present state of a system. In his perspective, this image is described as broad in scope, detailed, and comprehensive, dynamic, and descriptive of forces for change.

The base image is built up by delineating the system being studied, including a complete listing of the variables that should be taken into consideration. It should also take into consideration the subdivisions of these variables (for example, the internal and external variables, as descriptive of the general explanatory environment). This step is followed by a search for the principal determinants of the system and their parameters, often using structural analysis. The scenario process involves examining the current situation and identifying the mechanisms and the leading actors (influencers of the system, through variables) that have controlled or altered the system in the past (Godet 1993). This process continues with the development of actors' strategies. Construction of the database is then followed by construction of the scenarios. This author combines various futures research techniques in scenario development. For example, he finds that morphological analysis can be used in scenario construction since scenarios are, in essence, a configuration of identified components.

Both futures studies and strategic management are in favour today within most forward-thinking organizations, but these two complementary research traditions have grown in logically separate ways. Godet seeks to show that there are powerful synergies between the two approaches, since all types of strategic planning and goal-setting presuppose a prior exploration of possible, probable, and desirable futures.

The frequent errors that occur in forecasting, and the noticeable absence of forecasts of crisis events, bear witness to the crisis within forecasting itself. Causes of errors include inaccurate data coupled with unstable models, lack of a global and qualitative approach, and explanation of the future in terms of the past. The future must be studied with a view to illuminating the present, which is the basic idea that inspires futures thinking, or foresight (*prospective*). *"Foresight is neither forecasting nor futurology, but a mode of thinking for action and against fatalism, which supplies a key to understanding and explaining crises. In a world characterized by uncertainty and by the risk of trends being disrupted, intellectual investment in undertaking* la prospective *is more necessary than ever"* (Godet 1985).

Godet's study also includes a critique of forecasting, pluralism and complementarity, the scenarios method, identifying key variables with the MICMAC method (*Matrices d'Impacts Croisés*, a French version of the cross-impact matrix developed by Godet in 1973), analysis of past and future plans (showing why the first oil crisis was predictable), expert consensus methods to reduce uncertainty, the SMIC method (French acronym for Cross Impact Systems and Matrices), principal concepts of strategic management, internal auditing and external assessment, the choice of strategic options, reappraising strategic planning (*"The main focus of planning is not the plan, but the process of reflection and concentration which leads to it"*), the secrets of excellence (citing Peters and Waterman), and three methodological recommendations to avoid errors of diagnosis: 1) ask the right questions—do not hesitate to think against the grain; 2) the key to success in seeking excellence is as likely to be found in the human factor as in the technological and financial factors; 3) consider methodologies not as ends in themselves but as tools to stimulate thought and communications.

Other authors, in a book edited in 1992 (by Joseph F. Coates and Jennifer Jarratt) entitled *The Future: Trends into the Twenty-First Century*, organized topics that have received substantial attention from futures scientists, planners and strategic decision makers. This study demonstrated the richness of approaches in futures studies. The authors identify six streams of development in the study of the future: science and technology, military interests, business, sociology, history, and the literary tradition. However, they also underline methods to explore the future, i.e., the identification of key elements of the system being studied, the identification of driving forces toward change or to maintain stability, the assessment of the force and direction of these trends, the development of alternative futures that include preferable visions, the consideration of "wild cards" low-probability, and the identification of appropriate actions. Coates and Jarratt point out the benefits of a good futures study: it should reveal and test assumptions, widen the scope of thinking about the future, and enable interpretation of events and developments.

Scenario-Building Methods

Nevertheless, one knows that many forecasts eventually fail. The authors justify that on the grounds of different limitations: the existence of mechanical extrapolation of trends, or unexamined assumptions, but also problems of limited expertise and (with similar weight) lack of imagination. In the beginning of the 90's they recognized that four global trends would become more critical in the next decades: women status and gender issues, international relations, population growth, and the impact of information technologies.

The methods used for the purpose of foresight on policy making can be classified in the following way:

Table 9.1. Forecasting Methods

Method	By technique		By purpose	
	Quantitative	Qualitative	Normative	Exploratory
Environmental scanning	X	X	X	X
Cross Impact Analysis	X	X	X	X
Decision Analysis	X		X	
Decision Models	X			X
Delphi		X	X	X
Econometrics	X		X	X
Futures Wheel		X	X	X
Gaming and Simulation	X	X	X	X
Genius Forecasting		X	X	X
Morphologic Analysis		X	X	
Participatory Methods		X	X	
Relevance Trees		X	X	
Scenarios	X	X	X	X
Statistical Modeling				X
System Dynamics	X			X
Structural Analysis		X		X
Technology Sequence		X	X	X
Time Series Forecasts	X			X
Trend Impact Analysis	X	X		X

Source: Gordon 1994: 8

Thus, "scenarios" (as well as "environmental scanning" and "cross impact analysis") rely on either qualitative or quantitative techniques, and are normative or exploratory in terms of their purpose. In fact, in contrast with exploratory forecasting, forecasting *tout court* can be distinguished as being normative. Normative work is based on norms or values. Exploratory forecasting explores what is possible regardless of what is desirable.

Hence *normative* uses of futures methods answer the following type of questions: what is the desirable future? What do we want to become? Decision analysis, participatory methods or morphological analysis, for instance, are explicitly normative. Conversely, *exploratory* uses of futures methods answer the question: what are the possible futures - whether they are desirable or not? Decision and statistical models, system dynamics, time series forecasts or trend impact analysis, for instance, are explicitly exploratory.

At this point we can conclude that forecasting studies are not being developed in isolation, but in the context of a policy-making process. In most cases, they are integrated as key instruments in this type of decisional process. An exclusive emphasis on formal methods of forecasting, particularly on complex quantitative methods, will often prove self-defeating. Other authors, as William Ascher and William H. Overholt (1983), seek to do the following:

a) to locate forecasting as one logical component of the decision-making or strategic planning process;
b) to analyze the psychological and bureaucratic relationship between the forecaster and the decision-maker;
c) to identify the properties of different analytic methods in the context of different purposes and organizational settings;
d) to emphasize the importance of political assumptions in non-political forecasting;
e) to show how to interrelate political and non-political factors;
f) to offer an organizational approach to political forecasting that is systematic but non-quantitative;
g) to recommend the use of systematic scenarios and an emphasis on forecasting as heuristics, rather than an excessive emphasis on predicting discrete outcomes;
h) to describe how to present forecast results so as to ensure their maximum effective use.

A few forecasting techniques enable one to include perceptions about such events, thus modifying an otherwise deterministic extrapolation, for example Trend Impact Analysis (TIA). The technique produces a range of outcomes rather than just a single value. It begins with an extrapolation of a time series. This is taken to be a "baseline forecast"; that is the future of the variable if there were no future trend-changing developments of the sort listed above. Next a list of such developments is constructed, using the analysts' imagination, literature search, Delphi[3], or any other technique. These developments might include unique technology, societal changes, political actions or any other change that may affect the future course of the variable. Each development on the list is expressed in terms of its expected probability of occurrence over the future time interval of concern, and, was it to occur, its impact on the variable under study.

Although it may present a more realistic view of the future, this technique involves great over-simplification. For example, it omits any interaction among the future events (the occurrence of one may well affect the probability of other events); the list of future events will certainly omit some that in retrospect will be seen as having been important; and the variable is taken to exist in isolation but in reality will be affected by other variables. Another means for improving the forecasts of the variables would be to include a cross impact analysis – or possibly some variation of QCA of fuzzy sets analysis (but this hasn't been attempted as yet), as such techniques lay a key emphasis on the interaction or combination between variables.

Taking these examples one can establish a stepwise sequence for the scenario building process:

- Definition of the *scenario space*. A scenario study begins by defining the domain of interest. This can include visions and scenario topics and themes. These emerge from the identification of trends obtained by the theoretical framework.
- Within each scenario, certain *key measures* must be described. These measures include forces such as economic growth, political and legislative organizational environment, technology infrastructures, or labour market dynamics, among others.
- A *list of events* will also appear in each scenario. Of course, the probabilities of the events are different in each scenario, and for example, it can make certain policies (technological, educational, employment, etc.) more or less likely to be successful.
- Although some authors prescribe the need for probability analysis and quantitative forecasting for each measure, the contrast of implications of the *alternative futures* can be considered as sufficient.

3. THE TECHNOLOGY FORESIGHT IN JAPAN (TOWARD THE YEAR 2030)

The Ministry of Education, Culture, Sports, Science and Technology (MEXT)[4] has conducted a technology forecast survey to ascertain the future direction of technology in Japan from a long-term viewpoint which is regularly conducted once every five years since 1971. After the first Delphi experiences in the 1960s in the USA, these regular surveys confirmed the rising importance of such a tool for the decision-making process in the field of science and technology. The latest survey (2000-2001) is the seventh in the series.

Incorporating more than a thousand topics, Japan's technology forecast survey is indeed extensive, ranging from the elucidation of principles to the practical use of technologies in all kinds of fields. For the survey, MEXT established a steering committee within NISTEP, and the Institute for Future Technology (IFTECH) established 14 "technology field" and 3 "needs field" subcommittees headed by members of the steering committee. The technology field subcommittees comprised technological experts in the appropriate field, and the needs field subcommittees comprised experts in the cultural and social sciences.

In contrast with the Futur project (Germany), the steering committee examined the overall structure, such as the survey plan and implementation guidelines, and studied the survey results across all fields. The technology field subcommittees set the survey topics, selected survey participants, and analyzed the survey results in their respective fields of expertise. The "needs field" subcommittees identified possible future trends in socioeconomic needs over the next 30 years. After analyzing the results, the "technology field" subcommittees compiled reports for their respective survey fields. In a similar way, the "needs field" subcommittees compiled reports summarizing the results from a needs perspective.

The "technology subcommittees" set the topics, taking into account the consolidated needs items by the respective subcommittees that examined the future socioeconomic needs. First, the "technology subcommittees" set the scope of the survey in each of the fields, examined the future direction of technological development, and prepared a framework that would also ensure that the important topics were not omitted. They then drew up a list of topics. They finally settled on 1065 topics for the survey. The survey fields of the Japanese Delphi exercise were the following: a) Information and communications, b) Electronics, c) Life science, d) Health and medical care, e) Agriculture, forestry, fisheries and food, f) Marine science and earth science, g) Space, h) Resources and energy, i) Environment, j) Materials and processes, k) Manufacturing, l) Distribution, m) Business and management, n) Urbanization and construction, o) Transportation, and p) Services.

A conventional Delphi method was applied. In this sense, it was also a method of consolidating respondents' views by repeatedly submitting the same questionnaire to a large number of people. In the second and subsequent questionnaires the respondents received a feedback on the results of the previous questionnaire so that they could reassess their answers to the questions in the light of the overall trend of views.

The respondents were selected on the basis of the recommendations of members in each of the technology subcommittees, i.e. a cross-section of representatives from industry, the government and academia. The second questionnaire (December 2000) asked respondents about the same topics as in the first questionnaire (August 2000), and included the results of the first questionnaire for reference.

As is mentioned in the final report of the 7th Delphi application in Japan, *"from our experiences in past technology foresights, we know that respondents tend to give higher priority to technologies in their own expert domains (professional bias). So in designing survey fields, there is a need to exercise caution when adopting narrow domains as independent fields. At the same time, though, we also know from past results and comparisons of the degree of importance of topics between fields that the results tend to be rational, and there are hardly any cases where the true importance of topics that have been ranked highly has been difficult to comprehend"* (NISTEP 2001 : 13).

For this Delphi exercise in Japan, 3809 round 2 questionnaires were sent out, and 2849 responses (response rate of 74.8%) were received on the following question: *"Considering Japan's future, what fields of science and technology do you believe should be given a high priority?"* In the second round, the respondents were able to reassess their views after looking at the aggregate results from all respondents belonging to their own particular fields. With regards to the coming 10-year period, "Earth science and environment technology", "information technology" and "life science technology" were the top three current priority science and technology fields, while "material technology", "manufacturing and management technology" and "social infrastructure technology" were the three lowest rated technologies, barely managing to score a third of the responses of the top three. However, responses changed for the question on "priority science and technology fields after 2010". The proportion of responses indicating "earth science and environment technology" and "life science technology" rose, as more than 90% of respondents judged these two as priority fields. Response rates for "social infrastructure technology" and "material technology" increased 50% over their corresponding rates for "current priority fields", indicating a perceived need to increase the weight of research and development in these fields as well over the long term. On the other hand, the response rate for "information-related technologies" dropped by about 60%. Only about half of the members of the information experts group chose information related technologies, while among the other five groups, the percentage was no more than about 30%.

In terms of scenario topics, the top ranking topic was "Development of technology capable of forecasting the occurrence of major earthquakes (magnitude 7 or above) several days in advance" from the marine science and earth science field. It jumped from 7th position in the previous survey. Next was "Major advances in technology for disposing of disused manufactured products, leading to the emergence of commercial services capable of reducing the final disposal volume to one-tenth the current level" from the services field; followed by "Practical use of technology for the safe disposal of highly radioactive solid waste" from the resources and energy field; "Identification and classification by the molecular etiology of the genes related to diabetes, hypertension, and arteriosclerosis, which are typical lifestyle diseases that exhibit multiple-factor hereditary traits" from the life science field, and "Widespread use of highly reliable network systems capable of protecting the privacy and secrecy of individuals and groups from the intrusion of ill-intentioned network intruders" from the information and communications field. All top-ranking topics related to aspects of high social concern.

It is worth mentioning that the distribution of all 1065 topics was carried out according to the forecasted realization time, which was operationalized as the realization year corresponding to the response at the 50th percentile after the realization times were arranged in chronological order from the earliest to the latest. Half of all responses fell within the five-year 2011–2015 period, and 82% were forecasted to take place in the 2011–2020 period. In terms of fields, fields covering information technologies and their applications, such as "Information and communications", "Distribution", "Business and management", and "Services", were expected to be realized relatively early, while "Life science", and "Resources and energy" were expected to be realized relatively late.

The next figure shows the relationship between forecasted realization time and range of forecasted times.

Figure 9.1. Representation of Distribution of Realization Time Responses in First and Second Round of a Delphi Questionnaire

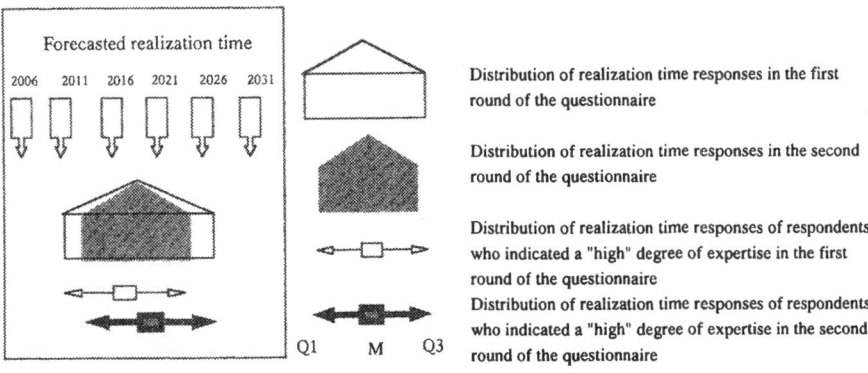

Source: NISTEP 2001: 7

Here the "range of forecasted times" is the width between Q1 in the figure below (forecasted realization year of the response at the 25th percentile of all responses) and Q3 (forecasted realization year of the response at the 75th percentile of all responses). The median 50% of responses fall within this range. A narrow width indicates a strong consensus among respondents. However, the values used for calculating forecast range include decimal values, so there may be some discrepancies between the pentagonal shape showing distribution and the values in this section. This survey looks at technologies up to 2030, so topics for which Q3 in the second round questionnaire (R2) is 2031 or later have been excluded. The number of topics covered was 1033.

The survey also examined the extent to which a consensus had been formed among respondents, and how forecasted realization times changed from R1 to R2. The Japanese report used the range of forecasted times as an indicator of the extent of consensus. As is mentioned in the Delphi exercise report, *"a convergence ratio [was calculated] for each topic as an indicator to determine the extent to which a consensus had been formed through repetition of the questionnaire. A smaller convergence ratio indicates a stronger consensus. For example, in the case of 'Practical use of biocomputers based on a new algorithm', the first topic in the information and communications field, the range of forecasted times was 11.5 years in R1 and 9.0 years in R2, giving a convergence ratio of 9.0/11.5 = 0.78. This comparison excludes topics in which Q3 (75th percentile of the R1 or R2 forecasted realization time) is 2031 or later. The number of topics covered was 1029"* (NISTEP 2001 : 35).

All Japanese technology forecast surveys have focused on the period running from the present-day situation to 30 years in the future. Already more than 20 years have passed since the first (1971), second (1976) and third (1981) Japanese Delphi surveys were carried out, so it is now possible to assess whether the topics forecasted in those three surveys have been realized or not. Indeed, an assessment of the results of the first and second surveys was carried out during the sixth survey, but it is now four years later and we believe it is important to reassess those results in the light of developments that have taken place since then.

Thus, of the assessed topics in the first survey, 185 are now (as of 2004) "realized", 222 "partially realized" and 209 unrealized", resulting in a combined realization and partial realization rate of 66%. By field, "industry and resources" and "information" displays high realization rates, while "social development" displays a low realization rate. Of the assessed topics in the second survey, 151 are now "realized," 244 "partially realized" and 218 "unrealized", resulting in a combined realization and partial realization rate of 64%. Fields with a high realization rate are "industrial production", "information", "space development", and "labor", while those with a low realization rate are "software science", "forest resources", "transportation", and "environment". Finally, of the assessed topics in the third survey, 135 are "realized," 348 "partially realized" and 196 "unrealized", resulting in a combined realization and partial realization rate of 71%. The realization rate is prominently high in the two fields of "space" with 54% and "communications, information and electronics" with 37%.

These results also enable one to confirm that the information and communication technologies (normally mentioned as "information", or alternatively as "communication and electronics") are the better know topics in terms of forecast, whereas "social development", "environment", "forest resources", etc., are less known.

4. THE EXPERIENCE FROM THE "FUTUR" PROGRAM

The experience of foresight in Germany is one of the most interesting from the methodological viewpoint, as several innovations were brought to the conventional Delphi method.[5] Germany ran its first foresight exercises with the Japanese Government (through NISTEP) in 1983, and a new exercise (2002-2006) is on the run. In the summer of 2001, the Federal Ministry of Education and Research (BMBF) initiated the "Futur" research dialogue with the aim to identify research priorities of the future (towards the year 2020) by means of a broad dialogue.

The key question was 'What is needed?' for the national science and technology system, i.e. in which areas must the German scientific community conduct research today, in order to fulfill society's needs tomorrow? Over 1500 economic, scientific and social experts have identified topics in areas that can play a decisive role in the development of German society.

Within this foresight program, the visionary ideas for research programs are developed in the form of interdisciplinary and problem-oriented (lead) visions. In spite of its target-orientation (lead visions), the so-called "Futur process" is open to new results. In comparison with existing programs, Futur can operate in an interdisciplinary way. Innovative links are drawn between complex subjects, and visionary thinking is stimulated.

The *lead visions* were developed through discussions involving a large number of actors from a broad variety of interdisciplinary backgrounds. The participating actors were motivated by the possibility to contribute to the development of BMBF research funding programs, and hence put a lot of effort into theme development. The process started out openly, offering the participants the possibility to introduce themes they considered as being important for the future. In the course of the process, promising themes were selected and their discussion was deepened in focus group sessions. From the executive team of the Futur project, the major objectives of the process were achieved (as mentioned in an assessment report). Nevertheless, BMBF is still on the way of evaluation of this process and several lead visions for research policy have since 2001 been created and are now being implemented in BMBF research support programmes. As the German federal minister for education and research Edeltraud Bulmahn stresses, *"only when we recognize and exploit our future opportunities at an early stage will we be able to optimally react to the challenges of tomorrow. This is why Germany needs a participatory foresight process such as Futur"*.

Lead visions are interdisciplinary and oriented towards societal needs. To stimulate innovativeness of themes, "visionary workshops" can be applied early in the process, and a targeted analytical input might be introduced at some stage. In the future, it is planned to introduce one lead vision every year so that there will be more time for topic preparation and development work in the focus groups. The structure of the lead visions is based in the following steps:

1. The Aim and the Vision
2. Description of the Topic and Its Significance for Economy and Society
3. Scenario
4. Future Research Priorities
5. The Present State of Research and Current Research Support Priorities

The first round themes were based on a common topic: Inventing the Future. 21 topic packages were defined and discussed (for example, "Young Life in the World of the Old: New Worlds of Living for Old and Young", "The Choice of Employment", "Understanding Thought Processes: Capacities of the Brain", "Germany as an Integrated Society of Different Cultures", or even "Mobility: Individually Attractive and Socially Sustainable?").

The second round established 12 topic packages, discussed in a new phase. These topics re-elaborated the first-round ones and are as follows:

- Farsighted Planning and Organization of Satisfactory Work in the Knowledge Society
- Germany as a Place of Learning: the Learning Society as a Factor of the Future
- Living in a Networked World: Individual and Secure
- Promotion of Intercultural Potentials
- Dealing with Knowledge
- Sustainable Mobility
- Individual Medicine and Health Care 2020
- Ways of Developing a Sustainable Nutrition Culture in a Changing Society
- Sustainable Agricultural Production With Global Responsibility
- Global Change/Regional Change: Recognizing the Challenges and Opportunities of Global Change and Shaping Them Regionally
- Decentralization/A Strategy for Sustainable Ways of Life and Work?
- Intelligent Products and Systems for Tomorrow's Society

The BMBF then selected 6 out of these 12 topic packages, so as to develop the process to the "lead visions": "Individual medicine and health 2020", "Access to the world of learning, Living in a networked world: personalized worlds of interaction", "Efficient processes of knowledge", "Intelligent processes" and "Understanding Thought Processes". Thus, those visions were established in the following way:

- Understanding Thought Processes
- Creating Open Access to Tomorrow's World of Learning
- Healthy and Vital throughout Life by Prevention
- Living in a Networked World: Individual and Secure

In fact, new research programs from the education and research ministry were launched following the topics discussed: Microsystem Technology 2000+, Nanotechnology, Basic Communications Technologies, Optical Technologies and Information Technology Research 2006. The last selection of the topics for the lead vision process took place in winter 2003: both the Futur participants and the BMBF submitted their vote. The final decision was made by the BMBF at the end of that year: The favorite topics were "The bionic house", "Needs-specific consumer products and innovation through cooperative customer integration" and "Healthy nutrition". These lead visions were further developed and supplemented by expertise and scenarios in creative workshops and Focus group meetings. The completed lead visions should be recently available.

A factor that had an important influence on the course of the whole process was the time frame, which can be important for the improvement of the Delphi method. One and a half years is a relatively short time span, especially considering the pioneer status of the process, and also considering that no themes were pre-defined, but the process was initiated without preconceived results in mind. Due to the complex demands of the task (which participants, how to select the themes, what expertise is necessary, etc.) more time was needed in order to properly plan and organize the different phases of the process.

One can agree that, because the participants of the Delphi process stem from different disciplinary backgrounds (for example, in our study on fisheries in Portugal – the MARHE project; cf. Moniz et al. 2000), they were coming from biology, sociology, economy, engineering, as well as from stakeholders, such as trade unions, business associations, public administration). Because the lead visions are interdisciplinary, this topic (interdisciplinarity) should be regarded carefully. In other words, too much interdisciplinarity and focal dispersion can hinder the discussion and the individual motivation of participants, which in turn may alter the discussion results. This being said, the interdisciplinary composition of the groups is usually stimulating for the discussions, supporting the development of research themes across disciplinary boundaries

Besides careful consideration in the selection of participants,, targeted expertise should be added in order to support the debates. This is a general problem, also experienced in other Delphi exercises; we have the Portuguese experience to confirm this (MARHE, IS-Emp, TeleRisk and WorTiS projects). Thus, one can conclude that more innovativeness of the lead visions has to be implemented into the process. Some authors underline the need for the application of stimulating visionary methods in the process of theme generation, by fitting in information in a provocative way and by improving the consensus mechanism prevailing in the discussion groups. Others prefer not to intervene in this process moment. Furthermore, as the general selection procedure constitutes a sensitive phase in a participatory process; the role of the different actors should be clear and transparent.

Eventually, the Delphi process stimulated the discussion of the themes from multiple perspectives, which constitutes one of the most important dimensions of the knowledge process of foresight. This discussion integrated different disciplines as well as different actors of the discussion process. Another interesting issue is that the planned implementation of the lead visions enforced that traditional actors (researchers, public administration technicians) had to recognize the achievements made at the research level (mostly technological ones) and integrate them into their work. Some of most updated technological developments could be connected to unusual application field, and discussed much more closely to the stakeholders needs. This proved to be a very difficult step, but a decisive one. This being said, traditional actors did play a role in the selection process of the themes, and provided external expertise. This was true for the case of the fisheries Delphi project in Portugal. In the German Futur project, the lead visions which were developed also took socio-economic dimensions into account (besides scientific-technical dimensions), and were need-oriented.

The focus groups in Futur were composed of persons from different circles and communities (scientific, economic and social experts, innovative thinkers, researchers, established scientists and young scientists; all were co-operating in developing concepts and ideas relative to key future topics), in order to focus on a topic of common interest for these persons while working on different questions (need for research, sub-themes, status of research, visions in the themes etc.). The focus groups were established during the Open-Space Conference in 2001. These groups were adequate instruments to perform the expert work, especially for scenario planning, i.e. to mediate between specialist expertise and interdisciplinary perspectives. This procedure was seen as preventing that technology and science lobbyists could prevail in the choice of the research topics needs. These theme profiles were used as basis for the lead visions. The work of the facilitators and thematic tutors was usually very much appreciated by the participants.

According to the organizers of the Futur project, this process is conceived as a participatory process. The participants were selected following the "co-nomination" method. As mentioned before, they stemmed from a broad variety of professional backgrounds (e.g. science, academic sector, private business sector), and a majority of them hadn't previously been involved in such processes. The participants developed lead visions, which are supposed to be implemented. As those participants in the various project-related activities were experts from different disciplines, this lead to a *reciprocal "inspiration"* of various perspectives. The positive effect was emphasized by all actors questioned during this Futur exercise. In spite of the fact that the facilitators supported the communication within the heterogeneous groups, the discussion groups needed more time to overcome communication problems and to reach agreement on themes.

The *co-nomination* method makes it possible to assemble expertise in the width and depth necessary for the process, even if this implies that no theme-specific nomination is possible. This creates an interdisciplinary circle of participants, in which "new" actors also take part (e.g. not the usual participants in such activities). As mentioned by the project team, the co-nomination method proved a good means to spark off the process, but additional database searches was necessary to add specific expertise in the course of the process. The participants were very interested in the process and therefore motivated to contribute their knowledge. They put a lot of effort into the activities. The phases of the process were structured along a continuous logic: theme generation, consolidation, profiling, focusing/enriching.

On one hand, workshops on future issues (or topics) enabled visionary ideas to be developed, extending beyond pure extrapolation and proving helpful for further work in focus groups, as well as for the development of lead visions. On the other hand, scenarios were helpful for the development and visualization of lead visions. They could be developed on the basis of the results of the focus group sessions and the lead vision discussion workshops. The aim was that scenarios should be integrated into the lead visions, thus visualizing the core theme of the lead vision.

Following this method, the workshop participants were asked to write down, on a mind map, what they thought society might look like in the year 2020. The second step was about how they think about how their own field might develop, to be written down in a kind of brainstorming (not methodologically strict) session. This part of the process was called *trend collection*. After the workshops, trend clusters were identified. After the definition of 12 most-wanted topics, focus groups were later formed and were given the task of re-focusing their topic according to pragmatic criteria, identification of perspectives, driving factors and frame conditions of their area. Building upon this material, consistent scenarios had to be elaborated and highlighted as "pictures of the future".

More recently (June 2004) a series of fourteen workshops were held, in which the "Futur" participants defined the direction of the future thematic work in the German research dialogue. The aim of that activity was to further develop the existing theme proposals and define their profile. The topics for discussion were chosen through an online voting procedure (in late 2003), in the course of which the participants were able to select and rate the various topics. In the individual work groups, the experts generated ideas which, after further development, were meant to become potential lead visions.

The use of various methods should be integrated in such a process, as they complement each other reciprocally, and as they may foster a continuous discussion. These methods were sufficient to develop the lead visions and scenarios, while also being stimulating for the participants. Additional visionary phases, alternating with more rational and information-based phases might be realized in future conferences of this process. Nevertheless, when the subjects (scenarios) are clarified, the topics have to be deepened (in terms of rationally, of information-based structure, and analytical form). This clarification should be made so that the research questions of the future can be dealt with by the research stake-holders.

The design and the questions posed by the methods (workshops, open-space conference, workshops on the future research and focus groups) were on the whole suited to identify particularly innovative approaches for research. The questions presented to the experts and participants were target-oriented (method, situation, workshops); this should be generalized to other foresight exercises, once it can be understood as an innovative methodological issue related to participatory foresight platform.

The questions for the Delphi questionnaires in the Futur exercise in Germany were also specific enough to be worked out in the different workshops (the most recent at the Congress 2004 already mentioned). It was sometimes difficult to do so, often due to the missing focus of the subjects. Some of the leading visions were too generic, loosing some links between the possible research applications and the future trends designed in those vision topics.. The vocabulary used in the process had to be simplified and to be clarified through examples. From the point of view of the persons in charge of this German foresight exercise (Futur co-ordination committee, BMBF officers), the visionary methods had to be used to generate the themes, which were then elaborated further by discussion groups.

The selection criteria of themes were also used for the selection of visionary ideas (not dependent on existing "lobbies" in the research and academic arenas). These criteria were also supportive to select and develop interdisciplinary and demand-driven themes. The possibility of online voting existed. In this case, the selection criteria had to be translated early into clear and simple questions. They had to be designed in such a way that rankings (e. g. via indexing and weighting of the criteria) could be computed.

To sum up, the Futur process was considered as a means of priority-setting for future innovation-oriented research policies (mainly aimed at the BMBF policy). The new innovative element of this program is that it is oriented towards the identification and inclusion of societal needs in future research agendas. The foresight process was based on surveys or workshop panels. It was also an iterative process which could be modified, should experiences make this necessary (reflexivity). In addition, it was conceived as a participatory process, and the participants were selected by the co-nomination method. The sketching of "pictures of the future" and "leading visions"

(*Leitvisionen*) now constitutes a guide to innovation-oriented research policy decisions of the German Ministry (a major decision-maker in the process). Thus, a link to implementation is included.

5. THE UNITED NATIONS "MILLENIUM" PROJECT

The Millennium Project of the United Nations University (UNU) is a global participatory futures research think tank involving foresight experts, scholars, business planners, and policy makers who work for international organizations, governments, corporations, NGOs, and universities. This international project produces the annual "State of the Future", a series on "Futures Research Methodology", and specific studies such as the Future Scenarios for Africa, Lessons of History, Environmental Security, Applications of Futures Research to Policy, and other annotated scenarios bibliographies.

It was initiated in 1996 by the Smithsonian Institution, The Futures Group International, and the UNU. The first phase of the feasibility study began in 1992 with funding from the US Environmental Protection Agency (EPA) to identify and link futurists and scholars around the world to create the initial design of the Project and conduct a first test on population and environmental issues.

In 1993-94, during the second phase, a series of reports were produced on futures research methodology and long-range issues of importance for Africa, funded by the United Nations Development Program (UNDP). The third phase was conducted in 1994-95 under the auspices of the United Nations University/World Institute for Development Economics Research (UNU/WIDER) and funded by United Nations Educational, Scientific and Cultural Organization (UNESCO) through the American Council for UNU, and was concluded with the final feasibility study report.

It was in 2001 that the Millennium Project introduced the State of the Future Index (SOFI). This index is a statistical combination of key indicators and forecasts (such as the well-known Human Development Index (HDI), also from UN), gathered in 19 variables. Building upon the previous work of the Millennium Project (including direct forecasts of important future developments and developments that appeared in various scenarios), a list of some 80 future developments was assembled and, when appropriate, extended and sharpened. The developments were chosen on the basis of their apparent potential to affect the future course of the 19 SOFI (State of the Future Index) variables.

According to a UN Millenium research report, *"the goal of generating scenarios is to understand the mix of strategic decisions that are of maximum benefit in the face of various uncertainties and challenges posed by the external environment. Scenario building, in conjunction with a careful analysis of the driving forces, fosters systematic study of potential future possibilities—both good and bad. This forecasting approach enables decision makers and planners to grasp the long-term requirements for sustained advantage, growth, and avoidance of problems"* (1999 : 3).

The SOFI differs from other indexes in several important respects. All indexes that have been reviewed deal with the present or past, whereas this one is designed to measure the promise of the future. Further, in contrast with most existing indexes that are cross sectional and are designed to compare countries to countries or various groups of countries at some point in time (usually as recent as possible), this index is longitudinal and is designed to track and forecast change over time. Since the SOFI is to display future as well as historical values, it is necessary to forecast each one of the series. A 10-year time horizon was selected, a period half as long into the future as the historical database once this database has the reference of 10 years (1991 and 2011).

The time series of each variable contains information which can be used to gauge uncertainty intrinsic to the SOFI forecast. For example, the observed errors between the "best fit" curve and the actual data points (i.e. "residuals") provide a measure of scatter, and one can assume that the residuals of the sort that existed in the past will also surround the extrapolation (Gordon 2002: 56).

The methodology for the study on the 2002 State of the Future on science and technology research established a first step where it was asked *"What are the most important questions to ask about science and technology, given our interest in emerging issues and forces that are likely to influence the future of science and technology programs and their management?"* The research strategy in this case is not to start with the question "What is needed?" but trying to identify the main questions.

To this end a meeting was organized with Science Attachés. It resulted in the choice of a set of initial lists of questions. These were further discussed with the Millennium Project Planning Committee and rated by this study's Steering Committee. Based on this feedback, round 1 was designed. In this round 1, the panel was asked to rate the questions in terms of both their global importance and the priority to their own country. In addition, panelists were asked to suggest other questions and to judge some staff-generated answers/actions to address these questions in terms of importance, likelihood and confidence, and, most importantly, to add questions to the list. The final section asked the respondents about science and technology priorities in their countries.

In the report of the last exercise, the authors confirm that *"better means should be explored for forecasting the variables, including perturbing extrapolations with future developments and cross-impacts among the variables. In addition, for at least some of the variables, agent modeling and multi-equation feedback models should be considered*" (Gordon 2002). In fact, using past work of the Millennium Project (including direct forecasts of important future developments and developments that appeared in various scenarios) a list of some 80 future developments was assembled, and when appropriate, extended and sharpened. The developments were chosen on the basis of their apparent potential to affect the future course of the SOFI variables. These developments were used to modify the forecasts of the variables. The analysis method produced not only a new median forecast but also the range of the variable in view of the developments that were expected to affect it.

The computation of SOFI involved the use of judgments of the Global Lookout Panel in 2001 about what the best (norm) and worst (dystopic) state was for each indicator in 2011, and about the importance of reaching the norm or dystopic state. The criteria for assigning a high weight to a variable were:

a. the number of people affected;
b. the significance of the effect;
c. whether some groups seem to be affected differentially;
d. the time over which the effect will be felt;
e. and whether the effect is reversible.

The computation also involved the scaling of the data by assigning the value of 100 for the most desirable (normative state in 10 years) and 0 for the least desirable values (dystopic state in 10 years). Finally, the computation involved the weighting of the data using an S-shaped function that allowed the weight of a variable to vary with the value of the variable.

The following table summarizes pertinent information about the 2002 baseline forecasts:

Table 9.2. State of the Future Index--2002

	Variable	Fit Equation	R^2	Number of Data Points
1	Infant Mortality Rate (deaths per 1,000 live births)	NA: Used US Census Bureau Projection	NA	NA
2	Food availability Cal/cp Low Income Countries	Linear	.968	20
3	GDP per capita, PPP (constant 1995 dollars)	Linear	.775	20
4	Percentage of Households w/ Access to Safe Water (15 Most Populated Countries)	S Shaped	.612	6
6	Mean Monthly Carbon Dioxide in Atmosphere (ppm)	S Shaped	1.00	22

7	Annual population additions millions	NA: Used US Census Bureau Projection	NA	NA
9	Percent unemployed	Linear	.749	20
10	Literacy rate, adult total (% of people aged 15 and above in low and middle income countries)	S Shaped	.996	20
14	Annual AIDS deaths (millions)	Power Function	.976	20
15	Life Expectancy (World)	NA: Used US Census Bureau Projection	NA	NA
23	Number of Armed Conflicts (at least 1000 deaths/yr)	Exponential	.218	21
24	Debt to GNP Ratio: (%) Developing Countries	Power Function	.943	9
25	Forest Lands (Million Hectares)	Linear	.801	10
26	People living on less than $2 per day (Billions, less China)	Power Function	.932	4
27	Terrorist Attacks, number of people killed or wounded	S Shaped	.266	21
28	Violent Crime Rate, 17 Countries (per 100,000 population)	Inverse V	.294	20
30	Percent of World Population Living in Countries that are Not Free	Linear	.379	20
38	Net school Enrollment, secondary (% school age)	Inverse V	.294	20
39	Percentage of population with access to local health care (15 most populated countries)	S Shaped	.856	5

Source: Glenn and Gordon 2002 : 99-100

These baselines were then modified using trend impact analysis (TIA) to account for the impacts of possible future developments towards 2012. Thus, the 2002 SOFI was estimated given all of the variables forecasted in full consideration of the future developments that could affect their course.

6. CONCLUDING REMARKS

Foresight is a process of studying the future. In other words, it is the study of potential change. It can be applied either to technology, or to social relations systems. That does not mean only to establish trends, but what is likely to make a systemic or fundamental difference over the next 10 to 25 years or more. In this sense, the interest for policy (in the field of science, or technology development, economy, or even public administration) decision making is evident. The futures analysis, in scientific terms, is not simply economic projections or sociological analysis, or even technological forecasting. Instead, as the three examples above can demonstrate, it is a multi-disciplinary examination of change, in order to discover the interacting dynamics that are creating the next generation. As Grunwald underlines, *"in many fields, it is not a question of prognoses as predictions of future outcomes, but of scenarios as illustrations of possible futures, in order to structure the spectrum of further developments, identify 'worst'- and 'best' cases, and to gain strategic knowledge for drawing up action strategies"* (2004: 152).

Futures research (or futures studies) is not a scientific discipline; it rather utilizes information from all of the sciences. A value of futures research is not discovering new factual knowledge (as in the scientific disciplines), but producing perceptions, visions and insights to that body of knowledge. A specific value can be understood when these perceptions and visions are a basis for political analysis. The possible use of "futures" studies for political forecasting is still challenging, but still weak in its formalization.

This approach can be based on some causal chains of decisions and circumstances that lead from the present, emerging dependent variables. The display of the variable conditions can reveal the quantitative dimensions that will enrich the narrative of those "futures". Defining a large number of alternative worlds is often neither necessary nor desirable. In the final selection of "future worlds", one should consider it sufficient to present a range of opportunities and challenges. Nevertheless, this range should be small enough in number to handle. Four to five scenario "worlds" seems ideal to capture that range.

The concept of "causal complexity" presented by Charles Ragin (1987, 2000, 2004) illustrates the possible use of causal analysis for the construction of scenarios, when in a relation between two variables, no cause is either necessary or sufficient. Then one is in presence of asymmetric causation (i.e. when a variable leads to an output, this does not mean that its reverse leads to the reverse output), where QCA or fuzzy-set analysis can play a significant role. And here the construction of possible scenarios is a field for QCA and fuzzy-set applications. There is probably more potential for the fuzzy-set method in this field (instead of QCA), as it allows to integrate the kind of "richer" data (more fine-grained measurement; see also Kvist, in this volume) which is most often used in futures research.

The key measures and variables need to be selected with care. Every scenario must include projections of the same measures in order to clarify the implications for decisions. For instance, in the field of technology forecasts, the significance of such forecasts lies in the fact that, through assessment and analysis of realization time and importance of various technologies, they give an indication of the direction and objectives of research and development, which in turn provides basic data for the promotion and development of science and technology. While the national Delphi exercises in Japan and Germany presented here are suitable examples of this, it is not so evident in the case of UN Millenium project.

The goal of generating scenarios is to understand the mix of strategic decisions that are of maximum benefit in the face of various uncertainties and challenges posed by the external environment. Scenario building, in conjunction with a careful analysis of the driving forces, fosters systematic study of potential future possibilities — both good and bad. This forecasting approach enables decision makers and planners to grasp the long-term requirements for sustained advantage, growth, and avoidance of problems.

In Portugal, after four Delphi exercises (in the fisheries social-economical system, on information society and employment, on tele-working and on the automotive sector), just two had a two-round survey. That means that those two exercises were further developed, using the same expert panel and an in-depth evaluated scenarios. This was the case for the fisheries system, and for the information society and employment linkage. The other two exercises were important experiences, but would need a further step, re-evaluating the scenarios topics with an enlarged panel.

Further, the policy action developed by stake-holders based on some of the main conclusions of these foresight exercises was evident. For instance some incentives system programs (with the support of European funds) were designed taking into account some of those conclusions. One reason thereof could lay in the political significance of some consensual futures. The other reason is that some policy makers were themselves involved in the foresight process, and hence they have also integrated some of the conclusions in their own activity, especially in two of the above-mentioned cases: fisheries (MARHE project) and information society and employment (IS-Emp project). In these cases a national operational program on fisheries (MARE) was integrating some of the main recommendations of the mentioned project, and the Ministry of Labour integrated in the policy agenda some of the IS Emp project recommendations. This means that to some extend the policy making strategy can use features from the scenario building methods. This has been the main practice for most cases illustrated in this article.

NOTES

[1] The author expresses his thanks for all the observations, comments and suggestions made particularly by Benoît Rihoux and Heike Grimm to this article, and to the participants that made interventions on this topic at the ESF Workshop in Erfurt. None of them are, of course, responsible for the errors and mistakes that can be eventually found in the text.

[2] In 1967, this study was developed under the Commission on the Year 2000 and sponsored by the American Academy of Arts and Sciences

[3] The modern renaissance of futures research began with the Delphi (word taken from the Greek location where the oracles for forecasting events took place) technique at the RAND "think tank" (at Santa Monica, California) in the early 1960s. These researchers

explored the use of expert panels to address forecasting issues. The principle was based on the idea that experts, particularly when they agree, are more likely than non-experts to be correct about questions in their field. Thus, the key to a successful Delphi study lies in the selection of participants. These regular exercises were very soon followed in Japan by the Ministry of Industry and Technology, and later in Germany by the Ministry of Education and Research. Nowadays, this foresight methodology is used in most countries for policy making.

[4] Called the Science and Technology Agency since December 2000.

[5] Here I would like to mention the inspiring talks and exchanges of ideas that I gratefully enjoyed during my sabbatical leave at ISI-FhG (Karlsruhe) during 2003, specifically with the department (TI) lead by Professor Dr. Stefan Kuhlmann, and all the support that I received since then from those colleagues.

PART THREE

INNOVATIVE COMPARATIVE METHODS FOR POLICY IMPLEMENTATION AND EVALUATION: APPLICATIONS

Chapter 10

A NEW METHOD FOR POLICY EVALUATION?
Longstanding Challenges and the Possibilities of Qualitative Comparative Analysis (QCA)

Frédéric Varone
Université catholique de Louvain

Benoît Rihoux
Université catholique de Louvain

Axel Marx
Hogeschool Antwerpen

1. INTRODUCTION

According to E. Vedung (1997: 3), evaluation is *"the careful retrospective assessment of the merit, worth and value of administration, outputs, and outcome of government interventions, which is intended to play a role in future, practical action situations"*. Thus, the purpose of evaluation research is to measure the effects of a policy against the goals it sets out to accomplish. Hence, it implies the application of systematic research methods for the assessment of program design, implementation and effectiveness.

In fact, several handbooks are dedicated to evaluation designs, which constitute the technical part of an evaluation process and relate to the collection and interpretation of empirical data on policy outputs and outcomes (see analytical distinction below). Various methodological designs are possible, such as longitudinal and/or cross-sectional quantitative research, different types of experimental designs (including quasi-experiments and natural experiments), or different types of (comparative) case research. With each design also come specific types of data (from the most quantitative to the most qualitative) and data analysis techniques. Although there are many ways in which outputs and outcomes assessment can be conducted, these methodological options are not all equivalent: some produce more credible estimates of policy effects than others. Therefore, it is not surprising that there is still a deep divide and fierce academic struggle among the advocates of quantitative versus qualitative methods of policy evaluation.

In this exploratory chapter, we investigate the potential added-value of QCA in such a methodological debate. Indeed, up till now, QCA and policy evaluation have very seldom been explicitly linked[1], and never in a systematic way. This is quite surprising, as clear parallels can be drawn between some key features of QCA (and, hence, the preoccupations of its initiators) and key preoccupations of policy evaluators.

The following two sections set the stage of "policy evaluation" and "QCA": we first provide a brief definition of policy evaluation, and then lay out the fundamentals of QCA. Next, we identify four methodological challenges that policy evaluators typically face. From there on, we examine to what extend QCA may offer some innovative answers to these longstanding methodological issues. Finally, we identify some of the remaining challenges for QCA, if it is to become a very useful tool for policy evaluation.

2. DEFINING POLICY EVALUATION: MEASUREMENT AND VALUE JUDGMENT

We define a public policy as a body of decisions and activities adopted and carried out by interdependent public and private actors – with varying values, beliefs, interests, institutional allegiances and resources – in order to resolve, in a coordinated and targeted manner, a collective problem that has been socially constructed and politically defined as public in nature (Knoepfel, Larrue and Varone 2001). Each public policy is thus based on some "causal theory" that consists of assumptions about the causes of the problem to be solved and about the intended impacts (on actors' behavior) of the implemented policy tools.

Numerous authors have tried to create a diagram conveying the unfolding of the decision and implementation processes involved in a public policy. The overall impression that emerges from the literature is one of a "policy life cycle" starting with the emergence and perception of a public problem, followed by the agenda-setting stage, the policy formulation, the implementation phase and, finally, the evaluation of the policy effects (Jones 1970). At this last stage of a policy cycle[2], the policy analyst aims to determine the results and effects of a public policy in terms of the production of administrative acts (policy *outputs*), the changes in behavior of target groups, and problem resolution (policy *outcomes*). Thus, policy evaluation represents an empirical test of the validity of the "causal theory" underlying the public policy.

Consequently the emphasis is placed on links between the administrative services responsible for implementing the public policy, the target groups whose behavior is politically defined as one of the (in)direct causes of the societal problem to be solved, and the final beneficiaries who endure the negative consequences of this public problem. For example, public environmental protection agencies, as well as industry, impose decontamination measures on polluting industrial companies in order to improve the quality of the air breathed by people living in the vicinity of factories, whilst the economic promotion and finance agencies grant tax exemptions to small and medium-sized companies which employ job-seekers by creating new jobs.

The main tasks of a policy evaluation are, on the one hand, to measure the outputs and outcomes of the public policy and, on the other hand, to formulate a judgment on the value, merit or worth of these policy effects with reference to criteria and explicit standards. As it were, there are numerous different such criteria. For example, the criterion of *relevance* (or appropriateness) examines the link that exists – or should exist – between the goals as defined in the policy design, on the one hand, and the nature and pressure of the public problem to be solved, on the other hand. Thus, a policy is described as relevant if the goals implicitly formulated in the laws and regulations, and sometimes concretized in administrative action plans (i.e. policy *outputs*), are adapted to the nature and temporal and socio-spatial distribution of the problem that the policy is intended to solve. The criterion of *effectiveness* is directly connected with the category of policy *outcomes*. It refers to the relationship between the anticipated effects of a policy and those that actually emerge in social reality. The evaluation of the effectiveness of a policy is generally carried out on the basis of a comparison between the target values (i.e. goals) defined in the policy design and the effects actually triggered among the policy's end beneficiaries. The criterion of *efficiency* focuses on the relationship between the resources invested during policy implementation and the effects achieved. It describes the ratio between the costs and benefits of a policy. The criterion of *economy*, which is rooted in a more managerial rationale, relates the administrative outputs produced to the resources invested. Thus, it evaluates the efficiency (in a narrow sense) of the administrative implementation processes. Further evaluation criteria are also discussed in the literature and applied in concrete evaluations. For example, E. Ostrom (1999: 48-49) refers to policy evaluation in terms of six criteria namely: economic efficiency, fiscal equivalence, redistributional equity, accountability, conformance to general morality and adaptability.

In this chapter, we mainly focus on the first ambition of a policy evaluation (the production of a valid and reliable measure of policy effects) and do not consider explicitly the aspect of value judgment (which always requires a previous measurement of the policy effects). The four methodological challenges of policy evaluation that are discussed in the third section are all related to the measurement of policy effects. Before addressing these challenges, we briefly introduce some fundamental notions of Qualitative Comparative Analysis (QCA).

3. QCA IN A NUTSHELL

Qualitative Comparative Analysis (QCA) is a method that was launched some 15 years ago by Charles Ragin in a prize-winning volume (Ragin 1987; Ragin and Rihoux 2004; Rihoux 2003). It is both an approach (and research design) and a specific technique for the analysis of data.

3.1 QCA as an Approach

As an approach, QCA develops a "synthetic strategy", which ambitions to «*integrate the best features of the case-oriented approach with the best features of the variable-oriented approach*» (Ragin 1987: 84).

Indeed, on the one hand, QCA meets some key strengths of the qualitative approach (Ragin 1987: 12ff; De Meur and Rihoux 2002: 20ff). The first one is its holistic character: each individual case is considered as a complex entity (a «whole») which needs to be comprehended and which should not be forgotten in the course of the analysis. Thus it is a case-sensitive approach. Furthermore, it develops a conception of causality which leaves some room for complexity. This is a truly central feature of QCA: multiple conjunctural causation. This implies that : A/ most often, it is a combination of conditions[3] that eventually produce a phenomenon (the « outcome »[4]); B/ several different combinations of conditions may very well produce the same outcome; and C/ depending on the context, on the « conjuncture », a given condition may very well have a different impact on the outcome. This implies that different « causal paths » – each path being relevant, in a distinct way – may lead to the same outcome (De Meur and Rihoux 2002: 28-30). Causality is viewed as context- and conjuncture-sensitive (as in policy evaluation indeed; see below). Hence, by using QCA, the researcher is urged not to « *specify a single causal model that fits the data best* » (which is often done with most conventional statistical techniques), but instead to « *determine the number and character of the different causal models that exist among comparable cases* » (Ragin 1987: 167).

On the other hand, QCA also ambitions to meet some key strengths of the quantitative approach (Ragin 1987: 12ff; De Meur and Rihoux 2002: 20ff). Firstly, it allows one to analyze more than a few cases, and from there on to produce – to a certain extent – some generalizations. Secondly, it relies on formal tools (Boolean algebra) and is analytic in nature, in the sense that each case is reduced to a series of variables (a certain number of *conditions* and an *outcome*). At the same time QCA is not radically analytic, as it leaves some room for the holistic dimension of phenomena. Thirdly, it is a replicable analysis, in the sense that « *a researcher B who uses the same variables and makes the same choices as a researcher A will reach the same conclusions as the latter*» (De Meur and Rihoux 2002: 27ff). This replicability also opens up the way for other researchers to verify or falsify the results obtained in the analysis. Finally, the Boolean technique allows one to identify «*causal regularities*» that are *parsimonious*, i.e. that combine only a few conditions, and not all the conditions that have been considered in the model.

Besides constituting a middle way between the holistic and analytic strategies, QCA is particularly well-suited for « small-N » or « intermediate N » situations and research design (De Meur and Rihoux 2002: 24). Moreover, QCA allows one to consider both phenomena that vary qualitatively and phenomena that vary quantitatively. Both of these phenomena can be operationalized in the conditions and outcome variables used for software treatment (De Meur and Rihoux 2002: 32). So, while « cases do matter, and each case matters » in QCA (in this sense, it has a strong « qualitative » preoccupation), QCA really lies at the crossroads of qualitative and quantitative analysis.

3.2 QCA as a Technique

QCA has been developed in the form of a software. The latest version (the «crisp» part of the fs/QCA software) is still under development, but already available as a freeware; so is TOSMANA, a software developed at the Marburg University, that performs similar analyses with some additional features (see also Cronqvist and Berg-Schlosser, in this volume).[5]

The key philosophy of QCA as a technique is to « *(start) by assuming causal complexity and then (mount) an assault on that complexity* » (Ragin 1987: x). The tool which is used for this purpose of reducing complexity is Boolean algebra, the « algebra of logic ». It would be impossible to give a clear idea of all the technical details and steps in this article.[6] In a nutshell, the researcher must first produce a raw data table, in which each case displays a specific combination of conditions (with «0» or «1» values[7]) and an outcome (with the « 0 » or « 1 » value). The software then produces a *truth table* which displays the data as a list of *configurations* – in a more synthetic way, as several different *cases* may very well display the same configuration[8]. Then the key step of the analysis is Boolean minimization: by using Boolean algorithms, the software reduces the long Boolean expression (which consists in the long description of the truth table) into a much shorter expression (the *minimal formula*) that shows the causal regularities – the different causal paths, called *prime implicants* – that were, in a way, « hidden » in the data. It is then up to the researcher to interpret this minimal formula.

Two more strengths of QCA as a technique deserve to be mentioned. On the one hand, it can be used for at least five different purposes (De Meur and Rihoux 2002: 78-80). The most basic use is simply to summarize data, i.e. to describe cases in a more synthetic way (by producing a table of configurations). Hence it can be a useful tool for data exploration, for instance to construct typologies in a more inductive way (for a more detailed discussion of typology-building with set-theoretic methods, see Kvist, in this volume). It can also be used to check the coherence within the data: when the researcher discovers contradictions, this allows him/her to learn more about the individual cases. The third use is to test existing theories or assumptions, i.e. to eventually corroborate (validate) or refute (falsify) these theories or assumptions. QCA is hence a particularly powerful tool for theory-testing (for example for testing the "causal theory" underlying a public policy). Fourthly, it can be used to test some new ideas or assumptions formulated by the researcher (i.e. not embodied in an existing theory); this can also be useful for data exploration. Last but not least, it allows one to elaborate new assumptions or theories : the minimal formula obtained at the end of the analysis can be exploited and interpreted – i.e. confronted with the cases examined – and eventually lead the researcher to put forward some new segments of theory, in a more inductive way.

On the other hand, in the course of the procedure, the researcher is confronted with choices. For instance, he/she must decide whether or not he/she wants to obtain the shortest solution possible (i.e. achieve a maximal level of parsimony). If this choice is made, this means that some *logical cases* (also called *remainders*, i.e. cases that exist logically, but that have not been observed in the data) will be included in the «black box» for the Boolean minimization[9]. The point is that the researcher may very well reject this option, and hence prefer more complexity over more parsimony.[10] One also has to make clear choices on which variables to include and how to dichotomize them. The bottom line is that QCA is a particularly transparent technique, insofar as it forces the researcher not only to make choices on his/her own (he/she decides, not the computer), but also to justify these choices, from a theoretical and/or substantive perspective.

Hence QCA really forces the user to always keep an eye on theory... and the other eye on the real-life, complex cases behind the coded data, not only on the tables and formulae produced by the software. Thus QCA is both theory-driven and inductive: although induction does play an important role, there is quite a significant input of theory in QCA (Ragin 2004; see also Befani and Sager in this volume). For instance, quite clearly, the selection of variables that will be used for the analysis – and the way each variable is operationalized – must be theoretically informed (De Meur and Rihoux 2002: 40).

4. METHODOLOGICAL CHALLENGES OF POLICY EVALUATION

Every public policy or action program evaluation faces (at least) four methodological challenges that are intertwined: How to identify the causal mechanisms underlying the policy "outcomes line"? How to measure the net policy effects? How to produce counterfactual evidence? How to triangulate methods and data? In the following sections, we summarize these traditional evaluation issues.

4.1. Explaining Policy Effects: "Testing the Program Theory"

Each program or public policy is based on (most of the time implicit) "outcome line", "causal chain", "theory of action", "policy rationale", etc. This outcome line consists in beliefs, assumptions and expectations about the nature of the change brought about by program action and how it results in the intended policy outcomes. Thus, every policy can be interpreted as a theoretical construction whose consistency and rationality must be questioned analytically by the evaluators: *"a policy can be interpreted as a theoretical construction, in the sense that it implies an a priori representation of the measures implemented, of the actors' behaviour, of the sequence of measures undertaken and of the effects produced on society "* (Perret 1997: 292, our translation). The first task of a policy evaluator is thus to re-construct this program theory.

Such a *program theory* is generally understood as a causal theory: it describes a cause-and-effect sequence in which certain program activities (administrative outputs) are the instigating causes and the social benefits (policy outcomes) are the effects that they eventually produce. Within a program theory one can further distinguish an *impact theory*, relating to the nature of the change on outcomes brought about by program action (links between outputs and outcomes), and a *process theory*, depicting the program's organizational and resources plan (links between the implementation arrangement and outputs).

The model of causality of a public policy is always a normative representation of the "operation" of society and the State. Proof of its validity comes through implementing and evaluating the effects of public policies. For an empirical analysis it is therefore necessary to distinguish the elements that constitute this outcome line. Program evaluation thus involves empirical testing of the validity of the causality model on which the program is based. The analysis concerns both the relevance of this program theory and the scope of its practical implementation.

Evaluation studies might (often) identify failures within the program designs and, thereby, explain missing policy outcomes. The ineffectiveness and adverse effects of certain policies often derive from false or incomplete hypotheses of the impact and process theories. Several ineffective policies can be found in the field of urban traffic planning. For example, nowadays, the management of *public* parking spaces is one of the solutions adopted in order to direct, level off and reduce private motorized transport and, in particular, the volume of traffic arising from commuting. As a new transport policy measure, residents' parking disks are intended to restrict the periods during which non-residents can park in certain city neighborhoods. The aim of this policy measure is to remove commuter traffic from residential neighborhoods and to improve the quality of life of local residents and traders. Evaluation studies on the contribution made by the residents' parking-disk model to the reduction in the volumes of commuter traffic in the cities of Zurich, Basel and Bern (Switzerland) conclude that this measure remains largely ineffective (Schneider *et.al.* 1990, 1992, 1995). Between 70% and 85% of commuters using private means of transportation already had *private* parking spaces prior to the introduction of the disk. A clear majority of the target groups (i.e. commuters) have their own private parking spaces or the use of one owned by their employers, thus they do not have to adapt their behavior (by ensuring their mobility using public transport). This is an example of the incorrect choice of policy instruments, of the bad formulation of the action hypothesis of the impact theory.

Hopefully, evaluations can also conclude that a public policy is effective and produce the intended effects. Anyway, such an assessment should also be based on a careful investigation of the outcome line. An example of an effective policy is that of public support for home ownership in Switzerland. In 1970, an average of 28.1% of households were home owners (three quarters of the Swiss people are tenants; they have to rent their place of residence). This percentage was very low compared with other European countries. Thus, the Swiss Confederation passed a bill (1974) supporting residential construction and access to home ownership. This bill contained the following measures to reduce the initial costs incurred by future home owners: a federal guarantee, a reduction in the price of land, and non-reimbursable supplementary reductions. The main objective of this policy was to increase the rate of individual residential property owners in Switzerland. According to an evaluation of this bill (Schulz *et.al.* 1993), the federal support of access to home ownership had the desired effect. Up to 1991, some 15.747

construction projects were financially supported by the Confederation (outputs). Access to home ownership with the help of public support was primarily of assistance to young households which, in view of their limited finances, would not otherwise have had a opportunity to become home owners. Thanks to this measure the proportion of home owners increased during the study period (around 15 years) to reach 31.3% (i.e. outcomes in accordance with the objective). Furthermore, the bill had other indirect positive effects: in a period of recession, the support of access to home ownership constituted an important asset for the economy. This was the case for example in 1991 (a weak period in the construction sector) because 20% of family housing built was supported by federal aid.

These two examples illustrate how useful it is to follow - both conceptually and empirically - the whole outcome line of public policy, in order to find out and explain where the program theory could be incomplete or even absolutely false.

> Challenge 1: *"The evaluator should test the program theory of the public policy to be evaluated. He/she should reconstruct the outcome line of the public policy even if it remains implicit in the policy design"*.

4.2. Isolating Net Policy Effects: "Purging the Confounding Factors"

The starting point for an evaluation of a public policy is the identification of one or more measurable outcomes that should represent the goals of the program (see examples above). A critical distinction must be made here between gross outcomes and net outcomes. *Gross outcomes* consist of all the changes (in an outcome measure) that are observed when assessing a public policy. Gross outcomes are normally easily measured as the differences between pre- and post-program values on outcome measures.

Net outcomes, also referred to as *Net effects*, are much more difficult to isolate. These are the changes on outcome measures that can be reasonably attributed to the program and not to other contextual variables. In other words, gross outcomes include net effects of course, but they also include other effects that are not produced by the program to be evaluated, i.e. that are produced by *other factors and processes* occurring during the period under consideration (such as other public policies, contextual events, etc.).

The evaluation of a public program that aims at reducing energy consumption by industry and households provides one example of this difficulty. The instruments of that policy are typically information campaigns to enhance energy efficiency of industrial production processes and of the use of heating systems in individual houses. The evaluator may analyze the evolution of the energy consumption statistics before and after the information campaign. He might observe that there is a clear decrease in the overall energy consumption of both the industry and household sectors. However, he/she cannot conclude (without further in-depth analysis) that this decrease is directly linked to the energy policy put in action. It may well be the case that the industry decreases its energy consumption because there is an economic recession and thus less industrial production. In the same way, the decrease in household energy consumption can result from a less cold winter and thus lower heating needs. Alternatively, it may well be that both industry and households face an important increase of energy prices and decide – for financial reasons that have nothing to do with the information campaign – to reduce their energy consumption. It may also be the case that a more complex combination of all these other evolutions (i.e. not linked to the program) is at work.

> Challenge 2: *"The evaluator should purge the confounding factors (other public policies, external factors)"*.

4.3 Estimating the Policy Deadweight: "Producing Counterfactual Evidence"?

The crux of the evaluation of a program with respect to a particular outcome is a comparison of what did appear after implementing the program (see points 3.1 and 3.2 above) with what would have appeared at the outcomes level had the program *not* been implemented. This pivotal element of any evaluation, which can never be observed and can never be known for certain, is known as the *counterfactual*.

The counterfactual (that should be estimated by the evaluator) is the quantitative score or level at which the outcome of interest would have be found had the program (to be evaluated) not taken place. In other words, the evaluator should compare a *policy-on* with a (fictional) *policy-off* situation. The real impact of the policy is then considered to be the difference between the real changes (at the outcome level) after the policy intervention with the fictional changes estimated in a situation without the policy intervention. Such an analysis prevents evaluators from over-estimating the effects of the public policy.

For example, the evaluator should determine the extent to which a public financial assistance scheme for job creation did make it possible to create new jobs and how much the absence of public financial assistance would have affected the creation of new jobs. If, say, public assistance has taken the form of job creation grants given to companies which would have created jobs anyhow (i.e. even without public assistance), the term *deadweight* is employed for those who have benefited from the financial support. The net effect of the policy is then obtained by substracting the deadweight effect from the gross effects.

The evaluation of rural development policy in Denmark provides another example. Farmers were to receive a subsidy for the purpose of diversifying their activities. In a survey carried out as a part of an evaluation, the farmers were asked whether they agree with the following sentence: "the support received conditioned the implementation of my diversification project". About 75% of the assisted farmers gave a positive answer. An initial estimation of the deadweight would therefore be around 25%. However a complementary survey was carried out on farmers who had requested assistance but had been rejected for various reasons. The results revealed that all the farmers had implemented their diversification project even without the public assistance. Deadweight can therefore be considered to be 100%. This conclusion is nevertheless hasty, in so far as some of the farmers were not selected for assistance precisely because the project selection committee judged them capable of realizing their project without public support. In such a case, a more in-depth analysis would be necessary to gauge the real deadweight (European Commission 1999:113).

> Challenge 3: *"The evaluator should estimate counterfactual evidence (in order to identify the deadweight of a public policy)"*.

4.4. Comparing Comparable Cases: "Triangulating Methods and Data"

Policy evaluation within the European context (enlarged EU, clusters of regions, etc.) or within a federal country (several federated entities such as Belgian regions and communities, Swiss *cantons*, German *Länder*, etc.) is generally based on interregional comparisons. Various evaluations are launched by funding bodies (e.g. the EU or the central level of power in federal states) to evaluate how a similar program (e.g. a European Directive or a federal law) is implemented, and whether it has produced effects in various countries and/or regions. As a matter of fact, the Europeanization of domestic public policies, namely the response of the domestic policies to the EU policies (minimalist definition in Featherstone 2003), is a growing political reality. The definition of Europeanization is still under discussion in the literature (Cowles *et.al.* 2001; *Héritier et.al.* 2001; Featherstone and Radaelli 2003; Börzel and Risse 2003; Radaelli 2004) and it still covers a very broad range of theoretical and empirical issues. However, in order to explain the impact of a European policy on the domestic policy outputs and outcomes, one must above all scrutinize the behavior of domestic policy actors. Indeed,

Europeanization processes are always mediated by the domestic implementation networks, following different paths.

The methodological challenge is then to compare one (similar) European program, its implementation by domestic actors and its effects in a « small-N » design, with a limited number of various countries, regions and/or administrations implementing the same (causal mechanism of the) European program in various political, administrative, economic and social contexts. The methodological issue consists in identifying all the conditions (at the European level as well as at the domestic level) leading or not leading to the expected policy outputs and outcomes.

As a matter of fact, the evaluator may identify more than one unique (causal) path to the policy outputs and outcomes: more than one combination of (domestic) conditions can account for favorable policy effects. This is quite obvious within the European Union or within federal countries, as practical experience shows that policy effectiveness is often strongly dependent upon national and/or regional settings as well a upon sector-specific features, and that different cultural, political and administrative traditions often call for differentiated implementation schemes.

Furthermore, policy evaluation ideally requires additional comparisons in time (before and after the program implementation; see challenge 2) and space (regions with the program and regions without the program; see challenge 3). Thus, the triangulation of several comparisons is a crucial factor for the methodological quality of an evaluation design. The question is how to develop an evaluation design that combines diachronic and synchronic comparisons and, simultaneously, is still feasible from an economic point of view (e.g. costs of data collection and analysis). Furthermore, the evaluation should ideally compare comparable cases. In real-life policy evaluations, however, the empirical cases to be compared by the evaluator (for example the same policy implemented in all Swiss cantons) are defined by the political reality and not on the basis of methodological considerations. This hinders the development of a comparative evaluation design within a well-defined set of comparable cases.

Challenge 4: *"The evaluator should triangulate many comparisons (before/after program, with/without program, cross-countries/regions/ public administrations/sectors, etc.) within a set of cases that are not (always) comparable."*

A New Method for Policy Evaluation?

5. QCA ANSWERS

5.1 Introduction – Trying to Order Challenges and Answers

A proper QCA analysis consists out of three strategies to address the four methodological challenges of policy evaluation. First of all, since QCA is, in essence, a case-oriented strategy, it allows researchers to conduct a within-case analysis, in order to grasp dynamic within-case processes and identify causal mechanisms which link policy-design (in configuration with contextual conditions) to outcomes (cf. arrow "1" in figure below).

Figure 10.1. Policies and Comparative Strategies

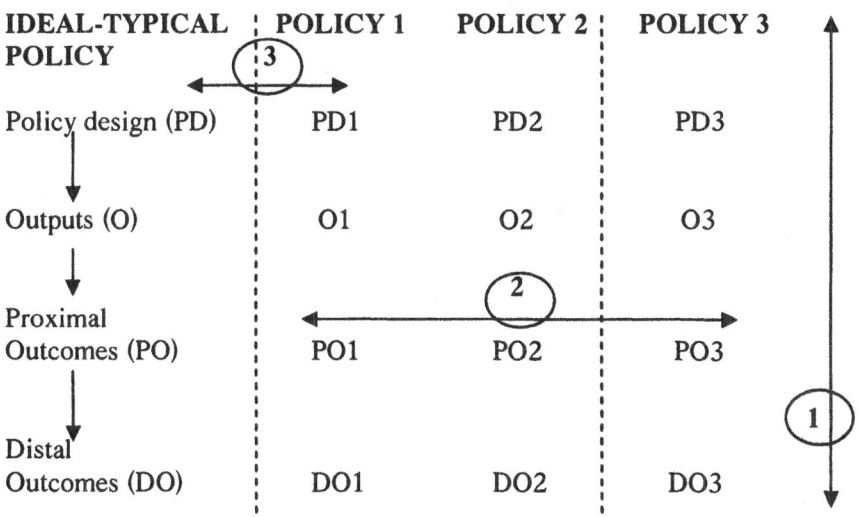

Note: Practical example (of concept of the outcome line) for a public policy: widening of a road to boost the development of an isolated valley
- <u>policy design</u>: budgets allocated, bills used for compulsorily purchase of land (expropriation), information campaign, etc.;
- <u>outputs</u>: kilometers of new roads, enlarged intersections, improved road surfaces;
- <u>proximal outcomes</u>: number of cars using the road, reduced traveling time between two destinations, reduced number of accidents (but also more pollution for people living near the road etc.);
- <u>distal outcomes</u>: more rapid economic development of the towns served, improve access to leisure activities offered the regional capital (but also decreasing value of the neighboring land, etc.).

Secondly, QCA is comparative in nature, which allows researchers to identify differences and similarities across cases (cf. arrow "2"). Finally, both in relation to within-case analysis and cross-case analysis, QCA allows researchers to assess policy implementation vis-à-vis an ideal-typical policy-design. This Weberian ideal-type comparison is especially interesting for policy-evaluation of outcomes in theoretically well-developed fields (see also Kvist, in this volume). For example, in the case of the impact of institutions for the governance of common-pool resources, each institution can be compared to an ideal-type institution such as one constructed by Ostrom (1990). This strategy enables researchers to identify where the actual policy differs from the policy theoretically hypothesized to be effective (cf. arrow "3").

5.2. Challenge 1: Explaining Effects, Testing Program Theory

We will mainly examine the "process theory" side of this challenge, i.e. the challenge to analyze processes, and more specifically to identify *causal* processes linking explanatory conditions to outcomes.

In fact, such issues are very much discussed in the recent literature, also beyond the policy evaluation literature *stricto sensu*. Much attention has been paid recently to the importance of specifying causal mechanisms in order to open the black box of how interventions relate to outcomes (Hedström and Swedborg, 1998). In addition, many authors have argued that 'time matters' due to path-dependent and sequential processes (Abbott 2001; Pierson 2004) and that this should be taken into account in research designs. In contrast to general assumptions that the effect of a policy intervention can be observed after its implementation Paul Pierson (2004) argues that the time horizons of causes and outcomes are far more complex and interact in different ways. The general assumption is that the time horizon of the cause and the time horizon of the outcome are short. However, there are many instances in which this is not the case. A policy outcome can occur shortly after an intervention, but can also be spread out over a long time-period. In addition, policy interventions can have a non-linear impact in the sense that they first generate a shock, which then fades away.

The inclusion of these 'process' challenges in a research-design is not straightforward, especially as the N increases. One possibility is to focus analytic attention to the causal processes as such. This has led some authors to argue that researchers should focus more on "causal process observations" (Brady and Collier 2004; Bennett and George 2005). In order to do this, researchers need to get to grips with the cases under investigation and gain case-specific knowledge.

In this context QCA is a suitable research strategy since, while being a *comparative* strategy, it also in essence a *case-oriented* strategy which pays much attention to "case-based knowledge" (Ragin 2004) and to gathering different types of data on each case. In addition, the configurational minimal formulae produced by QCA identify the key components (conditions) of an explanation and in this way identify the main variables which are important for a mechanism based explanation. It is important to stress, at this point, that QCA as a technique (the software and its Boolean algorithms) does not identify, by itself, a "causeA → causeB → causeC" sequence which eventually produces a certain outcome. QCA does not *include* process as such. What QCA does provide, through the minimization procedure, are key "configurations" of factors (conditions). It is then up to the evaluator to interpret the minimal formula(e), e.g. in terms of sequence ("outcome line", as defined above) between the key conditions identified

Marx and Dombrecht (2004), for example, evaluated why some forms of work organization generated more repetitive strain injuries of the wrist than other forms of work organization for a limited though comparable set of cases. In a first step they compared different forms of work organization and identified different configurations which led to repetitive strain injuries of the wrist. The QCA results showed for example that, in organizations where people had to work at a steady pace, do not rotate between jobs but are able to individually decide when they can take a break, repetitive strain injuries occur. These results were at odds with existing literature which stressed that the possibility to individually insert a break is a good design principle to prevent repetitive strain injuries from occurring. The results/configurations from the QCA analysis were used to return to the cases to analyze which mechanism(s) played between the different variables to produce the outcome. By specifically focusing on causal process observations the researchers found that the key mechanism producing strain injuries was free-time maximization. Most workers saved up all their free time to go home earlier. Hence, the possibility to insert a break at own decision combined with a demanding job in which there is no variation in terms of rotation results in the occurrence of repetitive strain injuries.

Another interesting feature of QCA in this respect follows from its "multiple conjunctural causation" conception of causality (see above). Eventually, in most QCA analyses, the minimal formula will provide not only one configuration; most often, it will provide 2, 3 or 4 configurations ("terms") leading to the *same* outcome. Hence the researcher will be able to interpret (reconstruct) not one, but 2, 3 or 4 (partly or totally) different sequences. This is also coherent with real-life evaluation practice: it gives an added value vis-à-vis most quantitative methods which lead to the identification of "one best way".

In addition, with QCA, the evaluator is 'forced' to operationalize a dichotomous outcome (e.g. success v/s "non-success" or "failure"). Hence the evaluator can also, in a separate analysis, systematically identify the configurations – also to be *interpreted* as a sequence, as above – which lead to a "negative" outcome. Most often, with QCA there is no symmetry between the explanation of a "1" outcome and that of a "0" outcome; this also is in line with evaluation theory and practice.

5.3. Challenge 2: 'Net' Effects; Purging Confounding Factors

Assessing an outcome implies taking many potential different explanatory conditions into account. In order to assess the impact of the factors under investigation, the evaluator should carefully construct a research population. Indeed the careful construction of a research population is an important step in a QCA analysis, too. This can be done by applying the Most Similar Different Outcomes (MSDO) design for constructing a research population (Przeworski and Teune, 1970). This design applies two key principles:

- Principle 1: Maximize the variation on the outcome and conditions (explanatory variables) under investigation.
- Principle 2: Homogenize as much as possible on other possible explanatory conditions.

These two principles imply that the evaluator draws a clear distinction between the conditions that will be included in the model (to be tested through QCA) and those that will be left out. This implies, in turn, that the evaluator carefully constructs the research population in such a way that some possible relevant explanatory factors (apart from the program-linked conditions) are held constant in order to 'neutralize' their effect (see also Collier 1993). Hence the evaluator should come as close as possible to an "experimental" design. Those principles (and practical consequences thereof) are of course common to all well-thought comparative research designs, but they are especially relevant in the context of evaluating policy relevant outcomes which are not linked to a specific policy program.

In practical terms, these requirements are probably difficult to meet in real-life policy evaluation work, as some variation in contextual variables is still most likely to remain. One of the reasons thereof is that the research population may be a "given", e.g. defined *a priori* by the public authority (see also above). For instance, the European Commission may request the evaluation of a specific policy in all 25 EU countries. In such a situation, the evaluator will most probably consider that (national) contexts display a lot a variation – hence several contextual variables will have to be added to the main program conditions (e.g. those identified by theory, by previous studies etc.). The problem, then, is that the evaluator will find him/herself in a problematic "few cases, many variables" situation.

One methodological strategy to meet this difficulty is to run separate QCA analyses on different clusters of cases that are sufficiently similar in terms of context, e.g. 3 clusters: Northern European EU members, Southern European EU members, and the 10 new (Central and East European) EU members. The problem with such a strategy is that it will make it more difficult to reach sufficiently general/comparable conclusions. So while being methodologically sound, this strategy may prove less interesting from the policymaker's perspective.

Another alternative strategy would be to include only *one* additional overall contextual macro-condition to the model for the QCA analysis. If, say, the evaluator is able to distinguish 2 main clusters of cases (say : the 10 new EU member states versus the 15 other states) that differ on quite *several* contextual variables, then he/she can add a condition [NEW], with a '1' score for the new EU members states and a '0' score for the other countries. If the minimal formulae reached at the end of the minimization procedure do not contain this [NEW] or [new][11] condition, then one may conclude that the contextual variables may be left out of the model. If it does contain this [NEW] or [new] condition, then the evaluator has a problem, and some of the (more detailed) contextual variables will need to be added to the model initially tested.

A third way to address this difficulty is to use QCA in a more inductive, iterative way. The first step would consist in producing a truth table adding up both all program and all contextual variables (not an exaggerated number of conditions altogether, of course). Provided there are no contradictory configurations[12], the second step would be to take out of the model, one at a time, contextual conditions, until this eventually causes contradictions. Then, finally, the evaluator can run the QCA analysis (minimization) with the shortest operational model possible, i.e. the model containing as few contextual conditions as possible, and yet still displaying no contradictory configurations.

Eventually, at the end of the second or third procedure explained above, if we take it for granted that *some* contextual variables will have been included in the model (for the reasons explained above), if the minimal formulae do not contain any of the contextual conditions, then the evaluator will be able to evacuate contextual conditions altogether (i.e. concluding that the outcome is really linked to the program – or some specific conditions within the program) and thus identify a high net effect. If not, then the researcher will most likely have to conclude that, in *some* cases (those cases covered by the prime implicants in which contextual conditions show up), the net effect is much lower than in some other cases. In any event, QCA will not allow the evaluator to actually quantify the net effects of the program.

Hence QCA can indeed be useful to make some progress towards an assessment of 'net' effects, especially when they are configurational in nature.

5.4. Challenge 3: Counterfactual Evidence

On a more general level, the use of counterfactuals (broadly defined, i.e. "non-observed" cases, called "remainders" in QCA jargon) lies at the heart of the QCA minimization procedure. It is actually the resort to counterfactuals which allows one to reach more parsimonious minimal formulae. One of the strengths of QCA is also that it *explicitly* addresses the issue of counterfactuals in the course of the analysis (De Meur and Rihoux 2002, 2004; Rihoux and Ragin 2004).

This original feature of QCA can be exploited for evaluation research, as follows:

1. The evaluator should choose, in the minimization procedure of the "1" outcome, to include remainders. This allows the software to select some non-observed combinations of conditions, to which it attributes a "1" outcome score (this is a "simplifying assumption"), hence allowing to express most parsimoniously the regularities (combinations of conditions) shared by the *observed* cases with a "1" outcome. The evaluator then asks the software to produce a list of these simplifying assumptions.
2. The same goes for the minimization procedure for the "0" outcome.
3. When this is done, the evaluator can interpret these lists of non-observed cases selected by the software. If there are no contradictory simplifying assumptions (NB: this is a key requirement; for technical details, see De Meur and Rihoux 2002; Vanderborght and Yamasaki 2004), this means that the evaluator will have at his/her disposal a list of non-observed cases with a "0" outcome. Within this list, he/she will be able to check whether or not one of these non-observed cases comes close to the "absence of program" situation.

Example: consider a simple model such as: [A + B + C = OUTCOME], where A, B and C identify 3 program conditions. If, say, the following non-observed case were to be selected by the software to minimize the "0" outcome:

a b c = outcome

(to be read as follows : a "0" score for condition A, combined with a "0" score for condition B and a "0" score for condition C, leads to a "0" outcome score): this would mean that the absence of program is very likely to lead to a "negative" outcome.

5.5. Challenge 4: Triangulating Comparisons

Another QCA procedure which could be usefully exploited would be to "cross" (= intersect) actually observed cases with "hypotheses". For instance, it is possible to cross the minimal formula for the "1" outcome with the following hypothesis: "a b c = outcome" (for practical examples of this intersection technique, see Peillon 1996; Watanabe 2003; Yamasaki 2003).

All this being said, the informed use of counterfactuals with QCA will not allow the evaluator to actually quantify the level at which the outcome of interest would have be found had the program (to be evaluated) not taken place – for the obvious reason that QCA is dichotomous. This might be attempted by using MVQCA or Fuzzy Sets (however, in these two latest options, the number of potential counterfactuals will become huge, so it will be much more difficult to examine these counterfactual cases in a systematic way).

5.5. Challenge 4: Triangulating Comparisons

As far as the number of cases is concerned, it is quite obvious that QCA is "tailor-suited" for a small-N (meaning: "intermediate-N": from ca. 10 to ca. 40-60[13]) research design. Hence it is perfectly suited for policy evaluation at the cross-national level (e.g. within the E.U.) and cross-regional level (within a country or across countries in the EU). This statement should however be qualified. One the one hand, there should be enough information on what is shared (background, contextual characteristics) between all cases and thus can be left out of the model (see above). On the other hand, there should be enough information (qualitative and/or quantitative) on each case. In a EU or within-European national context, it is reasonable to expect that such conditions are quite often met.

In such a design, it is also perfectly possible, with QCA, to take into account program-linked conditions as well as some case- and context-specific conditions. Indeed, the evaluator should inject 3 types of conditions in the model to be tested:

- program conditions;
- sector-specific features;
- context-specific features (cultural, political or administrative traditions, constraints etc.), i.e. features that are specific to the case or the case's "environment".

As far as the (causal) conclusions reached at the end of the analysis are concerned, QCA will indeed identify, most often, *more than one* combination of conditions leading to the desired output or outcome (or indeed to a negative output or outcome). This central feature of QCA (see "multiple conjunctural causation", above) is thus fully in line with the expectation that policy effects are often strongly dependent upon national and/or regional settings as well as upon sector-specific features, and that different cultural, political and administrative traditions often call for differentiated implementation schemes. Hence if the evaluator includes the right ingredients as conditions (see above), he/she will most probably identify at least 2 or 3 different (causal) paths.

Finally, regarding triangulation, both in time and in space, there are some practical ways in which QCA can be used to this end. One quite straightforward way to proceed is to include a condition such as "program implemented Y/N" [PROGR] in the model. This allows one to compare a set of cases (times 2) before and after implementation. Insofar as there are no contradictory configurations, this will also clearly show whether or not "the program matters" for a favorable outcome, and "how the program matters" – by looking at the other conditions that are associated with [PROGR] in some prime implicants (i.e. in the terms of the minimal formula).

The same sort of *modus operandi* can be applied for regions with and without the program. This can be operationalized by including one additional condition. Alternatively, one could distinguish 2 specific subsets of cases (regions), perform 2 separate QCA analyses, and then see whether the same (causal) combinations can be identified in the 2 minimal formulae.

Such triangulations are possible with QCA at a relatively low cost, but provided that enough data has already been collected. The best situation would be one where some good quality – and comparable – case studies are already available. In such a situation, QCA can then be used to systematically compare those cases.

6. REMAINING CHALLENGES AND NEXT RESEARCH STEPS

In the previous sections, we have demonstrated that QCA clearly has the potential to yield added value for policy evaluation, in particular within a comparative context. Of course, one limitation of our demonstration is that we have not (yet) proved our point on real-life policy evaluation data (see however Befani and Sager, in this volume).[14] This would be an obvious next step. In the meantime, let us point at some further potential benefits of QCA for policy evaluation, as well as some remaining challenges and difficulties.

One further interest of QCA for policy evaluation is that it could support the evaluation process itself, thereby enhancing the evaluation. Indeed, QCA is a very transparent tool. Thus, for instance, once the data has been dichotomized, the evaluator (and all the stakeholders participating to the evaluation) can very easily control the coding of the conditions, modify the dichotomization thresholds for further tests, include other conditions, discuss the robustness of evaluation results, etc.). Hence QCA is also potentially useful for pluralist, participative and empowering policy evaluation. This is also the case of the newly developing MVQCA (Multi-Value QCA; see Cronqvist 2004, and Cronqvist and Berg-Schlosser, in this volume) and Fuzzy Sets (see Kvist, in this volume), which display the further advantage that they can handle more fine-grained data (of course, the other side of the coin is that the data tables are somewhat more complex; but they are usually still not-too-complex for a more participative policy evaluation).

In addition, QCA is also useful for the synthesis of evaluations conducted on the same policy but by various evaluation teams and/or in various countries/regions. Relying on existing qualitative evaluation case studies conducted by different evaluation teams, QCA enables one to perform "systematic comparative case analysis" (see also challenge 4, above; and Befani and Sager, in this volume).

However, some challenges also remain to improve the use of QCA for evaluation purposes. The most important challenge concerns issues related to model specification and case selection. True, this is not only a challenge for a QCA-type of analysis. However, it is more important in QCA than for other types of analysis since QCA is more deterministic in nature.

In principle, it is recommended that QCA users go back and forth between theory and evidence to produce an explanatory model which might contain several causal paths to an outcome. It is important to note that multiple paths to a given outcome are all contained within an initial model which is a result of empirical inductive and theoretical deductive work. That is the reason why much attention is paid to the relationship between theory and data.

Such a research process does not really allow for contradictions to occur. All contradictions must be solved (see above) by developing an initial model on which a QCA analysis proper, i.e. Boolean minimization, can be applied (surely, contradictions can also be solved by other means; see below). Hence, in principle there is always a/one best fit model (BFM). However, it is not always possible to go back to the policy cases and collect additional data to develop this one BFM. Consequently, it is not always possible to fit the model to the data and evaluators need to work with the variables they have at hand. The problem is worse in a synthesis of evaluations where researchers are neither able to generate new data, nor to develop new explanatory conditions which require additional data-input.

The key challenge here consists in developing criteria for the selection of an explanatory model, which adheres to a configurational logic and can be used for a QCA-type of analysis that produces more or less parsimonious results. In other words, which initial model should be chosen to conduct a QCA-type of analysis? Given a number of variables one can develop many different models to be processed in a QCA-analysis. The total number of possible models is given by $2^k -1$ (with k = # variables). Since many policy evaluators are confronted with at least ten possible relevant explanatory variables (conditions), the number of models to choose from becomes very large.

In addition, it could be argued that QCA works best – in terms of parsimony and identification of multiple causal paths – when one works with between 4-7 variables. Yet, in many types of evaluation research more than 7 explanatory variables might be identified as potentially significant components to explain an outcome. Hence it becomes quite crucial to select a valid model to conduct a QCA analysis (see also Amenta and Poulsen 1994). The selection of the model is hampered by the fact that two problems occur when one works with either too few or too many variables in QCA.

On the one hand, if one includes too many variables, a problem of uniqueness might occur, i.e. each case is then simply described as a distinct configuration of variables. This results in full complexity and no parsimony, which might be of limited relevance to policy-makers. With a limited set of cases, this problem starts to occur from 8 variables onwards. On the other hand, if one uses too few variables the probability of contradictions, i.e. the fact that an identical model/configuration both explains successes and failures of policy, increases. This problem easily occurs with models of less than 4 variables, which indicates that there is an important omitted variables bias.

How can these two problems be solved? As far as the problem of uniqueness is concerned, the only solution is to develop limited explanatory models. This implies that the number of variables of an explanatory model should be significantly lower than the number of cases (see also Marx, 2005). With regards to the problem of contradictions, there are several possible ways to deal with it (see e.g. Clément 2004; De Meur and Rihoux 2002; Vanderborght and Yamasaki 2004). First, a new more homogenous and comparable research population can be constructed, by including new cases or removing cases (however this is not always possible when cases are "given"; see above). Secondly, new variables could be included in the explanatory model. Thirdly, existing variables – including the outcome variable, possibly – could be recoded or reconceptualized. A final way to deal with contradictions is to keep only those configurations which contain at least two or more cases for the minimization procedure, since it is often the case that contradictions are generated because only one contradictory case occurs. These contradictions are disregarded when one specifies that at least two or more cases should be covered by a given configuration. The drawback of this decision is that it decreases the number of cases in an analysis and hence excludes possible relevant configurations (and real-life cases, from the decision-maker's perspective). This is especially problematic when one works with (biased) samples and when the aim is to explore data and generate hypotheses. Concerning the latter it is best to exclude as few cases as possible and hence proceed with an analysis of all possible cases.

However, all the possible solutions we have sketched here often only produce partial solutions. Moreover, it should be noted that there seems to be a trade-off between the two main problems of contradictions and uniqueness. The shorter (i.e. the most parsimonious) the models, the more contradictions; the more extensive the models, the less possibility to summarize data and obtain parsimonious explanations. Hence, increasing the number of variables to solve the problem of contradictions is not really a solution. The risk with increasing the number of variables is not only indeterminacy but also uniqueness.

How then to proceed? How to select a suitable model or models for evaluating policies? One possible solution to the problem of model specification is to develop a "two-step approach" in QCA, i.e. to distinguish "remote" from "proximate" conditions (Schneider and Wagemann forthcoming). A problem with the two-step approach is that it is very sensitive to contradictions. A first step of the two-step approach, with a small number of "remote" conditions, will most often result in a very high proportion of contradictions.

Another possible way is to be tolerant of contradictions and try to identify the model which best fits the data in terms of balancing the number of contradictions and the number of configurations. In other words, the aim is to find a model with jointly the least configurations (reduction of complexity – parsimony) and the least contradictions. This means that one does not select the model with the least configurations or the least number of contradictions, but the model which scores best on the two criteria combined. This 'sub-optimal' model can then be used for further QCA analysis.

NOTES

[1] Some work by Sager (2002, 2004), Befani (2004) and Balthasar (2004) is, however, specifically dedicated to the field of policy evaluation. See in particular Befani and Sager, in this volume.

[2] Note that a policy evaluation can also be undertaken before the public policy is formally adopted (ex ante evaluation) or during its implementation process (on-going or mid-term evaluation).

[3] In QCA terminology, a *condition* stands for an « explanatory variable », or an « independent variable ». NB : it is *not* an independent variable in the statistical sense of the term.

[4] In QCA terminology, as indeed in evaluation terminology, the *outcome* is the ultimate « dependent variable ».

[5] For more information, see the "software" page on the COMPASSS resource site (http://www.compasss.org). See also Cronqvist (2004).

[6] For an accessible presentation of some key elements of Boolean logic, see (Ragin 1987: 103-163). For more details on the concrete steps of the analysis and use of the software, see (De Meur and Rihoux 2002; Ragin and Rihoux 2004; Rihoux et.al. 2003).

[7] The TOSMANA software also allows multivalue coding.

[8] To put it short: a *configuration* is a given combination of some conditions (each one receiving a « 1 » or « 0 » value) and an outcome (receiving a « 1 » or « 0 » value). A specific configuration may correspond to several observed cases.

[9] In technical terms: the software will give a « 0 » or « 1 » outcome value to these logical cases, thus making *simplifying assumptions* about these cases.

[10] Actually, some middle paths also exist, between maximal complexity and maximal parsimony (Ragin and Rihoux 2004).

[11] In QCA notation, [NEW] (uppercase) stands for a "1" score and [new] (lowercase) for a "0" score.

[12] A contradictory configuration is a combination of conditions with the *same* condition values that leads to *different* outcome values (a "1" outcome for some cases, and a "0" outcome for some other cases), thereby producing a logical contradiction. See also Cronqvist and Berg-Schlosser, in this volume.

[13] Actually it is also possible to use QCA with less than 10 cases. As for the upper limit, it is also possible to treat much more than 60 cases, as long as it is possible to gain some case knowledge for each case included (Ragin and Rihoux 2004).

[14] Note that QCA has already been used in quite numerous policy *analysis* applications (see full list via: http://www.compasss.org), but indeed not specifically policy *evaluation*, with a few exceptions (see note 1 above).

Chapter 11

SOCIAL SUSTAINABILITY OF COMMUNITY STRUCTURES: A SYSTEMATIC COMPARATIVE ANALYSIS WITHIN THE OULU REGION IN NORTHERN FINLAND

Pentti Luoma
University of Oulu

1. INTRODUCTION

The aim of my contribution is to analyze and compare social sustainability in thirteen residential areas in Oulunsalo by using statistical and crisp set analyses. The social sustainability can be here defined as social integration of people into their residential area. Thus the social sustainability implies that people are not willing to out-migrate to a large extent and that they are not marginalized in the community life.

One of the main objects of our research project is to develop planning methods for growing and especially for declining areas. The object of physical planning is always a regional unit even if many regional levels are involved. That is why it is necessary to have information on various regional levels including – at the micro level - the municipalities and residential areas. The areas have to be studied as wholes, which is one of the starting points of QCA: to study cases as totalities (Ragin 1987).

Secondly, it is an option to analyze the material inductively. One may ask whether QCA can produce unexpected findings, fresh hypotheses or theoretical ideas for further studies. This kind of inductive and heuristic use of QCA is also possible on top of testing hypotheses and theories (Ragin 1987). Thirdly, the idea is here to try to make empirical generalizations, when discussing the problems of social sustainability for the future studies.

The precondition to social sustainability is, of course, economic sustainability. The economic base of the area has to be strong enough to guarantee the material well-being and to prevent unemployment, marginalization and out-migration. That is why this article starts with an overview of the economic and spatial development in Finland and in the Oulu region.

2. THE ECONOMIC AND SPATIAL STRUCTURES IN FINLAND AND IN THE OULU REGION

Finland has been a small, export-oriented economy with low demand on the national market, which is a consequence of the small size of the population. Alapuro (1988) characterized the earlier Finnish society with its economy based on the forestry sector as a semi periphery in the world system with its own internal peripheries in the north and in the east. By now, the economy of Finland relies less on the forestry sector and more on the electronic and information technology (IT) industries (Oksa 1998; Yli-Jokipii 1998).

Since the fall of the Soviet Union and its bilateral trade with Finland, the IT sector has been the new motor of the Finnish economy and society. The investment in IT research and development has increased radically as a consequence. Globalization pushed forward the emergence of the IT industries, most notably Nokia with its subcontractors. The growth of this sector boosted the development of Oulu as a national and even international center of IT research, development and industry.

"The global age" is far more than just an economic issue. It includes among other things the issues of political and social control and the issues of the social and cultural "globalizations" and their appearance at the local level (Albrow 1998:4). In regard to political control globalization implies the weakening status of the nation-states as decision makers. Morin and Hanley (2004:370) claim that *"the Keynesian way of dealing with the economic problems at the national level is contested and the role of the state regarding social regulation is changing"*.

Globalization also involves a kind of localization (Albrow 1998: 93). It is the question about the global production of locality (Appadurai 1998: 188-199). According to Hyyryläinen (1999: 8) we are witnessing in Finland *"at the moment a simultaneous strengthening of both international and local ties"*.

Globalization has contradictory regional effects, in so far as some parts of the world and national regions gain and the others, with declining industries, lose in the accelerating international competition (e.g. Morin and Hanley 2004). This feature is embedded in our research plan which studies ecological, spatial and social sustainability in both thriving and declining municipalities and communities (Hentilä et al. 2004). How does the population mobility – expressed either as growth or decline – affect the ecological and spatial situation in the areas studied? On the one hand, some buildings and infrastructures are left idle in the rural areas, which lose population. On the other hand, the building of houses and infrastructure is extended to the uninhabited semi rural areas located around the centers. One of the major issues for physical planners is to achieve ecological and social sustainability.

The economic and social development of the Oulu region is even more tightly linked to the growth of IT research, development and production. This development is closely interrelated with economic globalization in IT sector. Located in the less developed northern Finland, Oulu could be characterized as a center on the periphery of a semi peripheral country. Even in the age of tar trade and shipbuilding, the city had close contacts to international centers. Thereafter, the city area was focused on export-oriented sawmills, pulp and paper production.

The growth of the city of Oulu can be described as a national success story in information technology research, development and manufacturing in a peripheral region. The development of the IT sector is based on the close cooperation between the University of Oulu, its science park, the local IT firms and the local authorities (more in Reinikainen 1998). This cooperation has sometimes been called a new urban regime, or "local development bloc", which refers, according to Oksa (1999: 72-73), to the power relations involved but absent in the more neutral conceptions such as "local cooperation" or "networking". In the Oulu region, this co-operation has been listed in the region's growth agreement between local authorities and firms (Oulu 2006: 2003).

Even if the IT-sector grows rapidly, the unemployment rate is expected to remain rather high in the Oulu region. For example, some of the assembly functions of the IT-industry have already been relocated to areas of cheaper labor, e.g. to Estonia and Russia[1], that is seen also elsewhere around the Western world. Except for assembly lines, even the research and development units of the IT-industries are facing new challenges.[2] The emergence of these industries has been beneficial to the economy of the Oulu region[3], but there are, however, economic pressures on relocating these industries to countries with lower production costs.

2.1 The Spatial Structures of Finland and the Oulu Region

The modernization of Finland began rather late. At the beginning of the 1960s more than half of the people lived on the countryside (e.g. Heikkilä and Järvinen 2002: 3) working in agriculture and forestry. This period was followed by the period of industrialization, the formation of a welfare state and urbanization.

Finland is very sparsely populated, with a dense population only in major city areas. The cities and towns are smaller and the share of the urban population is smaller than in the EU states on average (Heikkilä and Järvinen 2002:11).

The biggest urban area (including the surrounding municipalities) in Finland is Helsinki (URL: http://www.citypopulation.de/; cited 2004-03-24). The area is now growing very rapidly compared to bigger cities in Europe. According to recent estimations, there will be almost 25% more inhabitants in the area by 2015 than in 1995 (Heikkilä and Järvinen 2002:12). There are also some smaller urban areas, such as the Oulu region, which are growing rapidly. At the same time the population is radically declining on the countryside in the northern and eastern parts of Finland, as well as in some traditional industrial cities.The urban region of Oulu is the fourth biggest in the country after the Helsinki, Tampere and Turku regions (URL: http://www.citypopulation.de/; cited 2004-03-24). Almost 80% of the people in the Oulu region live in the city and the rest in the surrounding municipalities, which (like Kiiminki, Oulunsalo, Kempele and Liminka) have grown rapidly in recent decades. Measured in absolute numbers, the in-migration was highest in the Helsinki and Tampere regions (Virtanen 2003: 22). Even compared to the urban growth in the more populated Turku region, the absolute population growth in the Oulu region was higher (ibid.: 22; see also Jauhiainen 2004: 34). The Oulu 2006 Growth Agreement states that *"high technology plays a highly important role in the region of Oulu in terms of economy and employment. According to the statistics compiled by Statistics Finland, the five clusters of the growth agreement - that, in practice, cover the high technology in the region of Oulu - employ nearly 15,000 people and generate an annual turnover of about € 3.7 billion."* (Oulu 2006: 2003).

2.2 Oulunsalo – a Semi Urban Municipality

As a consequence of high growth in the whole Oulu region[4], the formerly much smaller surrounding rural municipalities (e.g. Oulunsalo) have witnessed even greater relative growth in population. Until the 1970s, Oulunsalo was a stagnant agricultural municipality. Its economy was earlier based on farming, fishing and sawmills products. Its population remained stagnant from the 1920s to the 1970s. Since then, the population in Oulunsalo has increased from 2000 to over 8000 from the 1970s to the present (Laakkonen-Pöntys et al. 2004:56).

In a recent profiling report Oulunsalo is seen as one of the high tech municipalities. In the survey report, the airport (situated in Oulunsalo) is seen as "the gate to the world" and as a support to the industries. Oulunsalo is also seen as a cozy living place close to the Gulf of Bothnia (Halonen and Korkala 2003:59-61.)[5] The population share of children and young people is very high. According to the statistics from the year 2002 (Copyright Tilastokeskus - Statistics Finland - ALTIKA 2003), children and young people (up to the age of 18) comprised 37% of the total population.

The economic structure of Oulunsalo has changed radically. On the one hand, the population growth in Oulunsalo can be seen as a consequence of the growth in electronic and IT industries. The largest of the Finnish software companies, the CCC Group - consisting of 20 firms and founded in 1985, which is producing customized software solutions for large-scale industry and administrations – could be mentioned as an example (for more information see URL: http://www.ccc.fi/index.htm).[6]

The spatial structure is *"inseparable from the overall process of social organization and social change"*, according to Castells (2002b:393). A comparison of the social and spatial structures of the Oulu region compared to the world mega cities (Borja and Castells 2003: 39-44) shows that the residential areas are not so sharply divided, even if there is a lot of talk about "the luxurious houses of IT-millionaires" in Oulunsalo.

Figure 11.1: The Population Change in Oulunsalo since the Beginning of the 20th Century

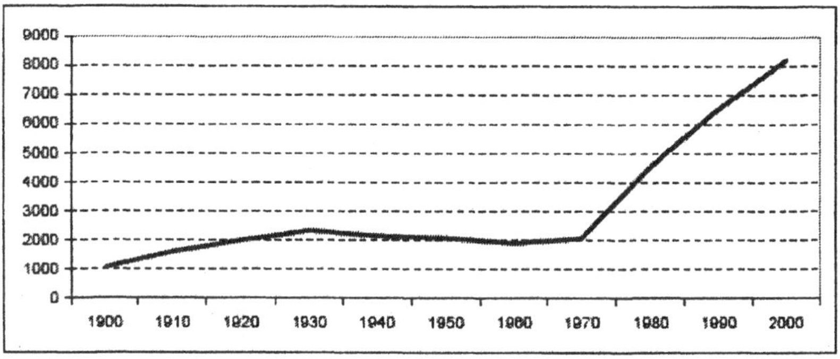

Source: Laakkonen–Pöntys et al. 2004: 56

In the 70s and early 80s, the growth of Oulunsalo was based on minor urban sprawl. The "early movers" to Oulunsalo were people living and working in Oulu but wishing to live on the countryside. These population movements took place after the great migration wave in Finland in the 60s and early 70s. At that time, people moved from the countryside to the cities, from the North and East to the South (and also to Sweden), and from agriculture to industry and the growing service sector. The out-migration from the rural areas decreased in general in the late 70s and in the 80s, but increased again noticeably at the end of the 90s (e.g. Jauhiainen 2004: 32).

Although many people moved to the cities they still kept their cultural heritage from the countryside. That is why also some of those living in Oulu wanted to move to the surrounding areas, from apartments to their own single family houses usually built by themselves. A special feature of the Finnish culture (found elsewhere, too) is still a strong longing to live on the countryside but close to the cities and their services. This assumption is supported by survey findings, where two thirds of the people living in urban or semi urban areas rated single house areas near the cities as their favorite living environment (cited in Viinikainen and Puustinen 2000: 46). Furthermore, many people often have a summer place of their own on the countryside (ibid.: 65).

3. THE RESEARCH METHODS

The data used in the following analysis was collected at the beginning of 2004 by postal survey. The survey was multifunctional. Aside from the usual background information of the respondents, data was collected a) about the people's conceptions and attitudes on their place of residence as well as b) about specific facts about the physical environments of the respondents. A random sample of 500 persons in Oulunsalo, born before 1988, was collected. The total number of people of this age group was nearly 6,000, which means that almost one tenth was sampled. The response rate was nearly 42%.

Quite a lot of open-ended questions were used in the questionnaire. The idea was to combine qualitative and quantitative data and intensive and extensive analysis of the data (Sayer 2000:19-22) in our analysis. A preliminary report based on the survey was published in Finnish at the end of 2004 (Hagman and Mäntysalo 2004). The material used in this article stems from this survey. The analysis is based on crisp set and statistical analyses. It is fleshed out by qualitative content analysis of the answers to the open-ended questions in the survey.

The data is analyzed using fs/QCA 1.1 (Ragin and Giesel 2002; see also http://www.fsqca.com). When using dichotomies, as in QCA or in the crisp set analysis as in this chapter, some information is lost (see also Cronqvist and Berg-Schlosser; Kvist, in this volume). Thus the findings presented here below should be seen as exploratory. In addition to fs/QCA, SPSS 11.5 for Windows (http://www.spss.com/) was used for the statistical analyses and NVivo 2 for Windows (Richards 2000) for the analysis of the answers to the open-ended questions. Thus the analysis moves between qualitative, comparative and statistical analyses, with references to some theoretical and empirical studies.

4. THE ANALYSIS OF SOCIAL SUSTAINABILITY

Social integration can be seen as a short-term indicator of social sustainability. One way to define it is to see people integrated if they embrace the values and norms of the societies they live in. This Parsonsian "pattern maintenance" approach concentrates on the study of the culture of the communities and societies. People are seen as well integrated if they act as "model individuals" of their communities. One of the well-known difficulties with this approach underestimates the social differentiation and conflicts in communities or societies. There are always contested and even opposing systems of values and norms, especially in modern communities and societies.

In contrast to this integrationist conception, social integration can also be seen in a more mundane way or as an indication of social sustainability. People can be seen as well integrated in their communities, if a) they are satisfied with their living conditions; b) if there are not large proportions of people excluded from the labor or housing markets and social support (more about sustainable housing in Green Eight 2004: 56-57); and c) if they are not going to move away for social, economic or cultural reasons. This conception is linked to the transformation of cities and communities caused by globalization. The issue is: what is the role of local communities in globalized societies? Is there enough social sustainability in the city areas to form preconditions for social cohesion and thus to produce social action when needed? Or are the societies and communities vanishing under the pressures of consumerism and individualization (e.g. Castells 2002a: 384-385; Borja, Castells et al. 2003: 136-137)?

Raising the issue of social integration does not equate with longing for the great age of community. Instead it has many pragmatic implications. Some degree of social integration is necessary for self-reflexivity and agency, which are socially structured (e.g. Lauder et al. 2004: 6-8). Self-reflexivity means that people have to know and to interpret what is happening in their neighborhoods. Otherwise they are individualized objects of abstract forces that are capable of influencing only their own living conditions. Agency means that there are moments in the development of communities and societies, when more or less spontaneous collective action is needed. A "spontaneous agency" develops when diverse social movements (such as environmental or urban movements) quickly emerge, so as to try to stop the undesirable changes in the community or society in question or to strive for some desired ends.

It is not, however, spontaneous agency solely that is at stake here.[7] This kind of citizen's agency is even called for in politics and planning. Politics cannot work without the support of the citizens. On the other hand, planning theory and practice have moved from the abstractly rational planning to more interactive planning, where the conceptions and opinions of the citizens concerned are taken seriously. For example, in physical and forest planning some forms of participation and interaction are even enacted by the law. These are not possible in a totally individualized world. The new, active citizenship is especially needed in the globalizing world (see e.g. Urry 1999).

This leads to the issue of social capital that is closely connected to the theory of social networks based on trust (e.g. Lin 2001). It means that staying in the area with the feeling "this is home" can be seen as a precondition for social networking, participation and social action. It is, however, important to remember that the social networks should not be seen in a too idyllic way. Power relations are always embedded in the networks as well as in the citizenship. The network view also divides the social networks into global and local (Savage et al. 2005: 6).

The aim in this chapter is not to study social integration through values and norms. Instead two indicators that to some extent measure the state of integration are employed. One is based on a survey question on whether the respondent is dissatisfied with or does not feel comfortable living in his/her residential area (NOSAT = the proportion of those who are only partially or not at all satisfied in living in their residential area is higher than the average). The second is based on the question on whether the respondent wants to move out of the residential area he/she is currently living in (MIGR = the percentage of those who want to out-migrate is higher than the average). The network aspect is measured by asking how well the respondents know the people in their neighborhood (NOKNOW = the percentage of those who do not agree at all with the statement that they know their neighbors well is higher than the average).

These are, of course, only rough indicators for social integration. However, they can be used as measures of non-integrationist integration mentioned earlier. In general, these indicators do not provide alarming findings for Oulunsalo. Rather, 75% of the people are satisfied with life in their residential area and only 23% want to move away. This being said, this willingness to move out can be interpreted as one of the greatest threats for the social sustainability of the rural municipalities of Ristijärvi and Suomussalmi in the east. The proportion of those in Oulunsalo who do not agree at all with the statement that they know their neighbors well is only 12%.

There are, however, statistical differences between the residential areas in Oulunsalo. In order to understand the combination of factors that influence the degree of social integration (as defined above), we study some preconditions for social participation and action to find out whether Oulunsalo inhabitants are attached to the area. If these conditions which are further explained in section 4.1 are not existent, people feel un-attached and may react by moving out of the area.

4.1 Factors Influencing Social Integration

There are at least three types of factors that may influence the attachment to the area. These types of factors are the:
a) locality of the population;
b) physical features of the housing; and
c) social characteristics of the population.

The locality of population supposes that those who have lived a long time in their area and in their house or apartment probably are better rooted in the area. This locality may lead more probably to social integration and thus also to social participation and action in the area. Those who recently migrated to the area have not yet integrated into the neighborhood. In the classical neighborhood studies, this latter view of anonymous suburban neighborhoods is emphasized and grounded by high mobility and rootlessness of the inhabitants who tend to engage in an instrumental and individualized behavior (Savage et al. 2005: 78).

Social mobility is based on the social choices of the individuals. These choices are structured by the development of the economy which, in the growing centers, is different from that in the economically and socially declining rural areas with weakening structural options. These push and pull effects have an impact on the structural conditions influencing the choices of individuals.

This is not, however, the whole story. The structural effects never determine the individual decisions, but they can be seen as *"causal mechanisms"*, present or absent in specific situations (e.g. Sayer 2000: 10-17). Thus it is also necessary to take into account the situations in which people make their choices. For example, both the personal environment and the local culture affect specific decision-making. A traditional theme in urban sociology has been that urbanism is culturally the driving force while the way of life in the rural areas is seen as a backward and vanishing cultural mode. This cultural effect of "urban ethos" causing out-migration has been recently verified by Baeck (2004) in her study of young people in the north of Norway.

A classical idea in the theory of physical planning is that the plans can sometimes affect the social life in residential areas. This relatively untenable view has been labeled as physical determinism. It is evident that social life can take different forms in various areas, whether they are well planned or not. Even in some areas of low quality housing a high level of social action can be detected. Accordingly, many local social movements are the products of deficient living conditions. Hence, in the well-planned and highly rated areas, individualization and consumerism may even hinder social action. At least the social action is different so that individuals with more economic and social capital try to participate by lobbying directly with the construction firms, planners and the authorities by using their direct contacts to the elites, whether those individuals are well-integrated or not.

Social characteristics of the population, too, may be hypothesized to affect the attachment to the residential area. A well-known fact is that those with lower financial resources cannot move away; instead they have to stay in the area and make the most out of it. The people with more resources – both material and social – in contrast, are not so dependent on their residential area and are more apt to move away for various reasons. They solve their problems of their everyday lives by out-migrating.

Residential areas, apartments and houses can also be studied by operationalizing the lifecycles of their inhabitants. There are new areas that are firstly inhabited by young families. When the children grow up, they usually move away. When the others, who stay, grow older they start planning to move away to smaller houses and apartments close to services. This is why age, as well as family structures, may affect the attachment to the area and migration.

The following factors are used as indicators of locality, physical environment and social characteristics:

a) Locality:
LONG = the proportion of the respondents who have lived in their current house or apartment for at least 10 years is larger than the average;
LOCAL = the proportion of the respondents who have lived in Oulunsalo all of their life is higher than the average;
OULUNS = the proportion of the respondents who work in Oulunsalo is higher than the average.

b) Physical features[8]:
NEW = the proportion of houses built in the 1990s is higher than the average in the area;
APART = the proportion of people living in apartments (not in single family houses) is higher than the average;
NOOWN = the proportion of rental houses and apartments is higher than the average;
BIG = the proportion of houses or apartments with at least 100 square meters is higher than the average.

c) Social characteristics:
YOUNG = the proportion of respondents who are younger than 45 years is higher than the average;
CHILDR = the proportion of respondents who have children (under 18 years of age) is higher than the average;
UNI = the proportion of respondents with a university education is higher than the average;
WELL = the proportion of respondents whose self-estimated level of income is high is higher than the average.

At this stage of the research only indicators that are easily obtained from the survey are used. The indicators used here are rather heuristic.

Social Sustainability of Community Structures 247

Table 11.1. The Distributions of the Variables[9] Used as the Basis of the Truth Table in the Residential Areas[10]

AREA	LONG	LOCAL	OULUNS	NEW	APART	NOOWN	BIG	YOUNG	CHILDR	UNI	WELL	NOSAT	MIGR	NOKNOW
Karhuoja-Niemenranta	62,5	12,5	62,5	14,3	0	12,5	86,7	31,3	66,7	12,5	12,5	12,6	6,3	6,3
Keskusta	57,6	18,2	23,8	9,7	8,7	15,2	48,4	54,6	53,2	22,6	31,3	18,2	27,3	12,1
Koura	53,3	18,8	36,4	33,3	7,1	12,5	71,4	66,6	68,8	25	43,8	25	37,6	6,3
Kylänpuoli	66,7	0	0	0	0	11,1	62,5	33,3	55,6	11,1	11,1	11,1	33,3	0
Lassila-Ranta	42,9	7,1	8,3	15,4	0	0	71,4	57,1	64,3	21,4	38,5	42,8	30,8	35,7
Airport Rd area	0	0	0	0	0	100	50	100	50	0	0	100	50	50
Lunki-Pellonpää-Karhukangas	14,3	25	20	85,7	50	25	50	62,5	37,5	12,5	12,5	37,5	0	0
Hailuoto rd. area	90,9	27,3	20	33,3	0	0	70	18,2	45,5	0	10	20	18,2	0
Pitkäkangas	24,4	7,3	18,9	65	40,6	29,3	52,5	80,5	70	12,2	17,1	26,9	17,5	15
Santaniemi	60	0	33,3	30	0	10	90	30	20	10	22,2	20	10	40
Varjakka	72,7	27,3	20	14,3	0	4,8	77,3	59,1	54,5	14,3	28,6	18,2	31,8	4,5
Vihiluoto	11,1	0	25	87,5	50	11,1	22,2	88,9	44,4	25	22,2	33,3	22,2	11,1
Örmi	33,3	11,1	14,3	44,4	18,8	33,4	66,7	66,7	55,6	5,6	11,1	27,8	27,8	5,6
All	47,8	13,4	21,9	34,5	13,8	16,8	62,7	58,7	56,8	14,9	22,5	24,6	23,2	12
Percentile (25)	19,4	0	11,3	12	0	7,4	50	32,2	45	7,8	11,1	18,2	13,8	2,3
Percentile (50)	53,3	11,1	20	30	0	12,5	66,7	59,1	54,5	12,5	17,1	25	27,3	6,3
Percentile (75)	64,6	21,9	29,2	54,7	29,7	27,2	74,4	73,6	65,5	22	29,6	35,4	32,6	25,4

CASEID	LONG	LOCAL	OULUNS	NEW	APART	NOOWN	BIG	YOUNG	CHILDR	UNI	WELL	NOSAT	MIGR	NOKNOW
Karhuoja-Niemenranta	1	0	1	0	0	0	1	0	1	0	0	0	0	0
Keskusta	0	1	0	0	0	0	0	0	0	1	1	0	1	0
Koura	0	1	1	0	0	0	0	0	1	1	1	0	1	0
Kylänpuoli	1	0	0	0	0	0	0	0	0	0	0	0	1	0
Lassila-Ranta	0	0	0	0	0	0	0	0	1	1	1	1	1	1
Airport area	0	0	0	0	0	1	0	0	0	0	0	1	1	1
Lunki-Pellonpää-Karhukangas	0	1	0	1	1	1	0	0	0	0	0	1	0	0
Hailuoto rd. area	1	1	0	0	0	1	0	0	0	0	0	0	0	0
Pitkäkangas	0	0	0	1	1	0	0	1	1	0	0	0	0	1
Santaniemi	0	0	1	0	0	0	1	0	0	0	0	0	0	0
Varjakka	1	1	0	0	0	0	0	0	0	0	0	0	1	1
Vihiluoto	0	0	0	1	1	0	0	1	1	0	1	1	0	0
Örni	0	0	0	1	1	1	0	0	0	0	0	0	1	0

4.1.1 The Local, Physical and Social Characteristics

At first it can be asked, which local, physical and social characteristics seem to explain social integration into the area. This distinction of the factor groups is of course artificial. It is a well-known fact in social geography that those factor groups are bound together in many ways.

In the first phase of the analysis, the Boolean formulae based on the truth table (table 11.2) were calculated by using the crisp set analysis method based on the Quine-McCluskey algorithm in the fs/QCA 1.1 program (Ragin and Giesel 2002; see also http://www.fsqca.com). All the contradictory configurations were excluded from the analysis. It is necessary to note that qualitative comparative analysis is used here rather mechanically. The aim is to inductively produce some hypotheses for further research. This is why contradictions are not systematically checked even if reported in some evident cases.

The conditions were classified in the analysis as explained earlier. Hence the locality, physical and social factors were analyzed separately. The results are summarized in table 11.3.

Table 11.3. Crisp Set Analysis: 9 Minimal Formulae

The factor group	The proportion of those satisfied with living in the area (nosat)	The proportion of those who do not want to migrate out of their residential area (migr)	The proportion of those who at least to some extent agree they know their neighbors (noknow)
Locality factors	(1) LONG ouluns + long OULUNS + ----- One of the Following ----- LONG local + local OULUNS ------------------------- Disregarding "OULUNS": nosat = LONG	(2) local OULUNS	(3) LONG local + long LOCAL + ----- One of the Following ----- LONG ouluns + LOCAL ouluns ------------------------- Disregarding "OULUNS": noknow = LONG + LOCAL
Physical features	(4) new apart noown BIG	(5) new apart noown BIG + NEW APART noown big	(6) NEW APART noown big
Social characteristics	(7) young childr WELL + young CHILDR uni well	(8) CHILDR uni well	(9) young childr WELL + young CHILDR uni well

In the next sections, the respective minimal formulae (the number of the formula, from 1 to 9, is mentioned in parentheses in the following text.) will be interpreted.

4.1.2 Feeling "Cozy"

In which kinds of areas are people most satisfied? Firstly, a high level of satisfaction correlates with the length of life time spent in one area while working more often outside the area, or vice versa. Satisfaction increases in the areas consisting of more than average people working outside Oulunsalo and having lived in Oulusalo longer. On the other hand there is quite a contradictory causal combination: working in Oulunsalo seems to increase satisfaction in areas consisting of newcomers more than average.

One might expect that the satisfaction with the working place would not affect very much the satisfaction with the residential area. Some people, perhaps, are not attached to the residential areas in which they live. The center of their life may be "at work" whereas the place of living is simply "at home" for them, no matter where it is situated. Also commuting is rather easy in the Oulu region due to the short distances and good connections.

Hence this factor may be "suppressed" in the analysis, as found in the classical example of elaboration in survey analysis (e.g. Rosenberg 1968: 87; referring to the article by Lipsitz 1965). That is why OULUNS is in the next step excluded from the formula, and the formula NOSAT = LONG + LOCAL is analyzed instead. This leads to the following crisp set solution: [nosat = LONG] - i.e. only the time lived in the current home increases the degree of satisfaction in the various areas in Oulunsalo. This also means that satisfaction with the area does not seem to depend on the regional origin of the people living in Oulunsalo.

Secondly, (4) people seem to be more satisfied in areas with big, elder single-family houses of their own. The owners themselves have usually built houses earlier for their families. The satisfaction ("feeling home") with the area may be hypothesized as being the product of one's own efforts of building the house.

Social characteristics (7) are more difficult to interpret since there are plenty of contradictory cases. However, the people seem to feel most satisfied in the areas with elderly, childless and wealthier people; or in areas with elderly people with children under 18, with less education and income. The first factor of this formula refers to wealthier and quality residential areas. The second factor refers to the areas richer with children than with status.

4.1.3 To Stay or Not

The first formula (2) on the willingness to out-migrate is linked to areas in which a great number of people live who moved to Oulunsalo from elsewhere, but work in the city. Working in Oulunsalo seems to lower the willingness to out-migrate, in conjunction with the higher percentage of those in-migrating to their living environments.

The next formula (5) for not out-migrating gives a contradictory picture, with more nuances. The areas where people like to stay are either the older areas with big, single-family houses or the areas with more new, small and self-owned apartments. The second factor perhaps refers to the fact that people living in these areas are young. They have probably moved from the house of their parents to the first apartment of their own and are not planning to move away in the near future.

By contrast, studying the effects of the social characteristics on staying in the areas (8) gives a rather simple result. People who like to stay in the lower status areas display a rather high proportion of families with children. It is understandable that moving with children is more difficult than without, especially if families are provided with fewer social and financial resources. Applying de Morgan's law, it is possible to calculate the formula for out-migration: MIGR = childr + UNI + WELL. This formula only gives support to the well-known fact in migration theories: people without children or with more resources (higher education or income) are more mobile.

4.1.4 Knowing the Neighbors

Calculating the formula of knowing one's neighbors in the areas (3) leads to rather contradictory results, which may be difficult to interpret. In the areas with a higher proportion of people who have lived for a long time in their homes and have in-migrated from outside Oulunsalo, or people born in Oulunsalo not having lived long in their present home, they knew their neighbors better. The next two optional factors show that, in the areas with more people working outside Oulunsalo, whether they have lived longer in their homes or were born in Oulunsalo, they knew their neighbors better than the average. This is rather difficult to interpret. Those people working elsewhere, however, seem to be well integrated into their residential areas.

Once again, by removing the "OULUNS" condition, a more reasonable formula is obtained: noknow = LONG + LOCAL. This shows that locality equates with more familiar social relations in the area. This refers to the rather self-evident fact that people in the areas with many newcomers and people born outside of Oulunsalo do not know their neighbors as well as in other areas.

Regarding the factors describing the physical factors of the areas, formula (6) produces an interesting solution, which is exactly the same as the second term of formula (5). People seem to know their neighbors better in the new areas in which they live in small apartments of their own. As noted earlier, the willingness to out-migrate is also lower in these areas, compared to the others. It is, however, important to notice, that there are 11 (out of 13 cases) contradictions in this formula. There is actually only one area (Vihiluoto) that fulfils this condition. Also the next formula (9) reveals as much as 10 contradictory cases.

Regarding the physical features of the areas, surprisingly, we observe a kind of polarization. The findings suggest, on the one hand, that people feel at home in more traditional areas and do not want to move out from such areas (4-5). On the other hand, the findings suggest a hypothesis that people do not want to move out and are socially well integrated in the areas with more small, new self-owned apartments (5-6). People may just be happy "living on the countryside", as one respondent suggested in an answer to an open-ended question.

At this phase the findings are only trend setting, and they should be elaborated in the future. In the following section, we search for statistical correlations through regression analysis, which in turn will be complemented with crisp set analysis of the factors in order to study the causal configurations of the factors whose effects are statistically significant.

4.1.5 Statistical Analysis

It is always challenging to draw general and unambiguous conclusions about a big number of factors that explain a social phenomenon. Even at first sight, it is difficult to explain social integration within the selected areas with the 11 explanatory factors used above by interpreting the Boolean formulae. That is why the reduction of the number of these factors is necessary. What justification seems plausible for this reduction?

The answer to this question is either theoretical or empirical. Theoretically it is hard to include some factors into a model, while excluding some other ones. That is why the next phase is to study empirically the correlations between the dependent and independent factors used in the crisp set analysis. Since the number of cases is small, the statistically significant correlations necessitate high correlation coefficients. It is also a known fact that statistical tests are rather conservative. For these reasons, even the correlations with significance level .10 are included in the following table (table 11.4). Furthermore it is necessary to point out that the simple (Pearson's) correlation coefficients describe only linear dependencies (thus the possible non-linear dependencies are not revealed here).

When studying the dependencies between the dependent variables, it is interesting to note that the indicator measuring the conditions for building up social networks (noknow) correlates only with the satisfaction of living in the area (nosat) and not with the willingness to out-migrate. It is, however, evident that "strong ties" in the area can be compensated with "weak ties" extending outside the area in question. In this regard, Granovetter (1985) writes about *"the strength of the weak ties"*. These ties may thus mean frequent contacts outside the residential area, which may even prevent out-migration.

The satisfaction of living in the area is, however, closely connected with out-migration. A kind of recursive model could be created, here: close contacts in the residential area make people satisfied with living in the area, but there are also other reasons. Dissatisfaction with living in the area causes out-migration. It can be hypothesized that these three dependent variables measure different dimensions of social integration. For this reason, they also have to be explained separately, as we did here above.

When studying the correlations between the independent factors, it can be noted that living in a house or apartment for a long time correlates strongly with the five other independent variables. They seem to refer to the same phenomenon, to a kind of adaptation to the area typical among the elderly people who own big, single-family houses in the older areas. These kinds of areas were built in Oulunsalo before the 1990s, in other words, before the recession in the Finnish economy. It would be easy to form three regression equations for the three dependent variables:

1) NOSAT = f (LONG, OULUNS, NOOWN, YOUNG)
2) MIGR = f (OULUNS, NEW, NOSAT)
3) NOKNOW = f (LOCAL, NOOWN, NOSAT)

The most satisfactory equations[11] can be expressed as follows:

1) NOSAT = 14,780 + .760*NOOWN ($r^2 = 0,74$)
2) MIGR = 40,435 - .417*OULUNS - .220*NEW ($r^2 = .54$)
3) NOKNOW = -0,753 + .499*NOSAT ($r^2 = .47$)

Before we consider the combinations of causal factors, we can observe that satisfaction with living conditions in an area is closely connected with one single cause factor: ownership of the houses (noown). For example, in the areas with a higher than average proportion of house owners, people were more satisfied in the area, and vice versa.

In their answers to the open-ended questions, the respondents often said they had moved to Oulunsalo to build a house of their own. This may have something to do with the rural ethos mentioned earlier. Respondents often referred to the freedom they have in their own houses, and to home yards being their favorite places. In the same vein they express that they dislike living in apartment blocks and in the cities. When asked about where they feel "at home", they also often mention the houses of their parents or parents-in-law.

NOSAT is excluded in the regression analysis from the final equation for the out-migration. Out-migration rates are lower in the case of those having a job in Oulunsalo and living in the new areas. The proportion of those knowing their neighbors increases with the satisfaction with the area. The causal relationship might, however, be understood the other way around, knowing the neighbors increases satisfaction with the area.

What about the configurations of the independent variables when using crisp set analysis? It might be expected that the causal mechanisms are not as evident as in regression analysis. These combinations can be studied by using crisp set analysis as in the following. The functions can be expressed in the same form as in the general equations above; is it then possible to draw some conclusions from these causal configurations of the factors?

Each of the equations suggested by the correlation matrix (Table 11.4) is introduced in the following form:

4) NOSAT = LONG + OULUNS + NOOWN + YOUNG
5) MIGR = OULUNS + NEW + NOSAT
6) NOKNOW = LOCAL + NOOWN + NOSAT

The contradictory and all the other cases are excluded from the analysis. The results of the crisp set analysis are expressed in the following formulae:

7) nosat = LONG noown young + OULUNS noown young + long oulans NOOWN YOUNG
8) migr = oulans NEW NOSAT
9) noknow = LOCAL noown nosat + LOCAL NOOWN NOSAT
10) NOSAT = long noown YOUNG
11) MIGR = oulans new NOSAT
12) NOKNOW = local NOOWN NOSAT

Most of the respondents satisfied with their living environment fall into the following categories: those who live in areas where a) there is a higher than average number of elderly house-owners who have lived there long-term; or b) there is a higher than average number of elderly house-owners in the area and the respondents work in Oulunsalo; or c) there are younger people who have lived for a short-term in their rental houses and work outside Oulunsalo (7). Owning a house and the locality seem to be important factors in increasing the level of satisfaction. However, there is one exception in the third configuration referring to young people, who live in their first apartment after "Hotel Mamma" (the term used by Sveinisson; cited in Kemeny 2004) and work outside Oulunsalo. Furthermore (10), the younger house-owners who have lived only a short time in their houses are the least satisfied.

	LONG	LOCAL	OULUNS	NEW	APART	NOOWN	BIG	YOUNG	CHILDR	UNI	WELL	NOSAT	MIGR	NOKNOW
LONG	1													
LOCAL		1												
OULUNS			1											
NEW	-0,478			1										
APART	-0,646			0,930	1									
NOOWN	-0,675					1								
BIG	0,662			-0,512	-0,711		1							
YOUNG	-0,865				0,507	0,644	-0,672	1						
CHILDR									1					
UNI										1				
WELL						-0,481				0,833	1			
NOSAT	-0,708		-0,476			-0,566		0,683				1		
MIGR			-0,563	-0,544		0,862						0,495	1	
NOKNOW		-0,593				0,522						0,688		1

As analyzed above, the factor of working either in or outside Oulunsalo might be removed from the analysis, because the distances to work are not very long in the Oulu region. Therefore, the formula (7) can now be expressed in a simplified form: nosat = LONG noown young + long NOOWN YOUNG

This refers to two opposing groups of areas, where the respondents are satisfied with their living conditions. Obviously, people are more satisfied if they have lived long in areas in which elder than the average people own their houses. The second configuration refers to the areas with a higher proportion of younger than elder people, who have not lived for a long time span in the area and who live in a rent apartment. Thus, Oulunsalo also seems to offer satisfactory conditions for young people who rent an apartment.

The willingness to move away (8) is not significant in the new areas with more than average people dissatisfied and working outside Oulunsalo. This is surprising, but maybe some of the inhabitants are not well attached to their residential community. Their center of life lies elsewhere, perhaps in their work: only the work matters and they live where they work. Another interesting feature (11) is that in the areas with more than average inhabitants born in Oulunsalo and having lived there long, there is yet more dissatisfaction and a stronger aptitude to out migration.

In the areas consisting of more than average people who are born in Oulunsalo, live in the house of their own and satisfied neighbors are known more often as in the average. On the other hand, and surprisingly, in the areas consisting more than average local people, living in a rental apartment and dissatisfied also know their neighbors more often (9). Contrariwise in the areas where there are more newcomers, living in rental apartments and not satisfied the neighbors are not known as often as in the other kinds of areas (12).

There are some areas with young people owning their houses who are not satisfied (12). This might be the case in the areas with rapid change, where new houses are being built. This might be interpreted as a cleavage between the old and the new inhabitants or between the old and new ways of living.

In addition to seeing Oulunsalo as an idyllic semi urban or rural municipality and the notions of the opposing lifestyles, there are also some other signs of contradictions. These contradictions are seen more clearly in the analysis of the answers to the open-ended questions. Firstly, many respondents refer to the fact that religion, Laestadianism[12], is a special issue in Oulunsalo that seems to cause contradictions between the inhabitants. The rather frequent comments on the open-ended questions in the survey[13] lead to the conclusion, that there is a kind of counter coalition against the traditional religious value system in Oulunsalo.

Secondly, there are also some other issues of disagreement. Some respondents living in apartment houses refer to the cold attitudes of those living in single-family houses towards them. Many respondents refer to the cities and to living in large apartment buildings in a very negative way in their answers. This is an indication of a more general discourse of biased opinions on those living in the apartment houses and on those living in cities) (see also Jacobs et al. 2002b: 441-442).

5. THEORETICAL AND METHODOLOGICAL IMPLICATIONS OF THE FINDINGS

After having performed comparative analyses, some conclusions and hypotheses can be elaborated. Social integration seems to correlate very strongly with homeownership. In the configurations, there is only one example in which the opposite is true (displayed by the correlation "young people who have not been living long in Oulunsalo" and by the formula: "nosat = LONG noown young + long NOOWN YOUNG").

According to Kemeny's (1981) original formulation, modern Finnish society has sometimes been characterized as a society of home-owners (Ruonavaara 1988). In the first half of the 1970s just over 60 per cent of Finns owned their own houses. The percentage started to rise in the second half of the 70s, because the great migration wave (see above) contributed to an increase of demand for housing and it was partly met by building rental houses. This was the period of construction in the suburbs with high apartment blocks in the cities' new areas. These kinds of suburbs also exist in Oulu. In 1990, almost 80 per cent of Finns owned their houses. Since then there has been a decrease of almost 5 percent. (Ruonavaara 2004)

This decrease in homeownership was caused by the recession and high interest rates in the 90's. During the recession, many had difficulties in selling their houses which were sometimes also mortgaged by the firms that went bankrupt. People had difficulties in selling their houses, and the price of property went down. This – together with the decline in production – was a phenomenon, which had never been experienced in Finland since World War II. It is probable that those with big cash reserves benefited from the situation and bought apartments for rent. The supply of rental apartments increased in the 1990s, even in the city of Oulu.

The development of homeownership may be related to cultural traditions. It somehow refers to the years of an intense resettlement policy from 1920 to 1960. In the 1920s, the rental crofters were able to buy their farm plots through state subsidies according to the settlement law. Also the evacuees from Russian Carelia and the war veterans were resettled on the countryside to farms created for them after the Second World War. Thus there is a long tradition of thriving to establish an independent life in Finland, starting from the agrarian society. For example Silvasti (2001: 269), who has recently studied the farmers' history, notes that there is something sacred in the way the farmers treat their own lands; the farmers see this rural landownership as inviolable. This cultural trait may explain this new model of homeownership found even in the late modern Finnish society. Even in the cities there are some people interested in buying and repairing wooden houses built just after the war by the war veterans. Hotakainen (2002) has described this phenomenon in his award-winning novel "Juoksuhaudantie" ("trench road").

This cultural tradition, however, is not the only explanation for the urban sprawl in the surrounding uninhabited areas, or for the interest in the old wooden houses in the cities. These attempts to own single-family houses is also a consequence of economic reasons and rational thinking, which may, together with new consumerist life style aspirations, be more usual among young people with higher standards of living. The interest rates have been rather low in recent years. At the same time the prices of plots for building new houses have been very low in the rural municipalities. As a matter of fact low land prices have been used as a way of attracting firms and people to move into the rural or semi rural municipalities. The municipalities compete for inhabitants or tax payers by offering cheaper prices for plots. At the same time, there is also fierce competition between banks for new customers in Finland. This cultural tradition together with financial reasons may be linked in this new wave of homeownership.[14]

In Oulunsalo the interest in homeownership can be verified in many ways. Referring to our statistical and QCA analyses, homeownership is the most significant single factor in the formulae explaining social integration. Secondly, in the open-ended answers the respondents often referred to the juxtapositions of living both a) in the cities and on the countryside and b) in apartment houses and single-family houses.

The answers to the open ended questions have a direct connection with the rhetoric of "nightmare neighbors" (Kemeny 2004) or neighborhoods in the cities and suburbs with big apartment houses. This rhetoric, common also among the authorities, is connected to the conceptions of the neo-liberal housing and planning policies. This is a way to consolidate the idea of homeownership, which is politically seen as a way to make the demands for state or municipal housing weaker, and to reduce welfare costs. This idea of single-house ownership can also be seen as a tool to reduce welfare costs by its implications to the idealized view of the nuclear family model (Jacobs et al. 2003b: 435-438).

These kinds of attitudes, however, are not unambiguous. Wiborg (2004: 419-426) gives a more detailed picture when analyzing the attitudes of Norwegian students. Among other things she refers to the students' attitudes to their rural home places as nostalgia, ambivalence and mixed attitudes of detachment and attachment.

The answers to our question on in which places people feel "cozy" or not, provide a clear picture of where people want and do not want to live. People are happy with living in the houses of their own. Many say they would not like to live in an apartment block in the middle of the city and more specifically in "the cement jungle" (the suburbs with tightly built and big apartment buildings are also mentioned in such a negative way). Some of the people are also concerned about the growth of Oulunsalo, and feel that buildings are built too tightly and that too many people are moving in.

The aim of living in single-family houses outside Oulu is easy to understand, since the land is less expensive in the surrounding areas (see above). The plots in the city are often only rented – also due to high prices – and not sold, and the building regulations in the city are tighter.

Compared to the Helsinki region, the housing situation in the Oulu region is different. In the Helsinki area there is a lack of land for building houses, which is the main reason why people often cannot build houses of their own. They can often only afford to buy an apartment of their own. The focus of housing interests thus often turns to terraced or mews houses. This leads some researchers to raise the question whether living in terraced houses in the Helsinki area is *"the fulfillment of dreams or a compromise of possibilities"* (Manninen and Hirvonen 2004). The latter option may be closer to reality, because many people are forced to move to the capital city region with much better job opportunities than elsewhere. Those who move to the Helsinki region have to compromise their housing needs both in terms of the quality and costs of housing.

The respondents to our survey gave quite unambiguous answers to the question of why they had moved to Oulunsalo: they wanted to live in a single-family house of their own, on the countryside. Also its closeness to the services of Oulu was emphasized.[15] Some also claimed that Oulunsalo is a better place to bring up children than the cities in general, and also referred to the peacefulness of the area as well as to its closeness to nature[16]. One respondent, who had moved to Oulunsalo from Helsinki, pointed out: *"I longed for a more peaceful living environment and a better standard of housing."*[17]

Oulunsalo seems to represent a successful way of local development in the global age. The respondents are satisfied with living in their residential area[18], and only a small minority wants to move away from their residential area. Besides, they seem to know their neighbors very well. All this gives a rather idyllic picture of Oulunsalo even if there are some variations between the residential areas. There are areas, mostly in the municipal center and its neighborhood, where people more often want to move away or are dissatisfied with their living conditions.

However, it is important to notice that about 85% of the respondents have moved to Oulunsalo from elsewhere, in the context of rapid in-migration over the last two decades. Furthermore, almost 80% of the respondents have a job outside Oulunsalo. Thus, the municipality has to be seen as a very dynamic growth area even if that growth is based on the growth of the region as a whole.

The areas under study differ from each other in many ways. On the one hand there are areas where people have lived for a long-term, as compared to people living short termed in the newly built areas. On the other hand, there are areas where almost none of the residents work in Oulunsalo. Finally there are areas of single-family houses, but also areas with apartment and rental houses. However, many of the areas are mixed types. The comparison between these areas is sometimes difficult. It is necessary to increase the diversity, which can be done by researching other municipalities with other kinds of areas. These will include declining and more rural areas where out-migration is threatening social sustainability.

It is also important to note that the age structure of the population, according to a recent national migration study (Virtanen 2003: 24), does not seem to correlate with out-migration. There might be many reasons for this. Firstly, the age structures may be polarized: on one hand, there may be many old and, on the other hand, very young people in the area. Secondly, the younger residents of Oulunsalo may not be ready to move, as would be more usually expected in such age groups, because they are better integrated than in many other municipalities in Oulu province. This could be because there are good opportunities to go to school (also to university) and to find a job in the Oulu region. Finally, the maintenance of single-family houses is often more difficult for elderly people, so they want to move to apartments closer to services, especially health services, which may even mean moving to the city of Oulu. This raises an interesting issue, which needs to be further studied: do the housing cycles, habits and preferences correlate with age?

Referring to the methodological issues, regression analysis and crisp set (QCA) analysis produce to some extent congruent findings. The results of the latter are often more complicated to interpret. The crisp set analysis was carried out only in an experimental way. However, it led to some interesting, if also complicated, theoretical questions. The main difficulty in the analysis was the numerous contradictory cases. It is also necessary to notice that the old problem of ecological fallacy is always embedded in the holistic analyses of cases (here the residential areas).

Arguably the material used in this exploratory analysis was not diverse enough. In a next step of the research, material will be collected in other municipalities. The new data will be analyzed by using statistical and qualitative contents analysis. The QCA or fuzzy set analysis is still, after this experiment, an option to be applied for future studies.

NOTES

[1] For example, the PKC Group Oyj (PKCG – earlier a part of Nokia), situated in Kempele, started subcontracting in Estonia, Russia and Brazil already in the early 1990s. The interim reports (in the URL http://www.pkcgroup.com/) give a more detailed picture of the development. In recent years PKCG has transferred its assembly to Estonia and to Kostamus in the Russian Carelia. – Kostamus is a new mining industry town with approximately 30 000 inhabitants situated close to the Finnish border. It was built close to the newly grounded mine in the late 70's and early 80's (Siuruainen 1981).

[2] The recent news in the national media (e.g. Kärki 2005) that Nokia will release employees also in its new multimedia research and development unit in Oulu is just one example. In the course of globalization, competition between firms will increase causing rising uncertainty among employees not only among the low-wage workers but also among the middle class and well educated.

[3] The high unemployment rate in the region is caused by the loss of jobs in rather traditional branches of the economy. The automation in the pulp and paper production and closing of some units in the food and beverages industry are examples for this development (Kerkelä and Kurkinen 2000).

[4] For a map of Oulunsalo and the Oulu region, see http://www.oulu.ouka.fi/ouluseutu/ .

[5] This closeness to the sea is accentuated by the fact that a well-known nature reserve and stopping-point for migratory birds, called Liminganlahti, is situated on the southern side of the bay of Liminka, south of Oulunsalo.

[6] Its headquarters are located in Oulunsalo with other offices elsewhere in Finland as well as in many other Western countries.

[7] These deficiencies in the organization of civil society (as well as citizen's agency) have been seen as a serious defect in the post socialist Baltic States (e.g. Alanen 2004:49).

[8] Perhaps it would be more appropriate to refer to "local culture" instead of "physical area", whereas local culture is a configuration of various spatial and social factors. Studying physical factors alone might hide the social factors and lead to a kind of deterministic bias. It is, however, probable that certain social forces or their combinations have differing effects on various cultures and areas. The material used in the following analysis is collected from our survey data (the original data presented in tables 11.1 and 11.2).

[9] Percentage is higher than the average in Oulunsalo data.
- LONG = 1, if the proportion of those, who have lived in their current house or apartment, at least 10 years > 47,8%
- LOCAL = 1, if the proportion of those, who have lived always in Oulunsalo, > 13,4%
- OULUNS = 1, if the proportion of those working or studying in Oulunsalo > 21,9%
- NEW = 1, if the proportion of those, whose house is built in the 1990's or later > 34,5%
- APART = 1, if the proportion of those living in an apartment (not single family) house (mostly row houses with 1-2 floors, not higher) > 13,8%
- NOOWN = 1, if the proportion of those living not in their own house or apartment > 16,8%
- BIG = 1, if those with a house or an apartment at least 100 square meters > 62,5%
- YOUNG = 1, if the proportion of those under 45 years of age > 58,7%
- CHILDR = 1, if the proportion of those having children in their family under 18 > 56,8%
- UNI = 1, if the proportion of those having a university exam > 14,9%
- WELL = 1, if the proportion of those telling their living standard is good > 22,5%

- NOSAT = 1, if the proportion of those, who only partly or not at all agree that they enjoy or are satisfied to living in the area, is > 24,6%
- MIGR = 1, if the proportion of those out migrating from their area or Oulunsalo, > 23,2%
- NOKNOW = 1, if the proportion of those, who don't agree at all, that they know their next door neighbors well > 12%.

[10] The classification of the residential area (the smaller areas included):
1. Karhuoja and Niemenranta (= Karhuoja, Niemenranta, Niemenväli and Pahajärvi)
2. Vihiluoto (= Vihiluoto, Vihiranta and Kallenranta)
3. Koura (= Koura and Kouranpelto)
4. Örni (= Örni and Ryytipuisto)
5. Lassila and Ranta
6. Pitkäkangas
7. Varjakka
8. Lunki, Pellonpää and Karhukangas (= Lunki, Pellonpää, Karhukangas, Karvola and Sarapää)
9. Oulunsalo Airport area (=Lentoaseman seutu and Mökkiperä)
10. Oulunsalo center (=Keskusta, Kirkonkylä, Kauppiaantie, Kirkonseutu and Päällystä)
11. Santaniemi (=Santaniemi and Santamäki)
12. Kylänpuoli (=Kylänpuoli and Letto)
13. The sparsely populated areas around Hailuoto road (= Salonpää, Ervastinkylä, Peherrus, Keskipiiri, Nauska and Pajuniemi)

[11] The statistical significance of the equations was tested with F-test and significance of the coefficients with t-test. The most parsimonious equations were derived by stepwise regression analysis.

[12] Laestadianism is a traditionalist religious movement inside the Lutheran church. It is based on the doctrines of Lars Levi Laestadius and other lay preachers from the second half of the 19th century. This movement was grounded in the peripheral parts in the north of Finland opposing modern and secular values. Laestadianism is also an influential political force in the municipalities like Oulunsalo (e.g. Sallamaa 1993: 144), and the Laestadians live a rather isolated life in their peer group.

[13] Just to mention two examples, those not Laestadians comment the question about the social contradictions between the people living in Oulunsalo as follows: "*Things like religion, agriculture and parochialism*", "*Religion, especially Laestadianism*" and "*Laestadianism causes certain polarization to dissenting camps e.g. in schools*".

[14] Kemeny (e.g. 2004; see also Jacobs, Kemeny and Manzi 2003) with others have analyzed the changes in the housing policies in some countries, which is nowadays based on neoliberalism.

[15] Pile (1999:28-34) writes about suburbs as "*a compromise between the city and the countryside*" and asks if it is to be seen as "*heaven or hell*"/"*paradise or prison*" to various people.

[16] This aspect is also mentioned by Wiborg (2004: 419) and others for Norway.

[17] NB: the housing costs in the Helsinki area are much higher than in Oulu, not to mention the surrounding municipalities.

[18] It was noticed in a recent Finnish study on internal migration, that the proportion of those satisfied with their living did not, in principle, differ at all between those who had moved and those who already lived in the areas under study (Virtanen 2003: 72).

Chapter 12

QCA AS A TOOL FOR REALISTIC EVALUATIONS
The Case of the Swiss Environmental Impact Assessment

Barbara Befani
University of Rome "La Sapienza"

Fritz Sager
University of Bern

1. INTRODUCTION

The aim of this contribution is to show that Qualitative Comparative Analysis (QCA) can be a supporting tool when using Pawson and Tilley's realistic approach to evaluation (Pawson and Tilley 1997). These authors apply the realist paradigm known among social researchers to the evaluation of public policy programmes, in order to stress the importance of context factors, provide room for different explanations of why a program works or not, and maintain the relevance of each single program in the course of systematic reviews of evaluations. The building blocks for realistic program evaluation are the so called CMO-configurations: program context (C) + program mechanism (M) = Outcome (O)[1]. A mixed QCA/realistic approach has been used in last year's evaluation of the Swiss Environmental Impact Assessment (EIA). This evaluation study is presented in the following as an example of how QCA can be used for a realistic evaluation.

2. THE EVALUATION OF THE SWISS ENVIRONMENTAL IMPACT ASSESSMENT

In 2002, the Federal Department of Environment, Transport, Energy and Communications commissioned a team of environmental policy experts with the task to evaluate the effects of the environmental impact assessment (EIA) on the implementation of environmental protection regulations and consent procedures (Sager and Schenkel 2004).

The EIA is a procedural regulation for big infrastructure construction projects with the objective to contribute in a significant manner to the final project meeting the environmental standards set by the Federal Law on Environmental Protection (*Umweltschutzgesetz* USG). The EIA is thus an institutional and not a substantial policy instrument, aiming at a substantial impact by regulating a procedure, i.e. focusing on the outcome. This idiosyncrasy found its expression in the guiding questions of the evaluation:

1. Does the EIA instrument contribute to the pre-assessment of the environmental quality of a project? (normative evaluation)
2. Which are the effects of the EIA on the planning process? (causal evaluation)
3. Which are the effects of the EIA on the official approval procedure? (causal evaluation)

In the following, we will first present our evaluation design developed as an analytical framework to answer these questions; second, we outline the empirical and the methodological approach, focusing on QCA; third, the main results from the QCA are presented; finally, we discuss the advantages and limits of the chosen methodology encountered in this evaluation.

2.1 Evaluation Design

Our aim was to focus not just on the results but also on the results' causes. We not only asked ourselves "what happened?" but also "how and why did it happen?". Our assumptions were that EIA gave rise to different results in different contexts, and we wanted to understand which mechanisms were activated in which contexts to produce those results. In a nutshell, our task was to test, refine, or discover a middle-range theory that could explain EIA outcomes by unraveling its inner workings. We thus started with our own selection of CMO configurations and tested them based on interview data and document analysis. In order to facilitate the transfer of ideas among cases that would lead us to the limitedly-general theory we were looking for, we operationalized our (supposedly) causally relevant propositions into Boolean variables or 'conditions'. This would enable us to perform QCA on our final data set and obtain a limited generalization that would cover all the available cases. To capture the different facets of the evaluation questions, we developed an analytical model embracing – along with several CMO configurations – three result variables to cover the different effect levels and three sets of condition variables. In short, we proceeded as shown in figure 12.1. In the following paragraphs, we explain the different steps of our design in detail.

2.1.1. Result Variables

We conceptualized the indicators for EIA success or failure with the classical three concepts in evaluation research of output, outcome, and impact[2] (Patton 1997: 193f.; see also Varone, Rihoux and Marx, in this volume).

Figure 12.1. Overview of the Evaluation Design

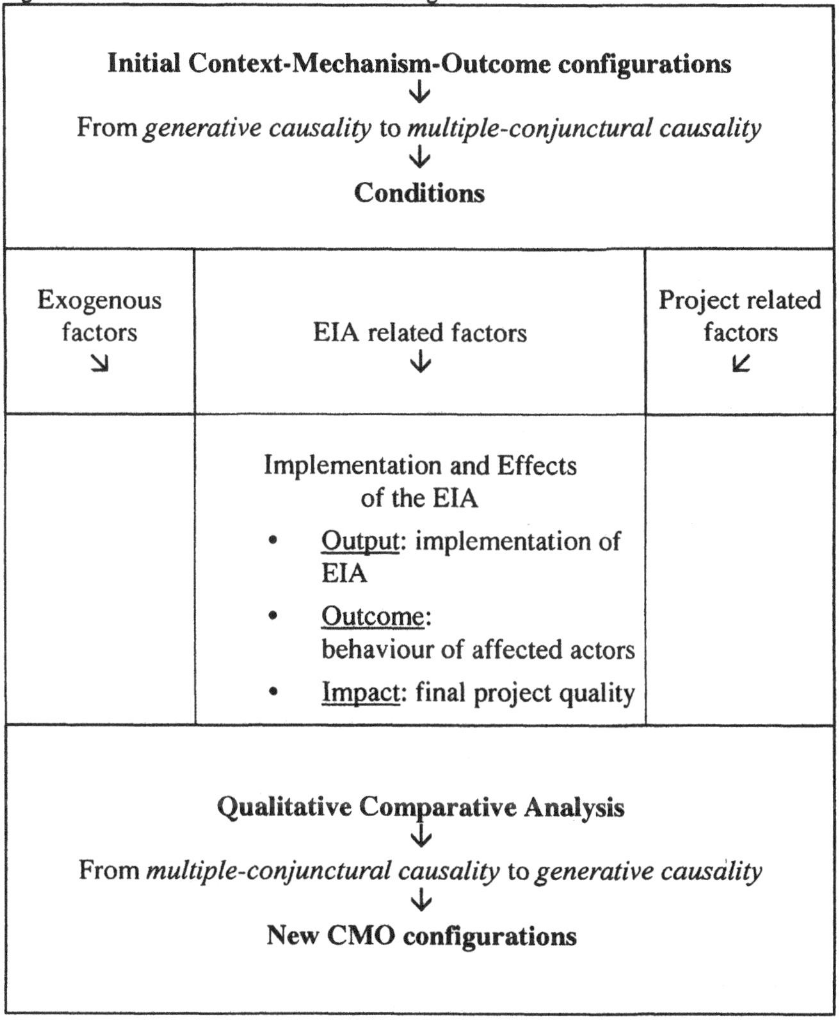

Initial Context-Mechanism-Outcome configurations ↓ From *generative causality* to *multiple-conjunctural causality* ↓ **Conditions**		
Exogenous factors ↘	EIA related factors ↓	Project related factors ↙
	Implementation and Effects of the EIA • <u>Output</u>: implementation of EIA • <u>Outcome</u>: behaviour of affected actors • <u>Impact</u>: final project quality	
Qualitative Comparative Analysis ↓ From *multiple-conjunctural causality* to *generative causality* ↓ **New CMO configurations**		

- The output of the EIA is defined as the quality of the application of the instrument. We asked whether we find implementation deficits or not, i.e. no delays in the fulfilling of the different obligations (pre-assessment,

handing in of the environmental assessment report, approval procedure) and substantial coordination of the different environmental services.
- The outcome to the EIA is defined as the willingness of the target participants to co-operate and coordinate with public agencies and potential complainants. Do potential complainants lodge a complaint against the project owners or not?
- The impact of the EIA is defined as the quality of the final state of the project: Has it been approved or did it fail? Does it meet the environmental standards? Is it financially bearable for the project owners?

2.1.2 Context-Mechanism-Outcome (CMO) Configurations

Not all our initial CMO configurations include a context, as some of our ideas were rough and in need of major refinement. In these cases we assumed that a mechanism was at work, that was 'equally available' in all the cases; namely the 'reasoning' it included was not 'weaved' to constraints or resources that were present in only a part of them. Below is a full list of our assumptions.[3]

1) For output:
   a) Existence of controversy about the interpretation of documents, arising from a lack of clarity in project definition, may result in delays, non-compliance of procedures and other implementation problems (bad output).
   b) The taking place of an early discussion between parties about all the relevant matters may smoothen the implementation process (and thus lead to a good output)
   c) Full deployment of institutional resources, coordinated by a highly motivated project management, can help avoid implementation problems (accounting for a good output)
   d) In a context politically and culturally sensitive to environmental issues, the parties involved (project owners and institutions) are more willing to acquire/provide knowledge on EIA, thus helping avoid the hampering of procedures (and lead to a good output).
   e) For big projects, EIA is more complex than for small ones; therefore owners of big projects have a deeper knowledge of EIA than those of small ones. This may help procedure compliance (and lead to a good output).
2) For impact:
   a) Why do projects finally meet environmental standards? Are they modified after EIA? Or does this policy instrument simply act as a deterrent, so that owners plan projects according to the standards right from the beginning? We assumed that the latter (EIA as deterrent)

could be a mechanism producing a positive impact: initial compliance is also final compliance.
b) A good EIA implementation can help identify the environmental weaknesses of a project – in case they exist – and lead to their overcoming (and to eventual achievement of standards).
c) When the project needs to be modified, the development of cooperation dynamics makes the process of modification easier and less problematic (thus facilitating the final meeting of standards).
d) A favorable, environment-friendly political-cultural context provides a higher general awareness of environmental needs, along with a higher propensity to respect them, whether from the beginning of the planning process or during the course of the impact assessment. Either way, the probability that the project eventually meets the standards is higher than in less favorable contexts.
e) Beside the above, the modification of projects' characteristics during EIA (that leads to approval) can proceed smoothly due to the following reasons: full deployment of institutional resources;
f) Early awareness of all relevant matters by the project owners and other stakeholders;
g) Absence of controversy in establishing the boundaries of a project (mainly due to a clear project definition).
h) Finally, EIA knowledge by the project owners – highly dependent from project size – increases the project's chance to pass the assessment (e.g., meet the standards).

At this point we finalized the "realistic part" of our initial phase: we stopped thinking "generatively" and started to reason in terms of multiple-conjunctural causality, asking ourselves which patterns of intersections or combinations of conditions were causally relevant to the outcomes. How do these different factors fit together? In doing so we attempted to "translate" our CMO configurations into configurations of Boolean variables, where each variable stood for a realistically-defined mechanism or context. This was possible because, in Pawson and Tilley's definition (1997), *'program mechanisms take the form of propositions (which will provide an account [...] about what it is within the program which triggers a reaction from its subjects)'*, the transformation of a proposition into a Boolean variable coming natural and immediate. Besides, while mechanisms regard people's choices and reasoning, contexts are about the capacities and resources they derive from belonging – being embedded – in an established layer of a stratified reality, that constrains those choices and modifies that reasoning; the belonging or not to a specific layer being also easy to translate into Boolean language (for a similar 'translation' approach with Fuzzy Sets, see Kvist, in this volume). Consequently, the conditions were built in a "proposition holds/proposition does not hold" style and "belongs to/ does not belong to" fashion.

2.1.3 Condition Variables

We developed three sets of condition variables regarding: first, the EIA as the policy instrument of interest; second, idiosyncrasies of the project that is assessed; and third, variables exogenous to both EIA and project.

- As EIA factors, we defined two sorts of variables: substantial factors and organizational factors.
    Substantial factors:
    o (def) clear definition of the assessed project
    o (disc) discussion of all relevant questions at an early stage
    Organizational factors:
    o (man) systematic EIA project management by the relevant public agency
    o (int) early integration of all affected actors by the relevant public agency
- As exogenous factors we defined:
    o (sens) political culture sensitive for environmental aspects in the respective political entity (canton or federal level)
- As project related factors we defined:
    o (beg) respect for environmental standards from the beginning of the planning process
    o (size) size of the project (small vs. large).

So far, we have come up with ideas on the mechanisms that may generate good or bad outcomes, and on the contexts in which they may or may not be activated. Moreover, we have produced a list of conditions in the form of Boolean variables to represent those mechanisms and those contexts. Now we need to translate our working CMO configurations into QCA models for us to test with the QCA 3.0 software (the more recent fs/QCA and TOSMANA software would produce the same formulae, for the crisp and dichotomous parts).

- Output model: output = def + disc + man + sens + size
- Impact model: impact = def + disc + man + sens + beg + size +
                        + output + outcome.

We have thus completed the passage from our initial generative type of causality to a multiple-conjunctural one; the next step will be to gather the empirical data and complete the Truth Table.

2.2 The Comparative Case Study Approach

In order to make sense of data regarding a medium number of cases, we chose the comparative case study approach. We proceeded in three main steps: first, case selection; second, case studies; third, comparison.

2.2.1 Case Selection

A great challenge for the chosen comparative case study-approach was the heterogeneity of possible test cases. The EIA is a very complex instrument that regulates different infrastructure projects in a different manner. While certain projects lie in the competence of the Swiss Agency for the Environment, Forests and Landscape at the federal level, most projects are treated by the Cantons. Also, large projects demand a two or even three steps EIA, while smaller projects have a one-step EIA.

The evaluation was supposed to deliver findings as generalizable as possible and, thus, had to select cases that covered the whole range of project types. In order to select the right and somewhat representative cases for the whole picture, we had to proceed differently for the federal and for the cantonal level.

At the federal level, we could use the existing controlling database for EIA projects with some 1500 cases. Based on a frequency analysis, we first decided which project types had to be considered because of their prevalence. Second, we coded all cases along chosen variables, such as the number of involved environmental services and the length of time for both the assessment and the approval. In a cluster analysis, we identified seven types of EIAs that had to be considered. The case selection at the federal level was then focused in that we drew a case in the first cluster and crossed the respective project type from the list of types to be considered. In the second cluster, we drew another case that had to cover another project type and so on.

At the cantonal level, the data situation was more difficult as only half of Switzerland's 26 cantons had statistics at hand. Again, we made a frequency analysis with the existing statistics, but additionally conducted a survey in all cantons to distinguish the most important project types as well as the way they are generally perceived among the cantonal environmental protection agencies. Based on these two surveys, we chose eight project types at the cantonal level. The cases were then selected along two criteria: first, we wanted both generally easy and generally difficult projects as perceived by the cantonal authorities. Second, we had to take Switzerland's four language regions into account to come close to representativeness.

Based on these analyses, we finally had fifteen cases to be studied in depth. The cases are enumerated in the following table.

Table 12.1. List of Test Cases

Type of project	Case study	Short title	Actors	Time
1. Natural gas pipeline (Erdgasleitung)	Section Ruswil-Brienzer Rothorn / LU, EIA 1. and 2. Step	erdgas	Project owner: Transitgas AG Decision: 1. Step Federal Council, 2. Stufe Swiss Federal Office of Energy (SFOE)	1997-2002
2. Chair lift (Sesselbahn)	New chair lift Arvenbühl-Brittertannen in Amden / SG, one Step EIA	sessel	Project owner: Sportbahnen Amden AG Decision: Federal Department of Environment, Transportation, Energy, and Communication (UVEK)	1999-2001
3. National Highway (Nationalstrasse)	Highway A8, Umfahrung Lungern / OW, 2nd and 3rd Step EIA	A8	Project owner: Canton of Obwalden Decision: 2. step Federal Council, 3. step cantonal goverment	1989-2001
4. Railroad (Eisenbahnlinie)	Alptransit Lötschberg, Basistunnel in Raron, three step EIA	alptrans	Project owner: BLS Alp Transit Deicison: 1. step Federal Parliament, 2. step Federal Council, 3. step UVEK	1986-2002
5. Power Line (Hochspannungsleitung)	Power line Mettlen / Gösgen, one step EIA	hochsp	Project owner: atel Decision: Federal Inspectorate For Heavy Current Installations (ESTI)	1984-2002

Type of project	Case study	Short title	Actors	Time
6. Hydroelectric power plant (Wasserkraftwerk)	Lauf- und Speicherkraftwerk Ferrerabach in Trun / GR, Konzession and two step EIA	wasser	Project owner: Kraftwerk AG Decision: 1. und 2. Stufe cantonal government	1989-1997
7. Airport extension (Flughafenausbau)	Dock Midfield, Flughafen Zürich / ZH, two step EIA	flug	Gesuch: Unique Decision: 1. and 2. step UVEK	1995-2001
8. Multy storey car park (Parkhaus)	Car park Berntor / SO, one step EIA	parkhaus	Project owner: Parkhaus AG decision: municipal and cantonal government	2000-2001
9. Domestic animal facility (Nutztieranlage)	Pouletmaststall Bözen / AG, one step EIA	poulet	Project owner: Farmer decision: commune and cantonal infrastructure department	2000-2002
10. Gravel pit (Kies-/Sandgruben)	Steinbruch Roc in Cornaux / NE, one step EIA	kies	Project owner: Juracime Decision: Département de la gestion du territoire	1989-1999
11. Main road (Hauptstrasse)	T10-Umfahrung in Gampelen, Ins und Müntschemier / BE, one step EIA	T10	Project owner: Cantoanle Service of civil engineering Decision: cantonale government	1996-1999
12. Shopping center (Einkaufszentrum)	Kino- und Fachmarktzentrum im Grüt in Adliswil / ZH, one step EIA	kino	Project owner: Saville Finanz decision: municipality	1996-2001

Type of project	Case study	Short title	Actors	Time
13. Inert waste disposal site (Inertstoffdeponie)	Disposal site Chrüzstrasse in Cham / ZG, one step EIA	depot	Project owner: Risi AG Decision: cantonal government	1998-2002
14. Waste treatment (Abfallanlage)	Waste incineration site Posieux / FR, one step EIA	kehricht	Project owner: SAIDEF Decision: Préfet du district de la Sarine	1993-1999
15. Golf course (Golfplatz)	Golf course in Signal de Bougy, two step EIA	golf	Project owner: Migros Decision: 1. step communes, 2. step cantonal infrastructure and building department	1995-1997

2.2.2 Case Studies

The case studies were conducted in view of the comparison of the cases and, thus, had to be comparable and consider the idiosyncrasies of each case at the same time. We, therefore, constructed a very strict operationalization framework for our variables to collect the data as well as a standardized analytical table to evaluate each case.

Empirically, the cases were based on document analysis and interviews with both experts and stakeholders.

The products of each case study were a text in which not only the guiding questions of the evaluation were answered as much as the case allowed for but also all other observations unique to the cases were reported on the one hand, and a table in which influence of each condition variable on each result variable was coded as a dichotomous variable 0-1 in view of the QCA.[4]

The data is presented in the following two tables.

Table 12.2. Basic Data for Output

	def	disc	man	int	sens	size	output
1.erdgas	1	1	-	1	1	1	1
2.sessel	0	0	1	0	1	0	0
3.A8	1	0	1	-	1	1	1
4.alptrans	0	1	1	1	1	1	0
5.hochsp	1	0	0	0	0	1	0

QCA and Realistic Evaluation 273

	def	disc	man	int	sens	size	output
6.wasser	1	1	1	-	1	1	1
7.flug	0	0	0	1	-	1	0
8.parkhaus	-	1	1	1	0	0	1
9.poulet	1	0	0	0	-	0	0
10.kies	1	0	1	-	0	0	0
11.T10	1	1	1	1	0	1	1
12.kino	1	1	1	1	1	0	1
13.depot	1	1	-	1	1	0	1
14.kehricht	1	1	1	1	1	0	1
15.golf	1	1	1	1	0	0	1

Table 12.3. Basic Data for Impact

	def	disc	man	int	sens	size	output	outcome	impact
1.erdgas	1	1	-	1	1	1	1	1	1
2.sessel	0	0	1	0	1	0	0	1	1
3.A8	1	0	1	-	1	1	1	1	1
4.alptrans	0	1	1	1	1	1	0	1	1
5.hochsp	1	0	0	0	0	1	0	0	1
6.wasser	1	1	1	-	1	1	1	1	1
7.flug	0	0	0	1	-	1	0	1	1
8.parkhaus	-	1	1	1	0	0	1	1	1
9.poulet	1	0	0	0	-	0	0	0	1
10.kies	1	0	1	-	0	0	0	1	1
11.T10	1	1	1	1	0	1	1	1	1
12.kino	1	1	1	1	1	0	1	1	0
13.depot	1	1	-	1	1	0	1	1	1
14.kehricht	1	1	1	1	1	0	1	1	1
15.golf	1	1	1	1	0	0	1	1	1

2.2.3 Comparison of the Cases

For the comparison of the cases, we chose the QCA-approach for the known reasons. We had a limited number of cases and a great number of variables we could handle in each single case, but in a merely qualitative way for the comparison. Also, we were not only interested in the general effect of the EIA, but – following the realist paradigm – wanted to find out under which conditions the EIA works as it is supposed to, and under which conditions it does not.

We thus performed QCA on the final matrix, analyzed the results and evaluated how they would eventually modify our initial working theories. The results are presented in the following paragraphs.

2.3 Main Findings

The findings are presented along two of the three result variables as we focus, first on the intersections of conditions responsible for success or failure; and then, more specifically, on the choices and reasoning that stakeholders make when having established capacities and given resources.

2.3.1 Quality Of EIA Implementation (Output)

The output has been defined as the quality of the implementation of the EIA. We consider compliance with the EIA regulations positive (9 cases), implementation deficits or complete non-compliance negative (6 cases). QCA leads to the following solutions that cannot be further minimized:

- OUTPUT = DEF.DISC + DISC.sens + DISC.size + DEF.SENS.SIZE + DEF.MAN.SIZE + DEF.MAN.SENS
- Output = def.SIZE + def.SENS + def.disc + disc.man + disc.sens + disc.size

Our attention is captured, in particular, by the configurations we obtain by isolating (this operation is performed by hand) the "sens" and "size" conditions:
- Sens: OUTPUT = sens.DISC + SENS.DEF.(SIZE + MAN)
                 Output = sens.disc + SENS.def
- Size: OUTPUT = size.DISC + SIZE.DEF.(SENS + MAN)
                 Output = size.disc + SIZE.def.

When isolating the "sens" condition, the findings weaken our initial assumptions that a good output derives directly from "political will" (CMO configuration d), absence of document-related controversy (CMO configuration a), or a good timing of stakeholders' discussion (CMO configuration b). In particular, QCA results show a negative output associated with a favorable political environment, as well as additional conditions needed for DISC and DEF in order to produce a positive output: they are, respectively, political context non sensitive and sensitive to environmental issues. Interestingly enough, we notice that:

1. in a context politically and culturally sensitive towards environmental issues, a clear project definition is responsible for a positive output, while the absence of that condition for a negative one;
2. in a non environment-friendly context, an early discussion of all relevant issues is what determines implementation quality (if it takes place, we get a positive output; if it doesn't, a negative one).

We thus conclude that, depending on the cultural/political context, the quality of EIA implementation is affected by (two) different factors. At this point (switching from the multiple conjunctural type of causality to the generative type), we start wondering what this means in terms of capacities and choices that stakeholders make; namely, we search for new CMO configurations that are compatible with our QCA findings.

Our conclusions are summarized in table 12.4 (below). Why is project definition so important in environmentally-aware contexts? In particular, as we have seen, a clear project definition determines a successful EIA implementation, while the opposite of the former yields the opposite of the latter. We explain this as follows.

In a sensitive context, an environment-friendly project is regarded as having an intrinsic merit, deriving directly from its ecological qualities. Therefore, as a valid instrument to measure the degree of "environment-friendliness" of projects, EIA is considered a serious and important step for them to undergo. Now, when the impossibility to correctly determine the sphere of application for the assessment procedure arises, because of the fuzzy boundaries that a badly-defined project possesses, the stakeholders perceive the risk of pursuing an "approximate" assessment that may lead to acquire the wrong information on the project. If procedures cannot be rigorously applied, EIA loses its validity as an instrument to assess the actual "environmental" merit of a project; thus, since that is what stakeholders are really interested in knowing, EIA is no longer useful. Until one is able to restore the validity limits within which the instrument can be accurately employed, one has no point in proceeding further with it. In this sense, in this context, implementation is not successful.

In a non sensitive context, on the other hand, the reasons why projects are considered worth undergoing are independent from their environment-related characteristics. The lack of interest in the specifically environmental merit of a project allows more tolerance towards the existence of conditions under which EIA validity is maximized. Even if it were valid, in fact, EIA would still give information that stakeholders are not interested in providing to potential complainants as it increases the risk of a costly complaint; they regard EIA rather as paperwork to be overcome in the path to project fulfillment. Whether that kind of business is quickly taken care of, then, depends on how much the project is a priority for them; in case it is, they will likely meet well in advance to discuss all relevant matters concerning the assessment, in an effort to avoid unexpected problems that might arise during implementation. Conversely, if the project does not gather enough interest on behalf of stakeholders, no other factor contributes to a good EIA implementation that, as a consequence, will be severely neglected. As table 12.4 shows, we assumed that condition "disc" (early discussion of all relevant matters) is, in a non sensitive context, an indicator of the level of priority a project enjoys among stakeholders.

As table 12.5 (below) shows, QCA yields further interesting results as we isolate the "size" condition. Among our initial assumptions was that project size could be determinant, due to the higher knowledge of EIA that big project owners entertain; but our cases, nonetheless, showed that a good output is also associated with small projects, and a negative output with big ones. In particular, implementation fails in badly-defined big projects, while it succeeds in early discussed small ones. How can we explain this? Why is project definition more important than discussion as project size increases – and discussion more relevant than definition as size decreases?

Big project owners are learned for a reason: EIA is much harder to apply to big projects, as they often include sub-projects that might need separate assessments. In this case, the conditions for EIA to be correctly implemented are more difficult to meet. In particular, a clear definition of project boundaries provides an essential basis for the application of procedures. It is worth to note that the reason for failure here that is "inspired" by the "def" condition is not the same as the one above; there, the delays were caused by the loss of validity of EIA, by its newly acquired incapacity of judgment, so to speak; something of special concern for stakeholders. Here, on the other hand, they derive from insurmountable problems of technical nature. The reason for this difference lies in the presence of two different conditions: "size" and "sens", in that they represent two different contexts in which two similar occurrences acquire two different meanings, thus triggering two different mechanisms (though to achieve the same outcome).

In the case of small project owners, technical problems are not particularly relevant; it is the speed at which the stakeholders acquire essential knowledge about EIA that is relevant. Small projects present greater flexibility and can be easily adjusted "along the way"; the speed at which this is done determines the presence or the absence of implementation problems.

Table 12.4. New CMO Configurations and Related QCA Conditions Accounting for Implementation Quality with Regard to Political/Cultural Context

CONDITION	CONTEXT	CONDITION	MECHANISM	CONDITION	OUTCOME
Political/cultural context sensitive to environmental issues (SENS)	EIA is expected to assess the intrinsic merit of a project	Clarity of project definition – negative (def)	With fuzzy project boundaries, EIA validity (and thus its usefulness) is compromised. Until validity limits are restored, EIA does not provide the wished for information (is a project good or not?)	Output (negative)	EIA implementation delayed
Political/cultural context sensitive to environmental issues (SENS)	EIA is expected to assess the intrinsic merit of a project	Clarity of project definition – positive (DEF)	Absence of "technical" faults; EIA confirms itself as a valid and rigorous instrument to assess a project's merit	Output (positive)	EIA implementation successful
Political/cultural context non sensitive to environmental issues (sens)	EIA is paperwork: an obstacle to be overcome on the way to project fulfillment	Early discussion of all relevant matters – positive (DISC)	High motivation to fulfill the project on behalf of stakeholders prompts them to meet early in order to avoid EIA failure	Output (positive)	EIA implementation successful
Political/cultural context non sensitive to environmental issues (sens)	EIA is paperwork: an obstacle to be overcome on the way to project fulfillment	Early discussion of all relevant matters – negative (disc)	Lack of motivation to fulfill the project on behalf of stakeholders allows EIA implementation to be neglected	Output (negative)	EIA implementation neglected

Table 12.5. New CMO Configurations and Related QCA Conditions Accounting for Implementation Quality with Regard to Project Size

CONDITION	CONTEXT	CONDITION	MECHANISM	CONDITION	OUTCOME
Big sized project (SIZE)	Owners have a high degree of EIA knowledge but big sized projects are articulate and complex to define.	Clarity of project definition – positive (DEF)	Owners succeed in clearly defining the project, laying the basis for the smooth application of procedures	Output (positive)	EIA implementation successful
Big sized project (SIZE)	Owners have a high degree of EIA knowledge but big sized projects are articulate and complex to define.	Clarity of project definition – negative (def)	Owners fail to provide a clear project definition, laying the basis for procedural complications and technical problems during implementation	Output (negative)	EIA implementation retarded
Small sized project (size)	Small project owners have little knowledge of EIA requirements and regulations, and ignore how to plan their projects in order to pass the assessment	Early discussion of all relevant matters – positive (DISC)	By getting involved in an early discussion with other stakeholders, project owners quickly learn what they need to, modifying the project and still meeting their deadlines	Output (positive)	EIA implementation successful
Small sized project (size)	Small project owners have little knowledge of EIA requirements and regulations, and ignore how to plan their projects in order to pass the assessment	Early discussion of all relevant matters – negative (disc)	Project owners fail to quickly learn what they need to, unable to meet their deadlines while trying to modify the project	Output (negative)	EIA implementation is delayed or retarded

2.3.2. Environmental Project Quality (Impact)

Impact is here defined as the actual project quality of the final project to be constructed; this includes the accordance with environmental standards, hence the EIA final approval. We found a positive impact in fourteen of the fifteen test cases. QCA leads to the following solution for positive impact that cannot be further minimized:

- IMPACT = BEG + output
- impact = beg.OUTPUT

In switching from QCA to CMO configurations, the first thing we notice is that our assumption 2a on the "EIA as deterrent" mechanism (see above) is confirmed: a project is finally standard compliant if it is initially so. Assumption 2b, however, is not confirmed: far from contributing to success, a good EIA implementation is a necessary condition for a negative output. We thus glimpse the existence of two different mechanisms able to lead to project approval: in the first case, the project passes because it meets the standards; in the second case because, after implementation has failed and project quality has not been assessed, it is given a chance. In other words, the two paths leading to approval incorporate either project merit – notably present for a long time – or the impossibility to assess it.

Likewise, rejection is combined with initial incompliance and successful implementation. Our CMO assumption inspired by this finding implies that, when the project does not meet the standards from the beginning, we simply need a reliable instrument to find out: if we can count on a correctly implemented assessment, we are likely to discover that the project does not meet the standards. Hence it is finally rejected. These last findings are displayed in table 12.7.

2.4 Conclusions

In the following, the findings are synthesized and put into perspective regarding the guiding evaluation questions. As an overview, table 12.6 displays the QCA-solutions obtained for output and impact.

Table 12.6. Overview of Combinations of Conditions for Output and Impact

	Output	Impact
sens.DISC + SENS.DEF.(SIZE + MAN)	+	
sens.disc + SENS.def	-	
size.DISC + SIZE.DEF.(SENS + MAN)	+	
size.disc + SIZE.def	-	
BEG + output		+
beg.OUTPUT		-

As the table above shows, the quality of the EIA implementation (output) depends to a large degree on different EIA factors, both substantial and organizational. The EIA tends to be well implemented if the precautionary assessment treats all relevant questions, if compensation tasks are integrated into the planning at an early stage and if there is a systematic EIA management and an early integration of all affected actors by the relevant public agency.

In this respect, the study also identified weaknesses of the present EIA: particular opportunities for improvement lie in the area of procedural management and in the services provided by the authorities. The burden of the EIA could also be relieved if the consideration of the key environmental questions were to be commenced at the spatial-planning stage. Moreover, less-detailed environmental impact statements would be required during the consent procedures if environmental monitoring during construction and outcome reviews were to be given a firmer statutory basis.

On the other hand, the actual project quality (impact) seems to depend strongly on the project quality. I.e., an EIA leads to a good final project quality only under the condition that the assessed project respects environmental standards from the beginning, is well coordinated with land use concepts, and is well argued, in general. This finding implies that the EIA very well displays an effect on the final project quality, in that its regulations indirectly contribute to the project quality because construction project owners know in advance that they will have to go through an EIA. Therefore, they plan their projects accordingly in the first place, in order to avoid problems during the EIA procedures.

In the light of these findings, the evaluation study arrives at the conclusion that the EIA serves as a vital coordination tool, ensuring the enforcement of environmental legislation – and especially precautionary environmental protection in connection with consent procedures. The EIA also helps during the project planning process to ensure that the environmental impacts of major construction projects are reduced to an absolute minimum (Sager and Schenkel 2003).

3. REALISTIC EVALUATION AND QCA

So how do QCA and realistic evaluation relate to each other? First, they have many features in common. Both refer to the idea of "chemical causation" and assume the existence of the "right ingredients for change". Moreover, both acknowledge the enormous importance of the context. Realistic Evaluation regards it as that something which "turns (or fails to turn) causal potential into

Table 12.7. New CMO Configurations and Related QCA Conditions Accounting for Final Project Approval

CONDITION	CONTEXT	CONDITION	MECHANISM	CONDITION	OUTCOME
Standards met since the beginning – negative (beg)	The submitted project does not meet the standards	Output – positive (OUTPUT)	EIA Implementation is successful: the instrument is able to assess the project's merit	Impact – negative (impact)	EIA ascertains the project's faults; the project is consequently rejected
–		Output – negative (output)	EIA implementation fails; the instrument is not able to assess the project's merit	Impact – positive (IMPACT)	In doubt, the project is given a chance by being finally approved
		Standards met since the beginning – positive (BEG)	EIA does not change the assessment during the project; it acts as a deterrent before the project is planned	Impact – positive (IMPACT)	The project finally meets the standards

a causal outcome" or that "enables or disables the intended mechanisms of change". Similarly, in QCA (Ragin 1987):

"what makes a certain feature, a commonality, causally relevant in one setting and not in another is the fact that its causal significance is altered by the presence of other features (that is, its effect is altered by context). [...] By examining differences and similarities in context it is possible to determine how different combinations of conditions have the same causal significance and how similar causal factors can operate in opposite directions".

As for the centrality of causal mechanisms, Ragin (1987) calls them in a variety of ways: *"origins (of important qualitative changes in specific settings)"*, *"events [conspiring] to force [individuals to do something]"*, *"causal arguments"*, *"underlying commonalities"*, etc. His focus seems to be not so much on that 'weaving process' specifically binding together reasoning and resources, or the individual's choices and capacities; but rather on a more general "intersection" or combination of conditions. It is our view that this combinatorial structure can properly represent the interplay of mechanisms and contexts, only to the extent that structure- and agency-related propositions are correctly transformed into Boolean data.

This does not turn to be quite automatic and indeed, constitutes a step of the analysis whose importance should not be overlooked. One must keep in mind that the same factor can completely change its significance when combined with a different condition or result variable. For example, the "disc" condition has two different meanings depending on whether it is included in the output model or the impact model: in the former, it means that an early discussion of all the relevant matters among stakeholders contributed to smoothen the implementation process; while in the latter, it means that the taking place of such a discussion made a contribution towards a positive impact because it made project modifications easier. Another example is the meaning of the "def" variable when combined with the "sens" or the "size" conditions. In the latter case the lack of clarity in the project definition retards the implementation process because it produces formal problems which make the application of procedures technically impossible; the impeding barrier is of a legal nature. In the former case, instead, the process is retarded because the existence of technical problems alters the perception of EIA, now regarded as an instrument no longer valid to assess a project's merit, whether or not those technical problems constitute insurmountable legal impediments.

3.1 QCA and Realist Synthesis

Pawson and Tilley (1997) criticize the experimentalist approach to the systematic review of evaluations for its tendency to regard the cases as mere

quantitative additions to the sample total size. In its typical manner of sectioning the cases into generic sets of independent variables, this approach misses the singularity and wholeness of each case, along with its explicative features. On the other hand, these authors warn that *"what are transferable between cases are not lumps of data but sets of ideas"*, and regard the review of evaluations as a chance to *"test, refine and adjudicate"* middle-range theories. They maintain that cumulation in evaluation research is:
1. *"about producing middle-range theory, of a kind abstract enough to underpin the development of a range of program types yet concrete enough to withstand testing in the details of program implementation"*;
2. *"a matter of deepening, specifying, focusing and formalising our understanding of program mechanisms, contexts and outcome patterns"*;
3. *"a matter of increasing understanding of how these elements are connected"*;
4. *"a matter of traversing between general theory (abstract configurations) and empirical case studies (focused configurations)"*.

Our EIA study has been a sort of cumulation of evaluations, in that we performed a transfer and comparison of ideas about what made each of the 15 single project assessments work, unveiling many similarities and differences among cases. QCA allowed us to formalize a limited generalization of those findings which partly confirmed and partly modified our initial understanding of how the various elements were connected. And last but not least, making assumptions on a general theory about how EIA works – which was a necessary step prior to using QCA – allowed us to go back to the cases, or to a lower level on the 'abstraction-specification" scale: another step in the "traversing" mentioned above.

In fact, the evaluation of many programs can be regarded as a cumulation of single evaluations. The European Structural Funds projects, for instance, are selected according to policy priorities in the various sectors of unemployment, environment, research, social inclusion, etc.; its evaluations are carried out for single, as well as for groups of projects with similar objectives. In our study, the dimension along which our single projects were grouped, is that they were subject to and underwent the Swiss Environmental Impact Assessment; at the European funds level, however, projects may be grouped along several dimensions: regional, national, sectorial, sub-sectorial and so on. The same can be said for the other International institutions currently financing public projects and programs (eg., the World Bank, FAO, UNICEF, etc.): they can group their projects along several "axes" and expand the cognitive ambitions they hold about them, going from asking "what it is that made this single project work?" to "what it is that made this type or group of projects work?". Thus, QCA makes it possible to stop at many levels along the scale from abstraction to specification and back, not necessarily at the middle one. Adding even greater flexibility to the concept of middle-range theory, QCA enables us to easily commute between multiple-level theories: single-project theory, sub-group-of-projects theory, sectoral projects theory, national projects theory, and so on.

Perhaps the greatest added value that QCA can bring to realistic evaluation is this power to extend the transfer of ideas among up to several cases, so as to enlarge the empirical support of the theory. In simple terms, the "limited generalization" that QCA allows on twenty or thirty cases, is much "less limited" than that allowed in a classic case comparison. In this sense, QCA adds "power" to the realist synthesis, in that we are capable of obtaining a more comprehensive – quantitatively speaking – systematic review of evaluations, without abandoning the realist view. This means that, as we have already mentioned, this gain on the scope of the operation does not hamper its other several fundamental features: considering the cases as wholes; conceiving causation as 'internally' operating rather than 'externally'; avoiding the adoption of a successionist view of causality; dismissing the importance of the frequency of cases, regarding each single one as equally important; paying attention to the underlying mechanics of phenomena, etc.. Traditionally, all these features have been obtained at the price of considering only a few cases at a time, while the experimental, variable-oriented statistical methods that could handle many cases simultaneously lacked all of them. As Pawson and Tilley (1997) powerfully argue, these were crucial shortcomings as far as evaluators were concerned. But, as we have attempted to show, QCA can overcome these trade-offs and add usefulness and insight to evaluation research.

NOTES

[1] NB: Here we do not use QCA (Boolean) notation: '+' does not mean 'or', but rather 'and'.
[2] In the language of Realistic Evaluation, they are all "outcomes".
[3] For reasons of space we must omit configurations concerning the "outcome" result variable.
[4] In a second step of the presented research, we have calculated the solutions with ordinal data using TOSMANA software (see also Cronqvist and Berg-Schlosser, in this volume). The respective results will be presented in a subsequent paper yet to be published.

PART FOUR

CONCLUSION

Chapter 13

CONCLUSION
Innovative Comparative Methods for Policy Analysis: Milestones to Bridge Different Worlds

Benoît Rihoux
Université catholique de Louvain

Heike Grimm
University of Erfurt and Max-Planck-Institute of Economics, Jena

"If you like to have things easy, you'll have difficulties; if you like problems, you will succeed" (Laotian proverb)

1. TEN TANGIBLE PROOFS OF PROGRESS

At the outset of this collective enterprise, we had set ourselves a very ambitious task: to *"provide a decisive push to the further development and application of innovative comparative methods for the improvement of policy analysis"*. Have we been successful in performing this task? Though this might seem somewhat immodest from our part, we think we may answer in a positive way, for at least 10 reasons, which relate to both the concrete policy-oriented applications and more methodological and epistemological considerations. We have demonstrated that:

1. specific SCCA methods such as QCA (as well as MVQCA and FS) can indeed be *applied empirically*, in a useful manner, on policy analysis material. In fact, quite a few other such applications can already be found in the recent literature, but we have now demonstrated that such methods can be applied on a broader range of topics and data;
2. one key strength of these methods is their *transparency* – provided one gets acquainted with the specific jargon used in the technical steps of the procedure. On the one hand, this transparency lies in the fact that the key set-theoretic operations (be they "crisp" or "fuzzy") performed by the

software can be understood by the user – hence he/she really grasps what really happens in the "black box" of software data processing (unlike most statistical data processing, for instance). On the other hand, it also lies in the necessity to make clear-cut choices in the process, at different stages (e.g. case selection, model specification, operationalization of the variables, possibly dichotomization, concrete modifications to solve contradictions, etc.). From a policy analysis perspective, this opens up the possibility of a more informed discussion between the policy analyst and the "end customer" (e.g. political decision-maker, public administrator, etc.) of the study;
3. the *comparative research design* can be improved, especially in terms of case selection and model specification (i.e. selection of potentially relevant variables). Moreover, we have demonstrated empirically that some techniques such as MSDO/MDSO can be a key help in this difficult enterprise;
4. such methods do allow, starting from an intrinsically complex data matrix (which is itself the expression of still more complex, "thick" cases), to achieve *reduction of complexity*, and in particular to reach more parsimonious 'explanations' of policy-relevant outcomes[1] of interest. Of course the "price" to be paid for this is to accept a strong level of synthesis at some stage, what could be coiled as 'loss of information' by some. In fact it is not the case that information is 'lost' – it is only put between parentheses, during the 'analytic moment' in which some software treatment is performed. There is still a lot of complexity before this moment (e.g. "thick", complex case stories), and there is complexity again at the end of the analytic process (e.g. when the researcher has to 'interpret' the minimal formulae by going back to the complex case stories);
5. the conception of causality underlying these methods is very much in line with the experience of policy practitioners. It is not only an abstract conception, because these techniques do enable one to empirically identify (partly or fully) *different paths* producing an outcome of interest – what has been defined as "multiple conjunctural causation". This is a key added value as compared with most mainstream quantitative (i.e. statistical) analyses (see e.g. Ragin and Rihoux 2004). How some cases (say: regions or countries) cluster around one of these paths, while some other cases correspond to some other path, is very relevant from a real-life policy action perspective: different groups of cases, operating within different contexts, do require different policy intervention strategies (e.g. different 'policy mixes').
6. these methods allow one to exploit *different types of data*, from more quantitative, continuous measures to much more qualitative statements or

observations. Furthermore, one may choose different ways to operationalize the variables: purely crisp and dichotomous (for QCA), still crisp but with more categories (for MVQCA), or following the fuzzy-set logic. In many instances, one may try to test these different operationalizations and assess the pro's and con's of each strategy – in particular in terms of policy relevance of the minimal formulae;
7. these methods can be applied *at different levels*: supranational, national, sub-national (e.g. regional etc.) and local. Hence they are of potential interest for many different public agencies, political decision-makers and other policy actors, at all these different levels. There seems to be a particularly strong potential in the application of those methods at the level of supra-national regulatory bodies, who attempt to reach policy goals to be implemented in different national and regional settings – the European Union (even more so since its enlargement) is a case in point.
8. these methods enable one to infuse *"case-based knowledge"* in the analytic process, at all stages. In a way, it makes it possible to stick as close as possible to the complex, specific, idiosyncratic cases, while still performing an analysis – and reaching policy-relevant conclusions – on a larger number of cases;
9. these methods can be *combined* – and/or confronted – usefully *with other methods*, both qualitative and quantitative (see also below);
10. these methods are compatible both with more *"theory-driven"* preoccupations and with concrete, *policy-driven*, real-world questions. In fact, these methods enable, potentially, a rich dialogue between "theorists" and "practitioners" (see also below).

Hence, in short, we may argue that the four initial challenges (see introductory chapter) we had set ourselves have – at least to some extent – been successfully met. First, some key technical and methodological difficulties can indeed at least be "pragmatically" addressed (e.g. case selection, model specification etc.) – and one may build upon the experience of other researchers. This enables more cumulative knowledge, while 'best practices' (Rihoux et.al. 2003) in the use of these methods are becoming more widespread as well. Second, these methods are indeed particularly transparent (see above) and enable one to better exploit (in a SCCA manner) otherwise rather "soft" case studies. Thus SCCA methods are really useful to make more out of existing case study material. Third, these methods indeed allow one to perform different types of comparisons (see above), also at different stages of the policy process. They also bring "diversity" in, with different paths and differentiated "solutions" and implementation schemes; they allow one to engage in a systematic quasi-experimental design; and they are also compatible with more pluralist/participative policy analysis (as they are so transparent – see above). Fourth and finally, they indeed display some key strengths of both the quantitative and qualitative tools.

This is not to say, of course, that these are "miracle" methods" – in fact such a thing does not exist in real-life research (policy work is no exception). All methods have limitations, and researchers face trade-offs, some of which are more "tricky" than others (see below; and De Meur and Rihoux 2002). However we argue that these methods hold concrete promises both as a distinct, specific path – possibly a "third path" between the qualitative and quantitative strategies (Ragin 1987, De Meur and Rihoux 2002; Rihoux 2003) and in connection (possibly in sequence?) with some specific qualitative or quantitative methods (see below). Evidently, this is not to say that all difficulties have been lifted – indeed some further work is needed to better address some remaining challenges.

2. CHALLENGES STILL AHEAD[2]

2.1 Improving Comparative Research Design and Confronting Methods

Real-life comparative research design is a very challenging endeavor, full of caveats and apparently unsurpassable dilemmas – even more so if we ambition to put into practice genuinely *systematic* comparative analysis. This holds not only for policy-oriented research, but indeed for any comparative research effort in the social sciences broadly defined. SCCA methods are still quite recent, and hence they can still be consolidated and enriched in several respects (see also De Meur and Rihoux 2002; Rihoux 2003).

In spite of the progress we have made in this volume, one of the key difficulties still is case selection. Arguably, in social science research (and in policy research in particular), one should not broaden too much the variety of cases. In other words, the quest for generalization should always be 'bounded', e.g. by comparing cases which operate within sufficiently "comparable" contexts. This being said is of vital importance that cases display enough variation on the 'outcome' variable. For instance, if the outcome of interest is the relative success of a policy package in different regions (those regions being the cases), then one should make sure to select both cases of regions with successful and less successful policy results. In this respect, the Przeworski and Teune models are probably less powerful than the 'simple' Mill logic (which underlies QCA), as they do not take fully into account differences in the outcome.

Another difficulty – or rather several difficulties – arises with regards to model specification. The sheer selection of the 'condition' variables is of course a challenging task in most policy research, as the analyst is most often confronted with a potentially huge number of potential explanatory factors or conditions. In an ideal world, he/she would rely on some sort of commonly accepted, sufficiently parsimonious "theory" which would allow him/her to concentrate on a few key conditions. Alas, in real-life policy research, rival theories abound – so this also means that theories should be further consolidated and confronted. Actually, precisely on this point, SCCA methods such as QCA could be used more intensively to empirically test rival theories against real-life, policy-relevant data (see e.g. Sager 2004).

In quite direct connection with the difficulties of model specification, one potentially promising avenue is not to consider all conditions as belonging to one single 'package' of logically equivalent variables. First steps in this direction have been made by Schneider and Wagemann (forthcoming), who draw a useful distinction between some "remote" versus "proximate" conditions, and who also apply a practical 'two-step' procedure to implement this distinction. Incidentally, such a strategy also allows one to "filter out" some more remote (i.e. distant, more contextual) conditions, and hence to encompass more conditions in exploratory QCA or FS tests, for instance. In this respect, more work still needs to be done to refine and ground more solidly – empirically and theoretically – the distinction between "remote" v/s "proximate" conditions. One of the theoretical guides for this might be, for instance, Scharpf's actor-centered institutionalism, or the classical Coleman model (articulation of "macro" and "micro" determinants of some outcome of interest).

In addition, as with all empirical methods, concrete difficulties still arise when it comes to operationalizing and processing data stemming from real-life sources, for SCCA purposes. Here we should mention measurement errors, problems of validity and reliability of the data, and of course also practical difficulties in the dichotomization of "richer" data if one engages into crisp, dichotomous QCA. In spite of the progress we have made in this volume, among other things on the issue of dichotomization and categorization of the data, and in spite of the development of new tools which enable one to process "richer" data (such as MVQCA and Fuzzy Sets), there is still a lot to be discussed on how and why to categorize data (typically: where to place a dichotomization threshold).

One other promising avenue – and perhaps even more challenging than the others – will be to pursue the confrontation (or dialogue, rather) between SCCA methods and other methods, be they more qualitative or quantitative (i.e. mainly statistics-based). For instance, what is the added value of MSDO/MDSO as compared with "conventional" cluster analysis? What does

QCA add, in concrete terms, to statistical tools which may also process dichotomous data (such as conditional logit analysis[3])? Can we really combine QCA and SNA, as one may argue that SNA deals with interrelated cases, whereas QCA deals with interrelated variables/conditions? Which practical connections can be made with "thick" case analyses? How can one better integrate the time dimension, possibly combining somehow SCCA methods with sequence analysis methods such as optimal matching, comparative narrative analysis, event-structure analysis, process tracing etc. (see Krook 2005)? How could we, in practical terms, "sequence" SCCA methods such as QCA with other formal (quantitative) tools – maybe following some sort of "two-step" analysis as well? This last question is a rejoinder to growing debates on how to combine, or possibly even "mix" methods in real-life empirical research (see e.g. Tashakkori and Teddlie 2003).

These are only a few questions among many, many more. Actually most of these questions and difficulties – or rather challenges to be met – are not specific to policy analysis, but rather common to social science research, though the way these challenges are eventually met do of course orientate the final conclusions of the analysis (and hence this may, at least indirectly, have many important policy-relevant implications). Let us now turn to more directly and specifically policy-relevant challenges.

2.2 Developing Further Concrete Policy-Oriented Applications

In real-life policy-oriented research, any discussion of (past, current and future) methodological challenges cannot escape the paramount (and very "tricky") issue of measurement and coding. Both in QCA, MVQCA and FS, one often encounters difficulties when it comes to coding variables (see also above). However let us insist once again that this is a difficulty with all formalized methods which require numerical coding of data. In this enterprise, as a reminder, the specificity of SCCA methods is that such operations are carried out in a more transparent way. One more technical aspect is the placement of the dichotomization (0/1) threshold, in "crisp", dichotomous QCA. In this respect, in spite of the fact that one should only use statistical criteria (mean, median etc.) in last resort, one should still pay attention to the size of the two subsets (Herrmann and Cronqvist 2005). A rule of thumb (still to be fine-tuned) could be that each subset should contain at least one third of the cases. Note that this whole discussion is far from being only a technical and "academic" one: it has very direct and very concrete policy implications, as follows. As SCCA methods are tailored-suited for small-N and intermediate-N situation, they are evidently case-sensitive and variable-sensitive. Hence modifying the operationalization even only on one single condition, in dichotomous QCA for instance (say: "efficient" versus "less efficient" administrative system) may very well bring profound modifications to the minimal formulae. This will also lead to different research conclusions – and thus to different policy advocacy schemes.

Then comes another key methodological (but also policy-relevant) issue: that of logical contradictions: how important are they and how to deal with them? As is argued in this volume, it is actually good to obtain contradictions at some stages of the analysis: the researcher can learn from these contradictions, as it forces him/her to go back to the empirical cases and to theory. In practical, real-life policy research, one of the potential "signals" of the existence of such contradictions is that, most probably, the researcher has forgotten to include at least one key condition so as to explain variation in the policy phenomenon of interest (the 'outcome', in QCA terminology).

With regards to such contradictions, there are two practical ways to use QCA, in policy-oriented research in particular. The first way is to start with a "long" model (including many conditions), with very little chances of obtaining contradictions, and then to reduce the model following a stepwise procedure, until it is not possible to shorten the model anymore without creating contradictions. The second way is to start with a very "short" model (very few conditions), thus very likely to produce contradictions, and then to solve the contradictions by using techniques such as MSDO/MDSO to systematically compare the cases on many other attributes, and eventually add some specific conditions. Apart from this, using MVQCA may also help to suppress some contradictions, as one may transform a problematic dichotomous variable into a 3-category or 4-category variable (hence adding some differentiation between cases). In the process, frequency considerations can also be used to arbitrate (if one has to make a choice as to where to place some cut-off points). In a careful way, frequency considerations may also be used in the interpretation of the minimal formula. To sum up: there are no "absolute" rules as how to treat contradictions. It also depends on whether QCA is used for (empirical) hypothesis-testing or for theory-building.

Last but not least, a recurrent topic of SCCA needs to be further elaborated upon: the arbitration between parsimony and complexity. How much reduction of complexity should we aim at? This translates, in practical terms, in the following question: when and how should "simplifying assumptions" be used? It is argued that the most minimal (i.e. shortest, most parsimonious) formula should not always be aimed at, as it requests the use of very "hard" (v/s "easy") counterfactuals (Ragin and Sonnett 2004; Ragin and Rihoux 2004). In any case, especially in policy research, it is a virtue of QCA (v/s. most statistical methods) to obtain a solution which is not too simple (see our argument in favour of "multiple conjunctural causation", above).

In spite of all these difficulties, there is a broad potential for methodologically consolidated *and* policy relevant applications of SCCA methods, in many different settings and designs: across sectors, countries, regions, etc. This also calls for an enhanced dialogue between 'experts' (academics) and policy practitioners.

2.3 Nourishing a Dialogue with the Policy Community

If SCCA methods are to become more widely used and applied in real-life policy work, they have to be confronted with the preferences and needs of the policy-makers (political leaders and cadres, public administrators etc.). One of the quite crucial issues to be clarified in this respect may be stated as follows: at which point of the policy-making cycle are SCCA methods most useful? In the field of evaluation, for instance, should efforts be placed primarily on *ex ante* or *ex post* types of evaluation, or rather on *in itinere* evaluation? This discussion should be pursued. Secondly and more generally, some effort should be done to provide a more fine-grained mapping of SCCA methods in connection with the number of cases, with the number of variables, but also with the type of (policy) research questions. Ideally, this mapping exercise should include many different (qualitative, comparative-configurational, quantitative) methods. Some first attempts are being made at present. Third, and not least, more should be done to bring SCCA methods closer to policy practitioners. Two concrete ways will be to produce accessible textbooks for non-specialists (this effort is under way), to insert synthetic information about SCCA in compendiums of methods for policy analysis or evaluation, and also to provide training opportunities reaching beyond the purely "academic" circles. To cut a long story short: some practical steps still need to be taken in order to fully insert SCCA methods as part of the standard "toolbox" for policy analysis – alongside other methods of course.

3. INNOVATIVE COMPARATIVE METHODS: RECONCILING THEORY WITH PRAGMATIC POLICY NEEDS?

At the risk of over-simplifying, one may say that policy analysis is of interest to two very distinct publics: researchers ("academics") and decision-makers ("politicians"). Probably there is a continuum between those two extremes, but still the preoccupations and needs of these two publics are arguably quite contrasted.

An increasing proportion of 'academics' involved in policy analysis (among which, certainly, most contributors to this volume) would now contend that there is a need to bring more "theory" (back) in policy-oriented research, instead of being too inductive (too data-driven). This being said, as has been demonstrated in this volume, such theory-guided work is perfectly compatible with the pragmatic requirements of policy research – which are always, more or less directly, linked with the preoccupations of the policy practitioners and decision makers. For instance, it may be argued that SCCA methods resemble quite closely "analytical induction" (Rihoux 2003) which, by definition, is pretty much theory-guided. However these methods, as we have also demonstrated in this volume, do also produce relatively "short" (i.e. parsimonious) models, and consecutively minimal formulae, which is a major advantage from a policy action perspective. In a way, there is a need to inform policy practitioners that they can learn from (non-policy oriented) social science research – however this would imply that such social scientific literature is made accessible for (and thus understandable to) the policy community, which is easier said than done.

This is not to suggest that the respective goals of "academics" and "decision-makers" easily converge in a sort of harmonious movement. In many concrete situations, one is confronted with a dilemma between pragmatic requirements of policy operators, on the one hand, and methodological "purity" of academics on the other hand. One typical such situation occurs at the stage of case selection – at this stage, political process factors may, to various extents, influence the choice of cases to be included in the analysis. In fact, two opposite situations (but equally problematic from a methodological perspective!) often occur in real-life policy research. In some situations, the policy actors insist on including cases which should be discarded on methodological grounds – for instance, they would insist that all the regions of the country be covered, even if, say, some good sampling procedure (comparative research design) would be more appropriate. Conversely, in some other situations, policy actors demand that some "embarrassing" cases be dropped, in spite of the fact that those cases are methodologically and/or substantively[4] important from a sound comparative research design perspective.

Beyond this phase of case selection, policy researchers also face many other "political" constraints such as limitations in funding, time available, lack of transparency in data transmission, etc. As far as the 'resources' aspect (funding and time constraints) is concerned, we may argue that SCCA methods are altogether rather affordable, as they can build upon already existent (case) material. However one should also remember that a prerequisite of a good SCCA, in any field (policy analysis is no exception), is good, in-depth 'intimacy' with each one of the cases under consideration. This in turn implies that some good, reliable and thus 'comparable' data should be available for all cases of interest. If such data is not available, then indeed

SCCA methods become much more costly, if at all applicable – as they request intensive fieldwork for each one of the "thick" cases under consideration.

At the end of the process, there is also the difficulty of providing "easy-to-read" and "easy-to-use" conclusions to decision-makers. Probably one reason why mainstream quantitative techniques have become so popular over the last few decades is that they do provide such "simple" conclusions. How relevant and empirically valid these conclusions are is another question... We think we have made a strong case that SCCA methods do enable researchers to provide decision-makers with neither "too simple" nor "too complex" conclusions. For instance, in line with "multiple conjunctural causation", one typical SCCA conclusion would sound as follows: "among the 10 cases under study, one group of cases (cases 1, 3, 4, 5, 7, 8, 9, 10) reaches better results with the combination of policy instruments (policy package) A and B, whereas another group of cases (cases 2 and 6) reaches a better result with the policy package of instruments B and C". Such a conclusion is "complex", in a way, but still perfectly comprehensible and in line with the pragmatic needs of decision-makers.

At first sight, one might believe that this volume reflects more the preoccupations of 'academics' than those of "policy-makers" – yet we like to think that it opens a broad door for fruitful dialogues between these two different and yet connected worlds. One should not overstate the contrasts and the distances. There is no clear-cut dichotomy between, say, academics secluded in their ivory towers and pondering at the stars *versus* politicians dealing hands-on with everyday 'real-life' problems... though dichotomies are logically and analytically very powerful, so QCA clearly demonstrates!

NOTES

[1] Here the term "outcome" is used in the generic sense, with reference to QCA terminology. Needless to say, different types of phenomena (not only 'policy outcomes') may be of interest for policy analysts.

[2] Some of the points discussed below stem from the collective discussion at the end of the Erfurt ESF exploratory workshop, on 28 Sept. 2004. We thank all participants to this final discussion for their contribution in these reflections.

[3] In this respect, see the innovative attempt by Dumont and Bäck (forthcoming), who demonstrate on "real-life" data (governmental coalition formation) that, indeed, QCA does bring some additional insights as compared with conditional logit analysis.

[4] In fact, quite often the substantial interest of such cases lies precisely in the fact that they appear to be « outliers » which may be embarrassing for, say, some political decision-makers (e.g. because these cases contradict their political discourse, etc.).

REFERENCES

Aarebrot, Frank H. and Pal. H. Bakka (2003). "Die Vergleichende Methode in der Politikwissenschaft." In Dirk Berg-Schlosser and Ferdinand Müller-Rommel, F. (eds). *Vergleichende Politikwissenschaft*. Opladen: Leske + Budrich, 57-76.

Abbott, Andrew (2001). *Time Matters. On Theory and Method*. Chicago: Chicago University Press.

Adema, Willem (1999). *Net Social Expenditures*. Paris, OECD.

AICGS New Economy Study Group Team (2002). *The New Economy in Germany and the Unites States: Policy Challenges and Solutions*. American Institute for Contemporary German Studies: Washington, D.C.

Alanen, Ilkka (2004) "The Transformation of Agricultural Systems in the Baltic Countries – A Critique of the World Bank's Concepts." In Andrew Gilg et al. (eds). *Mapping the Rural Problem in the Baltic Countryside. Transition Processes in the Rural Areas of Estonia, Latvia and Lithuania*. Aldershot UK and Burlington VT, Ashgate.

Alapuro, Risto (1988). *State and Revolution in Finland*. Berkeley – Los Angeles – London: University of California Press.

Albrow, Martin (1996). *Global Age. State and Society Beyond Modernity*. Oxford: Polity Press in association with Blackwell Publishers Ltd.

Amenta, Edwin (2003). "What we Know About the Development of Social Policy: Comparative and Historical Research in Comparative and Historical Perspective." In James Mahoney and Dietrich Rueschmeyer (eds) 2003. *Comparative Historical Analysis in the Social Sciences*. Cambridge: Cambridge University Press.

Amenta, Edwin and Jane D. Poulsen (1994). "Where to Begin: A Survey of Five Approaches to Selecting Independent Variables for Qualitative Comparative Analysis." *Sociological Methods and Research*, 23,1:22-53.

Antonnen, Anneli and Jorma Sippilä (1996). "European Social Care Services: Is it Possible to Identify Models?" *Journal of European Social Policy*, 6 (2):87-100.

Appadurai, Arjun (1998). *Modernity at Large. Cultural Dimensions of Globalization*. Public Worlds, Volume 1. Fourth Printing. Minneapolis and London: University of Minnesota Press.

Ascher, William and William H. Overholt (1983). *Strategic Planning and Forecasting: Political Risk and Economic Opportunity*. New York: Wiley-Interscience.

Audretsch, David B. (2003). "Entrepreneurship Policy and the Strategic Management of Places." In David M. Hart (ed.). *The Emergence of Entrepreneurship Policy. Governance, Start-ups, and Growth in the U.S. Knowledge Economy*. Cambridge: Cambridge University Press, 20-38.

Audretsch, David B., Heike Grimm and Charles W. Wessner (2005) (eds). *Local Heroes in the Global Village. Globalization and New Entrepreneurship Policies*, New York: Springer Science+Business Media, Inc.

Audretsch, David B. and Roy Thurik (2001). "Sources of Growth: the Entrepreneurial versus the Managed Economy." *Industrial and Corporate Change*, 10:267-315.

Baeck, Unn Doris (2004) "The Urban Ethos. Locality and Youth in North Norway." YOUNG 12:99-115.

Balthasar, Andreas (2004). "The Effects of the Institutional Context of the Agency Responsible for Allocating Evaluations on the Utilization of Evaluation Results: Evidenced Using Qualitative Comparative Analysis (QCA)" (*unpublished manuscript*).

Barbalet, Jack (1988). *Citizenship: Rights Struggle and Class Inequality*. UK: Open University Press.

Baumgartner, Frank. R. and Bryan D. Jones (1991). "Agenda Dynamics and Policy Subsystems." *The Journal of Politics*, 53 (4):1044-1074.

Becker, Howard (1998). *Tricks of the Trade*. Chicago: University of Chicago Press.

Befani, Barbara (2004). "La Qualitative Comparative Analysis (QCA) e la valutazione basata sulla teoria: un connubio possibile." *Rassegna Italiana di Valutazione*, Anno VIII 29.

Bell, Daniel (ed.) (1968). *Toward the Year 2000*. New York: Houghton Mifflin Co.

Berg-Schlosser, Dirk (2001). "Comparative Studies - Method and Design." In Neil J. Smelser and Paul B. Baltes (eds). *International Encyclopaedia of the Social and Behavioural Sciences*, Oxford: Pergamon, 2427-2433.

Berg-Schlosser, Dirk and Gisèle De Meur (1997). "Reduction of Complexity for a Small-N Analysis: a Stepwise Multi-Methodological Approach." *Comparative Social Research*, 16:133-162.

Berg-Schlosser, Dirk, Gisèle De Meur and Charles C. Ragin (1996). "Political Methodology: Qualitative Methods." In Robert E. Goodin and Hans-Dieter Klingemann (eds). *A New Handbook of Political Science*, Oxford: Oxford University Press, 749-768.

Berg-Schlosser, Dirk and Sven Quenter (1996) "Makro-qualitative vs. Makro-quantitative Methoden in der Politikwissenschaft. Vorzüge und Mängel komparativer Verfahrensweisen am Beispiel der Sozialstaatstheorie." *Politische Vierteljahresschrift*, 37 (1):100-118.

Birkland, Thomas. A. (2004). "The World Changed Today: Agenda-setting and Policy Change in the Wake of the September 11 Terrorist Attacks." *Review of Policy Research*, 21(2):179-200.

Boole, George (1958)[1854]. *An investigation of the Laws of Thought on which are founded the mathematical theories of logic and probabilities*. New York: Dover Publ.

Borja, Jordi and Manuel Castells (coll. Mireia Belil and Chris Benner) (2003). *Local & Global. Management of Cities in the Information Age*. Based on a Habitat Report first presented at the Istanbul Conference, June 1996. Reprint (initially Earthscan Publ. Ltd., 1997]. United Nations Centre for Human Settlements (Habitat). London: Earthscan Publications Ltd.

Börzel, Tanja A. and Thomas Risse (2003). "Conceptualizing the Domestic Impact of Europe." In Kevin Featherstone and Claudio M. Radaelli (eds). *The Politics of Europeanization*. Oxford: Oxford University Press.

Brady, Henry and David Collier (2004) (eds). *Rethinking Social Inquiry: Diverse Tools, Shared Standards*. Berkeley: Rowman & Littlefield.

Bratton, Michael and Nicolas van de Walle (1997). *Democratic Experiments in Africa: Regime Transitions in Comparative Perspective*. Cambridge: Cambridge University Press.

Brazelton, T. Berry (1992). *Touchpoints: Your Childs' Emotional and Behavioral Development.* Reading, Massachusetts: Addison-Wesley.

Brüderl, Jürgen, Peter Preisendörfer and Rolf Ziegler (1992). "Survival Chances of Newly Founded Business Organizations." *American Sociological Review,* 57:227-242.

Brüderl, Jürgen, Peter Preisendörfer and Rolf Ziegler (1996). *Der Erfolg neugegründeter Betriebe. Eine empirische Studie zu den Chancen und Risiken von Betriebsgründungen.* Berlin: Duncker & Humblot.

Bulmer, Simon. (1994). "The Governance of the European Union: A New Institutionalist Approach." *Journal of Public Policy,* 13 (4):351-380.

Bursens, Peter (1999). *De impact van instituties op beleidsvorming. Een institutionele kijk op de besluitvorming in de communautaire pijler van de Europese Unie.* Doctoraatsthesis, Departement PSW, Universiteit Antwerpen (UA).

Bursens, Peter and Bart Kerremans (1997). *Loose and Tight Policy Networks. EU Decision-making.* PSW-Papers 97/3, Antwerpen: Universiteit Antwerpen (UIA), Departement Politieke en Sociale Wetenschappen.

Carvallo, Michel (1970). *Principes et applications de l'analyse booléenne.* 2ème ed. Paris: Gauthier-Villars.

CASA (1993). *Forbrugerstyrelsens familiebudget.* Rapport 1993:2. København: Forbrugerstyrelsen.

Castells, Manuel (2002a). "The Culture of Cities." In Ida Susser (ed.). *The Castells Reader on Cities and Social Theory.* Malden, MA, USA, and Oxford, UK: Blackwell Publishers.

Castells, Manuel (2002b). "Conclusion: Urban Sociology in the Twenty-first Century." In Ida Susser (ed.). *The Castells Reader on Cities and Social Theory.* Malden MA, USA, and Oxford, UK: Blackwell Publishers.

Castles, Francis (ed.) (1993). *Families of Nations: Patterns of Public Policy in Western Democracies.* Aldershot: Dartmouth

Clayton, Richard and Jonas Pontusson (1998). "Welfare-State Retrenchment Revisited. Entitlement Cuts, Public Sector Restructuring, and Inegalitarian Trends in Advanced Capitalist Societies." *World Politics,* 51 (1):67-98.

Clément, Caty (2004). "Un modèle commun d'effondrement de l'Etat? Une AQQC du Liban, de la Somalie et de l'ex-Yougoslavie." *Revue Internationale de Politique Comparée,* 11 (1):35-50.

Collier, David (1993). "The Comparative Method." In Ada W. Finifter (ed.). *Political Science: State of the Art,* Washington, D.C.: American Political Science Association, 105-119.

Cook, Thomas and Donald Campbell (1979). *Quasi-Experimentation: Design and Analysis Issues for Field Settings.* Chicago: Rand McNally.

Cowles, Maria G. and Thomas Risse (2001). "Transforming Europe: Conclusions." In Maria Green Cowles, James Caporaso and Thomas Risse (eds)." *Transforming Europe. Europeanization and Domestic Change.* Ithaca: Cornell University Press.

Cronqvist, Lasse (2003). "Using Multi-Value Logic Synthesis in Social Science." Paper prepared for the 2nd General Conference of the European Consortium for Political Research (ECPR).

Cronqvist, Lasse (2004). *Tosmana - Tool for Small-N Analysis*. Version 1.201, University of Marburg, Marburg <http://www.tosmana.net>.

Cronqvist, Lasse (2004). "Presentation of TOSMANA: Adding Multi-Value Variables and Visual Aids to QCA." COMPASSS Working Paper 2004-20, 17 pp. (online at http://www.compasss.org).

Cronqvist, Lasse (2005). *Tosmana – Tool for Small-N Analysis* [SE Version 1.202]. Marburg. Internet: http://www.tosmana.net.

Cuhls, Kerstin (2004). "Futur – Foresight for Priority-setting in Germany." *International Journal of Foresight and Innovation Policy*, 1 (3/4):183 – 194.

Cuhls, Kerstin, Knut Blind and Hariolf Grupp (2001). *Innovations for our Future*. Heidelberg: Physica publishers.

Dahl, Robert A. (1971). *Polyarchy: Participation and Opposition*. New Haven, CT: Yale University Press.

De Meur, Gisèle. (1996). "La comparaison des systèmes politiques: recherche des similarités et des differences." *Revue Internationale de Politique Comparée*, Vol. 3 (2):405-437.

De Meur, Gisèle and Dirk Berg-Schlosser (1994). "Comparing Political Systems – Establishing Similarities and Dissimilarities." *European Journal for Political Research*, 26:193-219.

De Meur, Gisèle and Dirk Berg-Schlosser (1996). "Conditions of Authoritarianism, Fascism and Democracy in Inter-war Europe: Systematic Matching and Contrasting of Cases for 'Small-N' Analysis." *Comparative Political Studies*, 29 (4):423-468.

De Meur, Gisèle and Benoît Rihoux (2002). *L'analyse quali-quantitative comparée (AQQC-QCA): approche, techniques et applications en sciences humaines*. Yamasaki, Sakura, collab. Louvain-la-Neuve: Academia-Bruylant.

De Meur, Gisèle, Benoît Rihoux and Frédéric Varone (2004). "L'analyse quali-quantitative comparée (AQQC): un outil innovant pour l'étude de l'action publique." *Pyramides*. (8):137-147.

Drass, Kriss. A. and Charles C. Ragin (1992). *Qualitative Comparative Analysis 3.0*. Evanston, Illinois: Institute for Policy Research, Northwestern University.

Dumont, Patrick and Hanna Bäck (forthcoming). "Green Parties and the Question of Governmental Participation". *European Journal of Political Research*.

Eckstein, Harry (1975). "Case Study and Theory in Political Science." In Fred I. Greenstein and Nelson W. Polsby (eds). *The Handbook of Political Science*. Reading: Addison-Wesley, 79-138.

Esping-Andersen, Gøsta (1990). *The Three Worlds of Welfare Capitalism*. Cambridge: Polity Press.

Esping-Andersen, Gøsta (1999). *The Social Foundations of Postindustrial Economies*, Oxford: Oxford University Press.

Esping-Andersen, Gøsta (2002). *Why We Need a New Welfare State*. Oxford: Oxford University Press.

Esping-Andersen, Gøsta and Walter Korpi (1987). "From Poor Relief to Institutional Welfare States: The Development of Scandinavian Social Policy." In Robert Erikson et al. (eds).

The Scandinavian Model: Welfare States and Welfare Research. New York: M. E. Sharpe, 39-74.

Eto, Hajime (2004). "Obstacles to the Acceptance of Technology Foresight for Decision Makers." *International Journal of Foresight and Innovation Policy*, 1 (3/4):232 – 242.

European Commission (1999). *Evaluating Socio-Economic Programmes. Evaluation Design and Management.* MEANS Collection, Volume 1, Luxembourg: Office for Official Publications of the European Communities.

Falter, Jürgen W. (1982). *Der "Positivismusstreit" in der Amerikanischen Politikwissenschaft: Entstehung, Ablauf und Resultate der sogenannten Behavioralismus-Kontroverse in den Vereinigten Staaten 1945 – 1975.* Opladen: Westdt. Verlag.

Faure, M. Andrew (1994). "Some Methodological Problems in Comparative Politics." *Journal of Theoretical Politics*, 63:307-322

Featherstone, Kevin (2003). "Introduction: In the Name of 'Europe'." In Kevin Featherstone and Claudio M. Radaelli (eds). *The Politics of Europeanization.* Oxford: Oxford University Press.

Featherstone, Kevin and Claudio M. Radaelli (2003). *The Politics of Europeanization.* Oxford: Oxford University Press.

Fischer, Claude S., Michael Hout, Martin Sanchez Jankowsk, Samuel Lucas, Ann Swidler, and Kim Voss (1996). *Inequality by Design: Cracking the Bell Curve Myth.* Princeton, NJ: Princeton University Press.

Flora, Peter et al. (1983). *State, Economy, and Society in Western Europe 1915-1975. A Data Handbook. Volume I: The Growth of Mass Democracies and Welfare States.* Frankfurt am Main: Campus Verlag.

Flora, Peter, Franz Kraus and Winfried Pfennig (1987). *State, Economy, and Society in Western Europe 1915-1975. A Data Handbook. Volume II: The Growth of Industrial Societies and Capitalist Economies.* Frankfurt am Main.

Florida, Richard (2002). *The Rise of the Creative Class: And How it's Transforming Work, Leisure, Community and Everyday Life.* Cambridge: Basic Books.

Freeman, Gary (1986). "National Styles and Policy Sectors: Explaining Structured Variation." *Journal of Public Policy*, 5:467-496.

Gallopin, Gilberto. C., Silvio Funtowicz, Martin O'connor and Jerry Ravetz (2001). "Science for the Twenty-First Century: From Social Contract to the Scientific Core." *International Social Science Journal*, 53 (2): 219-229.

George, Alexander L. (1979). "Case Studies and Theory Development: The Method of Structured, Focused Comparison." In Paul G. Lauren (ed.). *Diplomacy: New Approaches in History, Theory and Policy.* New York: Free Press.

George, Alexander L. and Andrew Bennett (2005). *Case Studies and Theory Development in the Social Sciences.* Cambridge: MIT Press.

Gerring, John. (2004). "What is a Case Study and What is it Good for?" *American Political Science Review*, 98 (2):341-354.

Gerring, John (forthcoming, 2006). *Case Study Research: Principles and Practices.* Cambridge: Cambridge University Press

Gilbert, Neil (2002). *Transformation of the Welfare State: The Silent Surrender of Public Responsibility*. Oxford: Oxford University Press.

Glenn, Jerome C. (1994). *Introduction to the Futures Research Methodology Series*. Washington D.C.: AC/UNU Millennium Project.

Glenn, Jerome C. (ed.) (1999). *Futures Research Methodology – Millenium Project*. Washington D.C.: AC/UNU Millennium Project.

Glenn, Jerome C. and Theodore J. Gordon (2002). *2002 The State of the Future*. Washington D.C.: UNU.

Godet, Michel (1985). *Prospective et Planification Stratégique*. Paris: Economica Press.

Godet, Michel (1990). "Integration of Scenarios and Strategic Management: Using Relevant, Consistent, and Likely Scenarios." *Futures*, 22, September 1990, 7:730-739.

Godet, Michel (1993). *A Handbook of Strategic Prospective*, Paris: UNESCO.

Goldthorpe, John H. (1994). *Current Issues in Comparative Macrosociology*, Department of Sociology, University of Oslo.

Goldthorpe, John H. (1997). "Current Issues in Comparative Macrosociology: A Debate on Methodological Issues." *Comparative Social Research*, 16:1-26.

Gordon, Theodore Jay (1994). "The Delphi Method." *Futures Research Methodology*, Washington D.C.: AC/UNU Millenium Project.

Gordon, Theodore Jay (1994). *Methods Frontiers and Integration*. Futures Research and Studies Methodology Series, produced by UNU Millennium Project Feasibility Study - Phase II and published by UNDP/African Futures.

Gordon, Theodore Jay (2002). *2002 State of the Future*. Washington, D.C.: AC/UNU Millenium Project.

Granovetter, Mark (1973). "The Strength of Weak Ties." *American Journal of Sociology*, 78:1360-1380.

Green Eight (2004). *Green Eight Review of the EU Sustainable Development Strategy. What Happened to the 80 commitments?* Brussels: European Environmental Bureau. Available in pdf-format [referred 2005-01-24] via URL: http://www.eeb.org/publication/general.htm

Greenberg, George D., Jeffery A. Miller, Lawrence B. Mohr and Bruce C. Vladeck (1977). "Developing Public Policy Theory: Perspectives from Empirical Research." *The American Political Science Review*, 71 (4):1532-1543.

Grimm, Heike (2004). "How to Turn Policies into Hands-On Strategies? Towards A Comprehensive Definition of Entrepreneurship Policies". Paper presented at the workshop "Space, Location and Agents", Max Planck Institute for Economics, on 14-15 May 2004, Jena, Germany.

Grimm, Heike (2004). *Abschlußbericht des Forschungsprojektes „Lo̊cal Heroes in a Global Village. Globalization and New Entrepreneurship Policies."* Bundesministerium für Wirtschaft und Arbeit, ERP-Transatlantik Programm, Erfurt, March 2004.

Grimm, Heike (2005). "Assessing Entrepreneurship Policies Across Nations and Regions." In David B. Audretsch, Heike Grimm and Charles W. Wessner (eds). *Local Heroes in the*

Global Village. Globalization and New Entrepreneurship Policies. New York: Springer Science+Business Media, Inc., 145-169.

Grimm, Heike and Robert Gamse (2004). "Entrepreneurship Policy and Regional Economic Growth: Exploring the Correlation." Paper presented at the ESF Exploratory Workshop on *Innovative Comparative Methods for Policy Analysis*, Erfurt, 25-28 Sept. 2004, 34 pp.

Grunwald, Armin (2004). "Strategic Knowledge for Sustainable Development: The Need for Reflexivity and Learning at the Interface Between Science and Society." *International Journal of Foresight and Innovation Policy*, 1 (1/2):150 – 167.

Guala, Francesco (2003). "Experimental Localism and External Validity." *Philosophy of Science*, Vol. 70, Supplement. Reference is to the internet document: http://philsci-archive.pitt.edu/archive/00001073/

Hagman, Minna and Raine Mäntysalo (eds) (2004). *EkoSuKaT -tutkimushankkeen väliraportti 1. Oulunsalon Karhuoja-Niemenranta.* Oulun yliopisto, Arkkitehtuurin osasto, Yhdyskuntasuunnittelun laboratorio. Julkaisu C 90. Oulu: Oulun yliopistopaino.

Hall, Peter A. (1993). "Policy Paradigms, Social Learning, and the State: the Case of Economic Policymaking in Britain." *Comparative Politics*, 25 (3):275-296.

Hall, Peter A. (2003). "Aligning Ontology and Methodology in Comparative Politics." In James Mahoney and Dietrich Rueschemeyer (eds). *Comparative Historical Analysis in the Social Sciences*. Cambridge: Cambridge University Press, 373-406.

Halonen, Veijo and Mikko Korkala (2003). *Oulunseudun profilointitutkimus.* Oulu: Head Consulting Oy. Available [referred 2005-01-24] in pdf format via URL: http://www.liminka.fi/sivu/fi/liminka-info/profilointi/

Hampel, Frank R. et al. (1986). *Robust Statistics. The Approach Based on Influence Functions*, New York: Wiley.

Hanneman, Robert A. (1999). "Introduction to Social Network Methods." Online Textbook Supporting Sociology 157. Riverside, CA: University of California. http://faculty.ucr.edu/~hanneman/SOC157/Index.html Retrieved 7 April 2005.

Hansen, Finn Kenneth (1998). "Forbrugerstyrelsens Familiebudget 1998." *Råd & Resultater*, 8:13-20.

Hansen, Hans (various years) *Elements of Social Security in 6 European countries.* Copenhagen: The Danish National Institute of Social Research.

Harkness, Janet A., Fons van de Vijer and Peter Ph. Mohler (2003). *Cross-Cultural Survey Methods.* Hoboken, New Jersey: John Wiley & Sons, Inc., Wiley Series in Survey Methodology.

Hart, David M. (2003). *The Emergence of Entrepreneurship Policy. Governance, Start-ups, and Growth in the U.S. Knowledge Economy.* Cambridge: Cambridge University Press.

Hasse, Raimund and Georg Krücken (2002). *Neo-Institutionalismus im Theorievergleich Netzwerkansätze, Theorien der Strukturierung und Systemtheorie*, Transcript.

Hedström, Peter and Richard Swedberg (eds) (1998). *Social Mechanisms: An Analytical Approach to Social Theory.* New York: Cambridge University Press.

Heikkilä, Elli and Taru Järvinen (2002). *History and Future Lines of Urbanization in Finland.* Paper presented in the 42nd ERSA-Congress August 27th – 31st, 2002, Dortmund. Available at: http://www.migrationinstitute.fi/db/articles/pdf/Heikkila-Jarvinen.pdf.

Hendrick, Rebecca M. and David Nachmias (1992). "The Policy Sciences: the Challenge of Complexity." *Policy Studies Review*, 11(3/4):310-328.

Hentilä, Helka-Liisa, Raine Mäntysalo, Jussi S. Jauhiainen, Pentti Luoma, Henna Ijäs, Janne Karjalainen, Jouni Kiirnamaa, Marja Mönkkönen, Marja Ryhänen, and Heli Villanen (2004). *Eco-Efficiency in Growing and Declining Residential Areas: The Physical, Social and Ecological Sustainability of a Changing Urban Structure. The Research Plan of EkoSuKaT–project.* Translated 31-05-2004. Oulu: University of Oulu. Available only via URL [25-08-04]: http://wwwedu.oulu.fi/sos/SuKaT/plan.doc.

Héritier, Adrienne (1993a). "Einleitung. Policy-Analyse. Elemente der Kritik und Perspektiven der Neuorientierung." *Policy-Analyse. Kritik und Neuorientierung.* D. V. P. W.. Opladen: Westdeutscher Verlag: 9-38.

Héritier, Adrienne (1993b). "Policy-Netzwerkanalyse als Untersuchungsinstrument im Europäischen Kontext: Folgerungen aus einer empirischen Studie regulativer Politik." *Policy-Analyse. Kritik und Neuorientierung.* D. V. P. W., Opladen: Westdeutscher Verlag, 432-450.

Héritier, Adrienne (ed.) (1993c). *Policy-Analyse. Kritik und Neuorientierung.* Opladen: Westdeutscher Verlag.

Héritier, Adrienne (2001). "Differential Europe: The European Union Impact on National Policymaking." In Adrienne Héritier et al. (eds). *Differential Europe. The European Union Impact on National Policymaking.* Boston: Rowman & Littlefield.

Herrmann, Andrea and Lasse Cronqvist (2005). "FS/QCA and MVQCA: Different Answers to the Problem of Contradicting Observations in QCA." *Paper Presented at the ECPR General Conference*, Budapest, 8-10 Sept.

Herrnstein, Richard J. and Charles Murray (1994). *The Bell Curve: Intelligence and Class Structure in American Life.* New York: Free Press.

Hinz, Thomas (1998). *Betriebsgründungen in Ostdeutschland.* Berlin: Edition sigma.

Hotakainen, Kari (2002). *Juoksuhaudantie.* Porvoo – Helsinki – Juva: WSOY.

Howes, Carollee (1997). "Children's Experiences in Center-Based Child Care as a Function of Teacher Background and Adult: Child Ratio." *Merrill-Palmer Quarterly*, 43 (3):404-25.

Huber, Evelyne, Charles Ragin and John D. Stephens (1993). "Social Democracy, Christian Democracy, Constitutional Structure, and the Welfare State." *American Journal of Sociology*, 99:3 (November):711-49.

Hunt, Charles W. (1989). "Migrant Labor and Sexually Transmitted Disease: AIDS in Africa." *Journal of Health and Social Behavior*, 30 (December):353-373.

Hunt, Charles W. (1996). "Social vs. Biological: Theories on the Transmission of AIDS in Africa." *Social Science & Medicine*, 42 (9):1283-1296.

Hyyryläinen Torsti (1999). "Finland – at Once Local and European. The Editorial." *New Rural Policy. Finnish Journal of Rural Research and Policy,* English Supplement 1999; 7: 6-9.

Indiana University. Network Analysis Toolkit, http://iv.slis.indiana.edu/sw/natoolkit.html, retrieved 7 April 2005.

Jacobs, Keith, Jim Kemeny and Tony Manzi (2003a). "Priviledged Council Tenants? The Discursive Change in Conservative Housing Policy from 1972-1980." *Policy and Politics*, 31:307-320.

Jacobs, Keith, Jim Kemeny, and Tony Manzi (2003b). "Power, Discursive Space and Institutional Practices in the Construction of Housing Problems." *Housing Studies*, 18:429-446.

Jansen, Dorothea and Mike Weber (2003). *Survival. Erfolgsbedingungen Neu Gegründeter Betriebe im Ruhrgebiet*. Forschungsinstitut für Öffentliche Verwaltung bei der Deutschen Hochschule für Verwaltungswissenschaften Speyer.

Jauhiainen, Jussi (2004). "Challenges for Growing and Declining Finnish Towns and Urban Regions." *Städte im Umbruch. Das Online Magazin für Stadtentwicklung, Stadtschrumpfung , Stadtumbau & Regenierung*, 2004:2:30-35.(Available in html format via URLs [16-09-2004]: http://www.thilolang.de/projekte/sdz/magazin/0402/4Finland.htm and http://stumpfende-stadt.de/index_de.htm).

Jones, Charles O. (1970). *An Introduction to the Study of Public Policy*. Belmont: Duxbury Press.

Kangas, Olli (1991). *The Politics of Social Rights. Studies on Dimensions of Sickness Insurance in OECD Countries*. Stockholm

Kärki, Vesa (2005). "Nokia karsii muldimediasta. Yhtiö vähentämässä Oulun 400 henkilön suuruisesta yksiköstä 140-160 työntekijää." *Kaleva* 2005–01–12.

Kemeny, Jim (1980). "Home Ownership and Privatisation." *International Journal of Urban and Regional Research*, 4:372-88.

Kemeny, Jim (1981). *The Myth of Home Ownership: Public Versus Private Choices in Housing Tenure*. London: Routledge and Kegan Paul.

Kemeny, Jim (2004). *Home Ownership Against the Welfare State: the Thesis and the Evidence*. The 5th July Plenary Address, European Network for Housing Research Conference, 1-6 July 2004, Cambridge University. Available in pdf format [referred 2005-01-25] via URL: http://www.ibf.uu.se/PERSON/jim/papers.html.

Kenis, Paul and Volker Schneider (1991). "Policy Networks and Policy Analysis: Scrutinizing a New Analytical Toolbox." In Bernd Marin and Renate Mayntz (eds). *Policy Networks: Empirical Evidence and Theoretical Considerations*. Frankfurt am Main and Boulder, Colorado: Campus Verlag and Westview Press.

Kerkelä, Heikki and Jorma Kurkinen (2000). *Työttömyys kasvukeskuksessa. Työttömyys ja työmarkkinat Oulun seutukunnassa*. Oulun kaupunkisuunnittelu, Sarja B 36. Oulu: Oulun kaupunki.

King, Gary, Robert O. Keohane and Sidney Verba (1994). *Designing Social Inquiry: Scientific Inference in Qualitative Research*. Princeton: Princeton University Press.

Kirchhoff, Bruce A. and Patricia G. Greene (1998). "Understanding the Theoretical and Empirical Content of Critiques of U.S. Job Creation Research." *Small Business Economics*, 10 (2):153-159.

Knoepfel, Peter, Corinne Larrue and Frédéric Varone (2001). *Analyse et pilotage des politiques publiques*. Genève, Bâle & Munich: Helbing & Lichtenhahn.

Korpi, Walter and Joakim Palme (1998). "The Paradox of Redistribution and Strategies of Equality: Welfare State Institutions, Inequality, and Poverty in the Western Countries." *American Sociological Review*, 63 (5):661-687

Kriesi, Hanspeter and Maya Jegen (2001). "The Swiss Energy Policy Elite: The Actor Constellation of a Policy Domain in Transition." *European Journal of Political Research*, (39):251-287.

Krook, Mona Lena (2005). "Temporality and Causal Configurations: Combining Sequence Analysis and Fuzzy Set/Qualitative Comparative Analysis", paper presented at the 2nd ECPR General Conference, Budapest, 8-11 September.

Kuhlmann, Stefan (2001). "Future Governance of Innovation Policy in Europe – Three Scenarios." *Research Policy*, 30:953-976.

Kuhn, Thomas S. (1976). *Die Struktur wissenschaftlicher Revolutionen*. Frankfurt am Main: Suhrkamp.

Kvist, Jon (1999). "Welfare Reform in the Nordic Countries in the 1990s: Using Fuzzy Set Theory to Assess Conformity to Ideal Types." *Journal of European Social Policy*, 9 (3):231-52.

Kvist, Jon (2002). "Changing Rights and Obligations in Unemployment Insurance." In Roland Sigg and Christina Behrendt (eds). *Social Security in the Global Village*. New Brunswick: Transaction Publishers, 227-245.

Laakkonen-Pöntys, Karoliina; Mari Moilanen and Ari Saine (2004). "Kaupungin eteläinen reuna – missä, millainen, milloin... " In Minna Hagman and Raine Mäntysalo (eds). *EkoSuKaT -tutkimushankkeen väliraportti 1. Oulunsalon Karhuoja-Niemenranta*. Oulun yliopisto, Arkkitehtuurin osasto, Yhdyskuntasuunnittelun laboratorio. Julkaisu C 90. Oulu, Oulun yliopistopaino.

Lauder, Hugh, Phillip Brown and A. H. Halsey (2004). "Sociology and Political Arithmetic: Some Principles of a New Policy Science." *The British Journal of Sociology*, 55:3-22.

Lehmbruch, Gerhard and Philippe Schmitter (eds) (1982). *Patterns of Corporatist Policy Making*. London: Sage.

Leira, Arnlaug (1992). *Welfare States and Working Mothers*. Cambridge: Cambridge University Press.

Lempert, Robert and Steven Popper (2002). *Shaping our Long-Term Future: Policy Analysis Under Conditions of Complexity and Deep Uncertainty*. Seminar for the RAND and Woodrow Wilson International Centre for Scholars, available at http://www.complexityandpolicy.org/dial.htm.

Levi-Faur, David (2004). "Comparative Research Design in the Study of Regulation: How to Increase the Number of Cases without Compromising the Strengths of Case-oriented Analysis." In Jacint Jordana and David Levi-Faur (eds). *The Politics of Regulation*. Cheltenham: Edward Elgar, 177-199.

Levi-Faur, David (2006). "Varieties of Regulatory Capitalism: Getting the Most of the Comparative Method." *Governance*, Forthcoming.

Lieberson, Stanley (1991). "Small N's and Big Conclusions: an Examination of the Reasoning Based on a Small Number of Cases." *Social Forces*, 70:307-320.

Lieberson, Stanley (1994). "More on the Uneasy Case of Using Mill-Type Methods in Small-N Comparative Studies." *Social Forces*, 72:1225-1237.

Lijphart, Arend (1971). "Comparative Politics and the Comparative Method." *American Political Science Review*, 65:682-693.

Lijphart, Arend (1975). "The Comparable Cases Strategy in Comparative Research." *Comparative Political Studies*, 8:158-176.

Lin, Nan (2001). *Social Capital. A Theory of Social Structure and Action.* Cambridge (UK) and New York, Cambridge University Press.

Lindblom, Charles E. (1959). "The Science of 'Muddling Through'." *Public Administration Review*, 19:79-88.

Lipsitz, Lewis (1965). "Working-Class Authoritarianism: A Re-Evaluation." *American Sociological Review*, XXX:106-08.

Lizaso, Fernando Guido Reger (2004). "Linking Roadmapping and Scenarios as an Approach for Strategic Technology Planning." *International Journal of Technology Intelligence and Planning*, 1 (1):68 – 86.

Loveridge, Denis (2004). "Experts and Foresight: Review and Experience." *Internationational Journal of Foresight and Innovation Policy*, 1 (1/2):33 – 69.

Lundstrom, Anders and Lois Stevenson (2001). *Entrepreneurship Policy for the Future.* Stockholm: Swedish Foundation for Small Business Research.

Lundstrom, Anders and Lois Stevenson (2002). *On the Road to Entrepreneurship Policy.* Stockholm: Swedish Foundation for Small Business Research.

Mackie, John L. (1974). *The Cement of the Universe. A Study of Causation.* London: Oxford University Press.

Mahoney, James (2003). "Knowledge Accumulation in Comparative Historical Research: The Case of Democracy and Authoritarianism." In James Mahoney and Dietrich Rueschmeyer (eds). *Comparative Historical Analysis in the Social Sciences.* Cambridge: Cambridge University Press.

Mahoney, James and Dietrich Rueschemeyer (2003) (eds). *Comparative Historical Research.* Cambridge: Cambridge University Press.

Majone, Giandomenico (1993). "When Does Policy Deliberation Matter?" *Politische Vierteljahresschrift*, Herbst. Special Issue on Policy Analysis: 97-115.

Majone, Giandomenico (2001). "Two Logics of Delegation. Agency and Fiduciary Relations in EU Governance." *European Union Politics*, 2 (1):103-122.

Manninen, Rikhard and Jukka Hirvonen (2004). *Rivitalo asumismuotona – toiveiden täyttymys vai mahdollisuuksien kompromissi?* Suomen ympäristö 694. Helsinki: Ympäristöministeriö.

March, James. and Johan. P Olsen (1984). "The New Institutionalism: Organizational Factors in Political Life." *American Political Science Review* 78 (2):734-748.

March, James. and Johan. P. Olsen (1989). *Rediscovering Institutions: The Organizational Basis of Politics*. New York: Free Press.

Marks, Gary, Liesbet Hooghe and Kemit Blank (1995). "European Integration and the State." *EUI Working Paper RSC No.95/7*, Florence, European University Institute.

Marks, Gary, Liesbet Hooghe et al. (1996). "European Integration from the 1980s: State-Centric v. Multi-level Governance." *Journal of Common Market Studies*, 34 (3):341-378.

Markusen, Ann R. (1996a). "Interaction between Regional and Industrial Policies: Evidence from four Countries." *International Regional Science Review*, 19:49-77.

Markusen, Ann R. (1996b). "Sticky Places in Slippery Space: A Typology of Industrial Districts." *Economic Geography*, 72 (3):293-313.

Markusen, Ann R. (1999). "Fuzzy Concepts, Scanty Evidence and Policy Distance; the Case for Rigour and Policy Relevance in Critical Regional Studies." *Regional Studies*, 33: 869-884.

Marshall, Thomas H. (1950). *Class, Citizenship, and Social Development*. New York: Doubleday.

Marx, Axel (2005). "Towards More Robust Model Specification in QCA Results from a Methodological Experiment." Paper Prepared for the 100th Annual Conference of the American Sociological Association. Philadelphia, 13th-16th August 2005.

Marx, Axel and Jan Dombrecht (2004). "The Organisational Antecedents of Repetitive Strain Injuries of the Wrist. A Systematic Comparative Case Analysis of Assembly, Sorting and Packaging Jobs." COMPASSS- Working paper 2004-21. Online at: www.compasss.org.

McKeown, Timothy J. (1999). "Case Studies and the Statistical Worldview: Review of King in Keohane and Verba's Designing Social Inquiry: Scientific Inference in Qualitative Research." *International Organization*, 53 (1):161–190.

Meadows, Donella and Denis Meadows et al. (1972). *The Limits to Growth*. New York: Universe Books.

Medda, Francois and Peter Nijkamp (1999). "A Combinatorial Assessment Methodology for Complex Policy Analysis." *Working Paper*, Department of Spatial Economies, University of Amsterdam.

Mill, John S. (1974). *A System of Logic*. Collected Works of J.S. Mill (vol. 7/8), London. (first 1843).

Mill, John S. (1967). *A System of Logic: Ratiocinative and Inductive*. Toronto: University of Toronto Press.

Ministry of Finance (1998). *Availability Criteria in Selected OECD Countries*. Ministry of Finance, Denmark, Working Paper No.6, November.

Mohr, John W. (1998). "Measuring Meaning Structures." *Annual Review of Sociology*, 24:345-70.

Moniz, António B. (ed.) (2002). *Futuros do Emprego na Sociedade da Informação*. Lisbon: DGEFP-MTS.

Moniz, António B. (2003). *Temas de prospectiva para o sector automóve.*, RPT_Delphi_03, IET/FCTUNL.

Moniz, António B. (2004). *Resultados do exercício Delphi WorTiS (1ª fase)*. RPT Delphi-WorTiS 06, IET/FCTUNL.

Moniz, António B. and M. Mira Godinho (2000). "Cenários prospectivos para as pescas: resultados da aplicação do método Delphi." In António B. Moniz, M. Mira Godinho and I. Kovács (eds). *Pescas e Pescadores: Futuros para o emprego e recursos*, Oeiras,: Celta Editora, 25-38.

Moniz, António B. and M. Mira Godinho (2000): "New Methodological Approaches for Change in Traditional Sectors: The Case of the Portuguese Fisheries Socio-economic System." *Économies et Sociétés* (Série "Dynamique technologique et organisation"), 5:63-77.

Moniz, António B. and I. Kovács (eds) (2001). *Sociedade da Informação e Emprego*. Lisbon: DGEFP-MTS.

Morin, Richard and Jill Hanley (2004). "Community Economic Development is a Context of Globalization and Metropolization: A Comparison of Four North American Cities." *International Journal of Urban and Regional Research*, 28(2):369-83.

Moses, Jonathon, Benoît Rihoux and Bernhard Kittel (2005). "Mapping Political Methodology: Reflections on a European Perspective." *European Political Science*, 4 (1):55-68.

Mufune, Pemplenani (2003). "Social Science and HIV / Aids Policies in Africa." *CODESRIA Bulletin*, (2-4):44-48.

Myles, John and Jill Quadagno (2002). "Political Theories of the Welfare State." *Social Service Review*, 76 (1):34-57.

Niedermayer, Oskar and Ulrich Widmaier (2003). "Quantitativ vergleichende Methoden." In Dirk Berg-Schlosser and Ferdinand Müller-Rommel (eds). *Vergleichende Politikwissenschaft*. Opladen: Leske + Budrich, 77-101.

NISTEP (2001). *The Seventh Technology Foresight: Future Technology in Japan toward the Year 2030*. Tokyo.

North, Douglass C. (1995). "Structural Changes of Institutions and the Process of Transformation." *Prague Economic Papers*, 4 (3):229-234.

North, Douglass C. (2004). *Institutions, Institutional Change and Economic Performance*. Cambridge: Cambridge Univ. Press.

Norusis, Marija J. (2002). *SPSS 11.0 Guide to Data Analysis*. Chicago, SPSS Inc.

NOSOSCO (various years). *Social Security in the Nordic Countries*. Copenhagen: NOSOSCO.

Oksa, Jukka (1998). "The Benign Encounter: the Great Move and the Role of the State in Finnish Forests." In Oksa, Jukka. *Syrjäkylä muutoksessa*. University of Joensuu Publications, Social Sciences Nr. 30. Joensuu: University of Joensuu.

Oksa, Jukka (1999). "For and Against the Windmills: Changing Concepts of Local Activity." *New Rural Policy. Finnish Journal of Rural Research and Policy*. English Supplement 7:69-74.

Orloff, Ann (1993). "Gender and the Social Rights of Citizenship." *American Sociological Review*, 58:303-28.

Ostrom, Elinor (1990). *Governing the Commons*. Cambridge: Cambridge University Press.

Ostrom, Elinor (1999). "Institutional Rational Choice: An Assessment of the Institutional Analysis and Development Framework." In: Paul A. Sabatier (ed.). *Theories of the Policy Process*. Boulder: Westview Press, 35-71.

Oulu 2006 (2003). *Growth agreement.* Available in htm-format [referred in 2004-01-24] at the URL: http://oulu.ouka.fi/kasvusopimus/, Oulu.

Owen, Gill (1995). "Policy Networks in a Changing World." Paper presented at the Political Science Association Annual Conference, University of York. Accessible at: http://www.psa.ac.uk/cps/1995.htm.

Palier, Bruno (2002). "Beyond Retrenchment: Four Problems in Current Welfare State Research and one Suggestion how to Overcome them." In Jochen Clasen (ed.). *What Future for Social Security? Debates and Reforms in National and Cross-National Perspectives*, Bristol: Policy Press.

Patton, Michael Quinn (1997). *Utilization-focused Evaluation*. 3rd ed. Thousand Oaks: Sage.

Pawson, Ray (2000). "Middle Range Realism." *Arch. Europ. Sociol.* XLI 2:283-325.

Pawson, Ray (2003). "Una prospettiva realista. Politiche basate sull'evidenza empirica." *Sociologia e Ricerca Sociale*. Anno XXIII 68-69:11-57.

Pawson, Ray, and Nick Tilley (1997). *Realistic Evaluation*. London/Thousand Oaks/New Dehli: Sage.

Peillon, Michel (1996). "A Qualitative Comparative Analysis of Welfare Legitimacy." *Journal of European Social Policy*, 6 (3):175-190.

Peisner-Feinberg, Ellen and Margaret Burchinal (1997). "Relations Between Preschool Children's Child-Care Experiences and Concurrent Development: The Cost, Quality, and Outcomes Study." *Merrill-Palmer Quarterly*, 43 (3):451-77.

Perret, Bernard (1997). "Les enjeux épistémologiques de l'évaluation." In Conseil Scientifique de l'Evaluation. *L'évaluation en développement*, Paris: La Documentation Française, 283-312.

Peters, Guy (1999). *Institutional Theory in Political Science. The 'New Institutionalism'*. London, New York, Pinter.

Pierson, Paul (1994). *Dismantling the Welfare State? Reagan, Thatcher, and the Politics of Retrenchment.* Cambridge: Cambridge University Press.

Pierson, Paul (1996). "The New Politics of the Welfare State." *World Politics*, 48 (2):143-179.

Pierson, Paul (1996). "The Path to European Integration: A Historical Institutionalist Analysis." *Comparative Political Studies* 29 (2):123-163.

Pierson, Paul (ed.) (2001). *The New Politics of the Welfare State*. Oxford: Oxford University Press.

Pierson, Paul (2003). "Big, Slow-Moving, and ... Invisible." In James Mahoney and Dietrich Rueschemeyer (eds). *Comparative Historical Analysis in the Social Sciences*. Cambridge: Cambridge University Press, 177-207.

Pierson, Paul (2004). *Politics in Time: History, Institutions, and Social Analysis*. Princeton: Princeton University Press.

Pile, Steve (1999). "The Heterogeneity of Cities." In Steve Pile, Christopher Brook and Gerry Mooney (eds). *Unruly Cities? Order/Disorder*. London and New York: Routledge in association with The Open University.

Pollack, Mark. A. (1996). "The New Institutionalism and EC Governance: The Promise and Limits of Institutional Analysis." *Governance* 9 (4):429-458.

Porter, M. Theodore (1995). *Trust in Numbers: The Pursuit of Objectivity in Science and Public Life*. Princeton: Princeton University Press.

Prescott-Allan, Robert (2001). *The Wellbeing of Nations: A Country-by-Country Index of Quality of Life and the Environment*, Washington: Island Press.

Przeworski, Adam and Henry Teune (1970). *The Logic of Comparative Social Inquiry*. New York: Wiley-Interscience.

Radaelli, Claudio M. (2004). "Europeanisation: Solution or Problem?" European Integration Online Papers, 8, 16.

Ragin, Charles C. (1987). *The Comparative Method. Moving Beyond Qualitative and Quantitative Strategies*. Berkeley: University of California Press.

Ragin, Charles C. (1994). *Constructing Social Research: The Unity and Diversity of Method*. Thousand Oaks, Pine Forge Press.

Ragin, Charles C. (1997). "Turning the Tables: How Case-Oriented Research Challenges Variable-Oriented Research." *Comparative Social Research*, 16:27-42.

Ragin, Charles C. (2000). *Fuzzy Set Social Science*. Chicago: Chicago University Press.

Ragin, Charles C. (2003a). "Making Comparative Analysis Count." Paper presented at: COMPASSS Launching Conference, Louvain-la-Neuve and Leuven, Belgium.

Ragin, Charles C. (2003b). "Recent Advances in Fuzzy-set Methods and their Application to Policy Questions." Paper presented at: COMPASSS Launching Conference, Louvain-la-Neuve and Leuven, Belgium, http://www.compasss.org/WP.htm.

Ragin, Charles C. (2004). "Innovative Causal Analysis and Policy Research." Paper presented at the ESF Exploratory Workshop on *Innovative Comparative Methods for Policy Analysis*, Erfurt, 25-28 Sept. 2004.

Ragin, Charles C. (2004). "La place de la comparaison: jalons pour la recherche comparative configurationnelle." *Revue Internationale de Politique Comparée*. 11 (1):118-129.

Ragin, Charles C. (2005). "From Fuzzy Sets to Crisp Truth Tables." Working Paper: www.compasss.org/wp.htm.

Ragin, Charles C. and Howard S. Becker (eds) (1992). *What Is a Case? Exploring the Foundations of Social Inquiry*. Cambridge: Cambridge University Press.

Ragin, Charles, Dirk Berg-Schlosser and Gisèle de Meur (1996). "Political Methodology: Qualitative Methods in Macropolitical Inquiry." In Robert Goodin und Hans-Dieter Klingemann (eds). *A New Handbook of Political Science*. Oxford: Oxford University Press, 749-768.

Ragin, Charles C., Kriss A. Drass and Sean Davey (2005). *Fuzzy-Set/ Qualitative Comparative Analysis*. Version 1.4. www.fsqca.com.

Ragin, Charles C. and Helen M Giesel (2002). *User's Guide to Fuzzy-Set/Qualitative Comparative Analysis 1.1*. Department of Sociology, University of Arizona, Tucson, Arizona. Available in the htm format [referred 06-12-2003] via URL: http://www.u.arizona.edu/~cragin/fsqca.htm)

Ragin, Charles C. and Benoît Rihoux (2004). "Qualitative Comparative Analysis (QCA): State of the Art and Prospects." *Qualitative Methods: Newsletter of the American Political Science Association Organized Section on Qualitative Methods*, 2 (2):3-13.

Ragin, Charles C. and John Sonnett (2004). "Between Complexity and Parsimony: Limited Diversity, Counterfactual Case and Comparative Analysis.", to be published in: Sabine Kropp and Michael Minkenberg (eds). *Vergleichen in der Politikwissenschaft*. Wiesbaden: VS Verlag fur Sozialwissenschaften (in press, 2005).

Redding, Kent and Jocelyn Viterna (1999). "Political Demands, Political Opportunities: Explaining the Differential Success of Left-Libertarian Parties." *Social Forces*, 78(2):491-510.

Reinikainen, Kalle (1998). "Information Society in the North: The Wizardry of High-Tech." In Leo Granberg (ed.). *Snowbelt*. Series B. Helsinki: Aleksanteri Institute & Kikimora Publications.

Reynolds, Paul D. and David J. Storey (1994). *Regional Characteristics Affecting Small Business Formation: A Cross-National Comparison*. OECD Working Papers, 2 (8).

Reynolds, Paul D., Michael Hay, William D. Bygrave, S. Michael Camp and Erkko Autio. (2000). *Global Entrepreneurship Monitor. 2000 Executive Report*. Kansas City: Kauffman Center for Entrepreneurial Leadership.

Reynolds, Paul D., Michael Hay, William D. Bygrave, S. Michael Camp and Erkko Autio. (2001). *Global Entrepreneurship Monitor. 2001 Executive Report*. Kansas City: Kauffman Center for Entrepreneurial Leadership at the Ewing Marion Kauffman Foundation.

Reynolds, Paul D., Michael Hay, William D. Bygrave, S. Michael Camp and Erkko Autio. (2002). *Global Entrepreneurship Monitor. 2002 Executive Report*. Kansas City: Kauffman Center for Entrepreneurial Leadership.

Reynolds, Paul D., Michael Hay, William D. Bygrave, S. Michael Camp and Erkko Autio. (2003). *Global Entrepreneurship Monitor. 2003 Executive Report*. Kansas City: Kauffman Center for Entrepreneurial Leadership.

Rhodes, Rod A. W. and David Marsh (1992). "New Directions in the Study of Policy Networks." *European Journal of Political Research*, 21 (1-2):181-205.

Richards, Lyn (2000). *Using NVivo in Qualitative Research*. Edition 2. Second Printing. Melbourne: QSR International Pty. Ltd.

Rihoux, Benoît (2003). "Bridging the Gap Between the Qualitative and Quantitative Worlds? A Retrospective and Prospective View on Qualitative Comparative Analysis." *Field Methods*, 15 (4):351-365.

Rihoux, Benoît, Gisèle De Meur, Sakura Yamasaki and Sophie Rorisse (2003). "Inventory of Good Practices in QCA", COMPASSS Didactics Working Paper, Online at http://www.compasss.org.

Rihoux, Benoît, Gisèle De Meur, Sakura Yamasaki, and Sophie Ronsse (2004). "Ce n'est qu'un début, continuons le... débat. Un agenda pour la recherche." *Revue Internationale de Politique Comparée*, 11 (1):145-153.

Rosenberg, Morris (1968). *The Logic of Survey Analysis*. New York, Basic Books Inc. Publishers.

Rueschemeyer, Dietrich, Evelyne Huber and John D Stephens (1992). *Capitalist Development and Democracy*, Chicago: University of Chicago Press.

Ruonavaara, Hannu (1998). *The Growth of Urban Home-Ownership in Finland 1950-1980*. Turku, University of Turku.

Ruonavaara, Hannu (2004). "Valtiovalta ja suurten ikäluokkien asumisurat." In Erola Jani and Wilska Terhi-Anni (eds). *Suuret ikäluokat aj 1960-lukulaisuus. Yhteiskunnan moottori vai kivireki?* Sophi 92. Jyväskylä, Minerva Kustannus Oy.

Russett, Bruce N. et al. (1964). *World Handbook of Political and Social Indicators*. New Haven: Yale University Press.

Sabatier, Paul A. (1993). "Policy Change over a Decade or More. Policy Change and Learning. An Advocacy Coalition Approach." In Paul A. Sabatier and Hank C. Jenkins-Smith. *Policy Change and Learning: an Advocacy Coalition Approach*. Boulder, San Francisco, Oxford: Westview Press, 13-56.

Sabatier, Paul A. and Hank C. Jenkins-Smith (1993). *Policy Change and Learning: an Advocacy Coalition Approach*. Colorado: Westview Press.

Sager, Fritz (2002). *Vom Verwalten des urbanen Raums. Institutionelle Bedingungen von Politikkoordination am Beispiel der Raum- und Verkehrsplanung in städtischen Gebieten*, Bern, Stuttgart and Wien: Haupt.

Sager, Fritz (2004). "Institutions métropolitaines et coordination des politiques publiques: une AQQC des arrangements politico-administratifs d'articulation entre urbanisme et transports en Europe." *Revue Internationale De Politique Comparée (RIPC)*, 11 (1):67-84.

Sager, Fritz, Michael Meyrat and Markus Maibach (2001). "'Boundary Delineation' in grenzüberschreitenden Policy-Netzwerken: Primat der ‚Policies' oder der ‚Polity'? Das Fallbeispiel des Policy-Netzwerkes zur 28-Tonnen-Limite." *Swiss Political Science Review*, 7 (1):51-82.

Sager, Fritz and Walter Schenkel (2004). *Evaluation der Umweltverträglichkeitsprüfung*. Bern: Bundesamt für Umwelt, Wald und Landschaft (Umweltmaterialien Nr. 175).

Sallamaa, Kari (1993). "Pohjoinen ruumis: seksi, viina ja urheilu." In Ilkka Marjomaa and Jukka Nykyri (eds). *Pohjoinen ihminen – pohjoinen mentaliteetti. Alueellinen yhteistyö Euroopassa. Raportti kolmannesta KULTI-seminaarista Oulussa 9.–10.10.1992*. Oulun yliopiston täydennyskoulutuskeskuksen julkaisuja 15. Oulu: Oulun Kirjateollisuus Oy.

Savage, Mike, Gaynor Bagnall and Brian Longhurst (2005). *Globalization & Belonging*. Series: Theory Culture & Society. Mike Featherstone (series editor). London – Thousand Oaks – New Delhi: Sage Publications.

Savolainen, Jukka (1994). "The Rationality of Drawing Big Conclusions Based on Small Samples: In Defense of Mill's Method." *Social Forces*, 72:1217-1224.

Sayer, Andrew (2000). *Realism and Social Science*. London – Thousand Oaks – New Delhi: SAGE Publications.

Scarpetta, Stefano (1996). "Assessing the Role of Labour Market Policies and Institutional Settings on Unemployment: A Cross-Country Study." *OECD Economic Studies*, 26:43-98.

Scharpf, Fritz W. (ed.) (1995). *Games in Hierarchies and Networks*. Frankfurt am Main, Campus Verlag.

Scharpf, Fritz W. (1997). *Games Real Actors Play*. Boulder, Colorado: Westview Press.

Scharpf, Fritz W. (2003). *Politische Optionen im vollendeten Binnenmarkt. Europäische Integration*. Markus Jachtenfuchs and Beate Kohler-Koch. Opladen: Leske+Budrich: 219-254.

Schimmelfennig, Frank. (2004). *The Impact of Democratic Conditionality in Central and Eastern Europe: a Qualitative Comparative Analysis*. Bologna, Second Pan-European Conference on EU Politics, 24-26 June 2004.

Schmitter, Philippe (1979). "Still the Century of Corporatism? Trends Towards Corporatist Intermediation." In Gerhard Lehmbruch and Philippe Schmitter. *Patterns of Corporatist Policy Making*. London: Sage, 7-49.

Schneider, Carsten and Claudius Wagemann (forthcoming). "Causal Complexity and fs/QCA: Making Use of Remote and Proximate Causal Conditions." *European Journal for Political Research*.

Schneider, Gerald and Mark Aspinwall (2001). *The Rules of Integration. Institutionalist Approaches to the Study of Europe*. Manchester: Manchester University Press.

Schneider, Stefan *et al.* (1990). *Pilotversuch Zürich Hottingen*, Zürich: Planungsbüro Jud.

Schneider, Stefan *et al.* (1992). *Parkierungsbeschränkungen mit Blauer Zone und Anwohnerparkkarte: Empfehlungen für die Einführung*. Zürich: Planungsbüro Jud.

Schneider, Stefan *et al.* (1995). *Erfolgskontrolle Blaue Zone Bern Kirchenfeld*, Zürich: Planungsbüro Jud.

Schön, Donald A. (1973). *Beyond The Stable State: Public and Private Learning in a Changing Society*. Harmondsworth: Penguin Books.

Schön, Donald A. (1979). *Generative Metaphor: A Perspective on Problem-Setting in Social Policy*. In Andrew Ortony (ed.). *Metaphor and Thought*, Cambridge, Cambridge University Press.

Schulz, Hans-Rudolf *et al.* (1993). *Wohneigentumsförderung durch den Bund. Die Wirksamkeit des Wohnbau- und Eigentumsförderungsgesetzes (WEG)*. Bern: Schriftenreihe Wohnungswesen, Band 55.

Schumann, Wolfgang (1996). *Neue Wege in der Integrationstheorie. Ein Policy-analytisches Modell zur Interpretation des Politischen Systems der EU*. Opladen: Leske+Budrich.

Schwartz, Peter (1991). *The Art of the Long View: Planning for the Future in an Uncertain World*. New York: Doubleday.

Segal, Adam and Eric Thun (2001). "Thinking Globally, Acting Locally: Local Governments, Industrial Sectors, and Development in China." *POLITICS & SOCIETY*, 29 (4):557-588.

Silvasti, Tiina (2001). *Talonpojan elämä. Tutkimus elämäntapaa jäsentävistä kulttuurisista malleista.* Helsinki: Suomalaisen Kirjallisuuden Seura.

Simon, Herbert A. (1981). *The sciences of the artificial.* (3rd ed.). Cambridge: MA, MIT Press.

Siuruainen, Eino ja tutkimusryhmä (1981). *Kostamus-projektin ja Tornion jaloterästehtaan taloudelliset ja yhteiskunnalliset vaikutukset Pohjois-Suomessa. Loppuraportti 1: Tutkimuksen ongelmanasettelu ja pääasialliset tulokset.* Pohjois-Suomen tutkimuslaitoksen julkaisuja C 35. Oulu: Oulun yliopisto.

Skocpol, Theda (1979). *States and Social Revolutions. A Comparative Analysis of France, Russia, and China.* Cambridge: Cambridge University Press

Skocpol, Theda (ed.). (1984). *Vision and Method in Historical Sociology.* Cambridge: Cambridge University Press.

Smelser, J. Neil (1976). *Comparative Methods in the Social Sciences.* Princeton, NJ: Prentice Hall.

Smith, Martin. J. (1992). *Pressure, Power and Policy.* London: Harvester Wheatsheaf.

Smits, Ruud and Stefan Kuhlmann (2004). "The rise of systemic instruments in innovation policy." *International Journal of Foresight and Innovation Policy,* 1 (1/2):4–32.

Spreitzer, Astrid and Sakura Yamasaki (2004). "Beyond Methodological Tenets – The worlds of QCA and SNA and their benefit to Policy Analysis." Paper presented at the ESF Exploratory Workshop on *Innovative Comparative Methods for Policy Analysis,* Erfurt, 25-28 Sept. 2004.

Sprinz, Detlef F. and Yael Nahmias-Wolinsky (2004) (eds). *Models, Numbers and Cases: Methods for Studying International Relations.* Ann Arbor: University of Michigan Press.

Stame, Nicoletta (2003). "La valutazione realistica: una svolta, nuovi sviluppi." *Sociologia e Ricerca Sociale.* Anno XXIII 68-69: 144-159.

Steinmo, Sven, Kathleen Thelen and Frank Longstreth (ed.) (1993). *Structuring Politics.* Cambridge: Cambridge University Press.

Sternberg, Rolf (2003). *The Regional Entrepreneurship Monitor (REM).* Drehbuch für einen multimedialen Kurs "Regional Entrepreneurship Monitor" im Auftrag der Universität Erfurt. Köln.

Sternberg, Rolf and Heiko Bergmann, (2002). *Regionaler Entrepreneurship Monitor (REM): Gründungsaktivitäten und Rahmenbedingungen in zehn deutschen Regionen.* Köln: Univ.

Sternberg, Rolf, Claus Otten and Christine Tamásy (2000). *Regionaler Entrepreneurship M (REM): Gründungsaktivitäten und Rahmenbedingungen in zehn deutschen Regionen.* Köln: Univ.

Sternberg, Rolf and Christine Tamásy (1999). "Munich as Germany's No. 1 High Technology Region: Empirical Evidence, Theoretical Explanations and the Role of Small Firm -- Large Firm Relationships." *Regional Studies,* 4:367-377.

Stokey, Edith and Richard Zeckhauser (1978). *A Primer for Policy Analysis.* New York: WW Norton and Company, Inc.

Storey, David J. (2003). "Entrepreneurship, Small and Medium-Sized Enterprises and Public Policies." In Zoltan Acs and David B. Audretsch (eds). *Handbook of Entrepreneurship*

Research. An Interdisciplinary Survey and Introduction, Kluwer Academic Publishers, Boston: 473-514.

Strauss, Anselm and Juliet Corbin (1990). *Basics of Qualitative Research.* Newbury Park: Sage.

Tarrow, Sidney (1995). "Bridging the Quantitative-Qualitative Divide in Political Science." *American Political Science Review*, 89 (2):471-474.

Tashakkori, Abbas and Charles Teddlie (eds) (2003). *Handbook of Mixed Methods in the Social and Behavioral Research*. Thousand, CA: Sage.

Taylor, Charles L. and , David A. Jodice (eds) (1982). *World Handbook of Political and Social Indicators*. New Haven: Yale University Press.

Thagard, Paul (1988). *Computational Philosophy of Science*. Cambridge, Mass: The MIT Press.

Thatcher, Mark. (1998). "The Development of Policy Network Analyses. From Modest Origins to Overarching Frameworks." *Journal of Theoretical Politics*, 10 (4): 389-416.

Tilly, Charles (1984). *Big Structures, Large Processes, Huge Comparisons*, New York: Russell Sage Foundation.

Tucker, Aviezer (2004). *Our Knowledge of the Past*. Cambridge: Cambridge University of Press.

Uhlaner, Lorraine M. and Roy Thurik (2004). "Post-Materialism: A Cultural Factor Influencing Total Entrepreneurial Activity Across Nations." *Discussion Paper on Entrepreneurship, Growth and Public Policy*, 07-2004, Max-Planck Institute for Research into Economic Systems, Jena.

United Nations Development Programme (1999). *Human Development Report 1999*, UNDP, Geneva.

United Nations Development Programme (2002). *Human Development Report 2004*, UNDP, Geneva.

United Nations Programme on HIV/AIDS (1998). *Report on the Global HIV/AIDS Epidemic*, UNAIDS, Geneva.

United Nations Programme on HIV/AIDS (2004). *2004 Report on the Global HIV/AIDS Epidemic. 4th Global Report*, UNAIDS, Geneva.

Urry, John (1999). "Globalization and Citizenship." *Journal of World-Systems Research*, V:311-324.

Van Buuren, Arwin (2004). "Knowledge for Governance in Complexity." Paper presented at the PSA Annual Conference, April 6-8, Lincoln.

Van Waarden, Frans (1992). "Dimensions and Types of Policy Networks." *European Journal of Political Research*, 21 (1-2):29-52.

Vanderborght, Yannick, and Sakura Yamasaki (2004). "Des cas logiques... contradictoires? Un piège de l'AQQC déjoué à travers l'étude de la faisabilité politique de l'Allocation Universelle." *Revue Internationale de Politique Comparée*, 11 (1):51-66.

Varone, Frédéric (2001). "L'évaluation comme démarche scientifique." In Christian De Visscher and Frédéric Varone (eds). *Evaluer les politiques publiques*. Louvain-la-Neuve: Academia-Bruylant, 29-42.

Vedung, Evert (1997). *Public Policy and Program Evaluation*. New Brunswick and London: Transaction Publishers.

Verba, Sidney (1967). "Some Dilemmas in Comparative Research." *World Politics*, 20:111-127.

Verkuilen, Jay (2001). "Measuring Fuzzy Set Membership Functions: A Dual Scaling Approach." Paper presented at the Annual Meeting of APSA, San Francisco.

Viinikainen, Tytti and Sari Puustinen (2000). *Kylä kaupungin kyljessä. Tutkimus maaseudun ja kaupungin vuorovaikutuksesta*. Yhdyskuntasuunnittelun tutkimus- ja koulutuskeskuksen julkaisuja B82. Espoo: Teknillinen korkeakoulu.

Virtanen, Vesa (2003). *Valta- ja vastavirtaan. Selvitys maassamuuttajien elinoloista, uuteen kiinnittymisesta ja arvotaustasta Suomessa*. Sisäasiainministeriön julkaisu 14. Helsinki: Sisäasiainministeriö.

Von Reibnitz, Ute (1988). *Scenario Techniques*. Columbus: McGraw-Hill Professional Publishing.

Wasserman, Stanley and Katherine Faust (1997). *Social Network Analysis. Methods and Applications*. Cambridge: Cambridge University Press.

Watanabe, Tsutomu (2003). "Where Theory and Reality Meet: Using the Full Potential of QCA by Exploiting the Intersection Function of the QCA Software. International Comparison Analysis About the Occurence of Social Movement." COMPASSS Working Paper 2003-13, 14 pp, online at: http://www.compasss.org.

Weiss, Carol (1997). "Theory-Based Evaluation: Past, Present, and Future." *New Directions for Evaluation* 76: 41-55.

Wellman, Barry (1988). "Structural Analysis: From Method and Metaphor to Theory and Substance." In Barry Wellman and Steve D. Berkowitz (eds). *Social Structure: A Network Approach*. Cambridge: University of Cambridge, 19-61.

Welter, Friederike (2005). "Entrepreneurial Bevahior in Differing Environments." In David B. Audretsch, Heike Grimm and Charles Wessner (eds). *Local Heroes in the Global Village. Globalization and New Entrepreneurship Policies*. Springer Science+Business Media, Inc., New York, 93-112.

Wennekers, Sanders and Roy Thurik (1999). "Linking Entrepreneurship and Economic Growth." *Small Business Economics*, 13:27-55.

Whewell William (1840). *The Philosophy of the Inductive Sciences, Founded upon Their History*. London: John W. Parker [Vol. 1].

Wiborg, Agnete (2004). "Place, Nature and Migration: Students' Attachment to their Rural Home Places." *Sociologia Ruralis*, 44:416-32.

Wilks, Stephen and Maurice Wright eds. (1987). *Comparative Government-Industry Relations: Western Europe, the United States and Japan*. Clarendon Press.

Windhoff-Héritier, Adrienne (1987). *Policy-Analyse. Eine Einführung*. Frankfurt, New York: Campus Verlag.

World Bank (2002). *2002 World Development Indicators*, New York.

Yamasaki, Sakura (2003). "Testing Hypotheses with QCA: Application to the Nuclear Phase-Out Policy in 9 OECD Countries." Paper presented at : *2nd ECPR General Conference, Section "Methodological Advances in Comparative Research: Concepts, Techniques, Applications. "* Marburg, Germany.

Yin, Robert K. 1994. *Case Study Research – Design and Methods*. 2nd edition. London: Sage.

Yli-Jokipii, Heikki (1999). "From Agrarian Society to an Information Society. A Background to the Recent Changes Experienced by Finland and Its Rural Areas." *New Rural Policy. Finnish Journal of Rural Research and Policy*. English Supplement 7:22–29.

Zadeh, Lotfi (1965). "Fuzzy Sets." *Information Control*, 8:338-53.

LIST OF CONTRIBUTORS

Barbara Befani is a European Ph.D. student in Socio-Economic and Statistical Studies (SESS.EuroPhD) at the University of Rome "La Sapienza". She studied statistics, economics and sociology in Rome, Brussels and Southampton. Her research interests include university policy, evaluation theory and methodology.

Dirk Berg-Schlosser, Ph.D. in Political Sciences, is Professor at the Institute of Political Science at the University of Marburg. His major areas of research and teaching include comparative politics, African and Third World politics, political culture, democratization, and comparative methodology.

Peter Bursens, Ph.D. in Political Sciences, is holding an appointment as Professor and Lecturer at the Political Science department of the University of Antwerp. He teaches European integration, foreign policy and multi-level governance. His research interests include Europeanization, legitimacy in the European Union and EU migration policy.

Lasse Cronqvist is Research Assistant at the Institute of Political Science at the University of Marburg. His research focuses on comparative methodology, party politics and comparative policy studies. He has also authored software for Small-N comparative analysis (TOSMANA).

Gisèle De Meur is Professor of Mathematics at the *Université Libre de Bruxelles*. She teaches mathematics for social scientists, methodology, introduction to computers and epistemology, and is Director of the Laboratory for Mathematics and Social Sciences (MATsch) at the ULB. Her more recent research interests include mathematical models applied in anthropology, as well as political science, methodology (quali-quantitative comparative analysis) and gender studies.

Alain Gottcheiner is Assistant and Lecturer at the Laboratory for Mathematics and Social Sciences (MATsch) at the *Université Libre de Bruxelles*. His fields of research include anthropology of mathematics, mathematics of games and mathematical methodology for social sciences.

Heike Grimm, Ph.D. in Political Sciences, holds the Research Lectureship for Public Policy at the University of Erfurt, Germany, and serves as research fellow of the "Entrepreneurship, Growth and Public Policy Group" at the Max-Planck-Institute of Economics in

Jena, Germany. Her research focuses on entrepreneurial public policies for the promotion of state, local and regional economic growth in comparative perspectives.

Jon Kvist, Ph.D. in Social Policy, Master in Public Administration, is Senior Researcher at The Danish National Institute of Social Research. His research interests include comparative social policy and welfare state research, methodology and the impact of the EU on national policy-making.

David Levi-Faur, Ph.D. in Political Sciences, is a Senior Lecturer at the University of Haifa and Senior Research Fellow with the Australian National University. He teaches comparative policy, comparative methods, political economy and regulatory politics and policy. His research interests include the expansion of methodological training and more reflexive methodological practices in the social sciences.

Pentti Luoma, Ph.D., is a Senior Lecturer in sociology in the Department of Educational Sciences and Teacher Education at the University of Oulu, Finland. He is a member of the "EkoSuKaT" project group studying eco-efficiency in declining and growing residential areas in Northern Finland. His research interests include local and regional socio-economic development, rural environmental issues and computer-assisted qualitative data analysis.

Axel Marx is Research and Development Manager for *Hogeschool Antwerpen* (Belgium). His research focuses on comparative case methods, institutional design and institutional effectiveness, in the fields of sociology, management and organizational studies.

António B. Moniz is Associate Professor of Sociology at *Universidade Nova de Lisboa*, and President of the Department of Applied Social Sciences at the Faculty of Sciences and Technology of that University. He is also the director of the research centre on Enterprise and Work Innovation (IET) coordinating, among others, the group on "Innovation Systems and Foresight Analysis". His main research interests are related to foresight methodologies, technological changes in industry, and work organization concepts.

Charles C. Ragin holds a joint appointment as Professor of Sociology and Political Science at the University of Arizona. His main interests are methodology, political sociology, and comparative-historical research, with a special focus on such topics as the welfare state, ethnic political mobilization, and international political economy. In 2001, he was awarded the Donald Campbell Award for Methodological Innovation by the Policy Studies Organization and in

2002 he was awarded Honorable Mention for the Barrington Moore, Jr. Award of the American Sociological Association.

Benoît Rihoux is Professor of Political Science at the *Université catholique de Louvain* (Belgium). His substantive research interests include political parties, new social movements, and organizational studies. He is co-ordinator of the COMPASSS research group (http://www.compasss.org) around systematic comparative methods, and joint convenor of international initiatives around methods more generally, such as the ECPR Standing Group on Political Methodology or the ECPR Summer School in Methods and Techniques

Fritz Sager, Ph.D. in Political Sciences, is Assistant Professor for policy analysis and evaluation at the Institute of Political Science, University of Bern. His research interests include metropolitan governance, organizational analysis of public administration, public policy research, and policy evaluation in the fields of transport, land-use, environment, public health, and foreign policy.

Astrid Spreitzer works for `Statistik Austria´ and is a Ph.D. candidate at the Institute for Sociology at the University of Vienna. Her main research areas are EU policy making, Social Network Analysis (SNA), political sociology, collective bargaining and sociology of the labor market.

Frédéric Varone, Ph.D. in Political Sciences, is Professor of Political Science at the *Université catholique de Louvain* (Belgium). His research includes comparative policy analysis (e.g. environmental policies, regulation of biotechnologies) program evaluation and public sector reforms (e.g. New Public Management, liberalization and privatization of public services).

Sakura Yamasaki is a Fellow Researcher at the National Fund for Scientific Research (FNRS) and a Ph.D. candidate at the Centre of Comparative Politics at *Universite catholique de Louvain*, Belgium. Her areas of interests include comparative methodology (especially QCA), network analysis, nuclear energy policy, policy change and new social movement theories.

ABSTRACTS

Charles C. Ragin: The Limitations of Net-Effects Thinking

Abstract: "Net effects" thinking dominates quantitative social science today. In this approach, researchers try to isolate the net, independent impact of each relevant causal variable on an outcome variable. While powerful, this way of conducting social science has serious limitations, especially in policy-relevant research. A key limitation is that this approach poses serious obstacles to viewing cases in terms of the different elements that are combined in each case, that is, to viewing cases as configurations of interconnected aspects. Charles Ragin not only criticizes net effects thinking, but also offers an alternate approach, fuzzy-set qualitative comparative analysis (fsQCA), a technique that takes the configurational nature of cases as its starting point. Using a large-N data set, his contribution illustrates the difference between calculating net effects and looking at cases in terms of combinations. The empirical analysis examines the different combinations of conditions linked to poverty in the U.S., using the *Bell Curve* data, and contrasts these results with a conventional, net-effects analysis of the same data.

David Levi-Faur: A Question of Size? A Heuristics for Stepwise Comparative Research Design

Abstract: There are some areas where size does not matter. Social sciences are not one of them. Size [Big /N/] is widely perceived as a necessary condition for the corroboration and falsification of generalizations, the larger is often considered the better. David Levi-Faur qualifies the fetishism of size and develops a heuristic of comparative research design that allows an increase in the number of cases without compromising the strength of case-oriented analysis. The discussion starts with several problems that he faced in his efforts to increase the validity of his inference. It continues with a critical overview of Lijphart and King, Keohane and Verba's solutions for the limits of the case-oriented approaches in general and the comparative method in particular. He identifies six issues that need to be addressed in order to develop a comparative heuristics that allow an increase in the number of cases without compromising the strength of case-oriented analysis. He then lays the foundations for a heuristic that is grounded in four principals. First, a distinction between different cases according to their inferential roles in the research design. Second, balance of external (via an in-depth study of primary cases) and internal validity (though a series of secondary and tertiary cases). Third, a step-wise research design with two major steps: the first step is based on a most-similar research design and aims to enhance internal validity, while the second builds on the most-different research design and aims to increase external validity. Fourth, a formalization of the analysis in order to improve the consistency and transparency of case-selection, and of the inferential processes.

Gisèle De Meur, Peter Bursens and Alain Gottcheiner: MSDO/MDSO Revisited for Public Policy Analysis

Abstract: Gisèle De Meur, Peter Bursens and Alain Gottcheiner describe an application of the Most Similar Different Outcome / Most Different Similar Outcome design in public policy analysis. More in particular, they elaborate on the use of MSDO/MDSO in an analysis of EU policy-making with regards to nine concrete legislative dossiers (regulations and directives), in the fields of social, environmental and agricultural policies. It is argued that the MSDO/MDSO method is a helpful tool to reduce the complexity of decision-making configurations to enable the researcher to make more informative evaluations of the way decision-making develops. In the final part some methodological observations with respect to the MSDO/MDSO are presented.

Sakura Yamasaki and Astrid Spreitzer: Beyond Methodological Tenets. The worlds of QCA and SNA and their Benefits to Policy Analysis

Abstract: The aim of this contribution is to present combinations of Social Network Analysis (SNA) and Qualitative Comparative Analysis (QCA) and their benefits to Policy Analysis. It is argued that QCA and SNA are particularly suited to explain complex macro-social phenomena, such as policies. SNA gives access to a set of actors and the relationships between them. The main goal is to model these relationships in order to study action and structure in their mutual dependence. QCA on the other hand helps to uncover regularities across cases while maintaining within-case complexity; it offers "multiple conjunctural explanations". In this chapter, the authors first present their understanding of Policy Analysis and of the problems research on the topic faces. The second part of the contribution focuses on how SNA and QCA are able to address some of these issues on a theoretical level. Finally, through an example dealing with the Swiss Transport Policy, the authors illustrate how the combination of SNA and QCA can be beneficial to the field of policy analysis, on both theoretical and pragmatic levels.

Heike Grimm: Entrepreneurship Policy and Regional Economic Growth. Exploring the Link and Theoretical Implications

Abstract: In her chapter focusing on entrepreneurship policy and regional economic growth in the USA and Germany, Heike Grimm develops several qualitative approaches focusing on `institutional policies´ a) to define the concept of `entrepreneurship policy´ (E-Policy) more precisely and b) to explore whether a link exists between E-Policy and spatial growth. She then implements these approaches with QCA to check if any of these approaches (or any combination thereof) can be identified as a causal condition contributing to regional growth. By using conditions derived from a previous cross-national and cross-regional qualitative survey (expert interviews) for respectively three regions in the USA and in Germany, no "one-size-fits-it-all" explanation could be found, confirming the high complexity of the subject that she had predicted. Summing up, QCA seems to be a valuable tool to, on the one hand, confirm (causal) links obtained by other methodological approaches, and, on the other hand, allow a more detailed analysis focusing on some particular contextual factors which are influencing some cases while others are unaffected. The exploratory QCA reveals that existing theory of the link between policies and economic growth is rarely well-formulated enough to provide explicit hypotheses to be tested; therefore, the primary theoretical objective in entrepreneurship policy research at a comparative level is not theory testing, but elaboration, refinement, concept formation, and thus contributing to theory development.

Lasse Cronqvist and Dirk Berg-Schlosser: Determining the Conditions of HIV/AIDS Prevalence in Sub-Saharan Africa. Employing New Tools of Macro-Qualitative Analysis

Abstract: There are some new attempts to bridge the divide between quantitative and qualitative methods in the social sciences. This contribution explicitly illustrates and tests some of these methods such as correlation analysis, multiple regression, etc., on the one hand, and more recent case- and diversity-oriented methods such as QCA and Multi-Value QCA (MVQCA), on the other. As an example, this contribution explores some possible causes of the differences of the HIV prevalence rate in Sub-Saharan Africa. In contrast to purely statistical "universalizing" procedures, the macro-qualitative analysis conducted by the authors highlights the necessity of differentiated policies according to levels of development.

Jon Kvist: Diversity, Ideal Types and Fuzzy Sets in Comparative Welfare State Research

Abstract: This chapter advances a new method for studying policy diversity, fuzzy-set theory, which is a framework that allows a precise operationalization of theoretical concepts, the configuration of concepts into ideal types, and the categorization of cases. In a Weberian sense ideal types are analytical constructs used as yardsticks to measure the similarity and difference between concrete phenomena. Ideal type analysis involves differentiation of categories and degrees of membership of such categories. In social science jargon, this means analysis involving the evaluation of qualitative and quantitative differences or, in brief, of diversity. Fuzzy set theory provides a calculus of compatibility. It can measure and compute theoretical concepts and analytical constructs in a manner that is true to their formulation and meaning. This chapter sets out elements and principles of fuzzy set theory relevant for ideal type analysis, and demonstrates their usefulness in a study of policy diversity.

António Brandão Moniz: Scenario-Building Methods as a Tool for Policy Analysis

Abstract: Scenarios can be considered as tools for policy analysis and they describe possible set of future conditions. When a research procedure is going to analyze the changes of scientific programs and of technology developments, this kind of tool can be decisive. The author takes this example as a reference, referring to the German, the Japanese and the UN foresight exercises. This approach can lay out some causal chains of decisions and circumstances that lead from the present, emerging dependent variables. The display of the variable conditions can reveal the quantitative dimensions that will enrich the narrative of those "futures". Defining a large number of alternative worlds is often neither necessary nor desirable. The method for its definition can be presented. The final selection of "future worlds" should consider the sufficiency to present a range of opportunities and challenges. The social actors can design their decision procedures over the provisions of information presented and constructed for these scenarios.

Frédéric Varone, Benoît Rihoux and Axel Marx: A New Method for Policy Evaluation? Longstanding Challenges and the Possibilities of Qualitative Comparative Analysis (QCA)

Abstract: The goal of this chapter is to investigate the potential added-value of QCA for policy evaluation. Up till now, QCA and policy evaluation have very seldom been explicitly linked. This is quite surprising, as some clear parallels can be drawn between some key features of QCA and some key preoccupations of policy evaluators. The first two sections set the stage of "policy evaluation" and "QCA": the authors first provide a brief definition of policy evaluation, and then lay out the fundamentals of QCA. They then identify four methodological challenges that policy evaluators typically face: explaining policy effects, isolating net policy effects, estimating the policy deadweight, and triangulating methods and data. To follow, they demonstrate that QCA may offer some innovative answers to these longstanding methodological challenges. Finally, they identify some of the remaining challenges and difficulties for the exploitation of QCA in policy evaluation, and discuss some further potential benefits of QCA from an evaluation perspective.

Pentti Luoma: The Social Sustainability of the Community Structures: The Case of the Oulu Region in the North of Finland

Abstract: This contribution includes, firstly, the presentation of the research subject of the multidisciplinary EkoSuKaT project sited in the University of Oulu (URL: http://wwwedu.oulu.fi/sos/SuKaT/ecores.htm) which focuses on the ecological, physical and social sustainability of a selection of residential areas in three growing and three declining municipalities in Northern Finland. Secondly, it presents preliminary results from a small-N study comparing thirteen residential areas and communities in Oulunsalo. In the study, the thirteen communities are compared for their level of social integration. The main findings suggest that the driving force of migrating to a municipality such as Oulunsalo is the "culture" of home-ownership. Thirdly, the author considers the potentials and limitations of comparative social research focused on communities. He applies mainstream quantitative methods, as well as QCA and a selection of qualitative data. Some methodological issues of QCA are discussed in relation to the empirical study, such as the problem of contradictions in the cases and the recurring problem of ecological fallacy.

Barbara Befani and Fritz Sager: QCA as a Tool for Realistic Evaluations. The Case of the Swiss Environmental Impact Assessment

Abstract: In their contribution Barbara Befani and Fritz Sager argue that the realistic approach to evaluation can highly benefit from its integration with Qualitative Comparative Analysis (QCA). In both approaches empirical observation is theory-driven, causality is complex and the pursuit of generalization limited. A mixed QCA-Realistic Evaluation design is implemented in the evaluation of the Swiss environmental impact assessment. In the process, the Context-Mechanism-Outcome (CMO) framework is adapted to fit in QCA's dichotomous structure. Eventually, QCA results are translated back into CMO form. This experience leads to the conclusion that, under certain conditions, realistic evaluation and QCA provide a powerful tandem to produce empirically well-grounded, context-sensitive evidence on policy instruments.

INDEX

Abbott, A. 46, 226
Abstraction-specification scale 279
Academics 2, 3, 9, 46, 179, 294-296
Accountability 215
Actors (policy) 6, 70, 95, 97, 102, 103, 167, 214, 223, 289, 295
Additivity 15, 24, 36
Adema, W. 167
Administration 87, 98, 131, 144, 186, 199, 200, 206, 213
Africa 7, 145, 146, 149-151, 155, 157, 159-164, 166, 203
Agenda-setting 4, 6, 214
Agriculture 72, 73, 83, 85, 153-155, 158, 159, 163, 192, 239, 241, 262
AICGS 129
AIDS 145, 149, 151, 153-155, 157-160, 163, 164, 206
Alanen, I. 261
Alapuro, R. 238
Amenta, E. 66, 167, 234
Analytical induction 295
Antonnen, A. 172
Appadurai, A. 238
Arbitrariness 29, 40, 47, 57, 92
Argentina 64
Aristotle 173
Armed Forces Qualifying Test (AFQT) 16, 17, 19, 23-37, 39, 40
Armed Services Vocational Aptitude Battery (ASVAB), 39
Ascher, W. 190
Aspinwall, M. 89
Assignment error 32
Assumptions 9, 14, 15, 21-23, 36, 50, 54, 100, 102, 105, 118, 119, 128, 146, 188-190, 214, 218, 219, 226, 230, 236, 264, 266, 274, 276, 283, 293
Asymmetry 29
Atlanta 131, 136
Attitudinal features 70
Audretsch, D. 3, 124, 127
Australia 43, 62
Automotive sector 208
Availability 131, 133, 145, 175
Averaging out 165
Baeck, H. 245, 296
Bagnall, G. 244-5

Bakka, P. 145
Balthasar, A. 235
Baltimore 131, 136
Barbalet, J. 168
Basel 220
Baseline forecast 190, 205
Baumgartner, F. 97
Bavaria (Bayern) 132
Becker, H. 44, 53, 170, 180
Befani, B. 9, 144, 184, 218, 232, 233, 235, 263
Belgium 223
Bell Curve 5, 16, 26-28, 36, 39, 174
Benchmark 20
Bennett, A. 2, 17, 226
Bergische Städtedreieck 131, 138
Bergmann, H. 127, 138
Berg-Schlosser, D. 7, 65, 67, 127, 142, 145-147, 165, 170, 217, 233, 236, 284, 242
Bern 120, 220
Best fit model (BFM) 238
Best practices 141, 285
Binary data (see Dichotomies)
Biology 198
Birkland, T. 97
Blank, K. 98
BMBF 184, 195, 197, 201
Bonacich's centrality measure 105; power 107
Boole, G. 120
Boole/Boolean algebra 9, 69, 90, 91, 94, 103, 109, 120, 126, 127, 138, 142, 148, 161, 166, 216,-218, 227, 233, 236, 252, 256, 264, 267, 268, 282, 284; algorithms 216, 227; distance 69, 99; literals 161
Borja, J. 241, 243
Börzel, T. 223
Brady, H. 2, 44, 50, 146, 226
Bratton, M. 151, 154
Brazelton, T. 177
Britain 48, 52, 64; colonies 151, 164
Brown, O. 243
Brüderl, J. 144
Bulmer, S. 89
Burchinal, M. 177
Bursens, P. 5, 67, 70

Business 54, 128, 129, 131, 132, 137, 144, 188, 193, 198-200, 203, 276
Bygrave, W. 123, 124, 127, 144
Calibration 28, 29, 37, 38, 39, 40
Campbell, D. 64
Cantons 223, 224, 269; environmental protection agencies 265
Capital venture companies 131
Carvallo, M. 120
CASA 177
Case selection 2, 4, 43, 45, 48, 56, 58, 59, 62, 64, 233, 269, 288-290, 295
Case-oriented approach/analysis 2, 3, 43, 45, 46, 50-58, 62, 64, 65, 165, 184, 216
Cases; categorization 169, 171; comparison 3, 50, 51, 214, 224, 225, 269-271, 290; complexity 2, 171; conformity 167, 184; contradictory cases 148, 156, 249, 251, 260; counterfactual cases 27; holistic view 182; homogeneity 181, 182; idiosyncratic 285; knowledge 228, 289; number of 6, 43, 48-52, 55, 63, 64, 285; positive cases 140, 141; primary cases 44, 62, 63; secondary and tertiary cases 63; thick analysis 284, 291
Castles, F. 172
Castells, M. 241, 243
Categorization 7, 69-77, 80-93, 109-111
Catholicism 150, 151
Causation/causality 4, 6, 9, 15, 23, 46, 50, 54, 98, 102-105, 120, 127, 141, 143, 147, 207, 216, 219, 220, 227, 265-268, 275, 280, 284, 288, 293, 296; asymmetric 206; chemical 102; causal arguments 282; causal chain 185, 207, 219; causal combinations 14, 20, 32, 36, 232, 250; causal complexity 15, 98, 99, 207; causal interpretations 102, 118; causal mechanisms 8, 245, 254, 282; causal model 216, 219; causal paths 218, 224, 232-234; causal processes 226, 227; causal regularities 217; causal significance 282
Cause-and-effect sequence 219
CCC group 241
CCI 130, 131

Central African Republic 160, 162, 163, 167
Central and Eastern Europe 229
Centrality 105-111, 118, 282
Centralization 120, 137, 128
Chambers of Commerce 125, 130, 131
Chambers of Handicrafts 131
Child care policies 170, 172, 175, 176, 178-184
Chi-Square-tests 146
Citizenship 168, 172, 173, 244
City areas 239, 243
Civil law 56
Clayton, R. 168
Clément, C. 234
Cluster analysis 106-111, 120, 143, 148, 154-156, 159, 223, 229, 240, 269, 291
CMO configurations 263-268, 275, 277-281
Coalition government 172, 296
Coding 138, 139, 232, 236, 292
Cognitive ability 26, 35, 36,
Coleman model 291
Collier, D. 2, 44, 50, 145, 146, 226, 228
Combinations of conditions 4, 18-23, 30, 32, 34, 37, 104, 117, 120, 216, 230, 236, 276, 279, 282
Combinatorial approach 95, 102, 118
Common law 58
Communication technologies 196
Communist movement 186
Community structures 237
Comparative analysis/comparative method 1-3, 13, 44-63, 65, 71, 95, 99-102, 119, 126, 127, 143-149, 155, 213, 216, 237, 249, 263, 290
Comparative case studies 3, 48, 52, 53, 65, 232, 269, 272, 283
Comparative research design 4, 5, 43, 57, 228, 288, 290, 295
COMPASSS 2, 120, 235, 236
Competition policy 129
Complement 5, 6, 173, 178, 179
Complement operation 179
Complexity 2, 6, 8, 26, 33, 49, 52, 56, 67, 95, 98-120, 128, 142, 143, 146, 169, 206, 214, 217, 239, 240, 241, 246, 289, 293
Compliance 266, 267, 274, 279
Comprehensive approach 124

Computer mediated methodology (CMM) 44
Concepts 6, 102, 126, 129, 132, 137, 140, 142, 168-178, 183, 188, 200, 265, 280
Conditional logit analysis 291
Confounding factors 8, 221, 222, 228
Conjunctures/ conjunctural logic 99, 147, 214
Conservatives 167, 172, 180, 182
Consilience 45, 55, 65
Consistency scores 24, 33
Consultative procedures/committee 73, 88, 89, 93
Consumption 221, 236
Content analysis 242
Context/contextual factors 1,2, 7, 9, 15-18, 45-47, 50, 53, 55, 70, 97, 98, 100, 102, 104, 123, 126, 138, 139, 142, 149, 155-157, 163, 190, 216, 221, 223-229, 231, 232, 259, 263-268, 275-283, 288, 290, 291
Contradictions/contradictory configurations 5, 138, 160, 161, 229, 232, 249, 250, 253,
Contradictory simplifying assumptions 230
Contrasting configurations 83
Control 26, 27, 43-64, 179, 186, 232, 238
Co-occurrence 113, 115, 116, 120
Cook, T. 64
Cooperation/co-decision procedure 73
Coordination 98, 266, 280
COREPER 67, 73, 83, 85
Corporatism 70, 71, 113, 117
Correlations 5, 15-17, 21, 49, 62, 88, 126, 127, 140-143, 147, 150-158, 164, 252-257
Correspondence analysis 148
Corroboration 43, 55, 60, 113, 116
Cost-benefit analysis 97
Cost-efficiency analysis 97
Counseling 96, 97, 126, 130-133, 137, 138
Counterfactuals 23-23, 33-35, 143, 219, 222, 223, 230, 231,
Cowles, M. 223
Crisis/crisis events 67, 169, 188
Crisp sets 20, 24, 30, 34, 41, 173-178, 237, 242, 249, 250, 254, 260

Critical event 64
Cronqvist, L. 7, 109, 145, 156, 160, 170, 217, 233-237, 242, 284, 287, 292
Cross impact analysis 189-191
Cross-case analysis 8, 109, 140, 141, 226
Cross-national analysis 62, 127, 130, 131, 140, 231
Cross-national quantitative research 62
Cross-over point 29, 39, 175-178, 181, 183
Cross-regional analysis 2, 3, 6, 125, 131, 137, 140, 142, 231
Cross-sector analysis 3
Culture/cultural factors 87, 89, 90, 129, 130, 149, 150, 154, 192, 239, 243, 245, 267, 275, 277
Cumulative effects 60, 98
Data exploration 218; matrix 9, 113, 288; space 68, 69; visualization 114, 117, 118
Database 2, 187, 201, 204, 269
Davey, S. 34
De Meur, G. 2-5, 65, 67, 120, 127, 142, 145-148, 216-219, 230, 234, 236, 290
De Morgan's law 251
Deadweight (policy) 222, 223
Decimal values 195
Decision analysis 189, 190
Decision makers 9, 70, 86-89, 186, 188, 204, 208, 238, 295
Decision making process 4, 70-73, 84, 96, 106, 120, 192, 245
Declining areas 237
Decontamination measures 215
Degree of centralization 137, 138
Degree of membership 24, 25, 29, 30, 32, 38, 40, 173, 175, 181, 183
Delphi 189, 191-202, 207, 209
Demand factors 114
Democratic countries 24
Denmark 58, 172, 181-183, 223
Department of defense 39, 40
Dependency 2, 151-153, 170, 171
Deterministic extrapolation 190
Deutsch, K. 146
Development Index (GDI) 152
Development policy 223
Diachronic comparisons 224

Dichotomies/dichotomization 21, 26, 71, 91, 92, 109, 113, 120, 148, 155-158, 160, 173, 184, 218, 232, 242, 291, 292, 296
Differences 87, 16, 17, 21, 24, 26, 45, 49, 57-67, 81, 83, 91, 92, 98, 103, 123, 126, 129-132, 137, 139-157, 164, 167, 170, 171, 180, 184, 206, 221, 222, 226, 274, 276, 282, 283
Disjunctive form 91
Disposable income 176, 177
Dissimilarity(-ies) 68, 71, 72, 76, 103, 148
Distance matrices 75
Diversity 3, 7, 21, 23-26, 37, 51, 53, 147, 170-172, 180, 184, 260, 289
Document analysis 264, 272
Dombrecht, J. 227
Domestic policies 223
Drass, K. 34, 147
Dumont, P. 245, 296
Earth sciences 192-194
Eckstein, H. 64, 172
Ecological fallacies 57
Ecology 57, 238, 239, 260, 275
Econometrics 189
Economic agents 129; costs 175; development 58, 123, 124, 129, 131, 135, 137, 138, 139, 141, 142, 172, 225; efficiency 215; growth 7, 123-128, 138, 140-143, 191; indicators 130; policies 59, 60; pressures 239; recession 222; sectors 59, 60; structure 186, 241; sustainability 237; system 151
Education 7, 17, 18, 20-23, 28-30, 34-41, 60, 62, 130, 151, 154, 163, 169, 177, 186, 191, 192, 196-198, 203, 209, 250, 251,
EEA-agreement 172
Effect(s) 5, 15, 16, 18, 21, 22-30, 37, 40, 50, 60, 63, 96-103, 120, 146, 151, 163, 179, 190, 200, 205, 213-230, 238, 245, 251, 252, 261-265, 274, 280, 282
Effectiveness 3, 209, 213, 215, 220
Efficiency 57, 215, 221
EIA 8, 263-283
Elderly people 250, 253, 260
Elections, electoral behavior 24, 62
Electricity sector 46, 48, 64

Electronic sector 234, 237
Employment 138, 142, 177, 191, 198, 208, 240
Empowerment Measure (GEM) 152
Energy 221, 222, 263, 270
Entrepreneurial environment 124, 125, 130, 136, 143
Entrepreneurship networks 131; policies 6, 124-143
Environment/environmental policies 44, 47, 71, 72, 88, 92, 99, 100,102, 106, 124-130, 136, 139, 143, 189-196, 203, 204, 208, 231, 238, 242, 243, 251, 254, 263, 267-270, 275, 277
Environmental impact assessment (EIA) 264, 280 ; issues 203, 266, 275, 277 ; protection agencies 203; scanning 189, 190; standards 264, 266, 268, 279, 280
Epistemology 49, 65, 105, 119
E-policy 6, 125-130, 136, 137, 140-143
Equity 98, 152, 154-159
Equity Index 152, 154-159
Errors 66, 99, 186, 204, 206, 208, 291
Esping-Andersen, G. 167-173, 176
Estimation technique 18
Estonia 236, 209
EU 2-6, 71-73, 89, 91, 106, 172, 223, 224, 229, 231, 240, 289 ; governance 89 ; policies/governance 89, 90, 223 ; policy networks 6
Europe 48, 150, 151, 240
European Council 72, 90-92; Directives 223; funds 208, 283; integration 70, 89, 96, 98, 100; Parliament 74, 87; Structural Funds projects 279
Europeanization 45, 223
Evaluation (policy) 4, 8, 96, 97, 120, 197, 213-219, 223-228, 231-236, 294
Evaluation design 213, 224, 264, 265
Events 50, 64, 185, 186, 188-191, 282
Evolution 104, 107, 185, 186, 222
Ex-ante analysis 96
Exogenous factors 265, 268
Expansion 96, 149, 169, 170
Experimental design 213, 289
Expertise/experts 69, 74, 83, 86-90, 130, 131, 136-139, 143, 188, 189, 192-194, 197, 199-203, 209, 263, 272, 294

Explanatory analysis/model 107, 233, 234; power 15, 18, 55, 70, 84, 86, 88, 164
Exploratory analysis 7, 14, 105, 125, 130, 136, 138, 142, 143, 189, 242, 260, 291
Export-oriented economy 238
Ex-post analysis 96
External environment 99, 204, 208 ; events 97; validity 62
Extrapolation 189, 190, 201, 204, 205
Extremal distance 77
Extreme configurations 68
Facilitators 200
Factor analysis 7
Factual knowledge 207
Failure 220, 228, 234, 265, 274, 276, 277
Falsification 43, 55, 60, 99
Falter, J. 146
Farmers/farming 258
Faure, M. 59
Faust, K. 95, 103, 120
Favorable/unfavorable conditions 17, 23
Feasibility study 203
Featherstone, K. 223
Federal policies/countries 130, 133, 134, 135, 196, 197, 223, 224, 263, 270
Feedback mechanisms 170
Finance agencies 215
Financial assistance programs 132, 134, 135, 136, 137, 138; resources 243, 246, 250, 251
Fine-grained data 233
Finland 8, 172, 181-183, 237-241, 261
Fiscal equivalence 215
Fischer, C. 16, 27, 28, 36-39, 41
Flexibility 144, 276, 284
Flora, P. 146
Florida, R. 129
Focus groups 197, 199-202
Forecasting 7, 187-191, 194, 204-209
Foresight 185-189, 192, 193, 196, 197, 200-209
Forestry 237, 238
Forestry sector 238
Formal language 174; policy aspects 70-75, 84-86, 88-90

Formal tools, formalization 45, 64, 65, 99, 100, 103, 119, 207, 216, 292
Forward-thinking organizations 187
Framework conditions 129, 138,
France 58, 64
Freeman, G. 67
Frequency analysis 146, 269
Fs/qca (software) 103, 217, 242, 249, 268
FUTUR (exercise) 196-202; co-ordination committee, BMBF officers 202
Futures research 197, 202
Futurology 188
Fuzzy set membership scores 24, 25, 168, 175-178, 181-183
Fuzzy set theory 174, 175, 178, 179, 184
Fuzzy Sets (FS) 2, 4, 5, 7, 8, 20, 24-30, 34, 37, 40, 167, 168, 173-176, 178, 179, 184, 186, 191, 231, 233, 260, 267, 287, 291, 292; subsets 25, 28
Gallopin, G. 120
Gaming and Simulation 189
Gamse, R. 137, 138, 143
Gas emissions 72
GDI 152, 157
GDP 113-115, 152-155, 157-163, 169, 205
Gender 67, 105, 152-159, 161-164, 186, 189
General theory 264, 283
Generalization 1, 3, 5, 6, 21, 43, 44, 46-54, 57, 62, 66, 99, 100, 103, 147, 149, 170, 178, 216, 237, 264, 283, 284
Generative causality 265
Generosity (allowances) 175-180
Genetic engineering 186
Genius forecasting 189
Geographical environment 92
George, A. 2, 17, 18, 226
Georgia 131
German foresight exercise 196, 202
German FUTUR project 192-202; regions and *Länder* 133, 136, 138, 139, 140, 141, 223
Germany 3, 6, 7, 52, 125, 130-135, 143, 144, 186, 192, 197, 198, 202, 207, 209
Gerring, J. 2, 120

Giesel, H. 23, 242, 249
Gilbert, N. 168
Glenn, J. 205-6
Global change 198; economy 135; environment 139; lookout panel 205; measure 69
Global Entrepreneurship Monitor (GEM) 129, 152
Globalization 45, 129, 137, 238, 239, 243, 261
Godet, M. 187, 188
Goldthorpe, J. 146
Gordon, T. 189, 204-206
Gottcheiner, A. 5, 67
Government 86, 90, 91, 113, 117, 126, 129, 138, 172, 193, 196, 203, 271, 272
Granovetter, M. 253
Graph relations 80
Graphical visualizations 104
Great Britain 48
Great migration wave 241, 257
Green E. 243
Greenberg, G. 98
Greene, P. 139
Grimm, H. 3, 6, 123, 126, 127, 137, 138, 143, 208, 287
Gross effects 223
Grunwald, A. 206 207
Guala, F. 63, 66
Hagman, M. 242
Hall, P. 50, 53
Halonen, V. 240
Halsey, A. 243
Hampel, F. 147
Hanley, J. 238
Hanneman, R. 107
Hansen, F. 177, 182
Harkness, J. 128
Hart, D. 126
Hasse, R. 103
Hay, M. 123-4, 127, 144
Health policies 83, 84, 105, 169, 186, 192, 198, 206, 260
Hedström, P. 226
Heikkilä, E. 239, 240
Helsinki 240, 259, 262
Hendrick, R. 98
Hentilä, H.-L. 238
Héritier, A. 96, 98, 119
Hermeneutics 148

Herrmann, A. 292
Herrnstein R.J. 16, 26-28, 35, 37-39
Heterogeneity 69, 99, 139, 141, 269
Heuristics 43-45, 140, 190, 237, 246
High tech municipalities 240
Higher-risk sex 152
Hinz, T. 144
Hirvonen, J. 259
Historical institutionalist theory 70
Historical-institutional trajectories 170
History 7, 141, 163, 188, 203, 258
HIV 7, 145-166
HIV policies 7, 149
Holistic approach 96, 100, 119
Homeownership 257, 258
Homogeneity 69, 140, 148, 169, 184
Hooghe, L. 98
Hotakainen, K. 258
Households 19, 35-41, 220-222
Housing 169, 243, 245, 257-262
Hout, M. 27
Howes, C. 177
Huber, E. 147
Human development index (HDI) 152, 203
Human factor 188
Hunt, C. 150, 151, 153
Hypothetical data 20, 21; generalization 149
Hyyryläinen, T. 238
Ideal type (analysis) 167-184
Idiosyncrasies 268, 272
Impact 7, 13-15, 18, 27, 28, 56, 58, 97, 98, 100, 123, 124, 126, 129, 137, 151, 153, 157, 163, 176, 184, 188-191, 205, 206, 214, 216, 219-228, 245, 263-268, 273, 279-283
Impact analysis 97, 189, 190, 206; theory 219, 220
Implementation 3, 4, 8, 73, 96, 105, 136, 138, 148, 192, 200, 203, 213-215, 219-226, 232, 235, 264-267, 274-283, 289
Income 17, 19, 20, 22-25, 28-39, 174, 176-178
Incremental change 170, 174
Incremental stepwise comparison 61, 64
Independence (variables) 63

In-depth (case) knowledge 5, 44, 45, 48, 53, 62, 63, 65, 99-101, 139, 143, 149, 208, 291, 295
Indeterminacy 235
Index 152-154, 157-159, 164, 202-205, 241
Indian Oceans 91
Indiana University 107
Indicators 169, 175-178, 244-246
Individual actors 70, 74, 103
Individualization 243, 245
Individual-level data 20
Industry 130, 131, 193, 196, 209, 215, 221, 222, 238-241, 261
Inequality measures 111
Inference 43, 44, 49, 52, 53, 57, 59, 60, 62-66
Informal mechanisms 88
Information campaign 221, 222, 225
Information society 208
Infrastructures 239, 264
Initial assumptions 9, 274, 276
In-migration 240, 262
Innovation 56, 65, 112, 196, 199, 202, 203
Institute for Future Technology 192
Institutional framework 96, 97, 125, 129
Institutionalism 291
Institution-linked policies 127, 130, 136-139
Institutions/institutional actors 5, 46, 73, 74, 84, 87, 88, 89, 99, 124, 125, 129, 131, 132, 138, 143, 283
Integration (policy) 2, 8, 70, 75, 85, 88, 89, 106, 199, 244-246, 250, 268, 280
Inter War Europe 67
Intercorrelation 21
Interdependence of actors 103
Interdisciplinarity 199
Interest aggregation 96; groups 70, 71, 73, 84-89
Intermediate N 217
International institutions 283; relations 189
Interpretative single case studies 70
Interregional comparisons 223
Intersection 173, 178, 179, 225, 231, 267, 274, 282
Interview data 131, 132, 137, 264
Islam 150, 151, 155, 156, 164

Israel 46
IT (information technologies) 189, 193, 194, 238, 239, 241
Iterative model/comparison 64
Jacobs, K. 257, 258, 261
Jansen, D. 144
Japan 7, 192-196, 207, 209
Järvinen, T. 239, 240
Jauhiainen, J. 238, 240
Jegen, M. 97
Jenkins-Smith, H. 97
Jodice, D. 146
Jones, B. 97
Jones, C. 214
Kaldor-Hicks criterion 97, 100
Kärki, V. 261
Kemeny, J. 250, 256, 261, 265
Kenis, P. 120
Keohane, R. 44, 46, 146
Kerkelä, H. 261
Kerremans, B. 70, 89
Key conditions/factors 75, 81, 291, 293
Keynes, J. 238
King, G. 44, 46, 146
King, Keohane and Verba (KKV) 46, 49-53
Kirchhoff, B.A. 138
Kittel, B. 2
Knowledge Society 198
Korkala, M. 240
Korpi, W. 172-173
Krook, M.L. 292
Krücken, G. 103
Kuhlmann, S. 219
Kuhn, T. 145
Kurkinen, J. 261
Kvist, J. 7, 167, 172, 173, 182, 207, 218, 226, 233, 242, 267
Laakkonen-Pöntys, K. 241
Labor markets 26, 35, 129
Large N 43, 49
Larrue, C. 214
Latent construct 125, 128
Lauder, H. 243
Law of non-contradiction 173
Law of the excluded middle 173
Lead visions 197-203
Left-libertarian parties 105, 112, 113, 116, 117
Legislative initiatives 71, 88
Leipzig 131, 136, 138

Leira, A. 177
Lempert, R. 99
Level of analysis 45, 54, 56-58, 65, 66
Levi-Faur, D. 5, 43, 62
Liberal welfare state 168
Liberalization 45, 46, 48, 54, 58-60
Lieberson, S. 145
Lijphart, A. 5, 44-56, 66, 145
Likert scale 130-133, 139
Limited diversity 21-26, 37
Limited generalization 264, 283, 284
Lin, N. 244
Linear-additive models 15
Linearity 36, 104
Lipsitz, L. 250
Literacy 151-166, 206
Living conditions 244, 246, 255, 259, 262
Lobbies 67
Local communities and policies 8, 98, 107, 108, 123, 125, 127, 129, 135, 137, 143, 238, 239, 244, 250, 256
Logical 'remainders' (non-observed cases) 103, 166, 218, 230; contradictions 293
Logistic regression 16, 27, 28, 30, 36-38
Longhurst, B. 244-245
Longitudinal data 7
Longstreth, F. 89
Loose networks 71, 72, 83, 85-88
Lucas, S. 27
Lundström, A. 128, 143
Luoma, P. 8, 237
Macro-level (macrosocial) analyses 101
Macro-qualitative methods 145-149
Majone, G. 119
Malawi 157, 160, 161-167
Management 132, 187, 188, 193, 194, 266, 268, 280
Manninen, R. 259
Mäntysalo, R. 238, 242
Manufacturing 239
Many variables' problem 49-52
Manzi, T. 257-8, 261
MARHE project 199, 208
Marks, G. 98
Markusen, A. 124, 142
Marsh, D. 70
Marshall, T. 168, 173

Marx, A. 3, 8, 96, 97, 99, 100, 138, 143, 165, 265
Mathematical language 174
Matrices 75, 106, 112, 113, 119, 188, 256, 274
Matrices d'Impacts Croisés 188
Maximum distance 76; principle 179
McKeown, T. 49
MDSD (Most Different System Design) 57, 59, 60, 63,
MDSO (Most Different Same Outcome) 5, 67, 70-73, 79, 83, 84, 91, 93, 288, 291, 293
Measurement, measurement errors 4, 66, 99, 100, 173, 207, 291, 292
Mechanisms 9, 97, 187, 199, 246, 256, 264-268, 276-283
Medium-range 165
MERCOSUR 3
Method of agreement 58, 59, 62, 63; of difference 58, 59, 62, 63
MEXT 186, 192
MICMAC 188
Micro-level analysis 148
Microsystem technology 198
Middle-range theories 264, 283, 284
Migration 153, 157, 238, 240, 241, 246, 253, 256, 259-263, 265
Mill, J. 5, 45, 56, 58-63, 66, 120, 147, 290
Millennium project (UN) 203-205
Miller, A. 98
Minimal formula 103, 116, 128, 138, 139, 217, 218, 227, 229, 230-232, 289, 293
Minimization procedure 138, 227, 229, 230, 234
Minimum distance 76; principle 179
Ministry of economics and labor (Germany) 125, 143
Ministry of Education, Culture, Sports, Science and Technology (MEXT) 186, 192
Miscalibrations 29, 37
Model specification 5, 16, 288, 289, 291
Modernization 161, 239
Mohler, P. 128
Mohr, L. 98
Moilanen, M. 241
Monetary policy 60

337

Moniz, A. 7, 185, 199
Morin, R. 238
Morphological analysis 187, 190
Mortality rate 7, 158, 159, 164-166, 205
Moses, J. 2
Most-Different Research Design 45, 65
Motivation 199, 277
MSDO (Most Similar, Different Outcome) 5, 67, 70, 71-73, 79, 83, 84, 91, 93, 228, 288, 291, 293
MSSD (Most-Similar System Design) 57-59, 62-64
Mufune, P. 150
Multi-colinearity 104
Multidimensional Scaling (MDS) 103, 114, 116, 117
Multi-disciplinarity 206
Multi-equation feedback models 205
Multi-level 57, 98
Multiple actors 98, 105; conjunctural causation 9, 98, 128, 129, 143, 216, 227, 231, 288, 293, 296; regression 13, 154-156
Munich 131, 136, 138
municipalities 3, 8, 237, 238, 240, 245, 259, 261, 263, 265
Murray, C. 16, 26-28, 35, 39
Muslims 151, 155
MVQCA 2, 4, 7, 8, 109, 155, 160-162, 231, 233, 287, 289, 291-293
Myles, J. 168
Nachmias, D. 98
Nahmias-Wolinsky, Y. 2
Nanotechnology 198
Nation states, national level 2, 47, 58, 62, 63, 98, 100, 105, 123, 126-131, 137, 139,
National Longitudinal Survey of Youth (NLSY) 16, 26, 27, 38, 39, 41
National Patterns Approach (NPA) 47
NATO 3
Natural gas market 186; language 172, 176, 184; resources 64
Negated scores 48
Negation principle 171
Negative correlation 151, 156; output 231, 274, 276, 279
Negotiation procedures 98
Neighborhood 8, 16, 17, 27, 244-246, 261, 262

Net effects (thinking; in policy) 8, 13-18, 2-29, 36, 37, 99, 100, 221, 223, 229, 230
Net impact 15; outcomes 221
Netdraw 113-118
Network visualization 113, 116
Networks (policy) 5, 6, 47, 59, 60, 70, 71, 74, 83-89, 91, 101-119, 131, 132, 194, 198, 239, 245, 255
New policies 124
New Social Democratic model 181
NGOs 203
Nijkamp, P. 100
NISTEP 192, 193, 195, 196
Nodes 102, 114, 116
Noise emissions 72
Nokia 238, 264
Nonexperimental data 20
Non-independence of variables 118
Non-overlapping effects 15, 16
Nordic countries 168, 172; welfare model 172
Normal distributions 146
Normative criteria 99, 100
North Carolina 131
North, D. 125, 131, 136, 143
Norusis, M. 126
Norway 58, 172, 181-183, 246, 265
NPA 47
NVivo 242
OECD 3, 112, 145
Oil shock 186
Oksa, J. 238, 239
OLS regressions 99
Olsen, J. 89
Ontologies, ontological divide 43-54, 65
Operationalization (variables) 3, 4, 7, 168, 169, 288, 289, 293
Optical Technologies 198
Optimal solution 22, 23
Optional factors 253
Organizational factors/organizations 72, 74, 86, 89, 90, 93, 101, 125, 131, 187, 190, 191, 198, 203
Orloff, A. 175
Ostrom, E. 215, 226
Otten, C. 125
Oulu region/Oulunsalo 8, 237-260
Outliers 147, 165

Out-migration 238, 241, 246, 253, 255, 256, 263
Output model 264, 278
Outputs 97, 99, 100, 136, 206, 209, 210, 212, 218, 219, 220, 224-227, 262, 264, 269-278
Over-generalizing 169
Overholt, W. 188
Overlaps 16, 19, 21, 56
Owen, G. 98
Pacific 95, 96
Package deals 90, 94
Packaging waste 72, 93
Palme, J. 172-3
Parental income 25, 28, 29, 32, 38-44, 50-56; SES 34, 36
Parsimony 9, 27-30, 47-49, 215, 216, 233, 238-243, 289, 291
Parsons, T. 240
Partial membership 169, 174, 182
Participatory methods 187
participatory process 195, 196, 198, 199, 201
Party formation 114, 117, 118
Patchy stepwise comparison 62
Path change/reversal 168; dependency 3, 168, 288
Pattern maintenance approach 240
Patterned relationships 103, 105
Patton, M. 265
Pawson, R. 259, 263, 278, 280
Pearson's correlation coefficients 252, 255
Peillon, M. 231
Peisner-Feinberg, E. 177
Percentages 149, 153, 173, 192, 220, 241, 250, 257
Percentiles 57, 58, 192, 193, 194
Perret, B. 219
Personal environment 242;
Physical environment 209, 238, 242, 247, 251; planning 233, 243
Pierson, P. 94, 165, 167, 168, 228
Pile, S. 262
Planning methods/process 233, 260, 263, 264, 276
Plausibility 27, 49, 65
Pluralism 44, 70, 71, 186, 237
Pluralist/participative analysis 5
Polarization 75, 92, 251

Policy action/actors 6, 70, 207, 284, 285, 291, analysts 1-4, 9, 118, 214, 288, 296; areas/domains/fields 3, 4, 84, 86, 88, 95, 100, 119, 139, 140, 169, 172; changes 97, 154, 184, 292; communities 2, 9, 47, 71, 295; cycle 4, 96, 214, 294; deadweight 222; design 215, 221, 225, 226; discourse 20; effectiveness 3, 215, 224; effects 100, 213-215, 219-224, 231; evaluation 4, 8, 96, 97, 213-219, 223-228, 231-233, 237, 238; experts 138, 139; formation/formulation 87, 96, 214; goals 289; implementation 4, 8, 84, 96, 105, 130, 197, 215, 226, 292; instruments 129, 220, 264, 266, 268, 292, 296; intervention 3, 8, 119, 222, 226, 288; makers 3, 6, 8, 47, 97, 99, 103, 118-124, 129, 185, 186, 229, 234, 294, 296; making process 46, 66, 190; needs 294; networks 5, 6, 47, 70, 71, 86-89, 97, 105-109, 111, 119; operators 295; orientation 7
Policy Outcome Evaluation (POE) 96, 97, 99, 100, 120
Policy outcomes 4, 91, 100, 105, 211, 212, 218, 219, 228; outcomes line 218
Policy Output Analysis (POA) 97, 99, 100, 97, 99, 100, 120
Policy outputs 2, 4, 96, 98, 119, 209, 211, 212, 225; package 286, 292; practitioners 2, 4, 99, 284, 289, 290, 291; process 6, 97, 102, 279, 285; programs 4, 67, 132, 133, 138, 167, 222, 259; relevance 285; results 9, 286; sectors 2, 47, 75, 105, 106, 225, 234, 235; styles 2; tools 185, 186, 214; traditions 125
Policy-off situation 222
Policy-oriented research 13, 18, 290-295
Political bargaining 96; change 47; economy 125, 170; forecasting 188; process 47, 58, 97, 295; science 70, 89, 145-147; systems 146; theory 89
Politicians 179, 294
Pollack, M. 89
Pontusson, J. 168

Popper, S. 98, 99
Population 9, 20, 53, 99, 130, 131, 149, 151, 154, 155, 158, 159, 162, 170, 187, 202, 205, 234, 235-238, 242, 243, 260
Porter, M. 66
Portugal 185, 199, 200, 208
Possible combinations 14, 18, 19, 24, 34, 37
Postal survey 242
Post-materialist values 113
Post-Positivism 96
Poulsen, J. 65, 66, 234
Poverty, poverty avoidance 16-29, 34-40, 41, 151, 153
Pragmatic evaluation 96
Pragmatism 97, 99, 101, 104
Preisendörfer, P. 144
Prescott-Allen, R. 152, 154, 155, 158, 159, 164
Price setting 87, 88
Prime implicants 218, 229, 232
Private business 54, 200
Privatization 52, 58
Probabilistic criteria 14, 20, 160
Probabilistic view/analysis 117, 118, 147, 160, 191
Probability analysis 191
Problem-oriented (lead) visions 197
Procedural management 280
Process theories 219, 220, 226; tracing 63, 292
Program theory 218-221
Project definition 266, 267, 275, 276, 282; quality 276, 279, 280; related factors 268
Property owners 220; space 128, 179, 180, 183
Proportional representation system 113
Prospective analysis 185
Protestantism, Protestant churches 150, 151-158, 163
Proximal outcomes 225
Przeworski, A. 6, 45, 48, 55-58, 64, 147, 228, 290
Public administration 186, 199, 200, 206; agencies 266, 268, 280; assistance programs 131, 133, 138, 223; expenditure decisions 97; institutions 131, 132, 138; ownership 129; parking spaces 220; problem 214, 215; projects 283; support 220-223
Public-private division 175
Puustinen, S. 242
QAP procedure 118
QCA (Qualitative Comparative Analysis) 3-9, 44, 70, 71, 95, 101-119, 126, 128, 137-143, 147, 149, 153, 155-161, 164, 165, 186, 191, 207, 214, 216-218, 225-237, 242, 258, 260, 263, 264, 268, 272, 274-284, 291-293
Quadagno, J. 168
Qualified majority 83, 84, 86
Qualitative approach/methods 7, 13, 18, 44, 49, 99, 100, 125-127, 147, 148, 160, 163, 167-171, 216; assessments 8; breaking points 138, 175-177; case-oriented methods 179, 184; changes 167, 181, 183, 282 ; interpretative methods 148 ; measurement 138 ; surveys 6, 125, 137, 140-142
Qualitative/quantitative divide 35, 40, 43-45, 49, 65, 214, 241, 289-291
Quality 3, 106-111, 120, 137, 168, 175, 176-184, 215, 220, 224, 232, 245, 250, 259, 264-266, 274-280
Quantitative approach/methods 7, 13, 54, 138, 146, 170, 190, 227, 290 ; change 167, 180 ; data 101, 242; forecasting 191; score 222
Quasi-experimental design 4, 289
Quenter, S. 164
Quine-McCluskey algorithm 249
Race 17, 38
Radaelli, C. 223
Ragin, C. 1-5, 13, 20-29, 33, 34, 44, 50, 53, 54, 95, 99, 102, 118, 120, 127, 128, 140, 142, 143, 146, 147, 160, 164, 168, 171, 175-180, 186, 207, 216-218, 227, 230, 236, 237, 242, 249, 282, 288, 290, 293
Random sampling 146
Rational planning 243
Raw data 113, 175, 176, 178
Realism/realist(ic) approach 8, 263
Realist synthesis 9, 280, 282
Realistic evaluation 9, 263, 280, 284
Recession 172, 221, 222, 253, 257
Redding, K. 112, 113, 120

Redistributional equity 215
Reduction in complexity 5, 103, 289, 293
Regional (economic) development, growth 7, 124-126, 129, 135, 138, 141, 142
Regional case studies 123
Regional change 198
Regional Entrepreneurship Monitor (REM) 138
Regional programs/subsidies 133, 134
Regions 6, 111, 123-143, 148, 153, 181, 198, 223-225, 231-233, 237-241, 250, 256, 259, 260, 261, 269, 283, 288, 289, 294, 295
Regression analysis 8, 27-30, 37, 154, 251, 252, 254, 260, 262
Regularities 95, 102, 107, 109
Regulation(s)/regulatory policy 52, 58, 72, 84, 85, 129, 132, 138, 259, 264, 269, 274, 280
Regulatory reforms 58
Reinikainen, K. 239
Related factors 268
Relational data 105, 109, 112
Relations (between variables) 13-30, 50, 67, 72, 76, 80-94, 102-109, 118, 120, 127, 138, 140-148, 150-164, 170-175, 179, 180, 184, 185, 187, 190, 203-207, 217, 218, 221, 227-229, 231, 253, 254, 264-274, 282
Relevance 15, 215, 220, 234
Relevance Trees 189
Reliability (of analysis) 152, 279
Reliability (of data) 215, 289
Religion/religious factors 150-158, 163, 256
Remainders' 21-26, 218, 230
Remote' v/s 'proximate' conditions 235, 291
Replicability 217
Representativeness 86, 269
Research design 2, 4, 5, 43-48, 53, 57, 65, 70, 71, 99, 119, 125, 147, 216, 217, 226, 288, 290, 295; policy 197, 203; programs 197, 198; strategy 1, 172, 204, 227; traditions 187
Research Triangle 131
Resettlement policy 257
Residential areas 8, 237, 241, 244, 245, 246, 250-253, 259, 260, 262

Residuals 204
Resilience 169, 170
Response rates 193
Result variable 264, 265, 275, 282, 284
Retrenchment 169, 170
Reynolds, P. 123-4, 127, 144
Rhodes, R. 70
Rice and fodder sectors 72
Richards, L. 242
Richness of approaches 188
Rihoux, B. 1-5, 9, 96, 97, 99-101, 120, 128, 138, 142, 143, 148, 164, 208, 216-219, 230, 234, 236, 265, 288-290, 293, 295
Risse, T. 223
Robustness 54-57, 63-66
Rokkan, S. 146
Rosenberg, M. 250
Royal Dutch/Shell 186
Rueschemeyer, D. 2, 147
Ruonavaara, H. 257
Rural areas 151, 239, 241, 245
Russett, B. 146
Russia 239, 257, 261
Sabatier, P. 97, 119
Sager, F. 8, 97, 106, 119, 144, 184, 218, 232, 233, 235, 264, 280, 291
Saine, A. 241
Sallamaa, K. 262
Sampling procedure 295
Satisfactory conditions 256
Savage, M. 244, 245
Savolainen, J. 145
Sayer, A. 242, 245
Scandinavia 7, 172
Scarpetta, S. 179
SCCA (Systematic Comparative Case Analysis) 2, 4, 8, 233, 287-295
Scenarios, scenario-building 4, 7, 8, 185-191, 194, 197, 199-208
Scharpf, F. 119, 291
Schenkel, W. 264, 280
Schimmelfennig, F. 70
Schmitter, P. 70
Schneider, C. 235
Schneider, G. 89
Schneider, S. 220
Schneider, V. 120
Schön, D. 98
Schools 17, 70, 145, 177
Schulz, H.-R. 220

Schumann, W. 96, 98, 119
Schwartz, P. 187
Science and technology research 198, 204
Scientific inference 44, 52, 63; instrumentalism 96; knowledge 13, 16
Scope conditions 15
Screening 51
Second World War 168, 257
Self-reflexivity 243
Semi periphery 238
Semi rural, semi urban areas 238, 239, 242, 256, 258
Sequences, sequence analysis 215, 219, 227, 228, 290, 292
Set intersection 23, 34
Set theory 14, 148, 171-182
Sexual behavior 150, 153-158, 163, 164
Sexually transmitted diseases 153
S-function 174
Shell Company 186
Significance level 20
Silvasti, T. 257-8
Similarities 57, 62, 63, 66, 69, 71, 73, 76-80, 83, 103, 112, 120, 130, 146, 148, 167, 226, 282, 283
Simon, H. 120
Simplification 139, 193
Simplifying assumptions 21-23, 230, 236
Single case studies 70
Single linkage cluster analysis 156
Single-project theory 284
Singularity 283
Sippilä, J. 172
Siuruainen, E. 262
Size 267, 268, 274, 276, 278-283
Skocpol, T. 147
Small and medium-sized companies/firms 126, 129, 131
Small sized project 276
Small-N 2, 3, 18, 43, 44, 64, 71, 72, 109, 217, 224, 231, 292
Smelser, J. 44
SMIC method 188
Smith, M. 70
Smithsonian Institution 203
SNA (*See* Social network analysis)

Social action 103, 243-245; affairs 169; benefits 219; capital 8, 244, 245; change 237; characteristics 245-251; citizenship 168, 172, 173; cohesion 243; Democratic model 167, 17, 173, 179, 180-183; development 239; differentiation 243; expenditures 169; geography 249; inclusion 283; inequalities 5, 17; integration 8, 233, 237, 243, 244, 245, 249, 252, 253, 257, 258; intervention 17; life 245; mobility 177, 244; movements 243, 245; network analysis (SNA) 6, 95, 98, 101-105, 111-113, 118-120, 293 (*see also* Network analysis); participation 244, 245; phenomena 1, 6, 14-17, 51, 53, 95, 101, 119; policy 71, 72, 88, 171; regulation 150, 238; relations systems 206; rights 172-174, 177; Science(s) 5, 13-15, 29, 43, 44, 50, 52-54, 57, 60, 101, 103, 167-169, 171, 172-174, 185, 192, 290, 292, 295; scientists 14, 16-18, 24; security expenditures 113; services 172; structure 103; sustainability 8, 237-239, 243, 244, 260; Theory 103; world 49, 54, 171, 180
Social-economical system 208
Societal changes 191; needs 197, 202
Society "intelligence" 26
Socio-economic challenges 136; factors 152-154, 157; problems 131; profiles 141; status 16, 26, 27
Sociologists 170
Sociology 188, 199, 245
SOFI forecast 203-206
Solutions 48, 22, 23, 26, 33, 48-54, 156, 160-162, 274, 279, 283
Sonnett, J. 21-23, 26, 34, 293
South Africa 149, 151
Southern European EU 229
Soviet Union 186, 238
Spatial growth 6; structure 241
Specification, specification error 15, 16, 28
Spontaneous agency 243
Spreitzer, A. 6, 95, 149
Sprinz, D. 2
SPSS 125, 127, 139, 141, 143, 242

Spurious relations 58
Stakeholders 199, 200, 232, 267, 272, 274-276, 282
Start-ups 127-143
State of the Future 203-205
State(s) 2-4, 48, 67, 74, 86, 90, 101, 127, 130, 132-135, 145, 146, 149, 156, 164, 167-170, 205, 219, 223, 229, 230, 238-240, 257, 258
Statistical approach/methods 3-7, 46-57, 64, 65, 100, 102, 118, 119, 126, 143, 146-148, 158, 164, 184, 186, 190, 203, 216, 235, 237, 242, 244,252, 258, 260, 262, 284, 288,292, 293,
Statistical worldview 52, 65
Steinmo, S. 89
Stephens, J. 147, 168
Sternberg, R. 125, 127, 130, 138
Stevenson, L. 128, 143
Stochastic modeling 99
Stokey, E. 97
Storey, D. 124
Strain injuries 227
Strategic decisions 7, 188, 203, 208; management 124, 187, 188; planning 187, 188, 190
Structural analysis 187, 189
Structured, focused comparisons 18
Sub-configurations 81
Sub-national economies 123; level 123
Sub-Saharan Africa 7, 146, 149, 150, 155, 164, 166
Subsets, subset relations 20-34, 69, 155, 156, 176, 292
Substantive and theoretical knowledge 20, 23, 26
Substantive knowledge 16, 20, 23, 26, 28, 38, 40, 174-181
Success 103, 112, 113, 117, 149, 157, 188, 228, 234, 275, 279, 290
Sufficiency 46
Survey analysis 192, 193, 240, 242, 244, 250, 256, 259, 261
Swaziland 149
Swedberg, R. 226
Sweden 172, 182, 183, 241
Swedish Foundation for Small Business Research 128
Swidler, A. 27

Swiss 28-ton policy 106; Agency for the Environment 269; cantons 223, 224; Environmental Impact Assessment (EIA) 8, 263, 283
Switzerland 106, 220, 269
Symmetric set 38
Symmetrical matrix 112
Synchronic comparisons 224
Synthetic matrix 77
Synthetic strategy 216; dynamics 190; properties 144
Systematic comparative case analysis (see SCCA)
Systemic factors 57, 58
System-level variations 64
Tamásy, C. 125
Tampere 240
Target groups 214, 215, 220; participants 266
Target-orientation (lead visions) 197
Taxation 169
Taxidistance 69
Taylor, C. 146
Technical problems 277, 280, 282
Technologies 189, 192-198, 207
Technology forecasts 188-191, 203, 205, 207
Technology infrastructures 191
Technology research 7, 199
Technology sequence analysis 189
Technology transfer institutions 131
Teddlie, C. 292
Telecoms 46, 48, 64
Telerisk 199
Test scores 16, 17, 29, 36, 39
Teune, H. 5, 45, 48, 55, 56, 147, 290
Thagard, P. 55
Thelen, K. 89
Theoretical and substantive knowledge 176, 183
Theoretical approaches, theories 46, 70, 98, 180, 218, 234, , 289
Theory development 7, 140, 143, 184; of action 219
Theory-guided research 148, 294; - testing 48
Thick case analyses 292
Thresholds 20, 29, 32, 38, 39, 71, 76, 77, 109, 116, 117, 120, 148, 155, 156, 159-161, 291, 292
Thurik, R. 124, 129

Tight (policy) networks 71, 72, 83-88
Tight configurations 71
Tilley, N. 263, 267, 282, 284
Tilly, C. 149
Time series analysis 189, 190, 191, 204
TOSMANA (software) 103, 109-111, 118, 156, 161, 217, 236, 268, 284
Traditions 224, 231, 232
Trainability 40
Trajectories 167, 170
Transfer system 172
Transitivity 106-108, 110, 111, 116, 120
Transparency (in methods) 45, 65, 87, 98, 144, 287, 295
Transportation policy 6
Trend clusters 201
Trend Impact Analysis (TIA) 189-191
Triangular (sub-)matrices 75, 76
Triangulation 224, 232
Truck Thesis 153
Truth table(s) 18-26, 33, 109-113, 116, 137, 139, 156-162, 180, 217, 229, 248, 249, 268
Tuberculosis 153
Tucker, A. 55
Turku 240
Two-round survey 208
Two-step analysis/procedure 291, 292
Typologies, typology-building 107, 109-111, 180, 218
UCINET 107, 108, 113, 120
Uganda 152, 153, 161
Uhlaner, L. 129
Umweltschutzgesetz USG 264
UNAIDS 149, 152, 155-164
Uncertainty 63, 97, 99, 119, 187, 188, 204, 261,
Uncontaminated effect 18
Uncontrollable variables 57
UNDP 152, 154, 155, 158, 159
Unemployment 7, 168, 237, 239, 261
UNESCO 203
Union government 91; operations 173, 179
Unions 186, 199, 224, 289
Unique (causal) path 224
Uniqueness 239, 240
United Nations 7, 186, 203, 204
United Nations Millenium project 204, 209

United Nations University/World Institute for Development Economics Research (UNU/WIDER) 204
United States (USA) 2, 3, 6, 48, 64, 129, 186, 192
Universality 146, 147, 149, 171, 173-180
Universal-statistical attempts 148
Universities 131, 203
Unstable models 188
UNU 203, 204
Urban areas/urbanization 238, 244, 245; sprawl 238, 258; traffic planning 220
Urry, J. 244
US Environmental Protection Agency (EPA) 204
Vague theory 15
Validity 29, 40, 43, 45, 48, 49, 52-55, 62-66, 100, 148, 214, 219, 220, 275, 276, 291
Validity (external) 6, 43, 44, 45, 62, 63, 65, 66
Validity (internal) 6, 43, 44, 45, 62, 63, 64, 65, 66
Value judgment 215
Van Buuren, A. 98, 120
Van de Vijer, F. 128
Van de Walle, N. 151, 154
Van Waarden, F. 70
Vanderborght, Y. 230, 234
Variable coding 292; selection 2, 148, 218
Variable-oriented approach/methods 18, 45, 53-55, 65, 66, 127, 140, 143, 171, 179, 184, 284
Variables (aggregative) 50
Variables (combination) 104, 147, 172, 179
Variables (contextual) 221, 225; 228, 229, 231
Variables (control) 56-59, 63, 64
Variables (critical, decisive) 58, 98
Variables (dependent) 3, 8, 13-21, 24, 26, 28, 37, 38, 52, 55, 57, 59, 60, 63, 70, 105, 120, 147, 148, 156, 157, 207, 253
Variables (dummy) 148
Variables (independent) 13-21, 24, 26, 28, 37, 38, 44, 50, 55-58, 63, 102-

106, 120, 147, 148, 252, 253, 257, 283
Variables (interval-scale) 28-30
Variables (multi-value) 109, 159, 160, 164
Variables (nominal-scale) 21
Variables (number of) 28, 51, 66, 69, 76, 275, 294
Variables (qualitative) 90
Variance 56, 59, 60, 63, 154, 155
Variation, variation finding 15, 18, 21, 36, 58, 62, 105, 139, 148, 171, 175, 179, 191, 263, 290, 293
Varone, F. 3, 8, 96, 97, 99, 100, 138, 143, 144, 164, 213, 214, 230, 234,
Vector space 25, 26, 30, 31, 37
Vedung, E. 213
Venn diagrams 104, 112
Verba, S. 5, 44-48, 53, 66, 144
Verbal concepts/labels 172, 173, 176, 178
Verkuilen, J. 168
Viinikainen, T. 242
Virtanen, V. 240, 260-261
Virus 149, 155
Visionary ideas/methods 197, 199, 201, 202
Visualization (tools, data) 6, 103, 104, 112-120, 201
Viterna, J. 112, 113, 115, 120
Vladeck, B. 98
Voss, K. 27
Wagemann, C. 235, 291
Warsaw Pact 90
Wasserman, S. 95, 103, 120
Watanabe, T. 231
Weber, M. 144, 167, 184
Weberian ideal types 184, 226
Weight, weighting 69, 80, 104, 189, 202, 205
Welfare State 7, 60, 167-172, 180-183, 239, reforms 167-170, types 169, 170
Wellman, B. 105
Welter, F. 125, 143, 144
Wennekers, S. 129
Wessner, C. 3
Western world 239
Whewell, W. 5, 55
Wiborg, A. 258, 261
Widmaier, U. 146

Wilks, S. 103
Windhoff-Héritier, A. 96, 98
Within-case analysis 8, 140, 141, 143, 225; complexity 95, 102; processes 226
Within-system variables 55
Work organization 227
World War II 257
WorTiS projects 199
Wright, M. 103
Yamasaki, S. 6, 95, 149, 230, 231, 234
Yin, R. 171
Yli-Jokipii, H. 238
Zadeh, L. 171, 178
Zambia 157, 159, 160-166
Zeckhauser, R. 97
Ziegler, R. 144
Zimbabwe 149, 151, 157, 159-166

CPSIA information can be obtained at www.ICGtesting.com
Printed in the USA
LVOW01*0933210713

343876LV00008B/199/A